MAPPING

YORÙBÁ

NETWORKS

MAPPING

YORÙBÁ

NETWORKS

POWER AND AGENCY IN THE MAKING

OF TRANSNATIONAL COMMUNITIES

Kamari Maxine Clarke

Duke University Press   Durham & London 2004

© 2004 Duke University Press   All rights reserved
Printed in the United States of America on acid-free paper ∞
Typeset in Galliard by Tseng Information Systems, Inc.
Library of Congress Cataloging-in-Publication Data
appear on the last printed page of this book.

TO CHIEF ALÁDÉ

FOR LIVING THE LIFE

YOU STRUGGLED

TO CLAIM

Contents

Note on Orthography

Ọ̀yọ́túnjí Village and Santeria speech communities are not native Yorùbá speakers. The residents of Ọ̀yọ́túnjí Village use Yorùbá as a second language and as a mechanism for cultural reclamation. In using Yorùbá, however, Ọ̀yọ́túnjí Village residents tend to differently pronounce words—and in relation to the standards of native Yorùbá speakers they would be seen as mispronouncing and therefore misusing many Yorùbá words and phrases. As a result, each speech act that I incorporated here was interpreted according to both pronunciation standards as well as differing social contexts. To reduce the ambiguities as well as to respect Yorùbá orthographic standards, the transliteration used here is based on modern Yorùbá orthographic conventions.

Yorùbá Orthographic Conventions

Yorùbá consonants are much like English consonants. However, some exceptions exist. The "p" is a double articulation sound [kp], called a voiceless labial-velar stop in phonetic terms; "gb" is its voiced counterpart. Both [kp] and [gb] are digraphs. [ṣ] is the same sound pronounced as "sh" in English. It has a phonetic value of [š]. The vowels "ẹ" and "ọ" are pronounced like the English vowels [e] and [o] in *get* and *fall*, respectively. Without the diacritical marks "e" and "o" resemble the initial vowel sound in the diphthongs [ei] and [ou] in *mate* and *drove*, respectively.

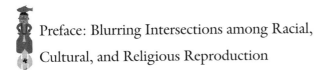

Preface: Blurring Intersections among Racial, Cultural, and Religious Reproduction

MY FIELDWORK MEMORY that best characterizes the interplay among race, difference, and the politics of authorizing knowledge occurred in an airport in Lagos in 1995. I had just arrived there with representatives from Ọ̀yọ́túnjí among whom I had spent fifteen months collecting fieldwork data. The arrival was a joyous occasion for them; despite their claims of a homecoming, however, their difference led to their precarious outsider status. A young Nigerian girl decided to openly express inquisitiveness: assuming that one of the men in our group was a visitor, she asked him if he was from America. In a celebratory tone he responded, "I'm from here," and pointed to the ground in front of him. When she responded with a look of puzzlement, he added, "But a long time ago, my people were taken away by white men and brought far away from here."

The little girl's mother pulled the girl toward her and instructed her to behave and stop questioning the visitors, but soon the girl broke away and again walked up to the man, responding to his answer as if they had never been interrupted. Pointing to his light brown face and glancing at his clothing, she declared, "But you are not black like me. *Màmá* says you are a visitor, *òyìnbó* [white man/outsider], and I am Ẹ̀gbá." With an emphatic insistence on her distinctiveness she pointed boastfully toward her chest, claiming membership in a particular Yorùbá ethnic group.

He playfully responded with further insistence, "No, we are the same," making circles of his arms, laying claim to no specific ethnicity but suggesting a commonality among us North Americans, the Ẹ̀gbá girl, her mother, and everyone in the line behind us. Pouting, she shook her head and crossed her arms as if she were unhappy. Pointing to his traditional dress, she asked, "Then why do you have those clothes on if you are really Yorùbá?"

Having undergone the requisite divinatory rituals with which priests in his community consult the oracle to determine the nature of their African roots, and thus confident about the generalities of his ancestry, he chuckled and nodded his head, as if suddenly understanding her confusion. "Ahh," he said. "But look at my black face, then look at my African clothes. These show you that I am African—I dress like an Ọba!"

"No," she retorted. "Poor people and òyìnbó wear those, and you're not poor. You can fly whenever you want."

Despite the apparent disjunctures in the politics of African American reclamation of an African homeland and African Yorùbá rejection of the legitimacy of those claims, the conjunctures of national belonging blur the vocabulary of national distinctions with that of the symbolic unity of blackness. The man's references to a shared racial identity with the young girl reflected his belief in race as the basis of shared national culture. But the young girl and her mother were not convinced that this Ọ̀yọ́túnjí chief was a direct descendant of an enslaved Yorùbá captive, for he could identify neither his ethnicity nor his kinship lineage, determinants that are important qualifiers of membership. Instead, laying claim to a generalized and temporally distant period long ago, the chief communicated the existence of a social rupture facilitated by transatlantic slavery. He invoked an alternative chronology of belonging that inverted her lineage-specific basis for membership to include a temporally cyclical link between Africans before their captivity into transatlantic slavery and African Americans today.

The man's insistence on black racial unity calls on a recognition of sameness. It requires that we relegate heterogeneity to homogeneity (Williams 1991). To the young Ègbá girl his declaration was comical, a playful trick in which he misrepresented his identity. Unlike what seemed to be familiar to her, his statement referenced neither his place of birth nor his parents' or grandparents' region of descent. For her and the majority of Yorùbá in Southwest Nigeria, notions of ancestral hometown remain important determinants for understanding Yorùbá belonging. His narrative of exile separated him from her, from them. Rejecting his reclassification of citizenship and, instead, deriving symbolic distinctions from his light brown face and his apparent practices, she classified him as fundamentally "Other."

When the research for this project began in the Yorùbá Ọ̀yọ́túnjí Village in South Carolina, I was interested in understanding the lure of the racial imagination as it related to the production of notions of ancestral belonging, especially in relation to the idea of "Africa" as a diasporic homeland for black Americans born and raised in the United States. I became intrigued by how the history of dispersals of slave captives around the world shaped black membership in African imaginaries in geographically distinctive ways and how one writes an ethnography about mobile subjects whose subjectivities are complex and whose social histories are sometimes unknown—in light of that history of capture and movement and its related regulation of racial difference. I wondered what such an ethnography would say about the limitations of single-site fieldwork and its ability to capture contemporary movements that may not be linked to empirically derived dispersals, but instead to social memories and imaginaries.

Research on today's communities of black and brown people around the world presents both classificatory and methodological challenges. Where anthropologists once embarked on sojourns around the world to study non-Western community settlements—the Other—today many from non-Western societies have claimed the rights to study "themselves." Yet, of late, even this we-they binary is no longer useful because those who claim the right to study "their" groups are far from representative of the communities they claim to represent. To make matters worse, the analytic conflation of racial sameness as a replacement for shared ethnic or cultural ancestry is equally fraught with classificatory problems.

The racial conflation that this ethnography addresses is that of blackness and the cultural politics of difference, though the focus is on the uses of religious, legal, and historical institutional strategies of power. In the context of the ways of seeing difference outlined in my first example, it is not simply that a similar ideology for classifying racial sameness, such as Pan-African blackness, was not a part of the Yorùbá girl's consciousness.[1] Rather, the event of contact between strangers is a disjunctural moment of articulation in which varied meanings are shaped by historically influenced ways of knowing. For even as identities are relational and social circumstances change over time, the authority on which knowledge is shaped is what contributes to particular logics of recognition in larger spheres of interaction. The young girl's recognition of ethnic difference underscored her need to preclude sameness from difference and distinguish herself with different boundaries of recognition. And though the man pointed to particular elements that for him were distinctive markers of racial membership, at the root of his authority of African membership was divination as an authorial form of knowing the past; at the root of hers was the sanctity of modern ethnic kinship.

Understanding when, how, and why people invoke sameness in the midst of difference is not always an easy task. It requires understanding the ways people legitimize membership in divinatory fields of power. The chapters that follow locate me, the ethnographer, as a non-Yorùbá, nonreligious practitioner, an academic—a cultural outsider whose family narrates its ancestral roots not from Africa at all, but from Canada by way of the Caribbean from a line of Jewish diamond traders from then-Palestine. These distinctions immediately set me apart from members of the Ọ̀yọ́túnjí Village community, and these conundrums of naming, origins, and cultural membership continue to present critical sites of difference from which I entered this work. Although I shared my interlocutors' desires for black solidarity, at the time, as a recent immigrant from Canada to the United States, I was neither comfortable claiming cultural solidarity nor satisfied with the unqualified description of me as either African or African American. Yet, despite my hesitation with those sites of difference, my informants accepted me as one of them; to them I was "black" and therefore implicated by transatlantic slavery and, as they often described it, "a victim of racist America, thus in need of redemption." Whereas I recognized that the disregard for my claims of difference was understandable, the claims of my interlocutors—black cultural nationalists—were fundamentally cultural and driven by a new movement in black American history, a post–Black Power movement, that was critically distinct from black Canadian politics of immigration and integration. At the heart of our differences was the problematic of the conflation of race with culture and an extended tradition in African American scholarship that accepted an a priori relationship between blackness and cultural sameness. As I contemplated that conflation, my interest in exploring the politics of desire that compelled some black Americans to use religious and legal-historical institutions as a means to look to Africa as their homeland increased and deepened.

In my experiences of blackness in eastern Canada from the early 1970s to the early 1980s, Africa was distant and unrelated to our lives. It was a place far away that had no relationship to our daily practices. Our African descent was taken for granted, but we were also of Caribbean descent, though we had as little contact with the Caribbean as we did with Africa. Yet, the prominent presence of increasing numbers of immigrants from English-speaking islands such as Jamaica, Barbados, Trinidad, and Guyana and the growing cultural and economic networks with those regions that led to the formation of black Caribbean identities as a dominant sign of blackness, as a heritage category, were central. Similarly, "black Americanness" had the same relationship to us: it was as distant as Africanness, yet culturally accessible. I remember watching American nightly television programs from Buffalo, New York, and various sit-coms' story lines that generalized a black American experience. Weekly prime-time shows such as *The Jeffersons* and *Good Times* highlighted not only how representations of race and class were conflated but also how foreign the characters seemed from my own experiences of blackness. Yet, despite my distance from what I often classified as U.S. workings of race, it was the institutionalized formations of global antiapartheid movements that swept through university campuses worldwide that offered young people of my generation—toddlers in the 1960s—a thematic basis by which we could form alliances with larger struggles around racial and economic oppression. This development of a transnational movement toward blackness as Africanness was central to the formation of conscientious movements of black Western students who formed coalitions with groups working toward African independence, in antiracism struggles, and in the antiapartheid movement in South Africa.

With the mainstreaming of computers and transnational expansion of television and radio programming things seemed to change. Information about Americans and black people became easier to access independently. The North American Free Trade Agreement (NAFTA) between Canada and the United States made the interconnections increasingly porous. And with the movement of various types of information technologies we saw reflections of who we were in the images being exported from the United States. They were models for conceptualizing our own experiences of racial marginalization, models that we attempted to incorporate as our own but that were not always relevant to our experiences, nor always useful. Nevertheless, these new knowledge technologies provided us with increasing leverage in narrativizing our experiences, ironically using American-based histories of slavery, categories for classifying race, and approaches for redemption.

It is no surprise that, despite being Canadian, as a graduate student and on moving to the United States, I, too, joined a camp of starry-eyed black middle-class students in their early twenties whose experiences of being the marginalized Other motivated self-conscious claims of Africanness as a form of empowerment and unity. Many of us often collapsed our allegiances to political organizing around political and contemporary issues related to Africa, for which the promise of black solidarity served as the symbolic basis from which we worked. Back then, some of us third-wave feminists, as well as latecomers to the Black Power movements of the 1960s, felt that, as much as we had benefited from the gains of earlier political movements, they had failed because participants lacked commitment to personal change. This, we argued then, led only to the further reproduction of new forms of institutional oppression.

Catching the end of the revival of Marxist intellectualism, I came of academic age long after the experience of the U.S. Civil Rights movement and at the beginning of the institutionalization of academic ethnic and racial heritage programs and centers of higher learning—very much corrective responses to a history of racial exclusion and curricular denigration of black people and cultural practices. The significant moment for my generation of black scholars, beneficiaries of the gains of antiracism struggles of the 1960s, was the eventual co-optation of blackness as a sign of struggle to blackness as a heritage category that was to be aligned with a corpus of "History" and a language for resignifying ancestral membership. As a result of coming of age during a time when there existed a popular shift in the black middle-class imaginary from Africa as the place of "distant primitives" to Africa as a metaphor for black noble roots, many of us were willing, albeit temporarily, to lay claim to such unproblematized attempts to claim social race and not actual complex cultural lineage as the basis for our formations of subjectivity. Instead, using language of enfranchisement, we integrated the symbolic language of social change. We borrowed from the earlier feminist refrain *The personal is political*, creating the possibilities for what would become the cultural revolution of the 1980s. We employed the constructs of blackness from the post–U.S. Civil Rights movement in an attempt to form alliances with what we thought, then, was a commitment to political uplift. For some, this meant "reclaiming their heritage"—perhaps Southern, perhaps Caribbean, perhaps Native American, as long as some form of ancestry was claimed. And, despite our cultural distance from African cultural worlds, returning to *roots* almost always invoked Africa as the foundational site of black roots: the place of "authentic" blackness, yet clearly a highly problematic conflation.

This period in the United States, the 1980s, was a time when deconstructions of anthropological imperial notions of culture began taking root with the institutionalization of cultural studies, ethnic studies, and African American, Africana, and African studies throughout U.S. universities. Yet, although these new programs recast the production of legitimate studies about the Third World Other, taking hold of their cultural traditions in their own terms, the faculty, including some of the "native" anthropologists, also engaged in further reproducing the very practices of racial and gender-based generalizations that they were trying to alter. By asking who should and could speak for whom, scholars tended to chart strictures of authenticity by which certain types of representations were narrowly tailored. Yet, despite the participation of increasing numbers of people of color and feminist interventions into the politics of cultural interpretation, studies of identity could maintain neither the weight of privileging experience nor classificatory generalizations.

Following these conundrums of origins, influence, and representational politics, my own self-understanding and therefore intellectual analysis came to reflect the ways that, despite their shared origins or seemingly similar subject positions, people participate in producing cultural norms in a way that creates sameness in the midst of difference. The obvious gaps in identity categories and cultural and personal experiences are relevant to the roles of culture and power in changing and producing new norms of linkage. A principal finding is that the production of black American descent narratives from the West African "homeland" is made real by historical, legal, and religious production, as well as other institutional mechanisms for charting legitimacy. Through the production of these formal institutional mechanisms, people in deterritorialized (or diasporic) communities map community, and in so doing make global issues locally relevant. As such, it is the creation of new norms that take on meanings across new boundaries that is relevant here. For in spite of the legitimizing rules of the nation-state, people mobilize particular conceptualizations of the self, the village, region, ethnic and racial group, and nation, even while they move beyond them. These processes of subject making produce increasingly autonomous mechanisms for local consumption. What we see with many black American claims to African cultural identity is a classic form of assimilation into American social life, yet the exaggeration of their cultural heritage is an attempt to establish claims to an ethnically relevant category.

Accordingly, as I demonstrate in the first part of this book, social theory today is increasingly rendering relevant the ways identity and culture are becoming dislodged from place and globalization is leading to new forms of regional autonomy through which socially relevant claims can be made. People from disparate communities can import information about other people and regions and adapt it to their own context, eventually using their own hegemonic position to reshape these "packages" and export them as more authorial than the original. The first part of the book sets the framework for understanding the context in which the political economy of "traditional" Yorùbá revivalism has emerged globally. Scholars articulate national identity as connected to given territorial origins and state designations of citizenship; they must explore the relevance of these categories in relation to people's reclassification of cultural belonging in time and place, how increases in the distance between sites of cultural origins and sites of cultural production are leading to changes in autonomy, and, in some cases, how these shifts in institutional power are enforcing new standards. We need to articulate how power shapes meaning and why, historically, this is so, as well as the mechanisms by which people produce and legitimatize transnational reclassifications of citizenship outside the parameters of traditional requisites of territorial contact. The focus of the second part of the book, therefore, is to demonstrate not just how these relations and meanings circulate and are transformed, but how they gain legitimacy in deeply historical realms of modern subjectivity. To reveal and analyze these processes of making, interpreting, and transforming social categories, I examine what I have identified as the institutionalization of a deterritorialized network of Yorùbá communities in which I chart how social institutions that exist in deterritorialized contexts play out in informal transnational contexts. These Yorùbá practitioners are not located in West Africa, nor were their parents born there. In most cases, the òrìṣà practitioners in this book are sixth- or seventh-generation black Americans, most of whom have never visited an African country, but who use deterritorial practices to transform social meanings in time and space. Through the reconceptualization of constitutional principles of national membership they use religious ritual, texts, and legal and racial discourses to participate in the production of a Yorùbá community outside of the African continent.

The critical goal of this project is to integrate useful but problematic assumptions endemic in highly localized studies that shape anthropological theory, race and diaspora theory, and the anthropology of religion in order to recast the ways we understand social relations as increasingly multisited, deeply historical, transnationally fragmented, and yet recognizable. Despite globalization and deterritorialized social change, the modernity of racial and spatial boundaries, central to the development of the modern state, has been unproblematically reinforced in twentieth-century protest movements. My modest hope is to clarify that this happens not because people simply exercise the freedom to express their ancestral heritage and do so at will, but because alongside these acts of agency are forms of historical domination that are both ideological and cultural and serve to negate the exercise of power seen as such. The making of subjectivity and communities involves the making and unmaking in particular hierarchies of value and distinction in the modern world. This argument explains how acts of agency are shaped by a priori values. Theories of agency thus need to be understood in conditions of possibility in particular fields of power, for power is a site of freedom and a space for the enactment of power as well as a site within which acts of agency are regulated. My argument highlights the role of institutions in the shaping of ideologies of seeing and belonging in particular temporal terms and, as such, highlights the importance of understanding social change in relation to identifying sites of variability, contingency, and sites for the reproduction of hegemonic forms.

Evolution of the Project

The research for this book emerged from my Ph.D. dissertation written at the University of California, Santa Cruz, but was inspired by an earlier project that I began in 1990 as a graduate student at the New School for Social Research in New York City. I collected data on Yorùbá religious revivalist networks throughout the United States, focusing on one community in the Bronx, some years before beginning research in Òyótúnjí Village in South Carolina. At the time, studies of African villages tended to focus on small settlements; studies of black Americans tended to focus on urban populations or patterns of change in rural and urban areas of the South. Although ethnographic approaches were responding to the crisis in ethnographic authority, there was an overwhelming interest in the role of the state and national discourses in shaping cultural practices in specific places, as well as the role of the individual in shaping cultural interpretations. Much of this work consisted largely of descriptive Third World ethnographies as well as texts that demonstrated the specificities of those local sites, without regard to how new modes of production and techniques of communication were changing the very mechanisms by which local sites were influenced by global sites and vice versa.

Over the course of this writing, there has been a proliferation of anthropological interest in legal, scientific, and political institutions and the interplay between the local and the global. Forced to rethink the social in the context of both its fragments and the orders within which they are embedded, I began this research because of my interest in what the study of communities of people who were laying claim to other nontraditional origins and practices necessarily entailed. I started by exploring the relationship of blackness, practice, and place to the production of practices said to be performed in the name of African traditions. The proliferation of Yorùbá drumming circles throughout New York communities served this purpose, and I charted how male and female drummers "performed Africa" through these practices.

My findings demonstrated that in these deterritorialized contexts, the dominant criteria for legitimacy surrounding questions of who had the right to play the African rhythms using conga and *bàtá* drums were organized along racial (read: black/Third World) and gender lines. Female drummers and nonblack drummers were often marginalized outside of the hegemonic boundaries of acceptable traditional practices. "Men drum and women dance" was the popular refrain used to explain the division of labor and ritual practice. Citing African traditions as the referential source of such taboos, many justified their ban on female drumming, for example, by referring to late-nineteenth- and early-twentieth-century anthropological village studies that outlined the lifeworld of the people studied. Sometimes new consequences accompanied these sources of traditionalist knowledge, such as warnings of biological reproductive consequences if premenopausal women transgressed these social rules. Although they knew they would be excluded from ritual and public events or dismissed as homosexuals and therefore not worthy of membership in a cultural organization, many women still pursued their drumming profession.

At the time, and to my surprise, the data also revealed that though some men certainly played a role in reinforcing these gendered taboos, many of the strongest enforcers of the exclusion of women from drumming were other women. They were invested in maintaining the gender division prescribed by what they felt was authentically African. Comparing data with West African drumming networks, however, it was evident to me that such rigid gender differentiation did not exist there in the same way as it was interpreted in the United States, which led me to ask why my American interlocutors were more intent on strict gender differentiation than were many in the African villages in which I traveled and visited. I became interested in not only the culturally constructed character of these male and female roles, but also in how they were allied in particular modern racial articulations, therefore serving to regulate daily social practices for those in the diaspora. This led me to examine the rhetorical or ideological process by which this traditionalism was both performed and legitimated, how these interpretations had been authorized and authored. Analyses of these factors made it clear to me that, despite the appearance of inflexible roles, even in the Americas, the rules were far from fixed. Instead, gender roles were variable and contested, as were other forms of interpretation. Various factors were embedded in the potential of ritual to change the referential meanings of signs, an understanding of which drew me to an investigation of the transformative power of African ritual for black Americans. I wanted to understand then, as I explore in this book, why and when traditional practices were transformed and what reasons were given, as well as what contingencies, such as timing and charisma, tell us about what components of sociohegemonic orders need to be present for some forms of variability to be seen as legitimate. In thinking through how we understand the features of deterritorialized communities that claim belonging to a home elsewhere, I continue to ask what signs need to be invoked for meanings to be resignified and accepted as authoritative, and why. By observing the making of traditions, I also documented the contestations of these acts. For whether one articulates the existence of tradition as the basis for an authoritative act depends on whether certain practices are seen as legitimately customary and, if so, embedded in the prestige of past practices. Therefore, the production of norms takes place through the referencing of contemporary social orders as well as through the formation of particular nontraditional institutions that are already in ideological alliance with preexisting social orders. Though the use of race, like the articulation of gender, may be intended to counter discrimination, it also invokes the articulation of a particular scientific or geographic order and so has the effect of reproducing the very practices that it was meant to alter. As a site of difference, race is necessarily present even in the rethinking of itself. Given the workings in these contexts of race as simultaneously reinscribing the modern and the postmodern, the sign of blackness draws its prestige from the moral authority of the trauma of separation or exile, dislocation and displacement, and the nobility of a preslavery African past. If this conceptualization of the African diasporic imagination is coupled with the will to claim or the impossibility of a return to Africa, the next questions are What are the features of transnational networks of Yorùbá religious institutions through which these narratives of connection are framed? and What types of ethnographic methods must we employ to capture the complexities of these transnational networks?

Methods

The data that resulted in this book were developed and collected over a ten year, four-phase period of participant observation in three countries, supplemented by my inspection of two and a half centuries of documents by missionaries, historians, anthropologists, sociologists, practitioners, and tourist eyewitnesses. My methods principally centered on participant observation in a multisited procedure in accordance with which I assumed that tradition, conceptions of Yorùbá, and race were locally and historically contingent. Upon describing my ethnographic interests in the workings of òrìsà practices outside of Nigeria, I gained permission to live in Òyótúnjí Village and participate in community life.

As the ethnographer living with and among my informants, conducting a local ethnography, I also traveled with them and some of the members of their network as they moved within their national and transnational networks: to Òyó, New York, Òyótúnjí, Houston, San Francisco, Milwaukee, Chicago, Washington, D.C., and elsewhere. I accompanied them from village to village, diviner to diviner, from one home to another, from one World Òrìsà Conference to another, and it became clear that the "pure" religious practices they were in search of were themselves hybrid reinterpretations of traditional practices. One such research encounter included following Òyótúnjí revivalists on a pilgrimage to Òyó, Nigeria, a region they see as their African homeland. Having been required to undergo necessary Ifá divination rituals to make the trip, I adhered to both their own local rules of participation as well as those of the anthropological tradition of local studies, thereby documenting localized ritual and decision-making processes that influenced social norms and formal lawmaking by their decision-making polity, the Ògbóni society. However, describing my compliance with both sets of rules may be misleading, as my adherence to Yorùbá traditionalism was through ritual participation without full belief in the cosmology. Nevertheless, I suspended my questions about the efficacy of ritual as I submerged myself into their complex worlds. In the case of anthropological methods, my characterization of Yorùbá cultural practices in the village in which I did the majority of this work was based in the United States. My overarching concern was with the conceptually transnational and morally racial religious movements through which I detailed the routes of connection that transcended local sites and national boundaries, crosscutting regions and trade routes.

While in the United States I documented social life in two communities through which I charted the transnational forms of revivalism that emerged out of Òyótúnjí's òrìsà voodoo focus. One was Òyótúnjí African Village in South Carolina; the other was an Òyótúnjí satellite community in the Bronx. The founders of Òyótúnjí Village established it as a means of finding their way back to Africa, back to a "homeland." Although the community is viewed as "strange" and "odd" by some other African Americans as well as a range of Americans, it would be a mistake to assume that in deterritorialized contexts, territorialized approaches to modern nationhood and racial membership are divested of territorial contexts. Rather, Òyótúnjí residents use reconfigured temporal and spatial notions of ancestral continuities to recast their conceptions of homeland as Africa in America. The challenge, therefore, in such transnational studies is to establish the geographic and temporal scales in which the globalization of such African-heritage practices play out.

Field Methods: Locating Racial Alliances in Ritual and Legal Institutions

The drama of calendrical and seasonal rituals and formal and informal regulations of daily life is the bread and butter of a long methodological tradition in anthropology as a practice intended to capture meaning in small places writ large. Just as conceptions of blackness as Africanness play a critical role in framing the parameters of black Atlantic membership to which Yorùbá revivalists in the United States lay claim, the ritualization of transnational religious practice and multisited legal and historical authority also provide the central forms of legitimacy on which Yorùbá belonging is established.

The first phase of my research began in September 1990 to September 1991 in the Bronx and resumed in February 1995 to spring 1996. During these two periods I documented the archival history of Yorùbá revivalism as well as daily social practices, recording the rhythms and rituals of everyday life in rural as well as urban contexts. During some of this time I lived with, observed, and recorded aspects of daily life among Yorùbá traditionalists on both sides of the Atlantic. As I documented their religious practices and examined these in relation to institutions relevant to American audiences, it became clearer that where race was the modality through which Yorùbá revivalism was lived, it was the invocation of spatial and temporal (chronotopic) reconceptualizations of their ancestors living alongside them that served as the modality with which deterritorialized Yorùbá revivalists claimed membership. Recognizing their beliefs that ancestral simultaneity is possible in the modern present, and in an attempt to understand the workings of ritual, I underwent a range of Yorùbá ritual initiations to fully engage in the transformative authority that religious ritual provides. By observing the power of the transformative sacred to enable the chronotopic reclassification of secular domains such as nationality and citizenship, I charted how "reality"—local, regional, national, transnational—was made and remade. This enabled me to explore the roles of power and interpretation in shaping how agents produced the ideological frameworks by which they interpreted their world.[2]

To understand the religious network of Yorùbá communities throughout the United States, I also traveled with Ọ̀yọ́túnjí villagers to affiliated communities in a range of other U.S. cities. By traveling with them in and out of communities in their network, I came to see how various cities were integral nodes in the larger network of Yorùbá practitioners in the United States. After spending phase 1 collecting ethnographic data about the daily enactments of Yorùbá traditions in and outside of Ọ̀yọ́túnjí, the next phase of my research involved understanding the Ọ̀yọ́túnjí network in relation to its transnational linkages in Nigeria and Cuba. Both Nigeria and Cuba are critical components of any study of Yorùbá transnational networks in the late twentieth and early twenty-first century. Phase 2 began with a voyage to Nigeria with an entourage from Ọ̀yọ́túnjí Village and a few members from the larger Ọ̀yọ́túnjí network and concluded in winter 1998 to spring 1999 with a return to the village.

The connections between Cuba and Nigeria, as points in the Yorùbá network, are symbolically powerful because the large majority of Yorùbá captives who arrived in Cuba were from the Benin region of the Ọ̀yọ́ Empire, forcibly enslaved and transported to the Caribbean and South America between 1760 and 1886. This period is characterized by the collapse of the Ọ̀yọ́ Kingdom, the civil wars in the Bight of Benin, and the interventions of the British, who eventually succeeded in overthrowing traditional governance and establishing a British colony in the New Nigeria. These conditions set the stage for the conditions of slave raids and slave trading along the West African coast and, eventually, the influx of captives to Cuba.

The historical development of networks of social and religious organizations led to the spread of òrìṣà worship in Cuba where there existed strong networks for religious practice. In Cuba today, òrìṣà worship exists as part of a larger continuum of religious change in the Americas in which religious practices, now known as Santería but also referred to as Lukumi and *regla de ocha*, have transformed the shape of òrìṣà worship outside of West Africa. Given the historical circulation of òrìṣà practices from West Africa to the the Americas, I realized that it was critical to understand how Cuban òrìṣà practices and practices in the United States are related. For the relationship between Cuban slavery and Santería as overtly Christianized continues to be a critical motivator for Yorùbá revivalism as a form of social protest. Thus, even as Santería has developed into a distinctive practice that combines the syncretization of òrìṣà and Catholic religious practices, there remain critical tensions between its genealogies of Ọ̀yọ́-Nigerian roots and the legitimacy of changing contexts and practices in the Americas.

My work related to Cuba and its place in the larger network of Yorùbá transnationalism was archival and relational; however, I spent six months in Nigeria in Ọ̀yọ́ and Abẹ̀òkúta, two small communities of Yorùbá traditionalists, where I collected ethnographic data on Yorùbá legal and religious practices.

Ọ̀yọ́ is a popular site of Yorùbá traditionalist practices and a location in which a range of Nigerian ethnic groups interact. It is a city that was rebuilt and relocated many hundreds of miles south of the demolished city of Old Ọ̀yọ́, which was the site of the capital of the Old Ọ̀yọ́ Empire. The demise of this empire in the late 1700s led to one stage of dispersals of Yorùbá-speaking people to other regions of southwestern Nigeria and to the Americas; thus, New Ọ̀yọ́ is considered to be the relocation of the ancestral Ọ̀yọ́ Empire and the reclaimed homeland of my informants in Ọ̀yọ́túnjí. In Ọ̀yọ́, I observed the interactions between Ọ̀yọ́túnjí villagers and their hosts, which allowed me to explore the convergences and divergences of transnational identities through which to chart the ways that Yorùbá tradition was interpreted, regulated, and authorized.

In Abẹ̀òkúta, Nigeria, I interviewed diviners, observed traditional court hearings, and participated in òrìṣàs thought to be traditional. This experience of extended fieldwork highlighted the postcolonial conditions of Nigerian poverty and widespread struggles for democracy and the ways religious ritual was called on to transform hardship. It became clear to me that most American revivalist practitioners were not that inclined to incorporate into their own struggles the contemporary postcolonial conditions of Yorùbás in Nigeria, such as the Ilé-Ifẹ̀ conflict of the late 1990s or the politics of democratic transition in the postdictatorship nation. The Ọ̀yọ́ past, not the present, was their focus. Disappointed with the residual impact that colonialism and Christianization had on Nigerian institutions and Nigerians themselves, most revivalists disregarded current problems of power and governance as a surviving condition of colonialism that will be eradicated only with the eventual overturn of European cultural imperialism, starting with Christianity, the central religious ideology against which their struggle for redemption is waged. Instead, they spoke in broad generalities about the richness of Yorùbá history and practices and reserved for private conversations their disappointment with the centrality of Christianity and Islam in people's lives.[3]

In the third phase of my research, I returned to Ọ̀yọ́túnjí Village. Here I realized that the pilgrimage home left my interlocutors with the resolve that the future of retaining Yorùbá cultural and religious traditions was no longer in the hands of Yorùbá in West Africa but in the future of black people in the African diaspora. "Ọ̀yọ́túnjí and black people of the Americas," they would say, "need to step up and take our rightful place." Otherwise interpreted, the future of Africa was in the hands of blacks in the Americas.

Having charted connections between òrìṣà practices in southwestern Nigeria and their contemporary connections to and differences from parts of the Americas (such as Brazil, Cuba, and the United States), in 1998 I began phase 4 of my research as a postdoctoral fellow. I went to London to conduct archival work, looking at historical evidence of the early building of religious and legal institutions and identities. Then in Nigeria again, at the National Archives housed in the University of Ìbàdàn, I focused on investigating Ọ̀yọ́túnjí claims that colonialism and the historical oppression of traditionalists by the Nigerian state led to the production of particular types of Western desires consistent with those that led to the earlier demise of the Ọ̀yọ́ Empire. In the British Library I also gathered data on the expulsion of slaves from Ọ̀yọ́ and the development of modern institutions that emerged out of traditionalist formations. Data from secondary sources on transatlantic slavery documented the "truth-seeking" practices of historians and missionaries, which, in combination with the primary archival records, provided a living statement of a complex past.

With the goal of completing the fourth phase of fieldwork almost ten years from my initial work in New York City, I returned to California to inspect data at the University of California, Berkeley's Bancroft Library, the site of one of the most important twentieth-century collections on the Yorùbá people of southwestern Nigeria, that of the renowned Dr. William Bascom. The holding consisted of meticulous fieldnotes, interview transcripts, letters, divinatory field recordings, traditional clothing, and art objects.[4] I explored the relevance and influence of such scholarly literature by examining the role of religious divinatory practitioners and teachers in shaping what has come to constitute Yorùbá history, religion, and cultural practice. This phase of research shaped my understanding of the centrality of Ọ̀yọ́ in Yorùbá revivalism and its reformulations in the United States as the symbolic site of Yorùbá slavery, prestigious governance, and hegemonic power.

Despite anthropology's single-site tradition, all locations in these four phases of exploration were ideal for studying the institutional production of African American reinventions of Yorùbá traditional practices and Nigerian Yorùbá contestations of those practices. To maintain and advance the role of ongoing movement as a hallmark of anthropological method, my method draws out the theoretical implications of data gathered in one site as the means by which to determine when and why a shift in sites is warranted as the means to highlight the importance of intersite dependencies and the recognition of fragmentation as holistic in anthropological studies. This processual and structural interdependence and the integrity of the symbolic and its relation to material conditions as both "real" and "imagined" are fragmented and complex. They point to how and why attention must be given to rethinking training and the expected length and forms of fieldwork necessary to cover the various scales of transnational interaction through which to produce holistic interconnections across time and space, fine-grained accounts that advance rather than undermine the centrality of holism as one of the long-standing goals of the discipline.

The complexity and time involved in carrying out such a study also raises important questions regarding the production of able students and the expectation of the timing of production for ethnographic accounts, mentoring, and training. The model of single fieldworkers at a single field site, as established in the early nineteenth century, still largely informs views of the time (typically twelve to eighteen months) thought to be necessary to develop skills for carrying out mixed qualitative and quantitative forms of collection, to build adequate rapport with a spatially hierarchically arrayed informant population, and to select the ways and means to integrate archival and other forms of secondary material and make use of new technologies. This model is also part of the problem with current dilemmas in ethnographic production and is itself embedded in the limitations set for us with the increasing professionalization of the American academy, which continues to be driven by consumer capitalism, or what David Harvey (1989a) has referred to as the "condition of postmodernity." Methodologically, therefore, we need to raise questions about and address issues concerning underlying expectations of expertise in area studies within which scholars are expected to locate themselves. For the reality is that now, more than ever before, globalization is leading to complex relationships between the local and the global, and therefore, what constitutes the field within particular units of analysis is changing also.

Classificatory Conundrums

The process of naming and classifying fields, national groups, concepts, and so on is a process of holding in time a moment that is constantly in flux. Any act of naming always participates in the act of fixing that object in time and space. And though there is no object that represents the totality of an absolute or the totality of that which it fixes, the task of naming is the challenge of identifying the ultimate values of a thing. Thus, the problem with discourse of all types is the problem of standardizing signs and meanings with which we necessarily communicate.

The act of writing is no different. Through the process of writing and documentation we analyze processes that are in flux and interpret them within historically legible norms. Similarly, I also engage in the necessary act of articulation, and in so doing employ classificatory distinctions that are relevant to the daily negotiations of the people with whom I work. However, because the limits of discursive fixity are not sufficient to undermine the necessity of articulation, I necessarily engage in translation, interpretation, and reinforcements of categories that describe processes that are in motion. Though I argue that the production of meanings in time and space is reflective of the production of particular ideologies of seeing, in naming and distinguishing between things I, too, make classificatory distinctions. Some of my distinctions may appear inconsistent; however, they are always strategic. At times, I use "African American" and at other times "black." Sometimes I define citizenship as a legal status governed by a social contract between the individual and the state, and sometimes I refer to citizenship in social terms, as cultural citizenship that indexes forms of social membership legitimized by social collectivities. I refer to American converts to Yorùbá traditional practices as "Yorùbá revivalists" or "òrìṣà practitioners." Reading this manuscript, my Ọ̀yọ́túnjí interlocutors disagreed with my classificatory interpretation of black Americans as ultimately "American." As in my interchange with forms of citizenship, sometimes, for ease of comprehension, I am forced to use traditional categories, the very categories of state power that Ọ̀yọ́túnjí practitioners work hard to contest. At other times, to distinguish between particular groupings of black cultural nationalists—ritual practitioners and social activists, and African practitioners who are engaged in similar practices but whose members do so under very different sociohistorical conditions—I use categories that reflect the spirit of revivalist protest. For analytic purposes I must insist on the relevance of the difference of place, yet to miss the opportunity to distinguish between the production of an African imaginary and the rule of the state in the legitimation and classification of personhood is to miss the politics of power and difference in daily lives. These people, who were born and raised in Nigeria, and those who, more often than not, speak "native" Yorùbá are clearly culturally different from those who converted to Yorùbá practices, were born outside of Nigeria (particularly in the United States), and approach òrìṣà traditions with the fever of reclamation rather than the banality of the everyday.

I use "African American" and "black American" interchangeably to refer to people who are often represented by the practitioners themselves as being of African origins or of African descent but who were born in the United States, live or have lived in the United States, or can claim belonging to generations of black American former slaves. Nevertheless, I often use "black American" instead of "African American" to refer to those persons in the United States who claim blackness as their identity but who, more often than not, claim neither African nor American as a primary overriding descent category. As a black Canadian living in America I would fit into this category. In general, I use the term "black" to mark the range of geopolitical, economic, and sociocultural routes of interaction that have constituted a black subjectivity within the expansion of the modern world. Yet, despite these constraints of representation and articulation, I demonstrate that, even in the articulation of distinctions, race is not something that one possesses, nor is it something that has remained the same over time. Blackness, for example, is not just a category that came to reference the "brown body." Rather, it is an index of particular hierarchies of meanings and a set of social distinctions that have changed over time. Like other categories, blackness is many things, including the cultural politics of seeing and the cultural politics of how race is seen. It is about the mutable alliances between distinctive hegemonic pronouncements of phenotypic features in space, as well as shifting designations of membership according to performative articulations and interpretations of sameness in relation to difference. It is about the ways people construct fundamental categories from which signs are shaped, boundaries are patrolled, and membership is secured and enforced.

What does it mean when the very classificatory acts that may have been designed to counter marginalization, as Reva Siegal (2002) has suggested, also participate in the "very practices [they seek] to alter and regulate"? To discover how this notion of the racially "real" is constructed in relation to the national is to recognize the tension between the ontological forces of its production and how its production is framed in institutions of power. Therefore, I also refer to territorialized communities to describe those who, like Nigerian Yorùbá practitioners, more often than not claim the national or ethnic identity of the region in which they live. My use of deterritorialized communities describes those who live in one place but claim origins and national/prenational belonging to another place, and therefore either live or see themselves as living outside of particular national boundaries. Reality is made and remade in a range of ways, and the imagination, a larger category, is regulated by the very ideologies of modernity that have come to constitute its bases for the intelligibility of subjects. Through explorations into the institutional influences that produce the imaginary, I demonstrate how people see themselves in relation to who they are legally and politically and in relation to how they reclassify group national identity in transnational terms. For even if race is easily constructed and imagined, it is not easily unimagined. Entering this terrain necessarily forces scholars to ask how the terrain of classification implicates us in lives that are not entirely defined in our own terms.

Taking up the challenge of understanding how Yorùbá practitioners participate in the necessary regulation of classificatory boundaries, I examine how we can employ the tools of multisited research to understand the processes of local interconnection by which people classify themselves along historically constituted conceptualizations. My only consolation for the violence of interpretation and the demarcation of distinctions that might be different from that of my interlocutors is to paint a description of the aesthetic landscape in each of the encounters that I describe. This act of description leaves room for the reader to see my role in providing both the analytic and classificatory lenses that have filtered all my encounters and the way my classifications are also a function of the historical shaping of concepts and relations over time.

Acknowledgments

The focus of this book is on Ọ̀yọ́túnjí òrìṣà practitioners and the knowledge they gain as a result of their transatlantic travel to Yorùbá-predominant regions in West Africa. However, my initial fieldwork conducted in a Yorùbá revivalist temple (or house) headed by the late Chief Aládé, an affiliated chief and political attaché of Ọ̀yọ́túnjí Village, would not have been possible without the welcome personal, political, and social insights that he shared with me over a two-year period. I dedicate this book to his memory, for I may not have moved from the òrìṣà community in the Bronx to pursue fieldwork in Ọ̀yọ́túnjí African Village in Beaufort, South Carolina, and then in Ọ̀yọ́ and Abẹ́òkúta, Nigeria, if it were not for him. I am also grateful to the many African American Yorùbá revivalists in the U.S. Northeast, especially those in the Bronx, with whom I spent many midnight hours in *bimbes* (òrìṣà parties), naming ceremonies, and long weekends traveling to funerals, conferences, and Yorùbá festivals. I am particularly thankful to the men and women of what was at the time Chief Àlàdé's sister temple, Ilé Onísẹ̀gùn, headed by the now Ọ̀yọ́túnjí chief, Dr. Adelerie Onísẹ̀gùn.

Though it is impossible for me to acknowledge all of the many individuals in Ọ̀yọ́túnjí who enriched my life while I was there, I offer my gratitude to all its residents. Her Royal Highness Ìyá Oritẹ́ embraced me as her surrogate daughter, as fictive kin, and for that I am thankful. I appreciate the kindness offered by her children, Adébísí, Adéyínká, Ọ̀sun Míwá, and Bahoon, and thank the women of the Ẹgbẹ́ Mọrèmi (the Ọ̀yọ́túnjí Women's Society) for accepting me into their cult despite my noninitiate status. I also had the fortune of critical support and clarity from Chief Alàgbà Ọláítán of Ọ̀yọ́túnjí Village, who played a foundational role in helping me make the transition to Ọ̀yọ́túnjí. And if Chief Alàgbà Ọláítán was a key interlocutor in the South, then the leader of Ọ̀yọ́túnjí, His Royal Highness Ọba Adéfúnmi I made the entry and terms of engagement possible. A charismatic spiritual and political leader, someone I have come to know both personally and politically and whose dedication to his community is an example of its success in a changing world, he deepened my understanding of the politics of nationalist desire and commitment to a cause to die for. I refer to òrìṣà practitioners by pseudonyms or titles instead of given names, but it was impossible for me to provide the Ọba with such anonymity. Instead, I accept his permission to identify him by his political title, His Royal Highness Ọba Adéfúnmi I, or, in some cases, the Ọba for short. I hope that my analysis of his role in the struggle toward black racial empowerment through cultural and spiritual redemption will raise critical questions about the complex place of Africa and African ancestry in the lives of black people worldwide. I thank him for his continued support of this project.

I am equally grateful to my informants in Nigeria, who, in the spirit of Yorùbá hospitality, went beyond all expectations. I offer special thanks to Wẹlẹ́ Olúmídé, Bísí Craig-Balógun, Làmídì Àyànkúnlé, Chief B. A. Ọbádínà, Dr. Rẹ̀mí Rájí Oyèlàdé, Dr. Egúnjọbí at the University of Ìbàdàn, Dr. Wándé Abímbọ́lá, the children at the Òyó Traditional Ifá School, the Ifá priestesses at Olúmọ Rock, and the Ọ̀yọ́túnjí, Ọ̀yọ́, and Abẹ̀òkúta, Nigeria *babaláwo*.

My distant guides throughout this writing process were the cultural artists and women drummers of New York. The rich tapestry of information that I gained from discussions with these women about African traditions, legitimacy, and gender issues are themes that continue to invigorate my own work. To Phyllis Bethel, Edwina Lee Tyler, Ubaka Hill, Debra McGee, Joan Ashley, Evelina Otero, Tracey Johnson, Frisner Augustin, Nicole Attaway, Marie Alice Devieux, Robin Burdulis, Maria Bryer, Montego Joe, Shango Adeserji, the women of the ÀṢẸ Drumming Circle, and the other individuals in the New York drumming community, I offer my special thanks.

During the years of conducting the research for this book, many friends offered their unwavering support: Ronald Crooks, Terry Day, Nancy De Graff, Mabinti Dennis, Ellen Farmer, Michael Horne, Jacqueline Odle, Joel Robertson, Nicole Thompson, and Jonathan Wosu. I owe special acknowledgment to Elena Georgiou, whose willingness to engage in difficult discussions with me about the politics of desire as it connects with race and the cultural politics of suffering was critical in inspiring the development of this project. I am also indebted to Monifa Bishop, whose hours of engagement and generous friendship from the beginning to the end of this project continue to inspire my work, and to Naomi Pabst, who has been a dear friend, a reliable critic, and an enduring colleague and interlocutor.

I am indebted to her as well as to Saloni Mathur, for both were tireless in reading and rereading different drafts over the years.

I thank the following institutions for their generous financial and institutional support: Leland Ferguson and the University of South Carolina at Columbia; the Wenner-Gren Foundation for Anthropological Research; the Social Science and Humanities Research Council of Canada; the University of California, Berkeley, President's Post-Doctoral Fellowship; the University of California, Berkeley, Center for African Studies; the Yale University Center for International and Area Studies (YCIAS); the Griswald Foundation; the Yale Social Science Faculty Research Fund; and the Hillis Publication Fund. I thank Ọrẹ Yusuf for his many hours of Yorùbá language editing and my field assistants, Dayọ̀ Àjàyí and Tiese Manigo, for their diligence in the field. I also thank Kadija Ferryman, Yetsa Tuakli-Wosornu, Jesse Givens, Oroma Mpi, Csilla Kalocsai, and Fèyí Adunbi for their research assistance. I appreciate the help extended to me by the staffs at the National Archives at the University of Ìbàdàn in Nigeria, the British Library in London, and the Yale University Sterling Collections in the United States. Thanks also to the publishers of the journal *Anthropologica* and to Broadview Press for permission to reprint here parts of the previously published articles "Governmentality, Modernity, and the Historical Policies of Ọ̀yọ́-Hegemony in Yorùbá Transnational Revivalism" in *Anthropologica* 44 (December 2002) and "To Reclaim Yorùbá Tradition Is to Reclaim Our Queens of Mother Africa: Recasting Gender through Mediated Practices of the Everyday," in *Feminist Fields: Ethnographic Insights*, edited by Rae Bridgman, Sally Cole, and Heather Howard-Bobiwash (Peterborough, Ont.: Broadview, 1999). I am appreciative of the tireless work of the wonderful editorial team at Duke—especially Ken Wissoker, Kate Lothman, Katie Courtland, and Christine Dahlin.

During the writing of this manuscript, the members of the University of California, Berkeley, faculty in anthropology, African studies, and African American studies welcomed me into their academic communities. I am indebted and deeply thankful to many people there, including Steve Small, Michel Laguerre, John Ọ̀jẹ́wọlé, Daphne Ann Brooks, Alan Dundes, Laura Nader, Marianne Ferme, Donald Moore, and Aihwa Ong. During various stages of this project, I also appreciated the substantial feedback and continued intellectual guidance of Carolyn Martin Shaw, who, being a central reader in the early stages, offered insight and guidance, pushing me to ask questions beyond my realm of comfort, yet questions that became critical to this study and its theoretical development. I thank her for ongoing and reliable feedback. I thank Níyì F. Akínnaṣọ for assisting in the early conceptualization and growth of this work and Brackette F. Williams for her conscientious reading of the many drafts of the later stages of this work. I am equally grateful for reflections and engagement by many colleagues, including Lisa Rofel, Don Brenneis, Steve Caton, David Anthony, Allison Sampson-Anthony, Brian Axel, Charlie Piot, Henry Goldschmidt, Ariana Hernandez-Reguant, Deborah Thomas, Barnor Hesse, Adé Àjàní, Chris Waterman, Eric Worby, Rogers Smith, Achille Mbembe, Betty Rodriguez, Ralph Austin, Jim Ferguson, Micheal Levin, Jacob Olúpọnà, Liza McCalister, Laura Nader, Ugo Nwokeji, Fẹ́mi Lawrence Adéwọlé, Stefania Capone, Pash Obeng, Sally Merry, Sarah Nuttall, Guillaume Boccara, Connie Sutton, Barney Bate, Paul Gilroy, Vron Ware, and George Baca.

I owe special acknowledgment to my writing groups in Santa Cruz from 1996 to 1997, in Berkeley from 1998 to 1999, and those at the New School for Social Research from 2000 to 2001. Most particularly, I am indebted to Cori Hayden, Galen Joseph, Jennifer Burell, and Mihri Inal. I also thank colleagues for their feedback at various institutions where I presented chapters: Wesleyan University; the University of California, Berkeley; Davidson College; Ohio State University; the University of Texas, Austin; the University of South Carolina, Columbia; the University of Toronto; the University of North Carolina, Chapel Hill; Duke University; Harvard University; and Princeton University. I am especially appreciative of the critical engagement by my colleagues at Yale, including the wonderful graduate students Ahmed Afzal, Csilla Kalocsai, Joe Hill, and Sheriden Booker.

Special thanks goes to my family, especially Kathy Clarke, Phyllis Yinka Walton, Eulette McKnight, Linton Clarke Jr., Evon Clarke, Sheryl Clarke, Viola and Linton Clarke Sr., and Herbert Williams. Thanks also to Steve Appea and Tiyani Behanzin, the central inspirations for this project from the beginning to the end. And, of course, a special appreciation goes to Ronald. This work is both a reflection of our personal progress and a measure of our growth.

Although many individuals and institutions contributed to the ideas and motivations that this work represents, only I am responsible for its shortcomings.

Kamari Maxine Clarke

New Haven, Connecticut

MAPPING

YORÙBÁ

NETWORKS

Introduction: From Village, to Nation, to Transnational Networks

ONE OF THE MOST EXPLOSIVE issues in transnational theories of revivalist movements today is the search for African roots. At the base of this trend are questions about how practices conducted outside of "homelands" become embodiments of other traditions. Given these shifts in the relationship between new localities and distant geographies of homelands and memberships, scholars have begun to investigate the ways that globalization is producing culturally portable practices through which new forms of innovations are being legitimated in new localities using various forms of knowledge. Not only are these shifts enabling changes in techniques of legitimacy, but ontologies of modern identities are increasingly finding expression in sociohistorical imaginaries alongside biological forms of identity. These identities are deeply embedded in historically constituted strategies of power through which the movement of capital, people, and ideas have spread throughout the modern world.

In the early twentieth century, as anthropology was increasingly shaped by scientific rigor, ways of sorting and typologizing subjects were connected to ways of making objects. With Bronislaw Malinowski, fieldwork became a rite of passage, and the increasingly professionalized work of anthropology involved the production of an original contribution—a comprehensive account of an isolated community. Anthropologists at both Oxford and Cambridge produced accounts of village life that sought both to test various universal principles and to detail theories of social reproduction. These theories were driven by scientific methods in order to derive general laws and eventually had the effect of shaping fieldwork techniques and producing the means by which the study of social order writ small took shape in seemingly isolated communities. The field became a self-contained unit, which became the basis for the production of what I call a *geography of subjects within self-contained spaces*. This form of seeing the "Other" led to ways of understanding the field as self-contained and self-perpetuating.

Given that such ethnographic and anthropological data-collection techniques as participant observation, ethnographic interviews, and surveying highlight the ways that people in particular communities understood their world, one might wonder how ethnography can be anything but local. How can researchers transcend national borders and map global processes? Understanding the making of transnational communities involves understanding how local communities are embedded in circuits of connections. Just as studies of local spaces involved the compartmentalization of social units in terms that made central the clan or the village or forms of sedimentation that rendered the nation-state secondary, so too does the study of transnational networks push us to rethink the ways that we understand the social units and people's relationship to them.

As anthropologists shifted from conceptualizing the field in terms of singular "sites" to studying not only multiple sites but also relationships between those sites as constitutive of the link between the local and the global, the artifact that had been the single site became the basis for ethnography as the study of "field."

Today, with the opening of national borders, transnational corporations and the movement of laborers from the non-West to the West, and the movement of labor camps from the West to the non-West, are leading to strategic knowledge forms that are becoming more salient in the development of new forms of identities that must be methodologically tracked. Thus, more than ever, these movements of people and circulations of knowledge are becoming more challenging to document because they are connected to a spatially expansive network of interconnection that goes beyond the nation and its history of sedimentation and because the formation of hierarchies of racial subjecthood and difference that preoccupied empires is being transformed along overlapping lines of mobility and immobility, investors and laborers, those who send remittances from the West and those who receive them. As such, human difference, once constituted by the symbolics of blood and biology, continues to be manifested in the United States in the myth of culturally distinct identities. In turn, major changes in categories of human ordering are being redefined in relation to forms of membership connected to new lines of mobility and access.

How we study such forms of movement, such new strategies of knowledge production, and such transformations of community is similar to and at the same time much unlike the methods of our predecessors of the early twentieth century. Today, the ways that people reclassify the boundaries of membership and the ways that time and space are reconceived have more to do with the mobility of our interlocutors who, over the past fifty years, have been displaced by war, are in search of labor, or are drawn to rapidly growing global cities of the developing world (Graburn 2002). Communities are far more fragmented and interrelated than they have ever been. Accordingly, it is becoming more difficult to conduct fieldwork among these mobile subjects, who are themselves on the move or whose cultural norms are increasingly both local and global (Graburn 2002). Thus, our ability to chart communities involves our ability to understand how people's networks are both historically shaped and institutionally legitimated and globally interconnected.

Yet, although we are witnessing the intensification of transnational alliances, with the formation of modern states we are also observing a strengthening, not weakening, of national distinctions and regional attachments to place and discourses of origins. This strengthening of autochthonous notions of ethnicity and race and the history of pannational and religious fundamentalist and revivalist movements raise questions about the newness of this contemporary phase of globalization. Nationhood and national sovereignty, as we know it, are not diminishing; the local is becoming increasingly internationalized in particular zones of power. It is becoming clearer that the modern is ever present in postmodern reconfigurations. As such, new forms of practice are taking shape alongside new institutional forms of knowledge.

What is popularly referred to as the globalization of cultural production is taking place not just on the level of shifts in the political economy of state power, but also in relation to shifts in commonsense approaches to place, practice, and identity. These issues are critical for understanding both the politics of transnational identity formation and the charting of the scope of inquiry. In what is to follow, I detail an anthropological study of a Yorùbá community constantly in the making. Ultimately, my questions are: How, in transnational studies of cultural production, might field sites be better conceptualized? In making the always necessary decisions of place and starting points, how and where should a single study follow processes of cultural production? How should we "locate," physically and analytically, spatial and conceptual boundaries and sedimentary forms without reliance on constructs of race as biology and culture as homogeneity (as many past and current diasporic studies do) that obscure rather than reveal the complexities of knowledge production and its circulation among "natives"?

In an attempt to trace the ways that black nationalists produced spatial indexations of African territoriality in particular fields of cultural production, I begin the first part of the book by exploring how ideologies of nationhood were formulated in the black Atlantic world, even as group formations outside of national borders led to diasporic linkages. Conceptions of culture, social change, migration, and diaspora are not new to twentieth-century social theory, but far less scholarly attention has gone into exploring the complexities of how knowledge circulates in precise and mediated forms within particular economic and political spheres. Particular ideologies of framing and classifying belonging must be understood in relation to the historical specificities that underlie the ways national imaginaries are intertwined with underlying forms of modern origins. These specificities of deterritorialized interconnection are producing intensified transnational networks which will tell us more about the nature of power as well as the conditions under which hegemony operates and agency is either possible or foreclosed in particular spheres of interaction. I approach the making of identity and place in deterritorialized fields of power to understand how colonial inscriptions continue to frame the interplay between national state boundaries and the achievement of ideological orders of membership that foreclose particular forms of intelligibility before they can be brought into being. One such example will be illustrated with this study: the place of the Yorùbá and their "elsewheres," specifically the relationship between the Yorùbá of Southwest Nigeria and the Nigerian state, and how we understand its elsewheres in the context of the modernity of linear temporal order, set alongside the simultaneity of the past, present, and future. As such, ways of seeing also involve ways of temporally ordering reality.

Yorùbá Networks: Deterritorialized Spaces

The Yorùbá people of southwestern Nigeria were popularly classified by sociologists and anthropologists of the twentieth century as an ethnic group. They have been described as having established their roots in West Africa, where they developed deeply sophisticated religious practices of communication between God, known as Olódùmarè, and humans. Thus, it is the West African countries of Benin and Nigeria that continue to be represented in the literature as the "traditional" origins of people of this group and òrìṣà practices that are represented as traditional. In documenting the people, their origins, and their cultural practices, studies of the Yorùbá often involved intensive fieldwork in which researchers lived with their informants and documented their life cycles, ritual practices, ceremonies, and death rituals. Scholars monitored the annual cycles of subjects year after year to understand the practices that constituted the group. The travel and movement of such African kinsmen and kinswomen were often secondary to the social reproduction of the settlements. Ironically, the forms of settlement that in the Third World seemed to exist prior to colonial governance were often described as constituting the "original" and "traditional" practices of the group.

As changes in research sites over the past fifty years reflected changes in people's mobility, so did the development of anthropological projects. Over the past four

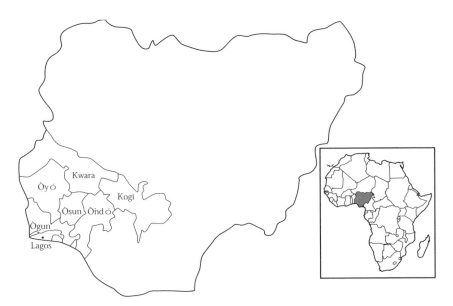

Map of Nigeria (Africa in inset).

hundred years, as African religions moved with the spread of African captives into transatlantic slavery, there developed a system of plantation slavery that transformed the ways ritual practices were applied to people's circumstances. These vast numbers of practitioners were from lines of predecessors who were transported from various parts of Africa to the Caribbean and North and South America and participated in the transformation of ritual and religious practices that have endured over centuries. One such grouping of people included Lukumi and Bantu speakers who were òrìṣà cult practitioners and over time came to be standardized as the Yorùbá people of West Africa.

Despite these discourses of origins, however, the twentieth- and twenty-first-century proliferation of groups of òrìṣà practitioners outside of West Africa continues to be expansive, ranging in the hundreds of millions of adherents of Yorùbá and Santería religious practices. Increasing numbers of these òrìṣà adherents are contributing to the growth of multiple networks of knowledge outside of the African continent. Though this history of traditional practice is deeply situated in the Nigerian "homeland," major changes in òrìṣà practices took shape over the past two centuries. Anthropologists started to take note of the transformation of òrìṣà practices in extensive communities in the Americas. In fact, since the publication of the first fieldwork-based account of Yorùbá communities in the United States by Carl Hunt (1999), *Oyotunji Village: The Yoruba Movement in America*, there have been significant changes in the form and content of òrìṣà worship.

Today, practitioners in West Africa, the Caribbean, and South America are increasingly in conversation with practitioners from the West, and now, more than ever, vast numbers of Americans in the United States are converting to Yorùbá religious practices and playing central roles in reshaping how òrìṣà traditions are to be practiced. Interestingly, this emergent group of practitioners continues to outnumber the practitioners in various West African regions. This disproportionality of new claims to òrìṣà practices is reflective of the prominence of Western practices that is fueling the growth of deterritorialized òrìṣà practices today. In Brazil, the spaces of interpretive production led to the development of a variation and became Candomblé; in Cuba, it became Santería; in Trinidad and Tobago it became Shango; and in the United States, among black American cultural nationalists, it became òrìṣà voodoo, or the Yorùbá religion.

The widening constituencies of changing Yorùbá òrìṣà practices, though not mutually exclusive, can be classified in four significant groups: (1) òrìṣà practitioners principally in Nigeria and Benin as well as various surrounding West African countries; they tend not to be educated in the West, have limited financial resources, and claim òrìṣà worship as their religious faith;[1] (2) òrìṣà/Santería/Lukumi practitioners in the Americas, who constitute the largest group of religious worshippers and tend to accept the hybridity of òrìṣà practices; they are spread throughout urban and rural Cuba, Haiti, Trinidad, Puerto Rico, Brazil, and the United States; (3) òrìṣà worshippers and Yorùbá or òrìṣà revivalists who are part of a relatively new (post-1960s) òrìṣà economy of practitioners who are interested in the return to a more orthodox traditional practice; and (4) òrìṣà modernists, a relatively new (post-1980s) group of initiates and practitioners, led by predominantly white American practitioners, who are part of a growing movement interested in the transcendence of racial belonging through the emphasis of ritual lineage. These four groups, overlapping in categories and purpose, constitute multiple networks of òrìṣà practitioners that have produced òrìṣà institutional practices throughout the Americas and reflect, to a greater or lesser extent, the African origins of òrìṣà practices.

Nevertheless, these relations are neither equal in impact, influence, and prestige nor evenly distributed. In West Africa, as interest in the practice and practitioners' acquisition of lifelong apprenticeships decline, New World practitioners' deterritorial participation in òrìṣà rituals is growing, and the industry of ritual knowledge and training is proliferating with the global spread of scholarly books and the institutionalization of Western distribution networks. Though the roots of Yorùbá traditions are seen as emerging from Africa, Nigerian òrìṣà practitioners are few in number. Nevertheless, procurement of new clients is building new networks between local sites and global nodes of connection. As Ọlábíyí Babalọlá Yáì (2001) has argued, the "òrìṣà tradition has its foot in Africa and its head in the Americas." The same Yorùbá practitioners who hold the symbolic roots of Yorùbá practices are becoming marginal to the production of new standards of practice in the global age. This has led to particular asymmetries in which West African òrìṣà practitioners who have limited access to electronic technology are having declining significance in their social worlds, which are increasingly dominated by Christianity and Islam. Their participation in global òrìṣà networks, although highly symbolic, is often limited in quantity of influence in Santería/òrìṣà revivalism in the Americas.

As with the proliferation of òrìṣà practices propelled by post-Fordist consumerism and a new òrìṣà consumption, the growth of transnational Yorùbá institutions has promoted the widespread availability of self-help books and videos, online òrìṣà chat rooms, and Internet-based services, by which people with differing levels of familiarity with Yorùbá practices are attaining the knowledge to become òrìṣà worshippers. These forms of knowledge production circulate within private ritualistic and public forums and are becoming increasingly embedded in global circuits of exchange and local sites of historically relevant variation. Thus, with the transnational circulation of Yoruba religious networks, formations of religious practices in the Americas are becoming more institutionally autonomous. Yorùbá revivalists are expanding their matrix of Yorùbá knowledge and not only participating in a transatlantic dialogue but also playing a central role in the production of Yorùbá institutions of knowledge. For example, the World Congress of òrìṣà Tradition and Culture, established in 1981 in Ilé-Ifẹ̀but, has traveled throughout the black Atlantic zones, ranging from Brazil to the United States to Trinidad, back to Nigeria and to Cuba, where debates over how òrìṣà practices should be regulated took place. These issues are highly contested, and both point to a problem with a discourse of "authentic origins" and people's discomfort with unregulated change. In 2002, a keyword search on the Internet using "òrìṣà practitioners," "Santería," "Yorùbá," and "divination" yielded over seven thousand Web sites. Such a vast index reflects the range of transnational òrìṣà institutions that could be called upon for obtaining online divinatory readings, information about the history and culture of the Yorùbá, the history of slavery, and adaptations of òrìṣà rituals by Africans in the Americas. Typically, an òrìṣà Web site offers links to òrìṣà/cultural marketplaces; on the site for the Awo Study Center run by Awo Fá'lokun Fatunmbi (http://www.awostudycenter.com/), selection options include home, classroom, forum, news, marketplace, gallery, links, and contact. The site boasts a mission statement, a Welcome/Ẹ káàbọ̀ salutation in English and Yorùbá, an opportunity to join the mailing list, a comments area, updated postings for learning Yorùbá words, divinatory interpretations, and general knowledge study material. The key players in the proliferation of òrìṣà practices in the United States sport sites that not only produce knowledge about òrìṣà rules and practice, but provide services that can be procured and consumed.

The Web site for Santería Batá Drumming (http://www.ochemusic.de/linklist. htm) provides a roadmap for knowledge about a wide array of òrìṣà practices, music forums, academic books, and institutions, including a link to the School for Oriental and African Studies (SOAS) in London, which provides a gateway to research on scholarly information on African and American Yorùbá-Santería-Candomblé practices. There are sites that provide network groupings and sites that provide information about the particular practices of a given group in the larger alliance. For example, the Church of Lukumi Babalu Aye, run by Ọba Ernesto Pichardo (http://home.earthlink.net/~clba/), is one site for Afro-Caribbean religion; Orisha Net (http://www.seanet.com/~efunmoyiwa/) is another popular Santería site that is dedicated to providing information on La Regla Lucumí, which provides postings for the divination reading of the year as well as general information about òrìṣà ritual practices. The Ọ̀yọ́túnjí African Village Web site (www.oyotunjivillage.net or www.cultural-expressions.com/oyotunji/default. htm) provides general information about their schedule of monthly òrìṣà festivals as well as postings outlining the reading of the year and general principles of Yorùbá traditions. The temple known as Ile Afalobi (http://www.yemoja.com/) is a traditional house of Lukumi òrìṣà worship headquartered in the Detroit area, with members principally from the Midwest. It is another African-centered òrìṣà site that provides updates for òrìṣà practices for its constituency. Representing Nigerian Yorùbá constituencies, the Alliance of Yorùbá Organizations and Clubs, USA (http://www.yorubaalliance.org/) was set up to foster the unity of all Yorùbá organizations, clubs, and religious groups through collaborative activities in the United States and around the world and to promote the economic, social, cultural, and political empowerment of all Yorùbá organizations, including information sharing. This site, more than the others listed above, is concerned with both religion (especially Islam and Christianity) and the governmental politics of Africa.

All these groups provide similar packages of knowledge, redemption, and individual and community empowerment. Therefore, any approach to understanding the globalization of Yorùbá religious practices not only must recognize the various geopolitical zones of interaction within which these practices have taken shape; it must also examine new institutional mechanisms, propelled by electronic technologies, by which new forms of practices continue to change over time. Approaching the study of religion this way involves approaching the production of knowledge and belief through the ways that regimes of "truth" are put in place toward the construction of rights to the creation of new spaces of religious practice. Thus, religious rituals and religious institutions, whether or not they are

Ọ̀yọ́ òrìṣà practitioners initiating an Ọ̀yọ́túnjí practitioner undergoing an Ifá initiation. Here they are mixing the herbs and preparing to wash the initiate with them.

supernaturally experienced or believed, are better addressed as symbolic and practical mechanisms for the articulation and reproduction of particular social logics. Today, with new knowledge technologies and the ability of people engaged in religious institutions to produce a nexus of deterritorialized networks, we are seeing the production of new meanings of place and practice and the compression of time-space distance for the sake of religious reproduction. This shift is reflexive of the spread of Yorùbá practitioners in the Americas, in which large populations of formerly enslaved practitioners are engaging in the institutionalization of òrìṣà practices. It also demonstrates how concepts and practices can either be intentionally invoked in the procurement of power or come to constitute social norms by which society is regulated through an attempt to align values and morals with social judgments. Ultimately, the emergence of these varied forms of practices has constituted new crosscutting networks of practitioners engaged in the reformulation of òrìṣà practices for the purposes of religious reproduction and the remapping of the religion in racially territorialized terms.

Although there is a growing divide in the Americas between people who align themselves with Santería-Lukumi traditions and those who align themselves with Yorùbá traditionalists, that divide is often constituted within racial imaginaries that are complexly territorial. Practitioners in these religious networks limit themselves to neither one school or affiliation nor one territory of influence. Many use recursive approaches to time and space and subvert racial hierarchies of order and influence to distinguish themselves from each other. Thus, membership in religious networks is being understood in relation to packages of ancestral knowledge that crosscut nations. Through new knowledge networks, citizenship categories are being transformed by new categories of ancestry legitimated through ritual practices, and new sects are being increasingly supported by more books, videos, and packages of ancestral validation produced for mass conversion and religious reproduction.

To understand the particularities of change in òrìṣà revivalism in this regard, and to make sense of these growing forms of deterritorialized and denationalized institutions of knowledge developing in the West, we need to recast our understanding of linkages—national and racial—not in modern terms, in which territory and place standardized our classification of Others, but in relation to the historically constituted ways that people see linkages. These linkages reflect the order of particular social logics and shape the formation of new knowledge institutions: religious, legal, historical. In this regard, this book is about the making of an imaginary within particular fields of historical power. It is an attempt to chart field sites through nodes of regional interconnections. In this case, it is the black Atlantic world that is being mapped to provide a model for how transnational communities are forged within histories of displacement and how people, in an attempt to forge alliances, produce the terms for membership within institutions of power. As such, in involves asking, What are the nodes, assemblages, and domains in which these formations are taking place, and why?

The primary location of this study, Òyótúnjí Village, is neither a local village, a neighborhood of a larger community, nor a homogenized population that can be reduced to a single location. Although the site itself is the kind of very small rural community that the sociological literature often refers to as an "intentional community," Òyótúnjí Village represents a regionally diverse, transnational network of people and practices within and outside of the nation. Indeed, it is an intentional community in the standard sociological sense, describing an intended creation of a separate domestic arena. It is a reconstructed Yorùbá village in the rural region of Beaufort, South Carolina. I identify it as a site within a network of Yorùbá revivalists throughout the United States. I neither locate it as a marginal site, which relies on black-white dichotomies, nor do I take its unit of analysis as a demographically small community as the end of the story. Rather, I treat it as the middle of an ongoing story about the cultural production of deterritorialized institutions of power that have a life outside state hegemonies and within which new networks of religious exchange are struggled over, contested, and produced in particular regional zones. Today, anthropology is shifting from single-sited ethnography to multisited fieldwork that is indeed regional, national, and transnational. However, to understand these new networks and flows we need to understand how concepts of space and place are being reconceptualized not simply through people's imaginations of spaces constructed through institutions but through the ways people use these institutions to reclaim, and thus produce, the domains—spatial, temporal, national—in which modern classifications of ethnic and racial ancestry are being both usurped and reformulated. Thus, the modern and the postmodern are interrelated and mutually constitutive and the power of the transformation of categories are found in institutions where they are naturalized and formalized. Seen thus, the creation of new categories of belonging are sites of social change, for it is in the intersection of history and contingency that the reformulation of meanings are negotiated.

Following Marcus's (2000) articulation on the importance of multisited fieldwork, and taking up Akhil Gupta and James Ferguson's (1997b) critical call to change our conceptions of the relation between "here and there," I locate the ethnographic "field" of òrìsà practitioners on both sides of the Atlantic Ocean. The significance of such multisited explorations is in the tales people tell of the making of historical-cultural identity in ideological spheres posited against the backdrop of metaphorical realities of racial and national categories and narratives of transatlantic slave trade routes. These uses of identity classifications and the content of history are inscribed onto Ọ̀yọ́túnjí practitioners' understanding of the role of race, not culture, in shaping alliances for who can claim to be African in a changing transnational world.

The global reconfigurations of the new rights and racial heritage movements have led to the development of increasingly deterritorialized and denationalized group claims to modern subjectivities. Rejecting modern U.S. citizenship as the basis of their government's sovereignty over national identity, the predominant numbers of Ọ̀yọ́túnjí-aligned òrìṣà worshippers claim a prestate form of belonging. This reclassification of their citizenship as Americans is not dependent on a recognition of state territory and birth in that territory as the basis for citizenship. Indeed, citizenship is popularly described as the legal relationship between the individual and the polity. Thus, citizenship takes on a formalized character through nationality, what Sassen describes as a "key component of citizenship." Both refer to the state but depend on different legitimating domains by which subject statuses are defined. Nevertheless, Ọ̀yọ́túnjí notions of citizenship are deterritorial and stand outside the legitimacy of the national state-granting apparatus. It is what Sassen has referred to as "denationalized citizenship"; Stuart Hall (1993; Hall and Jacques 1983; Hall and du Gay 1996; Morley and Chen 1996) has elsewhere referred to it as "cultural citizenship," and Aihwa Ong (1999) has called it "flexible citizenship." Lying five thousand miles from the western-most tip of West Africa, outside of the geographic boundaries of African nation-states, Ọ̀yọ́túnjí Village is symbolic of a time of royal governance long ago, prior to the colonial conquest of the Ọ̀yọ́ Empire and the formation of nation-states. In its current conceptualization, practitioners have created a deterritorialized kingdom in a nation situated on the outer perimeter of Beaufort, approximately sixty-five miles southwest of Charleston, South Carolina. These conceptualizations are fundamentally tied to a rejection of citizenship as territorially embodied. Instead, their conceptions of African ancestry highlight an embodied notion of ancestors living through them. By examining the uses of nationalism and invocations of transnational racial alliances, this approach decenters the significance of territory and state-citizenship status in demarcating the distinctiveness of a people. Yet, though nationalism is an act of consciousness—a form of cultural politics, a subjective feeling of community that uses the concept of a nation, an imagined political community, to build a nonstate mode of civic governance—Ọ̀yọ́túnjí Village as a node in a network of religious revivalists is constituted by both cultural and political forms of nationalisms through which to produce new forms of membership. And although their nation is imagined, as Benedict Anderson would agree, it is not easily unimagined (Croucher 2003).

Map of South Carolina (United States of America in inset).

Ọyọ́túnjí was born of complex controversies over both the conditions of slavery from the late fifteenth to the mid-nineteenth century that brought Africans to the Americas and the mid-twentieth-century contestations over the legitimacy of adaptations of West African practices between African American converts and Afro-Cuban Catholics. Through particular imaginings of belonging to the nobility of African empires of the past, their descent from Africa outlines the ideological framework for revivalist governance. However real or imagined this construction, under question is the play of power by which the cultural logics of race serve as a basis for legitimizing black American claims to African identities.

And meanwhile, back in Africa? Yorùbá traditional religious practices are often rendered secondary to Christian and Muslim institutions. Unlike the large numbers of Yorùbá traditionalist worshippers outside of West Africa, in places such as Cuba and Brazil, most Nigerian Yorùbá are either self-professed Christians (48 percent) or Muslims (47 percent); many fewer are òrìṣà worshippers. The declining numbers of òrìṣà practitioners in Nigeria represent the fundamental tension between Yorùbá of southwestern Nigeria and Yorùbá revivalist heritage travelers from the West. The knowledge and advancement of these voyages offer black Americans the cultural capital of diasporic heritage seen as a valuable component of ancestral citizenship. They travel to West African countries for three primary reasons: òrìṣà knowledge, the need for and consumption of educational training in rituals and texts, and the commodification of African knowledge with the hope of building institutions of expertise back home. Through these and other forms of

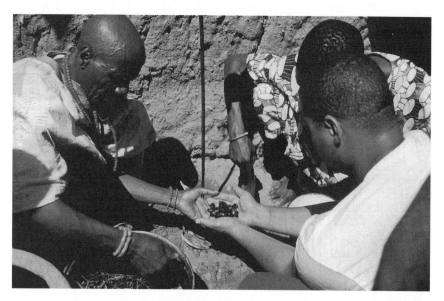

Ọ̀yọ́ òrìṣà practitioners initiating an Ọ̀yọ́túnjí practitioner undergoing an Ifá initiation. This phase of ritual involves prayers with kola nuts.

practice, Yorùbá revivalists participate in the making of African identities through the rendering of the homeland as ancestrally lived.

My findings indicate that despite these claims to Yoruba cultural citizenship, many Nigerian Yorùbá, however, insist on black American exclusion from Yorùbá membership, citing the popular trope that the transport of black people as captives to the Americas and the many generations of acculturation they endured led to the termination of cultural connections between Africans and African Americans. For this reason, black Americans, among many, no matter what their complexion, are often referred to as *òyìnbó* (meaning white man or outsider).

Ironically, Ọ̀yọ́túnjí travelers to Nigeria were equally inclined to classify Nigerians as "white black people," for they would say that the enduring power of colonialism and Christianity in the lives of their African-Nigerian compatriots led them to be far too willing to please, mimic, and uncritically adopt practices of "white people." Nigerian exclusions of Ọ̀yọ́túnjí are ironic because the Ọ̀yọ́túnjí argue that it is their legitimate right to reclaim and preserve the traditional authority of Yorùbá practices. As returnees to their homeland, they insisted that they were entitled to join the traditions of their ancestors and that the epistemological violence of European colonial history and religion rendered continental Yorùbá practices inauthentic.[2] Therefore, just as Nigerian Yorùbá rendered Ọ̀yọ́túnjí claims inauthentic because of their ancestral genealogies, Ọ̀yọ́túnjí practitioners rejected as

Nigerian Christian practitioners.

comical Nigerian adoption of "Western clothing"—pants, suits, hats—as well as foreign religious practices.

While some groups claim their distinctiveness as a result of the modernization of ritual and religious principles, and others recognize the relevance of transatlantic slavery in the substantive revision of Yorùbá practices, others, like Òyótúnjí practitioners, undermine the history of slavery that led to the radical transformation of Yorùbá orthodoxies. Instead, Òyótúnjí practitioners claim a racially exclusive orthodoxy, thereby deriving their source of inspiration from a Yorùbáland divinity.[3] Given these competing interests on both sides of the Atlantic, the interplay between different approaches and meanings of Yorùbá is important in the relationship between cultural production of membership and power—the power to change the terms of access and belonging and to mobilize resources in time and space. How do we chart what constitutes "the field" in a world of competing claims, especially when the implications of such a study is, at its core, about boundaries of demarcation or the expansion of increasingly autonomous practices?

Globalization and Yorùbá Religious Practices

Globalization is popularly characterized by two related processes. The first is the increasing economic integration of national economies through trade, product marketing, and capital investments. The second is related to the transformation of information technologies that mobilize computers, media, and telecommunications to reshape national and transnational economies. Attention to these global processes has often foundered on ahistoricity or has tended to render insignificant the ways locally constituted networks are transforming local practices. Globalization has led to changes that are altering basic components of social practices and, as Arjun Appadurai (2000) articulates, are leading to new institutional forms. One such component is the use of institutions to develop autonomous domains that borrow and create practices relevant to individual historical contexts and contemporary realities. These uses of closely related transnational knowledge institutions to produce new mechanisms for social change, while maintaining the appearance of continuity, are central to the relevance of the local in the global and the role of historical context in shaping how meanings are seen.

The global landscape is deeply historical and our structures of knowledge and power are shaped by inscriptions of the past. Similarly, new institutional formations are producing possibilities for imagining innovations in the distinctiveness of forms by which changes in particular practices are possible in an increasingly globalizing world; thus, the paradox of globalization is the centrality of locality and autonomy in making relevant the importation of different forms and meanings. Difference is blended into otherwise unrelated spheres and made hybrid. This transformation of meanings through mixing and moving grew with the development of increasingly independent institutions that made possible seemingly autonomous forms of practice.

If the globalization of Yorùbá revivalism is a production of increasingly autonomous practices, understanding the historical processes and divergent relations that shift the ways national belonging is reclassified by agents and local networks are built calls for an understanding of how practices shape the boundaries of membership. It calls specifically for an examination of the ideological processes by which agents produce a sense of place outside of traditionally recognized sedimentations of "community," "nation," and/or "nation-state." In the context of the formation of such a race-conscious movement as Òyótúnjí, attention to circum-Atlantic zones of exchange enables us to understand how membership is circumscribed within and outside of the nation and through the history of the forced migration of African captives.[4] By not claiming real distinctions between the validity of Òyótúnjí and Nigerian Yorùbá spaces as more or less "authentic," I identify the discursive strategies of both groups as they engage in the making of daily life, and I point to the historical particularities of divergent histories of Yorùbá cultural production.

Charting the zone of Yorùbá transnational cultural production, telling the complex tales of Òyó and Òyótúnjí contestations and negotiations, and the making of community through the development of new logics of special meaning cannot end with the varied stories about U.S. and African "natives." Òyó as a place in the Òyótúnjí imaginary represents histories and new sites of agency in constructing Yorùbá connections across time and space. However, because of the complexities of spatial and transnational interconnection, their story can neither be told only through pilgrimages and international conventions back to Africa, nor fully lived solely in Òyótúnjí. For, meanwhile, Santería practitioners are worshiping in New York City and in various locations throughout the United States and Cuba. Santería, a Cuban form of Yorùbá òrìsà worship and a symbol of a mestizo nation, is deeply enmeshed in plantation slavery in Cuba and the racialization of labor and speaks to the power of new innovations in religious social order. Santería practitioners—some claiming Hispanic roots, others claiming Afro-Cuban national identities, and still others claiming American or African heritage—are active participants in the production of Yorùbá-based practices in America. They too "travel," sometimes in body, sometimes through ritual, sometimes by electronic mail, to, through, or against Òyótúnjí and their African Yorùbá origins. There is a range of key nodal communities throughout the United States, including the Caribbean Cultural Center, whose longtime director, Marta Vega, brought it to national attention in the 1990s; John Mason and his Yorùbá networks in the U.S. Northeast; Ernesto Piccardo in Miami; and many other Yorùbá-Santería houses known for their drumming networks and ritual/possession power from the Bronx to Brooklyn, San Francisco to Seattle, Houston to Detroit, New Orleans to Buffalo.

Of late, however, controversies over the legitimacy of òrìṣà practices have centered around the 1990 orthodox pronouncements against Olúfadékẹ the Ìyánífá, a white American woman who became a priest of Ifá. Because she was not only a woman but was also seen as racially Other, the politics of race and gender brought to the fore critical questions about what constitutes Yorùbá practice, who should be included, and what are the legitimate mechanisms for inclusion and hierarchies of knowledge by which these practices are to be measured. Similarly, Olúwo Fágbàmílà, a white American priest of Ifá, was said to have transformed Yorùbá blood sacrifices. Rather than catch blood at the ritual site, he caught blood in the slaughterhouse and transported it as needed to the Yorùbá ritual site.[5] Such a reconstruction of ancient ritual is part of the many changes that are leading to the formation of and controversies surrounding new forms of practice in the Yorùbá "elsewheres."

Electronic technologies, circulating publications, and films about òrìṣà religious and cultural practices have played a critical role in enabling the expansion of Yorùbá transnational religions in North and South America, England, and Canada; the formation of Ifá College is one example. Such an institute is in competition with Ọ̀yọ́túnjí networks, as it is providing òrìṣà religious training to a new generation of practitioners formerly excluded from participation in African ritual practices. Boasting a wide spectrum of faculty members from the United States and Africa, Ifá College is creating increased horizontal linkages across Africa and the United States. With a stated mission of the dissemination of the *wisdom of ancient Africa to the Modern world* (see www.ifacollege.com/faculty.htm), the college is opening the parameters of òrìṣà membership to a broader clientele—this time, predominantly white American students and professionals—thereby creating a university mechanism for the teaching and accreditation of òrìṣà practices as well as an Internet resource for potential converts.

Whether to gain knowledge or to experience modes of contestations embedded in ongoing negotiations of sacred rituals—rituals of touristic presence, through text, orality, or computer technologies—the interrelationships among racial differences, gender restrictions, ethnic rivalries, and Santería- and Ọ̀yọ́túnjí-based differences are deeply historical and transnationally complex, requiring extensive mappings of movements both in relation to people and in relation to institutions of knowledge and their mechanisms for legitimacy. And ironically, Yorùbá traditionalism in Nigerian village communities and urban centers is increasingly dependent on the patronage of local and global practitioners and students, black and white alike. This increasing reliance on those in the circum-Atlantic region and their demands for ritual knowledge from African practitioners point to the power of preexisting interrelations among Yorùbá networks today, in which capital and information are being separated from place and transformed across national boundaries.

To address how both studies of and processes inherent in globalization are producing new methodological shifts from single-sited conceptions of "the field" to the field as emblematic of the larger networks of social organization is to mark the ways in which localized flows that were once the object of local studies are today troublesome objects of analysis. Today the village site, and all that constitutes it, is best captured through networks of interconnection between the rural and the urban, the regional and the national, and the national and the transnational.

Today, if an anthropological study of a "village," however rendered, can provide a statement about the world writ small, what message can the world at large render for a small village constructed on the historical abyss of the triangular slave trade, the reason black Americans were transported from Africa in the first place? Recognizing the centrality of place not just as location but as being centrally about ways of producing rights to seeing spatial meanings, I do not use the case of Ọ̀yọ́túnjí òrìṣà voodoo and its related urban networks as either a typical village or a radical example of social inventions. Rather, when examined in relation to the ways people make and produce meaning in their lives, òrìṣà voodoo is an example of how politics figures into the making of everyday life in particular conditions of history making and structures of hegemony. These are moments in which new norms are shaped with preexisting institutions. Therefore, understanding the conditions for legitimacy is critical for any analysis of transnational networks in which particular linkages are easily imagined and others either require additional mechanisms of legitimacy or are already foreclosed. Approaching notions of social change in these terms opens up possibilities for highlighting both the how and where of the hegemonic stability of spatial cartographies of belonging.

Authority, Change, and Institutions: How Deterritorialization Works

Since September 11, 2001, when the World Trade Center was destroyed by Islamic fundamentalist suicide bombers, religion has reemerged as an increasingly central force in international politics. Prior to September 11, however, issues connected to the rule of law, the age of treaties, the centrality of democracy, and social movements making claims for civil and human rights and new economic consequences of globalization preoccupied the international stage. Today articulations of religious groups and revivalist organizations are being called on to justify autochthonous claims to homelands and ancient civilizations. The state boundaries that, with the rise of the European empires, shaped the landscape of the modern world are being reinterpreted with new structures for promoting political power. These forms of political power operate with their own sphere of logic and provide practitioners with forms of knowledge by which to interpret and act upon their world.

Like other religious-legal systems, Yorùbá religious cosmology has its own processes for identifying and formulating which practices are to be considered legitimate and which are not. These sources of legitimacy operate in particular fields of logic and reasoning and are essential components of the varied reformulations taking shape in the West. Ultimately, there is no clear separation between the religious ritual system that shapes Yorùbá knowledge and the customary rules that frame which practices are acceptable. They operate in entangled institutions of knowledge and vary in hierarchies of sources. The differences in application lie in three domains: the interpretive authority of particular divinatory forms that shape the legitimacy of òrìṣà logic, the recognition of those forms of logic by others, and the methodologies by which practitioners achieve such logic.

Divination represents the central organizing mechanism through which the world of Yorùbá practitioners is understood. Diviners are critical, for not only are they key intellectual producers, but they possess the power of interpretation, thereby making divinatory verses applicable to the case at hand. It is believed that the divinatory sources—the stories of ritual knowledge—are sacred because they were communicated from Olódùmarè (the Yorùbá god) through intermediaries known as òrìṣàs (deities). As thus told, these proverbs and songs represent characterizations of òrìṣà, believed to have once been kings, heroes, and soldiers with human imperfections. Upon death, they are believed to have transformed themselves and reentered the human world in the form of the sky, sea, and earth, and they are represented by various colors, environmental conditions, and personality characteristics with the goal of divine guidance. Today, those who follow the teachings of Olódùmarè do so by interpreting verses through various divinatory oracles, such as Ifá.[6] These forms of divinatory teachings are constituted in the verses of the Ifá oracle and describe the lifeworlds of the òrìṣà, seen as Olódùmarè's messages to his sons and daughters and therefore timeless and a reflection of Olódùmarè's divinity. Ultimately, divinatory knowledge is the gateway into the cosmic world, and it is through such forms of ritual that narratives of ancestry are concretized.[7] However, differences in the interpretation of the divinatory corpus reflect differences in the field of cultural production within which practitioners are situated. In òrìṣà communities there are both personal divinatory rules and sociopolitical rules. The primary source of Yorùbá religious rules is derived from verses from the divinatory corpus, and the application is based on the diviner's interpretation of the verses (*odù*) for personal advice or to explain issues of larger social relevance.

Divinatory ritual plays a central role in producing sacred knowledge about the past, present, and future (destiny) and, in so doing, shapes social rules that have come to constitute particular norms in the circum-Atlantic world. In relation to the Yorùbá Ọ̀yọ́túnjí, these norms work to establish social rules that govern social life, such as rules of death, family/marriage, social obligation, civil law, and protocol and procedure. The rules developed out of these codes of social conduct, secular and religious, took shape in Ọ̀yọ́túnjí over a thirty-year period and were legitimated by the seat of Ọ̀yọ́túnjí governance, the Ògbóni society.

The Ògbóni society is one of the highest institutions of secular authority in both Nigeria and Ọ̀yọ́túnjí and establishes religious and secular rules in the community. Members of the society are also cult members and play a central role in the legitimation of which rules and practices should be incorporated for the purposes of òrìṣà religious reproduction. Today, as new networks of practitioners form governing bodies that distinguish them from others, contestations over the legitimacy of Yorùbá practices in the Americas are becoming more volatile. Complaints of misinterpretations of the divinatory oracle, criticism that initiations performed outside of the homeland are not being conducted properly, accusations of sexual exploitation as a result of interpretive abuse, and threats that if certain tasks are not ritually performed the person will suffer are all central to ongoing contestations over what constitutes legitimate Yorùbá interpretations and what should be the sources of knowledge for legitimate knowledge production.

In the 1960s and 1970s, racial differences between light-skinned Afro-Cuban immigrants who performed Santería rituals and black Americans who participated in them represented a typical divide in òrìṣà contestations in the Americas. Today, although at various times Santería leaders have been allied with òrìṣà voodoo practitioners, there is a growing division between the Ọ̀yọ́túnjí òrìṣà voodoo orthodoxy and those African and Santería practitioners who have affiliated themselves with modernists interested in Yorùbá traditions updated for universal access. Priest-intellectuals of òrìṣà religious laws, both inside and outside of Nigeria, have formulated rules applicable to the historical circumstances within which the practice was shaped and became acceptable by those involved. In line with Christian theology, the modernization of Yorùbá religion is taking shape in institutional structures of knowledge that are both in alliance with traditional formulations and responsive to new formations of migration and domains of access. There are many ways to chart the mechanisms of legitimacy through which these alliances are taking shape. These developments intensified over the last two decades of the twentieth century and are providing practitioners with the necessary tools to render secondary the fact of place in particular fields of power. Instead, new institutional mechanisms of religious ritual, ritual rules and doctrine, and the narratives of the customary past enable the production of Yorùbá spatial formations and make possible particular linkages between the West and the non-West. These sources of knowledge shape ways of seeing what is "legitimate" and, of late, are being propelled by technological engines, such as the Internet, and forming new gateways for òrìṣà knowledge transactions.

These formations of networks and forms of circulation are not without interpretive disagreement. With the consequent growth of various forms of electronic technologies, new forms of access to information and videos and films about Yorùbá religious cultural practices globally are contributing to the institutionalization of African-derived cultural identities being invented and procured for the reproduction of religious life outside of Africa. Of noteworthy mention are the widespread Yorùbá events, such as monthly festivals, national conventions for the standardization of rituals, conferences in rotating cities such as the biannual World Òrìṣà Conference, electronic information posted over the Internet, and the invention of new ritual institutions that are producing new forms of practices. These practices are increasingly being planted outside of African countries, contributing to the growing decentralization of knowledge production in various places and the production of particular discourses of òrìṣà practices that are fundamentally imagined in relation to transatlantic slavery and a widening interpretation of divinatory doctrine. Nevertheless, despite fragmentation in epistemologies and sources and the increasingly autonomous diasporic practices, such deterritorialized networks still constitute a unit of analysis for anthropological inquiry, though not in the classic area studies form.

Late-twentieth-century refashionings of what constitutes the field and what groups of people are bound, or not, are being reconceptualized through a rethinking of difference and geographical disunity as endemic to social life. Today's anthropologists now ask: What are the deterritorialized institutions of knowledge and power that link spatially disparate people? What are the fields of authority and customs that shape legitimacy? What are the conditions of historical possibility that shape particular ways of seeing linkage? Central to understanding the reconfigurations of anthropology's traditionally studied field sites and how people's uses of the imagination create new networks of linkage is a fundamental story of historical fields of change. This story is inscribing onto particular global movements what Lisa Rofel (2001) has argued are particular "historical characteristics" that frame particular forms of practices.

The processes of social change that we are witnessing today are in the backdrop of late-twentieth-century reconfigurations of global spaces in the wake of decolonization and the end of the cold war. The reorganization of capitalism into new institutional forms is producing new networks, new forms of practices, and shifts in technological means of communication. The spread of capital, pushed forward by electronic technologies and changing national and international commodity regimes, has increased distances between sites of production in Third World countries and sites of consumption in the West. The new millennium has seen an intensification of economic and technological development that has further contributed to shifts in the migration of people from rural to urban locations, from former colonies to former colonial governments, and from poorer to richer nations. These economic disparities and institutional reconfigurations in governments, corporations, and localities are influencing why and where people move, leading to new definitions of citizenship for religious, ethnic, and nationalist reproduction. Since the end of the cold war, various manifestations of transnational and multinational linkages between African nations and the West have revolutionized how Africans from various nations have engaged in transnational interactions across wide-scale capitalist economies. And these linkages and interactions are embedded in new institutions for legitimizing meaning.

Yet, despite the apparent newness of these shifts, the modernity of national origins of the nineteenth and early twentieth century, which fixed nomadic movement to sedimentation and *biologized* citizenship, has continued to inform how people link human belonging to national origins and racial groups to perceived racial and ethnic typologies. Even as governments and social scientists attempt to establish analytic standards by which to measure qualitative and quantitative meanings of these social changes, there is a continuing intellectual schism between emphasizing the expansiveness of the global while also increasing attention on the extent to which historically inscribed patterns undergird new formations. Similarly, scientific institutions of knowledge developed along with the formalization of modern territorial ideologies and the social sciences, as they took shape in modern conceptions of nationhood and further contributed to the standardization of particular meanings of personhood and physical attachment.

The development of the science of anthropology, therefore, involved the development of innovations in methods for documenting and charting social norms and behavior within particular narratives of origins and territorial belonging. Anthropology's village studies of the early twentieth century contributed to conceptualizations of territorially and biologically distinctive peoples and cultures in relation to nation-states. These notions of territorial placement were used by governmental and social scientific institutions to reinforce conceptions of belonging in relation to how bodies, space, and time were to be understood. Anthropology's original focus on local communities—as isolated microcosms—failed to capture social worlds that were becoming interconnected in increasing fields of interaction. The spatial domains within which these articulations were presumed to be "natural" were shaped just as much by ideologies of *seeing* connections as they were by *actual* connections.

Those at the forefront of the formalization of African studies in anthropology at the turn of the nineteenth century also witnessed rapid change out of mostly European contact and colonial governance, but their questions were inspired by the search to discover rules of change in relation to detailed articulations of space shaped by their own ideologies of seeing space. Approaches to studying Africa and its spatial organization are far from new; anthropologists were as conscious of space, place, and kinship in the early to mid-twentieth century as they are now. The difference is that kinship groupings were often detailed according to "unitary groups" and their designations in relation to attachments to "natural" territories (Gupta and Ferguson 1997b), whereas today the deterritorialization of group practices from homelands is shaping new ways of understanding subjectivity. My inquiry here builds on these insights to demonstrate how particular ideologies of *seeing* place, thus belonging, produced early anthropological conceptions of placement and membership. These forms of spatial practices (Clifford 1997) were reflective of particular ways of seeing subjectivity and reflected a general climate of ethnography as science and people as territorially constituted within particular measurable units. As the shifts of subjects on the move intensified, so did anthropology's approaches to understanding changes in spatial organization. However, the social scientists engaged in studying marginalized people in bound communities were the same social scientists whose attention to space and place was used to chart the function of particular practices in the reproduction of society. Anthropological fields of study were shaped by particular ways of seeing communities and groups for the purposes of scientific units of analysis. By charting this genealogy of place and spatial ideology in the history of anthropology fieldwork, I demonstrate how ideological understandings of territoriality have shifted—from that of spatial structure and organization to the process of producing space and identity with new technologies of knowledge—thereby calling for an anthropology of critical studies of transnational networks within particular historically inscribed fields of power.

Toward a Genealogy of Seeing Place: Formations of Territorialized Subjecthood

Since the early twentieth century, research on Africa has moved from concerns with the origins of the "primitive" as embodied in particular local sites to the survivals and changes of African cultural practices (see Tylor 1865, 1871/1958; Fraser 1922; Herskovits 1941; V. W. Turner 1969; Bascom 1969a, 1969b, 1980; Bastide 1971), to the ongoing contemporary investigation into the processes by which African warfare and displacement and the search for labor have produced people on the move (Nadel 1942; Mitchell 1956; Middleton 1966; Colson 1971), to the ways cultural practices are played out locally and globally (Mintz and Price 1976; Williams, 1991; Olúpònà 1991, 1997, 2000; Apter 1992; Akínnasọ 1983a, 1983b, 1995; Clarke 1997, 1999, 2002; Matory 1999; Piot 1999; Worby 1994, 1995, 2001; Capone 1999a, 1999b; Brown 2003). Over the past twenty years, as anthropologists moved from conducting the bulk of their research in "small-scale, face-to-face" societies to investigations of sites and topical issues in seemingly "complex" societies, the shift pointed to the need to address the methodological problems while understanding the intensified complexities of research in "class-stratified," "ethnically diverse" or "plural" and "racially fractured" contemporary societies.

Scholarly attention to the centrality of complex differences has led to the breakdown of bounded concepts of the village, nation, and "culture" that established the contexts for anthropological local studies. In part, these shifts were motivated by the contradictions of studying social production under the conditions of empirical investigation that ensued at the time. However, they were also motivated by empirical changes that resulted from frequent contact between people. With advancements in technology, the mid-twentieth century was a period of substantive increases in the extent to which people, ideas, and things traveled and interacted more quickly than ever before. These shifts in capital, institutions, historical trajectories, and rules of citizenship resulted in the need to rethink not only the ways that agents in deterritorialized contexts reshape spaces to produce new meanings of place, but, most centrally, the relationship between particular places and what Annelise Riles (2000) would refer to as the institutional "networks" that connect them. This shift from the local to the interplay between the local and the global to the multisited study (Marcus 1998) of institutional networks is critical for understanding how zones of interaction are not only imagined and shaped, but also aligned along domains of knowledge and power.

Many late nineteenth- and early to mid-twentieth-century ethnographies, especially some of the classic accounts, used the ethnographic present to describe the people they studied and often used intensive fieldwork focus on specific communities. This had the effect of structuring the field site in temporal and spatial isolation without attention to people's engagement with outside influences and historical contexts. The studies of villages by Bronislaw Malinowski (1932, 1935), Alfred Reginald Radcliffe-Brown (1922, 1952), and later generations of British social anthropologists, including Max Gluckman (1941, 1943a, 1943b), Meyer Fortes (1949), and E. E. Evans-Pritchard (1937) were often based on the long residence and intensive data collection from which systematic studies of villages emerged. In these studies, change was understood in relation to assessments of tradition as compared with the institutionalization of European colonial governance. As an academic discipline, anthropology was consolidated through the work of Malinowski, and questions of cultural change were understood by early ethnographers in relation to the cultural elements borrowed and transformed from distinct racial groups to create new cultural realities. From 1915 to 1918 Malinowski traveled in New Guinea in the southwest Pacific to study the Trobriand Islanders and to document the practices of clan/tribal groups and villages. With his systematic mapping of villagers and villages in relation to their clan units as his unit of analysis, he developed the early goals of anthropological fieldwork. Later, in 1934, he contributed to the systematization of social anthropology when, along with Radcliffe-Brown, he engaged this method and trained a generation of anthropologists to document the lifeworlds of people living in African villages.

Although both Malinowski's and later Radcliffe-Brown's generation of anthropologists were primarily concerned with developing social theories to chart African social organization and understand cultural change, their accounts of the African Other were also used to establish a coherent scientific logic for village studies in which their interest in locality was concerned with the precise reiteration of the spatial layout and the biological relatedness of their interlocutors. Space-related themes were grounded in specific localities and were shaped by larger missions of understanding the social organization of the Other. These studies reinforced the relationships among territory, authentic social groups, and kinship, perpetuating the study of coherent African social systems in isolated national or colonial borders. With these approaches to the uses of space, the publications that emerged out of detailed ethnographic research furthered the existence of "authentic cultures" that could be located in single sites far away in the bush or primitive jungle (for more, see Stanley Diamond's *In Search of the Primitive*, 1974). By producing social theories that articulated culture as a system of collective habits that fulfilled vital functions in the development of a working whole, various early anthropologists contributed to the critical production of ethnographic monographs by charting the coherence of "cultures" and "peoples" within place-based localities.

Two variants of functionalism, as these theories were later termed, served this purpose—especially the type of analysis developed by Radcliffe-Brown—after the death of Malinowski. Functionalism dominated much of social theory, playing a critical role in the development of methods and rationales for the study of kinship and social organization in the advancement of social anthropology as a science. Evans-Pritchard (1940, 1951, 1956), working among the Azande and Nuer tribes of the southern Sudan, built on classical tenets of functionalism and as a framework for exploring the causalities of beliefs, the structural cohesion of practices, and ways of understanding social change in ritual contexts. He studied the proliferation of witchcraft as symptomatic of the consequences of rapid change in African societies and demonstrated that Zande society did not exist in a state of stasis. Instead, developing a dialectical theory of change and continuity, he argued that the proliferation of religious beliefs followed particular patterns of cultural logic that developed as a response to the forms of social change experienced as a result of ideas, regulations, and practices introduced by colonial administrators or Christian missionaries. These approaches to documentation set up a system of articulation that consisted of a group of people and particular cultural practices. The area that Evans-Pritchard referred to as the Azande was actually a handful of tribal kingdoms bordered by bush land. The forms of governance in each kingdom were characterized by a royal dynasty. Despite these distinctions in group formation, in the context of the emergent world of colonial administration of native land, it was as critical for Evans-Pritchard to understand native logics of place-naming as it was to understand the role of place-naming in social organization. As he showed, the layout of kingdoms seemed to repeat the same logic—divisions into provinces and the administration of these provinces by younger male relatives and wealthy non-relative commoners. Yet, exploring the production of these forms of organization and linking them to divergences in other forms of place-making was irrelevant to the enterprise because the questions asked had more to do with an a priori existence of place and people than with the fragmentary and ongoing production and reclassification of meanings of place and identity in time and space.

Evans-Pritchard's approach became popularized in England as structural functionalism. As an analytic approach, it provided classical anthropologists with the necessary data to establish analytic accounts of the systems that ordered particular societies that presupposed a priori spatial sedimentation. Evans-Pritchard's ethnographies, as well as many of the other ethnographies of Africa written at that time, also included an interest in space but always in relation to the rules of social organization of daily life in village societies. With the critical role of missionization and colonial governance, the production of anthropological knowledge led to the understanding of the individual in relation to predictable behavior patterns of people spatially located in the territorial demarcations of those societies.

Following similar approaches to understanding the individual in relation to social organization, and pursuing questions of how to understand those changes in
relation to colonial governance, Max Gluckman (1941, 1943a, 1943b) documented
the influence of the practice and regulations of colonial rule on cultural meanings
among the people of the Lozi kingdom in rural Barotseland. Although Gluckman
began with assumptions about the static character of the precolonial African village, he analyzed cultural processes as variables to be used in understanding the
development of social rules and their changes over time. Similarly, anthropologists such as Meyer Fortes (1949) tried to understand social organization among
the Tallensi through ritual and filiation by charting descent groups in relation to
family lineage and totem beliefs. Detailing the politics of kinship and political alliances among the Tallensi, he explained their constituted spheres of obligation in
relation to their logic of filiation elaborated on the rules that shaped kinship (1970).
Like most anthropologists of his time, Fortes analyzed domestic kinship patterns
as they were connected to large-scale place units. According to his theories of standardized social systems, kinship and ritual units served to produce connected and
interlocking communities of individuals in time and place. For many British anthropologists engaged in village studies of the time, locality was produced through
social functions, and these functions existed for the purpose of reproducing social
life. With these new approaches to understanding "primitive societies," theories
of social change emerged from rapidly changing colonial institutions that were
taking form throughout African colonies.

Proponents of structural functionalism developed analytic concepts with which
to understand the social structures that reproduced operations transmitted
through "bundles and relations" (Lévi-Strauss 1963). For many who used these
structuralist approaches, culture was reproduced internally, by which they meant
from one cultural group to another, as well as from one individual to another
(Forde 1941, 1951, 1956;[8] Evans-Pritchard and Fortes 1940; Gluckman 1943a,
1943b, 1948, 1959; Colson 1949, 1958, 1960, 1962, 1974; Colson and Gluckman
1951). The resultant ethnographic monographs of these scholars as well as many
more early anthropologists served the goal of demonstrating the logic of structure
and form of African societies located in the territorial boundaries of the colonial
state. Most saw Africanness as primordial, reproducing particular patterns of social
organizations that were tied to place. Most tended to uphold the idea of African
societies as bounded by local kinship and village linkages that linked cultural practices to local territories, as Nelson Graburn (2002) described; some examined the
movement and displacement of people.

Most anthropologists who worked in Africa preferred to study their interlocutors in traditional settings until the pioneering works of Nadel (1942) on the

multiethnic Nupe city of Bida in Nigeria, Mitchell's work (1956) on the African migrant laborers of the Copper Belt, and Colson's (1971) study of the displacement of the Gwembe Tonga by the creation of the Kariba Dam. Until the 1935 publication of Linton et al.'s "Memorandum of Acculturation," many anthropologists were not officially interested in the dynamics of power and change; often, they assumed, for instance, that Reservation Indians in the United States were living "traditional" lives, or they focused on the idealized lives remembered by their older informants. It was only after World War II that the presence of modernity loomed large and became the dominant factor in the lives of anthropological subjects (Graburn 2002, 23).

As changes in people's displacement continued to intensify with the industrialization of communities, changes in what constituted the field in anthropological research took shape in the second half of the twentieth century. These shifts in what Gupta and Ferguson (1997b) referred to as the "association of citizens of states and their territories as natural" were transformed in relation to the rapidly growing urbanization movements, driven further by newly flourishing European empires. These new economic and political investments and the development of new sociopolitical institutions of the 1960s were at the center of anthropological questions of culture and the role of context and state power.

This book is not an attempt to reinstate village studies and particular naturalizations of spatial subjectivity to the center of anthropological work. Functional structuralist approaches can no longer sustain the complexities of understanding social organization in relation to changing cultural practices of the twentieth century. Despite the cartographies of warfare and governance, colonialism and boundary making that constituted these emergent nations, anthropologists presented associations of people and places as commonsensical and natural (Gupta and Ferguson 1997a, 1997b). Though it would be wrong to suggest that studies of space and place are new to anthropology, this genealogy serves to demonstrate that studies of place and social organization were as important to the anthropological enterprise then as they are today; questions of social change, whether inspired by early-twentieth-century changes as a result of European colonialism or early-twenty-first-century changes as a result of post–cold war intensifications of global institutions, were as critical to ongoing understandings of social theory as they are today. Building on these insights, I shift my trajectory to demonstrate how the process of institutionalizing particular forms of practices (academic, religious, ritualistic, etc.) shapes the ideologies within which spatial organization is understood and naturalized. For although notions of space and group classification have always been fundamental to the anthropological enterprise, the concept of space as produced through meanings of place, and of race as a classificatory construct with material consequences, are atypical of anthropological village studies of Africa. I return to the villages as field sites as well as discourses of race and their territorial connections to modern nations not as an attempt to identify them as sole units of analysis, nor as a means of theorizing the function of culture by focusing on a small-scale village obsessed with the introduction of race as culture. I return to them as a way to differently map cultural production and notions of territorial belonging by demonstrating how locality is ideologically mapped using historically constituted logics.

In the 1970s Laura Nader (1971) called on anthropologists to shift their gaze from village sites to institutions and corporations: "Studying up" was her call to study one's "own society"; she argued that "anthropologists might indeed ask themselves whether the entirety of field work does not depend upon certain power relationships in favor of the anthropologist." She asked how anthropologists would conceptualize reinventing themselves if they were to "study the colonizers rather than the colonized, the culture of power rather than the culture of the powerless, the culture of affluence rather than the culture of poverty." Thus, she called for an exploration of the sociopolitics of poverty as well as the institutions and organizations that participate in its reproduction. The 1980s and 1990s thus marked the beginning of studies by anthropologists investigating not only urban settings and institutions of economic power but also the transformation of anthropology as the study of the Other, Third World peoples, by the West.

Today, village localities are far from isolated and territorially bound and should be conceptualized in relation to transnational connections and vertical processes of local norm production. The circulation of anthropological knowledge about peoples and cultures, the role of state governance, and interdependent economies of race and capital continue to inform the authority by which contemporary Africans and African Americans understand their cultural past. These norms of traditional customs constitute the subject in relation to modern territorial attachments.

In the last decade of the twentieth century George Marcus (1995), in his essay "Ethnography in/of the World System: The Emergence of a Multi-Sited Ethnography," called for anthropologists to follow people and flows. Arjun Appadurai (1996b) developed an anthropology of flows to mark the transformation of the modern. However, today, as the classifications and values that once marked the colonization of territories are shifting and becoming more blurred than ever, the anthropology of the twenty-first century is increasingly marked by the reorganization of institutions and the questioning of related logics. These late-twentieth-century and early-twenty-first-century processes have highlighted the need for "mobile" ethnographies (Marcus 1995) that expand what constitutes the field, how the field looks, and what institutional mechanisms are called on to produce these linkages. It involves an understanding of multisited networks and how these linkages have been used by people to shrink space—such as the deterritorialization of Africa in the Americas—and to facilitate the production of diasporic imaginaries that are not only historically linked but that have become relevant through the invocation of variables such as race.

Under examination in the pages to come are explorations of the particularities of Yorùbá diasporic governance, in which practitioners remap space and time, thereby making a distinction between the lived and the imaginary, the real and the intentional production of "the real" as well as the politics of hegemony and agency that are productive of community formation. Such processes of community formation involve understanding the institutions that are called on to engage in space making—to create the socially "real." These shifts in ideology and movement call into question how we understand the particularities of place as well as how people use canonical hegemonies to reclassify human subjectivity, even as they reproduce them within deterritorialized networks. Historical inscriptions of canonical forms continue to undergird the complex zones of interconnection that enable us to map transnational relations through the complex making of space and place both within and outside of historical zones of origins. Given the nature of knowledge as fundamentally hierarchical and what constitutes legitimate forms as structurally hegemonic, we need to articulate what mechanisms in the circulations of knowledge in the late twentieth and early twenty-first century are at play in the zone of black Atlantic Yorùbá production. How have these mechanisms affected the way individuals understand and interpret their past? What role does history play in the demarcation of social boundaries? Such a focus calls into question the nature of "indigenous" knowledge in the first place; it provincializes the centrality of local origins and foregrounds the circularity of knowledge, and the particularities of its movement, and the forms of hegemony that shape its structure.

Taking theoretical inspiration from Carolyn Martin Shaw's (1995) *Colonial Inscriptions*, in which she documented how the early anthropological circulation of knowledge about Kenya was at the center of Jomo Kenyatta's Mau Mau liberation struggle, I demonstrate that colonial reinscriptions are fundamental to understanding how new practices are easily domesticated into local taxonomies. Today's formations of regional and transregional networks represent a return to the underlying formations of the development of modern capitalism. As such, we see how, in the process of integrating new postcolonial linkages, the inscriptions of colonialism continue to be deeply embedded in postcolonial articulations of the (post)modern future.

Understanding the ways that Yorùbá revivalist practitioners chart genealogies in particular confines of inclusion serves as a guide for understanding the ways that, despite displacement, practitioners use race as a form of liberation, even as they participate in producing the very practices of territorial and racial demarcations they had intended to undermine. This is not arbitrary, nor is it a product of choice or free will. How blackness and homelands are imagined has everything to do with the ideological formations of recognition that shape how they are seen, recognized, read, and interpreted. Indeed, Yorùbá transnational revivalism, like all articulations of contemporary cultural identities, is deeply embedded in modernist conceptions of space, nationhood, and family that construct notions of the individual in relation to fixed categories. These conceptions are historically constituted; through the reclassification of spatial meanings people engage in place making through the mappings of imaginary cartographies and particular modernist reinscriptions of belonging. Recent work on the interplay among the global, the local, and the politics of place has shown how ideologies of imagining are shaped by sociohistorical realities. Some scholars who explore theories of globalization suggest that contemporary processes of globalization are not new, that recent migration over the twentieth and early twenty-first century has affected only a small percentage of the world's population. Instead, they argue, earlier migration, with fewer restrictions on immigration, amounted to larger mass movements, thereby exceeding what is going on today. Such approaches often represent globalization not as a change in kind but as a change in degree, in which the development of those processes popularly articulated as distinctive are seen as part of a continuum that has been emerging over centuries (Llewellen 2002).

It is true that such transnational forms of capital have evolved and have been evolving over the development of capitalism worldwide (Patterson 1999), but there is a difference between charting the historical roots of national and transnational formations and charting the fundamental transformation of practices. Globalization is about both historical processes and distinct breaks in the texture of daily life. And the deterritorialization of capital, daily production, and technologically driven knowledge forms has produced ruptures in not only daily practices but also ideological conceptions of belonging that, through technology institutions, for example, allow people to communicate across borders and reinvent forms of belonging that are at once transnationally imaginary and deterritorial. Some, like Appadurai (1996b), have argued that the shift in subjective identification, from being based in nation-states to more transnationally interconnected forms, is revolutionizing the ways that new geographies of power are being culturally reconstituted through the deterritorialized imaginary.[9] Accordingly, they have referred to these processes as globalization, explaining them in strictly classificatory terms. Recasting the nation-state as the sole unit of scale for social science inquiry, this literature has charted deterritorializing transformations of space, community, and origins. Exploring such processes through new global formations (Ong 1999), this approach focuses on how groups that claim diasporic linkages to other regions or that are engaged in circular migrations are being transformed by interactions between the local and the global and between imaginary and lived social worlds (Appadurai 1991, 1996b, 1998a, 1998b; Martin Shaw 1995; Clarke 1997; Matory 1999; Rofel 1999; Piot 1999). While a conception of the imaginary looms large in this approach, this is often not without an understanding of the political economy that shapes the meanings embedded in these imagined worlds (Massey 1994; Gupta and Ferguson 1997a, 1997b; Ong 1999).

Those Africanists who remain skeptical of the novelty of late-twentieth-century global capitalism frame these processes in larger historical terms that mark prior moments in which revolutionary change in information technologies has contributed to the internationalization of markets. This approach has called for an analysis of domination and social change over centuries.

These two approaches to the study of globalization are not always distinct, but are overlapping and convergent. Where one argues that the period following the cold war led to the intensification of mass communication and that the reorganization of financial markets in the late twentieth century and early twenty-first century is distinct from what preceded it, the other emphasizes that the economic, cultural, and migratory movements and the formations of capitalism and related forms of governance that make up globalization are not new. Supporters of the latter position assert that populations have traveled and traded for centuries and that the revolution in telecommunications of today is an extension of the historical expansion of capitalism (Hart 1999; Latour 1993; Wallerstein 1983, 1986, 1991; Cooper 2001). Clearly, both positions have merit, and my argument is informed by both. The historical development of capitalism has set the material and ideological framework for contemporary capitalism and therefore underlies the regional circulations of labor, concepts, practices, and forms of identities as we have come to know them.

My point of convergence and departure is Appadurai (1996b), who theorizes the complexities of locality by framing the movement of capital, people, and ideas. However, I emphasize that understanding transnational movements and ways of seeing spatial and physical connections across boundaries involves understanding how historical inscriptions shape ways of seeing meanings and connections—even when there are few visible linkages.

In charting new terrain for understanding these complex processes of change and mobility, Appadurai (1996b, following Anderson 1983) asserts that the contemporary period is characterized by a rupture with the past in which the imagination and the imaginary are "no longer mere fantasy" but are constructed in a landscape of social practices, "a form of negotiation between sites of agency (individuals) and globally defined fields of possibility." This "unleashing" of the imagination, according to Appadurai, is itself "a key component of the new global order." As such, the global present can be described through the motion of people and images across the geographic boundaries that were previously overdetermined by concepts such as nation-state and ethnicity. These migrations and shifts in mass media capabilities are contributing to the reconfiguration of new imaginaries. Such an approach to the workings of culture and imagination demonstrates that culture is less a realm of reproducible practices and dispositions (*habitus*), and more an arena for the interplay between conscious choice and hegemonic power. It moves us from an approach to culture that focuses on the domination of the state through which objects are made, secured, and rendered intelligible, to culture as the historically constituted flows of cultural ideas and imaginaries. By arguing that the imagination is a space of contestation and that through the imagination groups are constituted and commonalities deployed, Appadurai shows how the boundaries of culture and nationhood are permeable and regimes of governance reshaped. In this light, he produces new mechanisms to analyze these local and global cultural processes and offers deterritorialization as a way to describe the reconfiguration of subjects within spheres that require neither the physicality of place nor the presence of nation-states.

Deterritorialization reflects shifts in geography, wherein territorial places, borders, and distances that were previously central to national state affairs are becoming increasingly significant outside physical territories. It provides us with an analytic for understanding people's practices in space and highlights the ways that new self-conceptions and self-fashionings are made, and remade, outside the structures of territorially based place alone. In this realm of deterritorialized possibility, the consumption of mass mediation is one of the modalities that contribute to the production of new imaginaries. Appadurai (1993, 33) introduces the term "scapes" as an alternative conceptualization of deterritorialized flows. By describing scapes as global cultural flows that carry with them the force of institutions, this argument is useful for its insights into the transformative possibilities of spatial and temporal fantasy. Thus, scapes are the irregular and disjunctural forms of perspectival constructs that once constituted scholarly concept of "culture," a thing bound in time and space or producing larger systems of meanings. Instead, today, Appadurai argues, cultures are deterritorialized. With shifts in the global cultural economy, scapes—ethnoscapes, mediascapes, technoscapes, financescapes, and ideoscapes—as new spatial and institutional mechanisms are being employed to reconstruct the boundaries of the nation.

I build on such approaches to deterritorialization to understand how the imaginary is put to work in relation to changing institutions of power, as well as the consequences of oppressive regimes that refract unintelligible formations. However, my point of departure is with Appadurai's use of the imaginary and how in that realm some productions of imagination and intelligibility are already foreclosed. Rather than the imaginary as an opening of possibilities, I argue for analytic limitations on the powers that we attribute to the deterritorialized imaginary and the freedom of mobility. This move toward imagining is intensified and more variable with increasingly mobile subjects who are more actively meshing the socially real with the production of the spatially real. Understanding these distinctions between social classifications of daily life and particular institutional productions of how life ought to be is about understanding the real that is itself constructed and, therefore, exists in imagined classifications of social norms, in relation to the production of the real, a process that involves different knowledge technologies. This focus on the production of the real breaks from the modern territorialized conceptions of time and space and, instead, focuses on the ways that global institutions are economically and historically aligned. Understanding the play of the imagination is about understanding the conditions of possibility that constitute knowledge networks through particular ways of seeing. For while deterritorial analyses are critically useful for understanding sites of innovation and change, I insist on a critical engagement of the extent to which the imaginary is historically constituted and therefore is mediated in specific conditions of material and ideological possibility. Thus, contours of globalization are embedded in historically produced zones of uneven development and are critical to how we understand place, movement, and relations of inclusion. The institutional relations produced out of particular identity forms may very well be in keeping with Appadurai's "conscious and imaginative constructions." However, it is the establishment of difference through various techniques of practice that shapes the ideological basis by which group sameness is produced. As such, the role of spatialized practices in constituting identity (Certeau 1984) and the production of meanings through the construction of place (Lefebvre 1991) combine with the centrality of historically inscribed contexts to produce particular forms of imaginations. Conceptions of deterritorialized cultural production are fundamentally connected to institutions of power that shape ways of seeing meanings. Not only is the imaginary historically contingent, it is also fundamentally influenced by ways of seeing place and belonging that reinforce preexisting forms of difference. These processes produce a social logic that is incorporated into particular master narratives that reproduce and legitimate meanings in particular ways.

Toward a Mapping of Yorùbá Transnationalism

The focus of this study—the development of networks of Yorùbá connections across national boundaries—highlights how late capitalist formations that are the context behind transnational Yorùbá cultural practices continue to be closely allied with territorially inscribed approaches to modern origins. Rather than assume that the imaginary of spatial belonging and national domains is embedded in unlimited conditions of global possibility, I demonstrate how new global imaginaries are reinscribed in relation to the modern notion of as the basis of territorial origins. What we need, then, is a conceptualization of deterritorialization that marks how formations of descent are historically constituted and how social memories, events, meanings of place, and social change work to reinforce particular inclusions and exclusions. It is critical to recognize how, in deterritorial spheres, meanings are embedded within particular axioms of power, as well as to establish the institutions of particular historical routes and contexts that shape the ways that place and meaning are legitimized in particular terms.

In charting how knowledge moves from one region to another and is produced, circulated, negotiated, and translated, I suggest that we approach deterritorialization in complexly territorialized terms. Drawing attention to people's spatial attachments while also highlighting how they are ideologically bound is critical for understanding the conditions of possibility that increasingly mediate local imaginaries within supranational institutions of power. Given this, we need to determine the underlying forces that enable some practices, and not others, and some people, and not others, to be seen as belonging "there" and not "here." This has implications for the way we understand power as well as how we understand how power shapes power. It enables us to ask both What are the institutions through which these transformations are taking shape? and Who has the power to claim membership in some regimes and not others?

The challenge for analysts of globalization today, therefore, is to understand how global circulations are tied to historical and geopolitical processes that have shaped ideologies of origins and place. Our failure to understand how local imaginaries are becoming increasingly embedded within supranational institutions of power while producing increasingly autonomous localities is our loss in determining the underlying forces that restrict some practices, and not others, some imaginings, and not others, and that make possible new hegemonies in new fields of power. This has implications for the way we understand power and the kinds of questions we should be asking about the convergences of ideology, late twentieth-century capitalism, and the uses of racial biology in contemporary life. In the case of the formation of new transnational Yorùbá networks of the late twentieth century, those questions include: What are the limitations of how whiteness is incorporated in black nationalist imaginaries? What are the conditions of possibility under which constructions of blackness can extend beyond African origins? What are the mechanisms that are being called on to implement these changes?

To answer these questions, I begin by charting the ways that agents deploy institutional mechanisms to bring into being alternative forms of belonging. These institutions actively shape new forms of practices and frame the conditions of possibility under which particular alliances are both imagined and rendered intelligible. We need to trace the genealogical formations of interconnection and fragmentation among transcontinental movements (Cooper 2001) to understand how the imaginary is propelled alongside changing institutional and historically inscribed formations. Drawing on the spatial networks of Yorùbá transnational webs, I demonstrate how these networks are mapped onto particular historical processes that exist in particular conditions and not others. I explore the ways that the political history of Yorùbá religious and regulatory practices serves to unite and prescribe Yorùbá revivalist membership as dialogically constituted in relation to African heritage. Deterritorialization, therefore, is useful in describing the particularities of shifting from an industrial to a technologically sophisticated electronic economy.

Scholarship on transnational Yorùbá practices has only just begun to highlight the cooperative efforts and historical and expansive networks that shape the complex interrelationships of Yorùbá transnational practices and rules of conduct and the terms of membership. These formations are no longer bound by the social organization of the nation-state and society alone. They are shaped, regulated, and enforced by transnational institutions that serve as forums for teaching and learning. By focusing on the deterritorialized institutionalization of Yorùbá networks, I argue that at the center of the development of early-twenty-first-century òrìṣà practices is both a historical order and a knowledge-producing regime that gives new network formations their temporal architecture. Yorùbá transnational relations, the Internet, heritage tourism, international conferences, publications, the distribution and circulations of books and videos, as well as the regulation of ritual practice and the terms of membership link localized areas to larger webs of institutional participation. Like the history of anthropology's village studies, similar mechanisms of place making and links to group membership continue to be operative in particular regional groupings and self-selected networks.

This study demonstrates that social imaginaries are shaped by contingent fields of power. At the center of these networks is the making of alternative conceptions of subjectivity through which people de-link themselves from homelands in order to constitute themselves in socially and historically relevant terms. In the case of the Yorùbá, transnational imaginaries, in keeping with historical linkages among the decline of West African empires, the rise of transatlantic slavery, and the development of hierarchies of scale in racial terms, and early capitalist formations led to the way new forms of social organization are made and remade through the institutionalization of religious ritual, the reconceptualization of traditional family through legal rules, and the charting of Yorùbá history as the antecedent to the present. These three—religious ritual, social rules and legal principles, and historical traditions embedded in particular political economic contexts—constitute the basic ways of creating transnational òrìṣà networks in particular histories of Americanness. These factors of institutionalization are relevant to the making of black Atlantic religious practices and constitute the architecture of Yorùbá transnational networks. They are enforced through participant adherence to institutional structures within related domains of religious reproduction.

Institutional mechanisms allow people to connect ritual and legal rules to practice, and practice to higher institutional authorities. The institutional domain of deterritorial transnational practices works because practitioners, who are mostly tied to black Atlantic rules of Yorùbá etiquette, are bound in conversation with subjectivities that are deeply inscribed in the history of slavery as the backdrop in which manifestations of the emphasis on heritage take shape. If we take for granted the mapping of new networks of interaction as already spatially ordered in particular ways, theories of globalization must clearly demarcate the historical contours that shape how particular hegemonic ideologies are incorporated and constitute new subjectivities. Similarly, in the realm of producing an anthropology of deterritorialized and historically inscribed networks that attend to the ways that transnational practices are differently deployed, we need to chart a framework of social change that highlights how people are able to claim homelands they have never visited or experienced. Ultimately, I argue that the making of new transnational institutions is about rendering the physicality of place secondary to the ideological circuits of knowledge and power that shape how interconnections are seen and legitimated and lead to new forms of denationalized and regionally autonomous practices.

Territorially specific ideologies of place play a central role in shaping deterritorial ideologies of belonging. One of the tasks ahead, therefore, is to highlight how both the historical formations of new geographies of identities, as a result of new knowledge technologies of intensified global-local interaction, are reshaping institutional forms, thereby producing possibilities for new forms of practices. I traverse historical periods of precapitalism, moving from the migration of Yorùbá practices to Cuba, to the colonial establishment of institutions of nationhood and power that contributed to the classification of distinctive Yorùbá identities in Nigeria, and then to a third moment of Yorùbá transnationalism, the post–cold war period, in which there has been a critical reorganization of the nucleus of òrìsà worship from Africa to the New World. Such movements are possible with the transmigration of African slaves, the development of movements calling for a return to Africa, black nationalism, and Pan-Africanism, which led to the internationalization of conceptions of blackness as Africanness. This third period, the Africanization of Yorùbá practices in the United States, makes clear my argument that the post–cold war period of Yorùbá revivalism is critically shaping the development of new practices and different interpretive schools within reorganized networks of power. The influence of the different interpretive schools that emerge out of the normative authority of different òrìsà religious systems, such as Santería and òrìsà voodoo, and the terms for which practices get to count as legitimate and which are decentered, depend on the sources of authority in relation to the hierarchy of variables at play. To understand how these shifts in connections have been established and legitimated in transnational national networks, we must understand the way that institutions of power have produced particular ways of seeing membership outside of modern nation-states. Approaching religion through an analysis of belief as fundamentally shaped by social institutions of power, this book explores the making of community through religious reproduction. How we approach religious practices has consequences for how we chart the field and how we understand the mechanisms by which we go in and out of field sites as well as implications for how we approach transnational methodologies. Demonstrating how transnational linkages and changing vertical practices within nations are connected to how people form institutions to legitimize new practices, I examine how religious/divinatory institutions, legal institutions, and customary/historical knowledge production are used by Yorùbá revivalists as instruments of transnational networking. I select these because they are central transnational mechanisms for the internationalized transmission of Yorùbá knowledge in the postindustrial and current period of late capitalism, and because ultimately their power lies in the ability of groups to incorporate these transnational norms in their own institutional structures, whereby new forms of practice are localized.

The first, literary/historical institutions, demonstrate the development of commonsense notions of national identity; the second, religious-magic institutions, highlight the reproduction of particular forms of knowledge; and the third, legal institutions as domains of property, marriage, and kinship, highlight the way that formations of personhood are looped through gendered distinctions that are productive of particular formations of family and nationhood. These institutions frame the ways that particular forms of social logics are understood, thereby producing particular master tropes through which truth and consciousness are legitimated by time and place. By laying the historical terrain for explaining how these new forms of institutional practices are shaped by fragmentary global economic processes of subject formation, I assert that new imaginings are far from arbitrary. Instead, the institutionalization of new forms of practices is producing innovative forms of "culture," historically constituted, colonially shaped networks of linkage. I explore how we can move theoretically and practically from the local to the global to understand what circulates when and how, and what does not and why. This calls on us to understand what Appadurai refers to as "the production of locality" through which to determine how meanings are differently imagined locally and executed globally, as well as how global circuits are unevenly engaging in particular routes of expansion and interconnection.

By continuing with religious ritual and charting how members of the larger network of practitioners who claim membership have done so in a changing terrain of U.S. racial to ethnic cultural identities, I ground my analysis in a range of general concerns that animate the relationship between the racial versus ethnic in processes of transnational cultural production and vertical incorporation of new transnational norms. The central questions are connected to how people establish practices without the enforcement mechanisms of the state through which to legitimate and institutionalize their norms. Three factors contribute to the development of the institutional elements of communities: (1) particular elements of fairness by which internal and external rules are used to establish the mechanisms for legitimacy and justice (i.e., redemption from slavery); (2) substantive rules and regulations that legitimate norms (i.e., dress codes, racial regulations); and (3) for communities to reproduce themselves they must have protocol and procedures by which norms can be derived (ritual practices).

The chapters reflect on the making of traditional knowledge of the anthropological village through examining the ways that practitioner leaders and the divining elite employ colonial and anthropological accounts to make their own village. This book explores the interplay of state governance, institutional apparatuses, and individual agents in the making of a Yorùbá transnational movement in a deterritorialized context. It does not represent a traditional ethnography as such. Rather, I present fragments of narratives and spaces of alliance, a metonymy of larger transnational zones, within which I examine the institutional formations that are operative in the making of Yorùbá communities in the late twentieth and early twenty-first century. By focusing on the making of institutions through which Yorùbá networks are sustained, I show that conceptualizations of national community are not simply in the domain of the state apparatus and conceptualizations of nations are not only validated through the authority of international organs. They are also not only in the realm of unitary territories. Instead, communities are produced through symbolic validation. They are groups of people who constitute themselves in singular, multiple, and diasporic locations, as well as within networks. Today, through a range of communication and contact mechanisms, various technologies such as the Internet and transportation are used to connect people more than ever before. And though indeterminacy is central to community formation, whether groups live alongside each other or far apart, they operate with interrelated core assumptions about their existence. These core assumptions shape the tenets of belief and the authority by which people incorporate and institutionalize norms.

Because this book deals with questions about how designations of the "idea of Africa" converge and diverge with globalization and changing approaches to cultural citizenship, at the core of my analysis is the argument that there are new geographies of membership being facilitated by new institutional mechanisms of knowledge. I address issues that have been at the center of research in the fields of African and African American studies, both pointing to the historical and contemporary particularities of traditional area configurations and arguing that area studies are not enough to understand how boundaries are crossed. I unravel how national identities have been tied to territorial attachments to place and how, through the symbolic imagery of biological belonging, such as blood and race, people traverse nations and codify membership in relation to larger institutions of knowledge production. Seen in the context of both the symbolic formation of the modern subject and post–cold war reconfigurations of governance, this fixing of human subjectivity in the context of the changing terrain of the national has produced new criteria for institutionalizing complex forms of territorialization and calls for more, not less, innovation in the writing and representation of these complex circuits and processes, most of which cannot be captured in their totality.

Writing Global Mappings

This book documents fragments across and within national boundaries and charts the ways race, religion, and gender take on new forms of meanings. Chapters are divided according to thematic mechanisms of ordering rather than thematic social organizational issues as objects of a totality. The first section, *Vertical Formations of Institutions*, explains the historical and political context for the development of Yorùbá networks; the second section, *The Making of Transnational Networks*, explores the institutionalization of Yorùbá transnational practices in the twentieth century. However, tracing networks does not always and neatly fit into conventional ethnographic structure. The chapters are augmented with a series of *contes-*

tations of various sorts that highlight the moments of disjuncture and disruption in the making of transnational networks. For I explore the ways new institutional productions of knowledge and capital flows (globalization) are evolving within deeply historical patterns of European colonialism.

In chapter 1, I examine the underlying routes of trade and repression that led to the political basis for African American claims to African homeland connections. I chart the complex set of cultural differences among Ọ̀yọ́túnjí, Ọ̀yọ́, and Santería cultural practices as they have arisen in Yorùbá communities in the Americas as a result of the transatlantic slave trade. By exploring the migration of Yorùbá captives from the collapsed Ọ̀yọ́ Empire of the southwestern region of Nigeria to the movement of enslaved Yorùbá captives to Cuba from the late eighteenth century to the twentieth century, and discussing the formation of Ọ̀yọ́túnjí Yorùbá revivalism, I detail how these transnational complexities of the present are not only embedded in the historical landscape of the past but continue to underlie the zones of interaction through which Yorùbá cultural production was shaped.

With data gathered from observations I made while traveling with Ọ̀yọ́túnjí practitioners to Nigeria, chapter 2 represents my attempt to examine the interplay between new geographies of identity and the cultural politics of globalization. I avoid telling a celebratory story about African and African American connections and try to render visible the tensions and problems with African Americans' reclassifications of themselves as culturally African. I analyze the role of telemedia as an engine of change propelled by global capital in contributing to the production and spread of new African imaginaries for Western consumption.

To historicize the role of various institutions of knowledge that have shaped the early production of sociological and anthropological texts about African history and culture that have now come to constitute anthropological communities, chapter 3 extends the conversation about the spread of literary institutions by examining how the texts were produced, who produced them, and how the symbolic codes and metaphorical renderings of images of those histories become both the impetus for and pose limitations on interpretation. I note how British colonial codes fashioned by Christian missionaries informed and structured the texts that through the international spread of historical knowledge now serve as canons for Ọ̀yọ́túnjí reclamation. By ending with an analysis of the ways that Ọ̀yọ́túnjí practitioners adopted the Ọ̀yọ́-centered history recorded primarily by Ọ̀yọ́-Yorùbá exslave captive returnees, I conclude my discussion of the historical specificity of these transatlantic cultural productions by highlighting the role of larger colonial and postcolonial institutions of power in shaping symbolic representations of race as the linkage to the Yorùbá past.

Many anthropologists working on either the Yorùbá in Nigeria or the anthropology of black America in the 1970s and 1980s were inspired by postcolonial critiques of race and empire. In chapter 4, I examine how another formation of knowledge and power, that of religious/magical institutions, was used by revivalists as a form of postcolonial redemption through which they reclassified their notions of national belonging, not through state criteria but through culturally historical ritualizations of history. I build on similar issues concerning the politics of ritual change in an attempt to theorize knowledge hegemonies through an engagement with the use of particular techniques of knowledge that revivalists call on to legitimize transnational connections. I demonstrate that individuals invoke the past to imagine the present and that, in so doing, cut across space and time and remap relations of belonging within and outside the hegemony of state boundaries and particular ritual forms. Such an investigation tells us more about the texture of the local processes through which individuals both adapt to and contest the hegemony of the nation-state than it tells us about the function of the nation as an instrument of elite power. My analysis of the language, forms, and structures of speech acts and processes of ritual incantations demonstrates dominant means by which the authorities of Ọ̀yọ́túnjí villagers create new alignments and prerequisites for transnational kinship ties aligned under the sign of blackness. By exploring questions of flexibility and instability underlying this apparent stability of Yorùbá identity, I explore how, despite greater access to technologies of knowledge by which an increasing number of African Americans learn African languages, the politics of primordial attachments and the structure of ritual forms still continue to characterize the boundaries of citizenship and ritual legitimacy, while also leaving space for particular variations.

The intrinsic value of Yorùbá ritual is in the ability of the diasporic practitioner to maintain the assumption of deterritorialized legitimacy and, in so doing, create meanings relevant to their lives. African Americans traveling to Ọ̀yọ́túnjí in search of spiritual guidance are able to obtain help in managing their daily life. Through my observations of spiritual divinations as both a client and an observer over a one-year period and more than one hundred divinations and pre- and postinterviews with clients, in chapter 5 I explore the role of divination in shaping relations of membership and belonging. I turn to issues of how these divinatory productions and positionings are maintained, and what such accomplishments can mean for conceptions of membership for and among individuals who were not born in Ọ̀yọ́túnjí, but who entered the community seeking a means of personal redemption by which to connect themselves to an African past. I show how Ọ̀yọ́túnjí practitioners use divination rituals to construct traditional knowledge. This includes a recent innovation in Ọ̀yọ́túnjí to determine heritage and ancestry known as the "roots reading." My analysis of these readings highlights how the authority of those who perform them is produced and how the readings serve to maintain articulations of the black American primordial attachments to Africa. The forms and practices of these modes are given shape by the diviner's ability to incorporate the hegemonic structure of the ritual and make it relevant to the type of client and the kind of request the client makes as he or she seeks assistance. From the numerous modes of divination available, I note that Yorùbá revivalists favor two critical modes of divinatory rituals: daily readings and roots readings. The kinds of requests made by these clients for an understanding of why Africans were enslaved ranged from why African Americans continue to experience conditions of social, political, and economic injustice, to how, through changes in their personal lives, these might be remedied for the clients' sake, for the sake of the diaspora as a racial community, or for both. The ritual process provides a means of redeeming the racialized future and ultimately points to how personal and communal suffering, wrought by transatlantic slavery, are interwoven, and as such, how—as key factors that shape the images of the past and the meaning of the symbols and codes of transatlantic slavery—suffering can be terminated by the proper realignments of ancestral lineage.

Anthropologists are people too, at least insofar as categories of their social identity are part of the process through which we look at "natives" who are looking back at us. After my participation in everyday activities and my experiences of women's rebuke, I reflect on how I came to understand women's reformulations of Yorùbá identity by examining how the concept of Yorùbá traditionalism in Ọ̀yọ́túnjí Village is fundamentally dependent on female traditional roles. In chapter 6, I return to questions of constructing and regulating Yorùbá traditions by examining kinship through the regulation of female gender. I analyze a classic dispute resolution case in Ọ̀yọ́túnjí to consider the ways that individuals use legal norms to regulate gendered codes of behavior. Like race, particular gendered practices are critical components of how people, diversely situated, make claims and enforce them. Here, by charting the way households and families are configured in Ọ̀yọ́túnjí—the heterosexual polygamous family—I demonstrate that although, on the one hand, Yorùbá revivalism was intended to create liberatory possibilities for Pan-African nationhood, on the other hand, it also reinforces a strict regulation of roles that might have the effect of exasperating already uneven relations between men and women. However, there are various ways of understanding gender relations outside of a standard configuration of male domination. Understanding the fluidity of gender designations in relation to status and roles is critical for locating the place of power and agency in the making of Yorùbá transnational networks.

Ultimately, these fragments of narratives about a group of people who claim Yorùbá as their cultural and religious identity are an attempt to address a set of methodological issues concerning how to link the zones of contact that constitute particular diasporic formations. However incomplete the story about subjectivity is here, globalization has rendered even more complex the meaning of identity in an increasingly transcultural world. By charting the intra- and intercontinental exchanges that constituted the formation of transatlantic practices, I end in the epilogue by returning to questions concerning the mundane significance of everyday life as it relates to the axes of power on which subjectivity is formed and unformed, seen and differently conceptualized. Considering what the achievements of my approach suggest for new directions in network studies in anthropology, I pull together disjunctures among the production of tradition in the field, analytic traditions in the academy, and the ways that technologies of knowledge change and are changing local sites. Indeed, in these diverse, transnationally linked spheres of power, individuals live the problematic about which I write. I close by examining our possibilities for studying locality while at the same time recognizing how local sites—which we analysts must, out of necessity, define—are themselves global, and how their global reach has critical implications for how we carry out ethnographies of globalization that are locally specific and historically constituted. I focus on the ways the proliferation of discourses on the local "native" past has served to create a standard from which the African Other not only has been represented by colonial and African native scholars but also has been narrativized by Western self-referential discourses of reclamation. To engage them is to offer a refinement intended to carry forward an ancient anthropological goal: to move the heart of the discipline to its core concern, a better understanding of processes of cultural production of a species constantly in flux.

Rethinking Spatial Relations, Rethinking Methods

Such explorations into knowledge networks are tied to methodological practicalities and make it critical for scholars engaged in social science inquiries to be similarly and increasingly committed to issues of method, theory, student mentoring, training, and research production time. For although anthropological village studies have been concerned with the role of place and the field in relation to developing ongoing patterns of standards, scholars today are struggling to achieve methodological innovations in conceptualizing the role of space and time in charting regions and zones of study. We must address issues in the discipline of anthropology in relation to methodological form and recognize that anthropologies of globalization should not attempt to chart all interconnections in a given field of study. Rather, whether anthropologists study at home or abroad, the transnational methodologies that we employ fall within a wider network of social relations that is historically inscribed. As such, we should engage in critical transnational mappings that rethink discrepancies between sedimentary formations and social imaginaries in historically specific ways.

In the case of this study, the late-twentieth-century shift in the internationalization of local Yorùbá practices has produced networks that, though not historically new, are different insofar as they have involved the institutionalization of new forms of practice. Thus, the Yorùbá religious connections that I examine span the regional movement of knowledge that links West Africa (the movements of Lukumi-speaking captives) to South American countries such as Brazil, to the mass migration of captives of war to the Caribbean (Cuba, Puerto Rico, and Trinidad in the mid- to late nineteenth centuries) to the migration of Cuban immigrants to the Americas from the early 1960s and the eventual mass mobilization of blackness as African heritage. The secondary purpose of studying networks, therefore, involves understanding how and why particular formations constitute particular zones of contact. These particularities of the local are connected to economic, social, and political zones. They tell us more about the larger forces that shape local domains than about the local as an isolated unit of cultural meaning.

By showing how ideologies circulate and how people create identity categories, and in that process regulate the avenues of possibility by which reality is rendered viable, I examine changes in self-understanding and self-justification of new Yorùbá social movements to think through the issues and implications for how we understand the particularities of what has come to be known as globalization. This is important in relation to the forms of ordering—legal, religious, national—within which identities and practices are, in the early twenty-first century, being reworked, differently aligned, and in some cases transformed. I chart the development of a new form of Yorùbá practice that took shape in the late twentieth century and led to the production of particular ideological forms of knowledge that became increasingly necessary in the circulation of new mechanisms of knowledge production. These modes of production—literary texts, books, and computer technologies—were used in the circulation of new pedagogies of Yorùbá doctrine and have set the basis for the modern production of new transnational subjectivities, subjectivities that we are only now beginning to understand.

I follow the circulation of African cultural production outside of the boundaries of the village, city, province, and nation-state and avoid the limitations of localized area studies that throughout most of the twentieth century tended to overdefine anthropological field studies as purely local and self-contained. To detail the circulation of people, things, ideas, and commodities and call into question the boundaries of culture, nations, and units of analysis that do not necessarily constitute the totality of the cultural groups being studied, I analyze the ways individuals reconfigure alliances outside of the borders of the nation-state. Here, I shift the unit of analysis to the interplay between microcultural production and the macro-circulation of ideas, commodities, and people and demonstrate that understanding the struggles over the right of black Americans to reclassify and claim membership in Africanness has comparative value for explaining global pancategory identity formations. I end by arguing that not only must we rethink local anthropological studies, but we need to recast the study of cultural practices of classification as not only translocal, and thus global, but in relation to the institutional specificities of zones of contact that have shaped the zones of black Atlantic alliance and produced a new cultural sovereignty detached from its modern origins.

The future of anthropology, especially with regard to diasporic and transnational studies, turns on the researcher's ability to maintain attention to the fine-grained and subtle analyses of everyday life—an emphasis that directed the goals and concerns of the discipline since its founding—while supplementing and integrating data thus generated into forms adequate to place it and its significance in larger processes of global circulation. By examining how the modern history of the economic and global circulation of people, commodities, ideas, and racialized notions of place have converged to form the spatial zone popularized by Paul Gilroy (1993a) as the "black Atlantic," I mark the ways that the Ọ̀yọ́, Nigerian, Santería, and Ọ̀yọ́túnjí Yorùbá practitioners engage in constructing and contesting "traditional" practices. And I demonstrate how Yorùbá traditionalists engage in producing and contesting national and transnational relationships regarding what constitutes Yorùbá practices. By detailing these ways through the tracing of history making, ritual, and legal processes, I show how individuals use narratives to incrementally change preexisting norms and to create new ones. Through a detailed examination of reconfigurations of descent in popular Yorùbá transnational movements, I demonstrate that in the context of the history of U.S. slavery and its forms of racial codification, notions of belonging both reflect and transcend national membership and continue to index perceived narratives of primordial origins. Thus, by examining the making of new Yorùbá deterritorialized institutions, we see that Yorùbá revivalism stands at the crossroads of the image of the enslaved African body in relation to the work of the redemptive hope of an ideological return to black enfranchisement.

PART ONE

Vertical Formations of Institutions

1. "On Far Away Shores, Home Is Not Far":
Mapping Formations of Place, Race, and Nation

WITH THE POWER OF RELIGIOUS RITUAL, Ọ̀yọ́túnjí Village awakens at night. Ritual initiations and rhythmic drumming echo in the endless hours of the night as residents remake their ancestral homeland outside of the territory of Africa. If Africanness is defined as doing, rather than simply being, then òrìṣà practitioners in South Carolina use ritual to produce a deterritorialized community in a U.S. landscape through which they become "African," in their terms. This making of Ọ̀yọ́túnjí Village as a legitimate site of Yorùbá traditionalism involves the recasting of time and space as a mechanism in which ancestral belonging is framed.

White candles along the community's private road lead participants toward the syncopated sounds of drums and the smell of frankincense. In the mystic aura of the moonlight, Yorùbá practitioners walk in and out of the palace courtyard, transposing themselves from African Americans to Yorùbá voodoo practitioners in sync with the mysteries of the occult from ancient times. The transformative celebrations begin with possessed dancers taken by the power of trance. Bare-breasted men and women with white cloths draped around their lower bodies invoke the ancestors through prayer, transforming ancestral death into life, into their ancestors living through them. Members chant songs announcing that, on these "far away shores, home is not far," for in the darkness of the moment lies the possibility of transformation. Although they are physically in the United States, they believe that they embody their ancestors in Africa. As such, the homeland is within them, allowing them to claim African ancestry regardless of their territorial affiliation. Prominently displaying reminders of slave captivity in sculptures that feature life-size broad-nosed, proud African ancestors, they study, worship, and wear the *ìlèkè*

Roadside sign announcing
location of Ọ̀yọ́túnjí
African Village.

(beads) of their initiation into Yorùbá òrìṣà rituals, believing that it is to ancient Yorùbáland, and not to America, that their souls will return when they die. Ultimately, the practitioners' willingness to believe is the fundamental condition for this reclassification of Americanness into Africanness. The value of spirituality as the basis for Ọ̀yọ́túnjí political and social life lies neither in the institution nor in the practice of religion itself. It lies in the belief that Yorùbá ancestral forces live within them, and it is through ritual that they communicate with them.[1] The links between southwestern Nigeria and life in the Americas is played out through invocations to transnational ancestors who were forcibly enslaved.

The day after, at the start of a standard workday, residents, many of whom live in polygamous family compounds, propitiate the gods and ask for blessings of good health, money, peace, and guidance. Announcing ritual completion and success, they spread rancid blood and remains of old animal feathers from earlier sacrifices throughout public shrines, unabashedly decorating ritual objects. During midmorning, the usual cacophony of men hammering, old engines, and tree droppings falling onto zinc roofs blends with the sound of people conversing, mixing

Tourist sign en route to Ọ̀yọ́túnjí.

both Yorùbá and English words in every sentence. The daily speech practices of Ọ̀yọ́túnjí villagers suggest that language is an ideological site for the reclamation of African ancestry. Mothers call out for their children, "*Àgò Yétúndé, Adémíwá, Yétúndééééé, WỌ̀LÉ*, come for lunch!" And children respond in Yorùbá, "*Òoooo!*" These sights and sounds may indeed transport the listener to a place seemingly far away, into an attainable reality: Africa in America.

The blended smells of livestock feed, fresh paint, and southern fried chicken refresh the community with the comforting banality of everyday life. In the heat of the day, while men in workgroups artfully decorate two-story buildings in the palace courtyard and children sit in classrooms learning African-centered humanities, sciences, and social sciences, clients pulling up in cars into the parking lot to seek spiritual guidance or healing are stopped by a young man on guard at the gate.

To announce regular clients, new visitors in tour buses, or simply local service repairmen, one of the boys beats the drum rhythmically, spelling out their message: *Àlejò ń bọ̀ wá, Àlejò ń bọ̀ wá, Àlejò ń bọ̀* (Visitors are here, visitors are here, visitors are here).

Site of alert for drumming communication to villagers.

Welcome to Ọyọ́túnjí. You are now leaving
the United States of America and about to enter
the Yorùbá Kingdom of Ọyọ́túnjí African Village.

This sign, posted outside the front gates to Ọyọ́túnjí, introduces a community that resembles the popular U.S. image of a quintessentially African village
somewhere on a faraway shore, whose articulations of subjectivity lie in the enactment of the imaginary. For many visitors, its artistic presentation, coupled with
the mementos of ritual, evoke nostalgic desires to see and experience ancient African village life. Named after the once powerful West African Ọyọ́ Empire of the
sixteenth to eighteenth centuries, Ọyọ́túnjí is a black nationalist community of
African American religious converts to Yorùbá practices who have reclaimed West
Africa as their ancestral homeland. Most Ọyọ́túnjí practitioners trace their origins
to the descendants of the men and women taken from West African communities
and exported to the Americas as slaves. As a result of the belief that they have a
right to control the African territory that was their homeland prior to European
colonization, residents of Ọyọ́túnjí Village have reclassified their community as
an African kingdom outside of the territoriality of the Nigerian postcolonial state.

In describing the power of indexical linkage to African homelands, I borrow
the terms "index" and "referentiality" from linguistic anthropology: terms that
are referential refer to things; terms that are indexical refer to truth-value. Such

derivatives connect things to concepts; thus, the spatiotemporal distance between the sign of Africa and the thing referenced by the sign, such as brown or black skin, flags, or African clothes, is integral to the sign system, which enables the production of a conceptual linkage between race and African ancestral descent. Ọ̀yọ́túnjí was born out of complex controversies over the slavery that brought Africans to the Americas and the contestations between African American converts and Afro-Cuban practitioners over the legitimacy of their adaptations of West African practices. Thus, three national flags in the Ọ̀yọ́túnjí palace courtyard represent black American emancipation from slavery, black nationalism, and the establishment of an ancient Yorùbá empire in South Carolina.[2]

The central theme of redemption from slavery is a direct reaction to the history of and continued hierarchies produced by U.S. racism. The flags, the meanings of the brown skin of the residents, and the aesthetics of African sign systems link conceptual relationships between people and sociohistorical meanings; however, this does not happen arbitrarily. The production of African aesthetic sensibilities is deeply connected to the establishment and strength of institutions that, through routinized practices, propel those meanings. Here, two institutions, that of religious ritual and legal regulations, are central to the entrenchment of linkages among race, citizenship, and hierarchies of scale that constitute historical patterns of exclusion and belonging. Yet, contemporary approaches to the convergences between religion and formal regulations of social law have been one of the most misunderstood areas of modern social life in the West. In an attempt to focus on religion as an object of study, scholars of religion have not only brought into being religion as a distinct conceptual element of social life, but they have also inscribed onto non-Western societies particular ontological categories ordered in particular domains that have not been reflective of their cosmology. Similarly, law has become an object of study, rendering secondary the processes of classifying the categories that have come to be scrutinized in legal analysis. By recognizing the ways that both religious and legal regimes co-constitute each other, we see how those regimes that developed alongside other institutions of knowledge contributed to the production of binaries that distinguish the secular from the nonsecular. It is important to note, therefore, that the similarities in these two forms of knowledge derived from religious and legal mechanisms relate to common requirements of solemn responsibility, training, and, most important, expected loyalty to principles of an originary founding moment as the basis of their authority.

In the case of religious worship, the founding moment of Yorùbá revivalists in the United States is both Olódùmarè's creation of the world and the eventual development of Yorùbá civilization in Ọ̀yọ́, which are further legitimated by Ifẹ̀-centered origin narratives and Ọ̀yọ́ narratives of greatness (see chapter 3). In rela-

Ọ̀yọ́túnjí (front gate).

tion to legal codes, the principles of constitutional doctrine, on which legal rules are based, are represented as having their origins in the founding of the Nigerian nation as a legitimating moment of statehood. These two originary moments figure critically in the institutional production of Yorùbá life. Òrìṣà practices/rules became absorbed into legal codes in Cuba and Protestant reform movements in Nigeria. Ọ̀yọ́túnjí revivalism, therefore, is an attempt to employ the power of origins with the return to premodern/prenational òrìṣà orthodoxies. However, in an attempt to reclaim these traditions, particular sources of institutional organization had to be established. History making as a domain of knowledge framed the basis for legitimating which origins and customs were to be followed. The second realm, religious ritual, which shaped the domain of ritual rules and developed alongside a society of priests, was established to interpret sources of divinatory interpretation. The third realm comprised the juridical political institutions that were established to secure "traditional" Yorùbá rules. The Ògbóni society was established to develop *ex-post* and *ex-anti* laws for the formation of coherent standards and methods for both forming and regulating transnational òrìṣà communities.

In an attempt to rethink traditional regions, in this chapter I examine the production of social meaning in the context of historically constituted forms of transnational social order. The black Atlantic region that I am describing does not fit neatly into the area studies model preset by the establishment of nation-states and the formalization of international organizations. Instead, it is shaped by the racialization of black difference in the Americas and the history of captivity of bodies from one region to another. Recognition of the black Atlantic as a viable area of study involves the recognition of the ways that subjectivity is inscribed both through origins discourses and through the regulation of new forms of belonging. Taking seriously the conflation of the two involves taking seriously the deterritorialization of subjectivity in historically inscribed forms, thus the need for rethinking the borders for the "area" so central to anthropological studies. As we will see in this chapter, the borders are more ideological and institutional than they are geographic.

The Village Network

Founded in 1970 and by the late 1970s boasting a residential population of 191 residents, Ọ̀yọ́túnjí Village represents the home of black people in the United States whose ancestors were enslaved, sold to traders, and transported to the Americas. The development of religious revivalist movements as part of a counterculture is not new and often reflects people's attempts to respond to particular unfair historical conditions they are attempting to correct. In this case, over a period of three hundred years, the United States became home to millions of black Africans sold into slavery. The community's claims to African ancestry are signified through its aesthetic organization, for it indexically references Africa as its homeland.

Lying outside of the geographic boundaries of African nation-states, it is a small community built to accommodate up to twenty-five housing compounds with a potential capacity of over five hundred people. It is organized into three main sectors: areas for religious ritual and organizations, for political governance, and for a small-scale market economy within which religion and politics are played out.

The degree to which Ọ̀yọ́túnjí has been incorporated into the political economy of the state of South Carolina can be mapped by the interplay between the historical formation of scales of human value and the politics of plantation slavery, the consequences of which are operative in the village and its networks. Ultimately, its force is in its network of national and international economic and political linkages. In the mid-1980s, the population of the community plummeted from two hundred to seventy, but this led to an expanding constituency of thousands of urban affiliates with growing loyalties to the community. During this period, as increasing numbers of practitioners left for better opportunities in urban America,[3] the community laid the seeds for the spread of new institutional forms of urban Yorùbá communities within a larger network of practitioners.

The decline in the number of residents and simultaneous growth of a national following produced the need to develop institutional infrastructures to standard-ize rules and norms of Yorùbá revivalism in the United States. Thus, through the creation of Ọ̀yọ́túnjí rural and urban nodes of connection, a larger deterritorialized network throughout the United States was constituted under the rubric of Yorùbá revivalism. Because of this added level of deterritorialized networking between Ọ̀yọ́túnjí Village and its satellite communities in urban centers, it became more important than ever for practitioners to claim belonging to a network of shared Yorùbá revivalists that linked them with Ọ̀yọ́ practitioners in Nigeria and like-minded and similarly descended practitioners throughout the Americas. Today, Ọ̀yọ́túnjí is connected to networks of hundreds of thousands of affiliated practi-tioners and millions of òrìṣà voodoo and Santería practitioners in the Americas. Compared with past numbers, fewer revivalists than ever resided in Ọ̀yọ́túnjí in the 1990s.[4] Thus, it is the circulation of the institutional network and movement of people related to Ọ̀yọ́túnjí and not just the local community (with fewer than one hundred practitioners) that constitutes the basis for this study.

Yorùbá revivalism in the United States was shaped by the historical formations of meanings of racial belonging that have their roots in a racial aesthetics of prac-tice. These aesthetics have taken the form of particular speech, dress, naming, ritual, and routinized practices that produced normative forms of Yorùbá expres-sion and drove practices that, in the late twentieth century, took shape through the production of literary texts, books, and computer technologies. Ultimately, with the development of a plantation, slavery machinery, racial hierarchies of value, and the historical regulation of òrìṣà ritual, the change in òrìṣà practices and the production of different forms of institutions of òrìṣà knowledge developed over time as a racially inscribed practice. These tenets of practice in Ọ̀yọ́túnjí and its related networks were reconstituted in the 1980s and 1990s through the spread of new religious forms. With these new circulations of knowledge, the movement, estimated by scholars of Yorùbá revivalism to exceed ten thousand adherents span-ning major urban and rural centers throughout the United States, reconstituted itself in culturally racial terms.

The politics of religious revivalism is centrally organized around ritual prac-tice, and it is here that the remapping of Ọ̀yọ́túnjí membership to African roots is made most explicit. Daily life in Ọ̀yọ́túnjí village revolves around calendrical celebrations of òrìṣà gods and goddesses known to have originated in West Africa but today is seen as living through black Americans as well. Each celebration is organized by a religious priesthood, technically referred to as an annual reli-gious ceremony and popularly referred to as a festival. Festivals are celebrated by the relevant order of priests in the community. Usually a senior priest presides

Kingdom of Ọ̀yọ́túnjí Village Organizational Chart

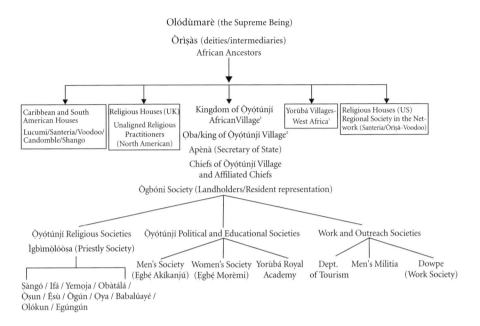

¹Yorùbá villages in Southwestern Nigeria are parallel to Ọ̀yọ́túnjí Village.
²Each head of compound or unmarried man pays monthly "taxes" to the Kingdom. Collected funds go toward the general maintenance of upkeep of the community, the King, and his family. Between January 1, 1995 and December 31, 1995, the monthly remittances ranged from $50 to $100 per month. Although some payments were occasionally late or sometimes bills went unpaid, or were directed toward expenses for other societies, the crown reported an estimated total of $7,000 for 1995. Members of regional societies in the Network are also expected to offer remittances on both King's Day in August as well as the òrìsà birthday of their godmother/father-priest.
³As of 1990 to the early 2000s, the relationship between West African Villages in Benin and Southwestern Nigeria and Ọ̀yọ́túnjí Village were stronger than that of Caribbean santería and candomble houses.

over the ceremony, leading the placement of offerings on the altars to the patron deity, or hosting and organizing the prayers, dancing, and general festivities. The celebrations are often highlighted by a series of ritual dances performed by costumed presentations, on-going drumming with bells, rattle-like instruments, and singing.

There are thirteen principal festivals and one prophetic day through which Yoruba social norms are shaped and new spaces opened up for the innovation of new meanings. The day of prophecy is the first day of each year and is designated as the day in which, after seven days of hibernation, the Ọba returns to the community and announces the divinatory predictions for the calendar year. This predictive pronouncement is made through the divinatory "reading of the year." Here, senior Ifá priests consult the Ifá oracle to reveal the state of the universe, and with this information people are warned, things to be anticipated are noted, sacrifices are performed, and prayers are undertaken.

The first of the festivals is the Olókun festival, a two-day event held in late February that is organized around the celebration of the goddess of the deep sea. In Yorùbáland, Olókun was venerated for its enrichment of Yorùbá soil in preparation for the planting season. Members of the Òyótúnjí network celebrate the soil, but also take the opportunity to venerate the ancestors who died during the Trans-Atlantic slave trade in the deep oceans. Following the Olókun festival is the Yorùbá New York, celebrated on March 20. On March 1, 2000, this celebration was in its 10,041st year. Here the prestige of the past is celebrated through the recognition of the antiquity of the Yorùbá people and the continuities of this ancient culture through their kingdom in the United States.

The Èṣu, Ògún, and Ososi deities are celebrated in the third week of March. This festival is run by the Men's Akínkọnjú society and many manhood initiation rites of passage take place during this time. In April the goddess of Òṣun is celebrated, and love and sexuality, promiscuity and pleasure are the themes throughout. The Egúngún festival is one of the longest celebrations and is usually held from the third week to the end of May, beginning with the U.S. Memorial Day holiday. During this festival the ancestors are vigorously revered. The Egúngún festival marks the beginning of the summer festival season, which draws thousands of tourists, practitioners, returnees, new initiates, and young children preparing to begin summer vacation and interested in summer long festival work.

Toward the end of June, the women's society, under the imagery of the goddess Mọrèmi, runs the women's festival known as the Yemọja festival. The celebration of the goddess Yemọja is often an attempt to recognize the survival of black women in America and the enduring importance of femininity and motherhood. Early July, during America's July 4 Independence holiday, is the period for venerating Ifá. The Ifá festival is one of the most prestigious festivals in which the god of destiny is celebrated.

In late July, the god of Ṣàngó is venerated with the Ṣàngó Festival. Ṣàngó is often referred to as the god of fire, power, and manhood strength. It is an important deity for Òyótúnjí practitioners because it is believed that it was the power of Sango that made possible their survival from the Old Òyó Empire to the Americas. Late August is the time that Òbàtálá—the patron god of Òyótúnjí—is revered. Òbàtálá, the god of white, of purity, of wisdom, is the Ọba's deity protectorate as well as the deity of many of the senior chiefs in Òyótúnjí.

In early October King's Day is celebrated—it is a time for praising the ancestors of royalty and revering the living Ọba. This is followed by the Ọya Festival in late October. This festival is often represented as a celebration of the royal goddess of death, storms, and transformation. The Hwedo Festival is celebrated on October 31. Instead of the western Halloween ritual, it is welcomed as a day for the solemn veneration of the unknown dead of the "African race." Parades of ghosts with candle light vigils characterize this festival.

Finally, the Ọbalúaiyé festival, celebrated in late December during Western Christmas, mainstream Kwanzaa, and other American holidays is a seven-day holiday, from December 23 to December 31. It marks the beginning of the winter solstice, thus the commencement of a new season. It is here when the Ọba of the community is sequestered, hibernating for seven days to pursue his own rituals; mischief is permissible and community rules can be broken. All these celebrations involve blood sacrifices, prayers, divination readings, and various forms of cleansings.

The community is spiritually sustained with all of these monthly events, for festivals are generative of new beginnings and new endings. They are seen as periods for the remembering of the past, the managing of the present, and planning for the future, an African-identified future where most believe that they will one day be redeemed from racist imperialisms that continue to marginalize them. By providing alternative celebrations made to represent their own image, they use ritual performances and market goods and services to create the spaces of black exception. Through the cycle of festivals, therefore, practitioners publicly celebrate their Yorùbá gods to sustain the building of an African-centered religious movement.

On a standard tour of Ọ̀yọ́túnjí Village the onlooker may see children in school uniforms—untucked and oversized—selling homemade jewelry to impressionable young tourists and associating that jewelry with ancestral heritage objects from years past. The tour guides often insist, "It is the ancestral powers that make Ọ̀yọ́túnjí what it is today." As one said, "The ancestors, what you guys call the dead, are our guides." Depending on whether guides think they need to further explain that point, they might add, as I heard one do for a group of white tourists, "Europeans also worship the dead. Yes, your ancestors are Abraham Lincoln and Thomas Jefferson. Ours are the Ọ̀yọ́ kings and millions of Africans sold into slavery."

Despite the successes of Ọ̀yọ́túnjí revivalists in resignifying the efficacy of their rituals as constitutive of their membership in African culture worlds, there are also serious tensions for many who visit or hear of Ọ̀yọ́túnjí, as they question the ethics of voodoo and the efficacy of ancestral worship or the legitimacy of residents' status as Africans.[5] Tourists in Ọ̀yọ́túnjí often make an attempt to identify things that are "authentically" African, and many who visit are disappointed by

An initiation room.

what they regard as the village's "inauthenticity." As they trudge in the summer heat behind tour guides, going in and out of public shrines and buildings, some smirk with disbelief. In a tone of chagrin, some visitors make statements and ask questions that make their judgments clear: "But they were born in America." "Are they into voodoo?" "But they don't believe in God." And although dirt roads and old buildings contribute to what many see as the necessary precondition of an African village's authenticity, any resemblance to Western Americanism makes tourists frustrated; like the tradition of twentieth-century area studies, their concepts of "Africa" as in the realm of the elsewhere resembled a purity distinct from Westernization. Nevertheless the community members have blurred those distinctions. Many wear African dashikis, and young teenagers in the community, as well as in African context, are often unabashedly engaged in hybridizing Africanness. Rather than playing one of the old tourist standards—a West African rhythmic great such as Fela or King Sunny Adé—young men often dance to black American rap songs by Tupac Shakur or Snoop Doggy Dog. The tourists' look of disapproval is an indicator of Ọ̀yọ́túnjí's failed attempts to maintain the stereotypes of Yorùbá authenticity, the ritual knowledge possessed by diviners, the spatial production of Ọ̀yọ́túnjí as a homeland long ago, and the making of traditional forms and efficacious productions of an "Africa" in the national imagination—rustic and "Other."

Ọ̀yọ́túnjí Village comes alive with the dreams of origins and doubts of authenticity of those who enter. In addition to the challenges of spatial marginalization and the villagers' absence of membership in an African citizenry, the hegemony of Christianity represents the backdrop against which Africanness is played out. Christianity set the stage for the norms and principles that continue to shape the everyday standards of practice in Òyótúnjí Village. These formations led to the development of particular types of subjects in a country that has historically supported the exercise of religious freedom. The value of religion as the basis for Òyótúnjí existence, therefore, does not lie in the religious institution itself but in the geopolitics of subjectivities produced and authenticated by its institutions as well as the conditions for the possibilities of social change that it conjures. Yorùbá belonging in Òyótúnjí exists in relation to modernist Euro-Christian hegemonies, and it is against the sign of whiteness that spatial legitimacy and the making of Yorùbá lifeworlds are played out. As such, they engage in practices in which meanings related to Europe, Christianity, and white dominance are resignified and new interpretations are produced—for truth is not a thing. Truth and reality are negotiated through the production of ongoing acts of remembering and forgetting. As such, it is no surprise that the majority of disbelieving tourists impatiently question the ethics of voodoo, the efficacy of ancestral worship, and the authenticity of black Americans as Yorùbá practitioners. Nevertheless, Òyótúnjí practitioners use redemptive strategies that depend on the moral force of freedom from slavery and the logic of reclamation of lost "culture" to establish their transnational alliances to West Africa.

Thus, ritual is a central institution for the transformation of the past into the present, and the history of the structural development of slave economies is central to the claims of African membership that produced black American politics of African belonging. As a result of transatlantic slavery, hundreds of thousands

Men's compound.

of captives settled on plantations in colonial South and North Carolina, and later, Mississippi, Alabama, Texas, Georgia, and Florida. Life then was structured in relation to citizens and slave subjects. These divisions further reinforced particular hierarchies of white settler superiority. Not only was the colonial history of labor and mobility highly racialized, but ideologies were deeply entrenched in demarcations of racial difference that overdetermined the slave economies in the Americas. By the late eighteenth century, as the colonial states converged and formed the United States of America, legal and economic forms of organization moved from slave to capitalist wage labor, to industrialized, and eventually to twentieth-century technological economies.

When the Declaration of Independence was written in the 1770s and adopted by Congress on July 4, 1776, plantation slavery was still integral to the logic of the social and legal order. Although by 1807 Congress had passed a law prohibiting the importation of slaves, which went into effect on January 1, 1808, slavery, as well as the ideological forms of classification that justified human bondage, became more entrenched through both the establishment of cotton and sugar plantations and the growth of state-based economies.[6] As more states entered the Union and more laws were mandated to enable the spread of pioneer settlers and their slaves, slavery became fundamentally central to the development of the U.S. economy. In relation to modern state formation, slave economies and their hierarchies of racial value formed the basis of early U.S. capitalism.

In spite of slave rebellions and growing numbers of antislavery societies over the first 250 years (1600–1850) of the Union, it was not until the American Civil War (March 4, 1861–January 1, 1863) that the North engaged in combat against the South to insist on the indivisibility of the nation. The Emancipation Proclamation, a military edict by President Abraham Lincoln, declared the freedom of southern slaves, stating, "All persons held as slaves within any State or designated part of a State . . . shall be then, thenceforward, and forever free." The North won the war and slavery was outlawed. However, it was the Thirteenth Amendment of the Constitution—passed by the House of Representatives on January 31, 1865, ratified by Congress on December 18 of the same year, and quickly signed by Lincoln—that abolished slavery throughout the United States and led to the establishment of a new regime of federal governance. Here, with new legislation and a postwar climate, the U.S. federal government played a central role in pushing for constitutional amendments that led to the enfranchisement of black people, the Fourteenth Amendment being one of them.[7] Because the North had won the war, the southern state governments of the defeated Confederacy, who had seceded from the Union, were made to rejoin. The return to a unified Union of

States marked the beginning of a new federation in which dramatic social changes took shape, especially in relation to new forms of trade, industry, technology, and social and legal consciousness.

After the 1865 abolition of slavery and the early formation of civil protections, large waves of black migrants moved to northern urban cities such as Chicago, New York, Philadelphia, Buffalo, Boston, and Detroit in search of employment and educational opportunities. However, legal racial segregation, known as Jim Crow, took the place of slavery and led to the development of racialized spaces. As an ideological and cultural practice, racial discrimination shaped the terrain on which the development of U.S. democracy took shape.

In general, the period following the Civil War was a period of difficult transitions; southern economies, still organized in relation to slave economies, were being compelled to change not only that system, but their ideologies of racial value. The struggle over the sovereignty of states that had led to the war continued to permeate American social life. It is in this historical context that the racial tensions of the twentieth century took shape and that the institutionalization of black nationalism and black African centrism employed black exclusion to forge racial linkages with Africa. It is important to see this connection as part of a moral process of racial redemption, and ritual serves this purpose.

As the object of practitioner pride in African heritage, ritual in Ọ̀yọ́túnjí Village is the means through which the Yorùbá nobility is held in tension with the dueling remnants of slavery. Ritual combines the realities of historically inscribed hegemonies in the realm of nobility and the grandeur of precolonial governance. It is through these dueling forces that a cartography of moral redemption is articulated, and the imagination becomes a conduit through which to articulate the past. Given that the politics of racialization have dominated black Atlantic zones of exchange, people in contemporary movements also reproduce typologies of racial continuities to debunk the cultural logics of white racial superiority. Similarly, because of the modernity of classifying national origins, the move to associate blackness with African homelands is far from unusual. The indexical references to African territorial origins are in keeping with popular cultural designations of black people as fundamentally originating from Africa. These approaches to constituting Yorùbá revivalism have produced òrìṣà revivalism as a form of moral redemption from the history of the torment of transatlantic slavery. It is the preoccupation with slavery and the instrumentalities of ritual that make Yorùbá revivalism a culturally American, rather than West African, movement. For, though born in the United States and therefore legally classified as U.S. citizens, the vast majority of òrìṣà practitioners in and outside of Ọ̀yọ́túnjí Village have realigned themselves with the iconic symbolism of the precolonial and noble kingdoms of West Africa. Insisting on their cultural heritage as descendants of West African towns, they claim belonging to the Yorùbá Ọ̀yọ́ Empire as their ancestral heritage.

Ọ̀yọ́túnjí Village is both a physical and a conceptual space for making history in the making of cultural practices. This "making" of Yorùbà practices reflects a heritage denied to the practitioners in the United States. It is productive of an imaginary Africa, because the real Africa was seen as being denied as a result of the history of slavery and continually thwarted in contemporary processes of American daily life. As a transnational concept, Ọ̀yọ́túnjí is increasingly interconnected with international urban and rural networks of ritual revival. With the work of the imagination, the conceptualization of Ọ̀yọ́túnjí as a home away from an African home operates by enabling subjects to become something else, somewhere else— though under particular conditions of possibility.

The development of òrìṣà voodoo in Yorùbá revivalism was self-consciously driven by the growing tide of black nationalism in the 1960s, in which black Americans reconceptualized Santería to disentangle it from its history of Spanish and Christian regulation. Ultimately, these changes meant symbolically "blackening" Santería and referentially indexing the West African empires and kingdoms that preceded the colonization of Nigeria by the British Empire. As a result of the belief that they have a right to control the African territory that was their homeland prior to European colonization, residents of Ọ̀yọ́túnjí Village, claiming diasporic connections to the ancestral history of the Great Ọ̀yọ́ Empire of the Yorùbá people, have reclassified their community as an African kingdom outside of the territoriality of the Nigerian postcolonial state.

On a basic level of signification, Ọ̀yọ́túnjí practitioners argued for the need to Africanize Santería as fundamentally Yorùbá and visibly African. Spurred by ideological clashes over the "whitening" of Yorùbá ritual practices in Cuba, Yorùbá revivalists in the United States (i.e., black American nationalists) renamed their version of Yorùbá-Santería òrìṣà voodoo, substituting Spanish-language words and pronunciations with African words. Using representations that incorporated the mythic visual imagery of the old empire from which Yorùbá people are known to have descended, the founders of Ọ̀yọ́túnjí created landscapes that resembled Nigerian Yorùbá religious and political institutions thought to be more authentically African. They substituted their Anglophone names with Yorùbá names, producing performative cartographies of Yorùbá membership. These reformulations of Africanness shaped the terms of contestation between early black nationalists and new Cuban immigrants to the United States. By the late 1970s, the membership of the growing Yorùbá movement comprised hundreds of voodoo practitioners spread throughout the United States and Canada.

This form of Yorùbá transnational religious nationalism, as well as the proliferation of Afrocentricity and African American cultural movements, can also be
seen as a sort of "culture industry," in which the production of local knowledge
is itself a part of many centuries of black reclamation of African-based cultural
practices. To understand how and why particular inclusions and exclusions are
introduced and sustained, we need to understand how the channels and circuits for
commodities (Hernandez-Reguant 2002) and the erasures of various kinds contribute to particular imprints (Tsing 2000) and shape and are shaped by particular
formations. As particular formations have been reinscribed onto new practices
and particular forms of social ordering are reflective of colonial inscriptions of
race and empire, particular hierarchies of racial aesthetics have been central to the
production of social imaginaries. These codes of logic have worked in religious
and legal institutions to structure meaning and order membership in particular
ways. These ideological orders continue to be driven by communicative mechanisms centrally connected to the movement, standardization, and circulation of
information. They have driven, reproduced, and changed how we understand the
religious underpinnings of secular life.

Examining the conditions for arranging social life so that agents behave in particular ways, Michel Foucault (1991) argued that governmental power operates
less by overt force than by covert forms of rationality, so that the role of government is to direct human relations with the aim of totally controlling them.
Modern colonial forms of social governance continue to regulate power and create distinctive spaces, values, and practices within them. Specific meanings with
which to read landmarks are not just signifiers; they become signs, and their meanings are produced in ways that differentiate between spaces and their ability to
secure the authority necessary to make their resignifications possible. Representations of these various practices are ultimately about how sites become locations
that are imbued with particular ideological meanings. As such, spatial localities
and the practices inhabited by them are produced through the transmission and
acquisition of ideological units of analysis from which people produce boundaries
and enact social distinctions. This process of reading signs—national, regional,
and racial—is constituted through the simultaneous conjuncture of institutions of
power in relation to the politics of agency that produces and resists change.

True, in ritual arenas, spaces of occult transformation exist within the vestiges
of hegemonic order. The seemingly contradictory presence of Christianity, Spanish and British cultural hegemonies, and colonial laws in the expression of Yorùbá
revivalist religious practices is fundamental to the reformulation of Yorùbá revivalism in Òyótúnjí and is part of the dialectic of a European colonial past and the
way this past is imbricated in the present. However, in understanding these pro-

cesses of producing meanings, I am not simply referring to the regulatory power of the state, its laws, or its codes of subjugation—this is a critical component of my analysis. I am also interested in examining the role of agents and the moral imaginary as historically constituted sites of micropower that reflect the tension between the historically configured, the governable, the imaginary knowable, and the inarticulable—the forms of place making that are not already part of particular hegemonic alliances and therefore never articulated but always present in their absence. Ultimately, whether agents bring into being particular innovations or reproduce those orders against that which is not articulated as "real" or "legitimate," the unarticulated also exists in the imaginary as a reminder of unspoken possibilities that are visible within the ordering of aesthetic value and spatial and temporal refractions. It is this unfixing of "reality," in which contradictory conditions are produced, that particular subversions are possible. People shape and resignify dominant meanings to create new or related subjectivities, and they do so in historically constituted terms.

In the context of the black Atlantic world, Ọ̀yọ́túnjí reclassifications of racial aesthetics are an example of how the African homeland is imagined in the United States. These forms of social uplift and making of denationalized communities outside of the African territory are reflective of particular formations of ordering that have contributed to the ideological reconfiguration of black cultural production. Considering the imaginary in relation to the ways it is shaped by complex social movements, we see that the linkage between racial subjectivity and people's imaginings of themselves in autochthonous terms produces qualifications of settlement and "real" notions of membership. In this regard, contra Althusser's (1971, 93) insistence that it is "only imaginary communities which are real," I suggest an analytic shift from the language of invention and the imagination as an individual process that is not real and that is without boundaries.

Influenced by approaches to the imaginary that incorporate the work of Lacan (1975, 1975/1988), Castoriadis (1987), Žižek (1996, 1998), and Bhabha (1983, 1990, 1994), and whose genealogy goes back to Hobbes's, Locke's, and Kant's approaches to theorizing the imagination in relation to subjectivity, we need to historicize the production of subjectivity in relation to the ways those meanings are embedded in sites of religious and legal regulation, contestation, articulation, and freedom. However, though people's imaginary plays a role in reclassifying subjectivity, I emphasize that these forms of racial conceptualizations of subjectivity locate the imagination beyond the individual domain. Charting the racial ideologies that developed in the Americas in relation to the imaginary requires looking at how the imaginary as mediated by institutions of power is always already foreclosed by larger processes of regimentation.

Emile Durkheim (1915) long ago suggested that the empirical basis for truth is secondary to the efficacy of social facts. Following this logic, productions of the imaginary are real because they are brought into existence through a larger process of constructing taxonomies of descent. The imaginary comes into being through the individual and society and highlights the particularities of how and when certain meanings flow across time and space and certain meanings remain unarticulated and unknowable. The ideological domain of deterritorialized Yorùbá governance is possible through the reorganization of institutional spheres of national belonging. For, even though the concept of the Yorùbá has changed over time, those changes were accompanied by particular ideological terms with which to create new forms of governance in new locales. Approaching the complexities of the transnational movement of Yorùbá revivalism in relation to the early formation of Òyótúnjí reclassifications of the regulation of Yorùbá practices as a result of plantation slavery calls for an analysis of three interrelated formations. These formations highlight three critical shifts: (1) colonial governance and the creation of related economic zones, (2) the relation among colonial governance, modern state formation, and changing religious and legal regulations, and (3) the historical production of symbolic codes that order hierarchies of value that shape new patterns of cultural meaning. By starting with the latter, we see that to discuss the deterritorialized production of Yorùbá locality in the Americas is to explore the ideological routinization of practices as they relate to the historical conditions under which particular formations were shaped. Linking these realms of religious, legal, and historical òrìsà networks provides us with a critical way of understanding how particular subjectivities are made, circulated, or rendered invisible within social institutions of power.

Race, Nation, and the Imaginary: Agency and the Making of Òyótúnjí Village

How does the sociology of bodily frames—the skin, the form of features—figure into the ways that bodies are understood in local and global contexts and therefore the ways they are incorporated into social life? Is there a way that the materiality of the body suggests that there exists a different politics of agency that lies outside of the realm of the public, the state? In what ways are corporal bodies, and the imaginaries that inhere, autonomous, and in what ways are they mutually co-constructed by individuals, cultural processes, and state institutions?

Many Yorùbá revivalists who live either inside or outside of Òyótúnjí advocate that black Americans should adopt Pan-African religious nationalism as the basis for their identity and should focus their worldly desires on their black ancestral solidarity, and not the contemporary nation-state and its constitutional struggles, as the basis for political equity. By maintaining the goal of eventually converting all black Americans to African religious practices, the prevailing belief is that through conversion and broad-based outreach, revivalist practitioners can subvert the legacy of slavery that has oppressed and historically impoverished black Americans. As a result, the image of a grand and noble black empire, as well as of Yorùbá practitioners being captured and taken away to the Americas, continues to be deeply embedded in the geographical designations of Ọ̀yọ́ as the precolonial empire and Africa as the homeland.

Given that it is the purpose of the institutionalization of society to erect complex forms of power by which norms may be individually regulated, it is no accident that deterritorialized communities often identify the prestige of tradition as the locus of authority. In recreating Ọ̀yọ́ in Ọ̀yọ́túnjí, for example, the leadership established strategies of governance that were aligned with the prestige of the past and forms of community that were embedded in the premodern hegemony of the nation-state. As such, Ọ̀yọ́túnjí is hierarchically divided into various levels, ranging from a political leader, the Ọba (king), to the chiefs, priests, and nonpriest practitioners. The Ọba, sophisticated and learned, is more commonly known by his followers, both in and outside the village, as Ọba Adéfúnmi I, the Yorùbá father of dispersed Africans. He claims a constituency of thousands of African Americans in the United States, hundreds of whom have lived and trained in Ọ̀yọ́túnjí.

In Ọ̀yọ́túnjí religious networks, the leader and Ọba is the charismatic leader. He is seen by most as a prophet and transmitter of god's message for general dissemination to black Americans. According to Max Weber's theory of charismatic leadership, to legitimize a break in an established order a prophet must invoke a moral authority with which he or she is able to establish a new norm by surpassing the old. The Ọba's mission is to break from the shackles of the slavery that many in the movement feel still overdetermines their fate. He is expected to intervene for the purposes of their inclusion into definitions of nobility and civilization and their ultimate redemption from stereotypes of black people as "slaves and savages." Ultimately, religious prophecy is a form of charismatic power that when aligned with a corpus of seemingly ancient knowledge works in religious revivalism to establish social norms that are reproducible because they are both morally and politically powerful.

Clearly setting the terms for the use of racial continuity to forge prestatehood claims to African nobility (empires and rulers), Ọ̀yọ́túnjí governance in South Carolina is organized into four central spheres of social life: political, religious, cultural, and economic. Within this very hierarchical movement there are various levels of leadership. Unlike the highest stature of the Ọba, others participate in making change through civic organizations (by nonspiritual means) or through personal change (by sociospiritual means). This hierarchy of spiritual influence is by design. In the mid-1970s, when some of Ọ̀yọ́túnjí's practitioner-specialists claimed that they were possessed and in that state tried to vocalize the need for correcting problems in Ọ̀yọ́túnjí's leadership, their claims were dismissed and the use of such forms of spiritualism, popular in Santería, were outlawed. Accordingly, the chiefs, priests, and spiritual followers who act as intermediaries between God and humans engage in spiritual communication in such ways that reinforce social order and sometimes push its boundaries.[8]

At the apex of its zones of governance is the palace, a signifier of ancient ancestral leadership. In keeping with the nobility of empire, Ọ̀yọ́túnjí is politically structured according to hierarchies of grandeur and social status. Embracing these symbols, embedded in the pride of African nobility (signs of Yorùbá institutional power), the formation of Ọ̀yọ́túnjí governance marked the development of a new kind of black nationalist governance in the 1970s that required an ideological framework to determine what counts as Yorùbá.

Notions of biological succession from one black ancestor to another have shaped the parameters for legitimating racial ideologies about African identities as constitutive of shared origins. Ultimately, Yorùbá revivalism stands at the imaginary crossroads of the enslaved African body, which reinforces remembrance of the forced migration of enslaved Africans and the redemptive hope of an ideological return to black governance. This approach to the realm of fantasy is critical to the ways agents become something else. However, the prestige of precolonial empire connections and the bodies that inhabit those deterritorialized spaces are not recognized simply through abstract imaginings alone. How they make and remake the imaginary within the boundaries of hegemonic conceptions of reality is deeply embedded in the institutionalization of reality. How the racial body is read and transformed into a sign of national belonging and how it is connected through the historical production of modern subjectivities is as much about the institutional representation of racial belonging as it is about the practices that constitute their differences. The processes of producing perceptions of identity are shaped by institutional ideologies that legitimize sameness and difference in particular ways.

The Development of Òrìṣà Voodoo as Cultural Heritage

Ọ̀yọ́túnjí revivalists often highlight the bringing of òrìṣà voodoo into the United States as the event in which Afro-Cubans were called on by the gods to give their secrets back to black people. In the narrative told to me by the Ọba, this moment took place in 1959, when the soon-to-be-founder of Ọ̀yọ́túnjí Village, then named Serge King, and his friend, a Cuban American named Chris Oliana, were the first two U.S. Americans to be initiated into the Afro-Cuban priesthood cult of Ṣàngó in Matanzas, Cuba. This ritual moment is seen as critical because the diviner identified King as protected by the patron òrìṣà Ọbàtálá, but in a negative configuration (ọ̀ṣẹ́ méjì in osobo). King was told that he should not assume a position of leadership. "Rather than initiating me into the Ọbàtálá cult," he explained, "the diviner declared that the gods prohibited me from initiating others into the Ṣàngó secret society and warned that I was to be careful to not share the secrets of Africa's gods with not only noninitiates but also non-Cubans." Relegating the interpretation of the odù (divinatory verses) to white Cuban racism, he noted that "white Cubans are afraid that black Americans will enter the Santería priesthood and Africanize it."

Once he established that in the past black Americans were outside the parameters of African cultural knowledge in the past, he repeatedly emphasized that the reason he entered the Santería priesthood was to gain the necessary ritual training to return Santería practices to their "purest African form." For this reason, King remained loyal to his Santería alliances in New York City and tried to abide by the basic cultural and political rules of secrecy and discretion—legacies from the disguising of Yorùbá religion during conditions of slavery.[9]

King and Oliana together established an òrìṣà religious organization and named it the Ṣàngó Temple. During this period, Santería networks began to proliferate, and there was a growing need to make available ritual products—inscribed saint candles, packaged herbs and remedies, òrìṣà objects, witchcraft protection, and good luck charms—as well as religious histories about òrìṣà practices. However, the more King learned about the origins and transformation of Santería, the more its Christian influences and the slave context that instigated its transformation became intolerable. By the mid-1960s, King had incorporated into his practice the fundamental principles of black nationalism that had been circulating in artistic and political circles of the time. He changed his name to Adéfúnmi and renamed his version of Santería òrìṣà voodoo and the temple the Yorùbá Temple, which emphasizes the African origins of Santería and not the conditions of slavery that led to the creation of Santería from Yorùbá-Lukumi. In the spirit of the black power fervor of the 1960s, he argued that such vestiges needed to be discarded "by all means necessary." As a result, most of the Santería consultants in New York City refused to support his increasingly overt race-centered declarations. Oliana too severed ties with him. The consequence of developing an Africancentric orientation was that over time he lost his constituency and, therefore, his potential economic power. The goal of Adéfúnmi's growing movement became, as he stated, to "return Santería to its African roots." Through routinized practices that emphasized the African origins of Yorùbá practices (from Africa to the Americas) Yorùbá revivalists recast Santería through the signs of African grandeur and Yorùbá aesthetics and performative nobility. To "purify" Santería of what they considered its problematic psychology of slavery and residual colonial hegemony, Yorùbá revivalists engaged in actively resignifying Santería in racialized discourses of African origins, especially the symbolic powers of òrìṣà, such as the iconic mothers or reproducers of the nation; these include the pantheon of deities such as Ọ̀ṣun, Yemọja, and Ọya. Adéfúnmi and other prominent òrìṣà voodoo leaders changed the mixed-race features on images of Santería saint-like deities to a stereotypical African image: dark brown skin and broad features, signs of authentic black purity (an ironic departure from his own and his family network's light-skinned physical features). To symbolically Africanize what is popularly referred to as the problematic European features of Catholic saints, they substituted the white or light-skinned faces of the saints with dark brown faces or, where appropriate, replaced the human features altogether with customarily symbolic objects from the earth. They painted portraits that emphasized thick lips and broad noses, began wearing West African dashikis and grand shiny fabrics and afros, and adopted Yorùbá names. Many practitioners involved in the early formation of Yorùbá revivalism identify their engagement in African-based practices as the only way of legitimately reclaiming their place as heirs to Yorùbá-related practices in the Americas. By restructuring Yorùbá identities in keeping with the signs of blackness, Ọ̀yọ́túnjí revivalists identified their ancestors as living through them, and because of the history of slavery they located Ọ̀yọ́túnjí in alliance with Yorùbá empires. As such, they saw themselves, and not their Afro-Cuban counterparts, as the keepers of Yorùbá rituals and, therefore, the only agents who had the legitimacy to bring about ritual innovations.

These interventions in religious and aesthetic representation were embedded in values connected to differences between whiteness and blackness. Dismissing Christianity and Lukumi reflected Adéfúnmi's attempts to return to a precolonial period of black pride and Ọ̀yọ́-Yorùbá governance. Fueling this was the conviction that the ideological return to African-based practices was the only hope for black Americans. However, by 1969, forging ahead toward the Africanization of Santería, Adéfúnmi started to feel the consequences of his political goals. He began to experience financial and personal traumas, and as a result of the thinning network of knowledgeable priests who would support the development of òrìṣà voodoo, he was forced to close the temple. The formation of the Yorùbá Temple had marked the official separation of a particular form of òrìṣà voodoo from Santería; its closing was transformative. Although dormant for six months,

Life-sized
Olókun statue.

Abeokuta—Ògbóni meeting place in King's palace.

Yemọja sculpture.

Òṣun òrìṣà shrine.

Life-sized Olókun carving in front of Olókun shrine.

when the leaders reemerged they changed the name from Yorùbá Temple to the African Theological Archministry (ATA). This time, referencing a return to African ways, the ATA became a branch of the larger African-based model they named Ọ̀yọ́túnjí African Village.

Ọ̀yọ́túnjí Village became a sign of the abrogation of Santería alliances from black nationalist Yorùbá practitioners, and the differences in meaning and racial value that were resignified by Adéfúnmi's use of temporal and spatial codes are reflective of the problem of power. That is, the changing meanings of what is authentic and legitimate were authorized through the spatial and temporal referencing of Africa in relation to Cuba, the past in relation to the present. These dynamics of memory also reference bodily meanings inscribed within the particularities of the political economy of governance. What is particular about the type of racial nationalism that emerged in the United States as a result of the increased circulation of history of the forced migration of slaves is that it contributed to the transformation of linkages between spatial belonging and race. These discourses led to the political proliferation of a nostalgia of racial suffering in the United States; they also allowed individuals to redraw cartographies of belonging, which related ideologies of contemporary racial alliances to race-historically constituted zones of subjugation and governance.

Race as Culture and Cultural Production in Ọ̀yọ́túnjí

By 1970, five families moved with Adéfúnmi to Beaufort with the goal of establishing a black separatist community in the bush of South Carolina. As he was the former spiritual leader of the Yorùbá Temple, the members decided that Adéfúnmi should become the leader of the entire establishment. The significant years of formulating the structure and layout of Ọ̀yọ́túnjí Village began after their second move in 1972, when they were forced to relocate from their initial, rented site on Brays Island Road to the new ten-acre site on Route 17, which they purchased collectively. Nevertheless, constructing a community that undermined Santero racism yet had minimal access to Nigerian Yorùbá traditionalists meant that practitioners had to depend on the scant publications about Yorùbá religious practices available to them. Unlike the intergenerational training of Santería, deeply entrenched in the social memory of families, the òrìṣà voodoo movement drew its strength from the deployment of educational institutional knowledge.

By the early to mid-1970s, the development of Yorùbá revivalism benefited from the rising tide of black history institutions in the United States as well as the development of different urban networks from which to disseminate knowledge of Yorùbá cultural history. Combined with the need to obtain and read African-centered textbooks, revivalists focused on the educational and ritual development of Ọ̀yọ́túnjí's Archministry in establishing the fundamental mission of Yorùbá revivalism. With the tasks of recasting Santería as not sufficiently African and of recreating a social organization that would resemble the practitioners' African-centered alliances, the formation of Yorùbá traditionalism in a new, intentional community in the bush of South Carolina—absent lived or historical knowledge about the particularities of Yorùbá cultural practices—had a difficult institutional beginning.

With advancing cultural relations between practitioners of various nations and the increasing affordability of travel for middle-class Americans interested in experiencing life in a homeland elsewhere, thousands of black nationalists embarked on pilgrimages to Mecca and heritage tours to various parts of Africa. In 1972, to strengthen their ties to Nigerian Yorùbá clan groups and to gain the ritual legitimacy of Nigerian rituals, Adéfúnmi joined many of those voyagers by traveling to Nigeria. With the goal of studying and learning about Yorùbá ritual processes, Adéfúnmi lived among families for a four-month period and learned the Yorùbá language to study the organization and history of Nigerian Yorùbá practices. He was initiated into the cult of Ifá (a ritual cult group) in Abẹ́òkúta, which provided him with the legitimacy he sought. The ritual process clarified for him the 1959 Santería interpretation of his initiation odù. Responding to his request that

Ọ̀yọ́túnjí school house and museum.

they clarify the symbolic meaning of ọ̀ṣẹ́ méjì in osoba, his Nigerian advisors told him that his configuration of ọ̀ṣẹ́ méjì did not represent someone who would be a dangerous leader. Rather, the Abẹ́òkúta-based Yorùbá priest who initiated him explained that the odù represented a highly powerful leader who would do many things that could have many consequences for his family.

When, at the end of 1972, Adéfúnmi completed his travels, he returned to Ọ̀yọ́túnjí, where his constituency crowned him Ọba, endowing him with the official Yorùbá title, Kábíyèsí. Often translated to mean Long Live the King or Your/His Royal Highness, Kábíyèsí is a marker of a leader—an Ọba or king—and signals the temporal and spatial power of Yorùbá governance, establishing symbolic codes that set the terms of particular social relations. With his ascent to the Ọ̀yọ́túnjí throne, Adéfúnmi became the leader of Ọ̀yọ́túnjí, a socially segregated democratic dictatorship governing Yorùbá revivalists in the United States in which the leader has veto power and community participation is represented through its house of landholding representatives and not through free and democratic elections. Along with the symbolic power of ultimate leadership, members of the community created an institution of black royal governance, with a traditional ruler and the decision-making power of landholders and chiefs referred to in Yorùbá as the Ògbóni society.

This crowning of an Ọ̀yọ́túnjí leader was an attempt to replicate the history of elaborate African monarchies that were ruled by kings. In the Yorùbáland of old, as it is often called, the Ọba presided over the state council and was advised by his closest priests and chiefs, all members of the prestigious Ògbóni cult. The Ògbóni cult of the mid-nineteenth century was an organization of member chiefs who venerated their ancestors through their worship of the earth spirit icon. Most cult members saw their worship as mediating between the living and the dead, both understood as living ancestral forces. In return for the ongoing sustenance provided by the ancestors of the land, worshippers throughout Yorùbá states offered libation to the earth spirits in the form of their first plate of food or their first drink at every meal. The Ògbóni earth cult society was the most politically powerful system, and member chiefs played a mediating role between the Aláàfin (the king of Ọyọ́) and the Ọyọ́-Mèsì (the kingmakers of Ọyọ́, literally, "The Ọyọ́ Chiefs know what answer to give"), as well as a judicial role with regard to community members (Morton-Williams 1960, 1967; Brandon 1993, 21). Its mostly male members were elders, and it was organized to perform all of the state functions, establishing an inner circle for those in positions of power (Fadipe 1970, 205). Those in the inner circle took an oath to create bonds of secrecy among the leadership, and this form of ritualized membership provided members with full access to the king. In contrast, the external chiefs, popularly known as being in the "outer circle" of the state council, had no executive duties or constitutional rights in the state-sponsored Ògbóni society. Chiefs in this category were the military chiefs and field marshals.[10]

Ọyọ́túnjí's leadership organization was designed to replicate the organization of Yorùbá customary towns. The community attempted to establish continuities in governance by creating an Ògbóni and chieftaincy structure. The people appointed to these posts assumed the authority to implement practical decision-making rules and procedures for the community. In relation to religious organization in prestatehood Yorùbáland, priests of the Ògbóni cult were called on to consult the divinatory oracle so that they could determine ritually if the Ọba's leadership was supported by the ancestors of the earth (Òjó 1967, 168). Similarly, in Ọyọ́túnjí, members interested in developing ancestral and òrìṣà rituals organized social and religious cult groups and a priest cult group for the formation of a divinatory authority structure.

Community leaders established political structures, legal codes, Yorùbá language training, and spatial designs to construct Ọyọ́túnjí as a village town. To represent Yorùbá social life, the architecture of governance and spatial design was organized around a large palace courtyard called the ààfin (palace) to replicate images of African kingdoms. Unlike the social organization of Santería as a covert practice incorporated into the structure of the nuclear family, the founders of Ọyọ́túnjí decentralized òrìṣà worship and initiation, creating a universe of gover-

Ọba of Ọ̀yọ́túnjí.

Òyótúnjí militia on guard and in line with three flags.

Òyótúnjí militia preparing to march.

Cars owned by Ọ̀yọ́túnjí royalty.

nance organized to incorporate distinct Yorùbáland towns as a means of drawing
a parallel between the towns and their accompanying patron òrìṣà.

When the builders engaged in the creation of the physical layout, they started
with small compounds that encircled the ààfin. They created a landscape that referenced the symbolic prestige of precolonial African village life in which they
replaced the symbols of Santería saints with disembodied òrìṣà shrines. They organized these reconfigurations to indexically reference key regions in West Africa,
from which nine of the most popular Yorùbá-American òrìṣà were known to
emerge, and the ààfin, and employed Yorùbá names and terminology.

Today, the village is divided into five main districts: the ààfin, igbóòṣà, ìká gbó
(ìkagbó), ànàgó, and igbàlẹ̀ (sacred forested district). Each is governed by a series
of town chiefs or a political or civic society (egbẹ́). Each district contains living
quarters, public buildings, and private and public temples and/or shrines for veneration by the practitioner. The ààfin, as the seat of leadership and the central, most
important district, was configured as a large compound that houses the Ọba, his
four wives' and children's houses, as well as the ancestral shrines. One such shrine
represents the embodiments of the Ọba's ancestors, as well as of the venerated unknown ancestors, damballah wedo. Other shrines housed in the ààfin include the
òrìṣà Ṣàngó (a symbol of kingship), the Ọba's òrìṣà of Ifá (the deity of destiny),
onílé (owner of the earth), and Ọbàtálá (creator of the human form). The ààfin also
houses the school complex, the museum, and guesthouses for new residents, in-

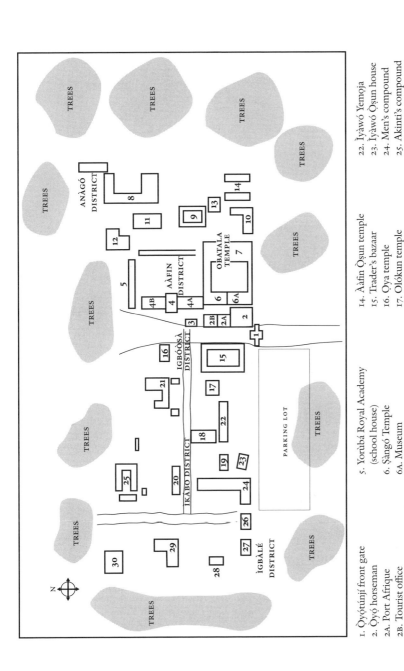

Ọ̀yọ́túnjí Village Map.

1. Ọ̀yọ́túnjí front gate
2. Ọ̀yọ́ horseman
2A. Port Afrique
2B. Tourist office
3. Drum house
4. Àfin gate
4A. Ọba's ancestor shrine
4B. Royal guest house

5. Yorùbá Royal Academy (school house)
6. Ṣàngó Temple
6A. Museum
7. Ilé di
8. Ilé Ọba's house
9.–12. Ọba's wives' houses
13. Royal guest house

14. Àáfin Ọ̀ṣun temple
15. Trader's bazaar
16. Ọya temple
17. Olókun temple
18. Yemọja temple
19. Ọ̀ṣun temple
20. Ògún temple
21. Ọlaitan compound

22. Ìyàwó Yemọja
23. Ìyàwó Ọ̀ṣun house
24. Men's compound
25. Akinti's compound
26. Ọ̀ṣàdélé compound
27. Akínwọ́n compound
28. Guest house
29. Women's house
30. Ifágbénró compound

Òrìṣà alley.

Chief Alàgbà's house.

Iya Orite's house.

Ọ̀yọ́túnjí Egúngún with chief Alagba.

dentured workers, and unmarried women (*ayaba*) who are betrothed or otherwise accountable to the Ọba.

The ànàgó district, named to honor the Nàgó of Dahomean people, is adjacent to the eastern border of the àdfin. At the front gate of the àdfin is the shrine of Eṣù/Ẹlẹ́gba. Extending westward, beginning with the igbóòṣà district, is the area popularly referred to as temple row. This district houses the temples of the Ọya, Olókun, and Yemọja òrìṣàs. The ìká gbó district begins with the Ọṣun temple and includes the shrine to Ògún and Ososi, as well as public and private buildings.[11] The òrìṣà Ọbalúayé is located in the forest adjacent to the ìká gbó district. The final district, the place of ancestral veneration for the community, is known as the ìgbàlẹ̀ grove, the home of the sacred *egúngún* (ancestors).

These configurations of community were developed to produce a sense of connection to Africa that was represented not only as ancestrally legitimate but also as indexically referential to an originary moment. Such signs of origins, of ancestry, have been resignified by Ọ̀yọ́túnjí Yorùbá practitioners to mark certain features about being Yorùbá, thus African. These signs of deterritorialized belonging link the territoriality of African ancestry to the figure of blackness as originary in the modern imaginary. It is critical, therefore, to recognize how these deterrito-

Ọba of Ọ̀yọ́túnjí meets Nigerian chief in Ọ̀yọ́túnjí. Two of Ọba's four wives are present.

rialized spatial layouts, structures of governance, and bodily imaginaries are both ideologically and historically embedded in modern attachments to place, and how narratives of racial belonging work alongside the modernity of discourses of territorial origins, that is, forms of sedimentation that work with tropes of state legitimacy.

The Ọ̀yọ́túnjí creation of new forms of belonging in the restructuring of a movement of post–Civil Rights heritage involves the ideological work of linking an originary moment to the project of deterritorialized place making. The history of religious and legal change in the circum-Atlantic region highlights the extent to which changing practices are connected to changing political and economic formations in the regulation and disciplining of new bodies that are raced, practices that are silenced, and aesthetics that are hierarchized in the modernity of circum-Atlantic state formation. For, while microanalyses of social imaginings involve the resignification and routinization of new practices, reclassifications of subjectivity must also be understood in relation to historically constituted modalities of power. Here, the plunder of resources for imperial accumulation and the development of new relations of human value must be understood in relation to the ways new logics of nationhood are shaped by particular routes of trade and formations of governance.

Passage Points of Revivalism: Slave Routes

The transatlantic slave trade of the sixteenth to the eighteenth century was the largest deportation of humans from one place to another and set in place the tenets of the first system of globalization in the history of modern international expansion (Deveau 1989). The modern state that set in place particular hierarchies of racial order took shape in the recent history of a mercantile order that was replaced by plantation slavery alongside the development of industrial capital and free market economies. The development of industrial and then capitalist economies produced early patterns of intensified contact between empires and newly forming colonies. This early wave of modern interconnections—the capture and transport of Africans to the Americas—developed alongside patterns of racialization that aided the justification of devalued bodies in exchange for low wages for labor and high returns on raw minerals for industrial development.

In the Americas, slave labor produced a high volume of crops. Some of the central products—sugar, tobacco, and cotton—were traded for other goods such as more slaves, gold, and alcohol. Next to slaves, gold was the leading commodity exported from the West African coast, and ivory contributed to almost a quarter of the trade with the Royal African Company (Eltis 1987, 1999, 2000). The transatlantic slave trade was predominant in the eighteenth century. The trafficking of large numbers of men and women from Africa to the Americas was central to the expansion of the European empires and contributed to the increased social interaction between European traders in West Africa and planters in the Americas. The forced migration of slaves was shaped by the politics of social and economic value, as forged by the preexisting trade webs. With the formation of capitalist slavery, settler colonialism and economic nationalism led to the success of the type of settler colonialism that reinforced the nationalism that territorialized new colonies (Arrighi 1994, 49).

With the growing trade routes, the rivalry among flourishing European countries, and the developing demand for laborers, African territories were raided for slaves by other Africans as well as non-Africans. On the West African coast, the Ọ̀yọ́ Empire, comprising the kingdoms of Dahomey, Benin, and Ọ̀yọ́, was one of the last West African empires to concede European conquest. It was the demise of the Ọ̀yọ́ Empire, coupled with the willingness of elite members of African groups to sell captives of war, that further enabled the possibility of transatlantic slavery. After the Òwu and Ẹ̀gbá wars of the nineteenth century, vast numbers of Ọ̀yọ́ Yorùbá prisoners were sold by predominantly Fulani traders first to European traders and then to planters in Cuba, Brazil, and the Caribbean.[12] The 1818 fragmentation of the Ọ̀yọ́ Empire occurred after the British abandoned slave-trading

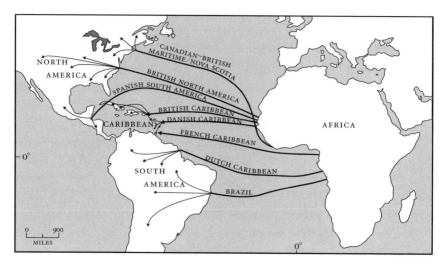

Map of slave route, 1790–1830.

castles along the coast of Gezo Dahomey. The British had annexed this region from the Ọ̀yọ́ Empire in the late 1700s, and after the fall of the Ọ̀yọ́ Empire, Yorùbáland became notorious as a slave-trading region on the West African coast.[13] From the late seventeenth to the early eighteenth century, merchants raided Yorùbá towns, captured men and women from large Yorùbá-speaking regions, and sold them, mainly to Portuguese traders. Yorùbá-speaking men and women, more than any other West African ethnic and linguistic group, were enslaved and exported to North America, Cuba, and Brazil in large numbers. The history of the dispersal of Africans to the Americas is a history of diverse people and commodities moved along multiple trade routes to new locales.[14]

Until the early nineteenth century, tobacco and beeswax were two of the most lucrative agricultural products in Cuba. However, by 1850, the majority of wealth from plantations came from the triangular sugar trade. The production of sugar in a global economy generated a rapidly growing cash-based economy. The formation of a new global network of trade using modern ship technologies for mass marine transport gave rise to the development of various triangular forms of trade involving particular European empires, such as Great Britain and France, that brought guns and gunpowder and forms of technological machinery to Africa in exchange for slaves and raw materials to the Americas and then back to Europe (Law 1991, 1997; Eltis 1987). The trafficking of slaves declined between 1680 and 1780 (Eltis 1987, 1999, 2000), and the legal abolition of transatlantic slavery began with the Danish in 1805. In 1808 British and North American acts abolishing slave trafficking were passed (Curtin 1969, 231).[15] But European consumption of coffee and sugar rose, and the transatlantic slave trade continued over a forty-year period, long after it was outlawed, even though, over time, it became difficult to trade captives across the Atlantic Ocean.[16] This difficulty signaled the end of the illegal trade of African captives to the Americas but also, by 1865, buttressed the development of a new form of plantation slavery in Cuba, the locus of one node of the transformation of òrìsà practices.[17]

With the development of European markets directly tied to the triangular trade of goods between Europe, Africa, and the Caribbean, the circulation of ideas about a racialized modern Atlantic world followed. The plantation-based economy led to the reinforcement of divisions between the landowners, who had political and economic power, and enslaved workers, who had very little material power, and, therefore, to the formation of racial hierarchies and parallel forms of national placement.

In charting the interrelationships between regimes of slavery and historical formations of religious regulation that inform the struggles over Yorùbá membership in the Americas, it becomes clear that the historical trade of transatlantic commodities shaped the nature of slave routes and served as the basis for the early internationalization of modern conceptions of subjectivity. Then, as now, the global circulation of Yorùbá bodies was driven by economic forces that shaped ideologies of value in particular ways. The formation of Yorùbá revivalist territorial alliances is thus connected to the modern capitalist development in the circum-Atlantic world. The variables central to how belonging and membership are imagined are as much a factor of the history of transatlantic slavery as they are factors of the power of histories of exclusion in shaping aesthetic signs of belonging. But, ultimately, there are ideological boundaries to the imagination that must be acknowledged if we are to understand the production and persistence of racial distinctions as historically contingent. Racial distinctions are not simply distinctions between black and white. Understanding the cultural politics of racial difference involves charting the ways particular types of moral geographies are incorporated to authenticate some practices over others, as well as the ways the particularities of aesthetic geographies of race play into the cultural economy of lightening and blackening in time and in space.

What can an understanding of the development of early capitalist subjectivities tell us about the interconnection between how the law was used to regulate ritual and how it produced a hierarchy of normative practice? The hierarchization of African subjectivities demonstrates why the historical formation of meanings of òrìsà voodoo as "pure," therefore "African," came into being as responses to the institutionalization of racial supremacy.[18] For it was not just African religious practices that were regulated by legal institutions. Notions of race were also ideologically shaped by hierarchical notions of human value and were reinforced in cultural institutions and the practices that constituted them. This regimentation of race was fundamental to the transformation of Yorùbá revivalist imaginaries and permeated the institutional basis by which African identities were and are incorporated into spatially relevant geographies of blackness.

What these zones of historical mappings demonstrate is that people connect different forms of meaning with different institutional models of practice. Understanding the transformation of African-based practices into the development of a Santería underground in Cuba and the United States is critical for understanding not only the changes in Yorùbá practices in Nigeria that led to the dispersal of Lukumi-Yorùbá, but also how Santería came into being and how it became silenced, criminalized, iconized as a hybrid, and eventually commercialized in the context of the cultural heritage industry. Determining how the Yorùbá past is constituted through institutions, therefore, lies in understanding the processes through which Yorùbá revivalists have devalued this history of Spanish Christian regulation (read: white) and employed racialized conceptualizations of Yorùbá origins to reconfigure their terms of belonging through the moral force of redemption from that past. As we shall see, even as black nationalist claims to African-based Yorùbá practices reflect a commitment to the symbolics of African homelands, Cuba and Afro-Cubanism were the points of passage for the development of Yorùbá revivalism in the United States. It was, therefore, the memory of slavery that produced Santería that had to be undermined to establish new ancestral connections to Africa. The moral geography of African centrism was justified by Adefumi and his followers because of the Christianization of Lukumi-Yorùbá in Cuba that created Santería.

The first critical moment, which occurred during the first generation of enslaved African captives in Cuba, was the establishment of the *regla de ocha* (mutual aid societies), which the Spanish colonial government encouraged enslaved Africans to create.[19] The second critical moment took place during the second and third generations of enslaved Africans who, in ongoing creolized formations, incorporated the symbolic conditions of slavery and a varying degree of Catholic ideological practices into their daily lives, eventually creating Santería, or *santería cubana*, as a reflection of Afro-Cubanness.

Genealogies of Racing Òrìṣà Voodoo:
Formations of Santería (Regla de ocha)

Historians have estimated that between 702,000 and 1 million African slaves were imported to the Americas from the Òyó, Dahomey, and Benin regions of West

Africa (Curtain 1969, 46; Brandon 1993, 43).[20] It was not until 1850–70 that the final phase of exporting African captives, then known as Lukumi and subdivided into Lukumi Èyò (from Òyó) and Lukumi Ifę/fee (from Ifę) from the hinterlands along the West African coastal trading zones, increased significantly.[21] A significant number of the Yorùbá-speaking captives who were exported to Cuba were most likely Yorùbá òrìsà cult practitioners, who, in contrast to captives along the West African coast, were unlikely to have come into contact with Christian missionaries. This distinction is critical, as it is likely that those Yorùbá-identified slaves who, during the final twenty years of plantation slavery (1849–69) relocated to the Spanish colony now known as Cuba, laid the seeds for the development of new Lukumi-Yorùbá practices.[22]

Newly imported captives in the islands and regions claimed by Spain and Portugal represented a cross-section of captives from different ethnic, cultural, linguistic, and economic regimes. Despite the reality that the diverse complexities of the forced migration of African captives refract the possibility of homogeneity on plantations, nevertheless owners of enslaved Africans classified them in distinctive racial groupings. In fact, they point to the diversity of adaptation that came to characterize regional variation throughout Cuba. Between 1790 and 1822, approximately 240,000 captives had been imported by the Spanish to their Cuban colony, and by 1850, approximately seven out of fifteen of the newly enslaved were Yorùbá women.

Large numbers of slaves lived on plantations in informal family communities, and ancestral cult worship was oriented in the family as the unit of governance. Catholicism succeeded in penetrating these pagan formations by leading to the introduction of saint-like imagery in African religious practices. Religious leaders forced legislation to mandate the conversion of slaves to Christianity,[23] and by the early 1800s, the Spanish colony was racially segregated and the Spanish Catholic Church was the only venue in which people from different designated racial groups could intermingle, if they so desired. Conversion efforts shifted from urban areas to the countryside, but Catholic priests did not succeed in quickly converting the rural masses, who could not easily go to church; further legislation banned work on church holidays. Even when the practice of African-based religions became illegal, slaves continued to practice their reconfigured cosmologies covertly, simply incorporating christening and church-based funeral ceremonies into their cult rituals. Still, this series of legal regimentations over many decades made it difficult for slaves to avoid joining Christian organizations. With the development of contemporary church institutions and civil society formations in various parts of Europe (especially Italy, England, France, and Spain) and later in the colonies (what would become Cuba, Brazil, and Trinidad) Catholicism became the institutional faith around which the family and agricultural life were reconfigured. As the growth of the colonies led to the importation of Catholicism in Spanish and Portuguese colonies, Christian religious rules were absorbed into European-based laws and the formation of religious life in the colonies involved the suppression of other religions as fundamental to the order of the law. Ultimately, what circulated was not just a language of social divisions and racial types, but a hierarchical aesthetic order by which notions of both racial value and moral logics took shape. As a powerful institution of governance, intolerant of pagan ritual life, Christian church institutions facilitated shifts from the occult and its relation to the family to the individual in need of leaving all else in search of individual salvation. The public display of ancestral totems and worship was silenced, and, with the rise of the nation-state and the reorganization of both the family and the political economy, local authorities established laws distinct from religious life. The struggles over Yorùbá membership in the Americas became the backdrop for interrelationships among regimes of slavery, ritual change, and new institutional spheres of governance.

Race, Space, and Changing Institutions of Practice

Enforcement of anti-African religious practices led to transformations in the already changing òrìṣà worship formerly associated with West Africa, and by the time of the mid-eighteenth-century missionary campaigns, enslaved communities had begun to incorporate Catholic sacraments of confirmation into secret societies, integrating Catholic saint reverence with Lukumi cosmologies. These new forms of practices proliferated throughout slave communities, and the Catholic Church became a leading institution working toward the integration of free and enslaved, black and white populations.

Principles of Catholicism spread from the monastery to society and provided the foundation for moral rules and later the formation of legal doctrine. Initially, priests administered penance, giving people the opportunity to discharge their sins. The Catholic Church in Cuba set the framework for principles of individual equality, justice, and guided access to God. Through confessions, priests began regulating people's conscience; once confession became institutionalized, basic ideas of guilt took shape. With both the encouragement of individual responsibility and the development of a European canon law system alongside Cuban state formation, canon law produced itself in relation to the moral standards of Christianity, ironically helping to create Santería alongside a popular system of Christian moral virtues that was consistent with Enlightenment forms of civility. Here, as in West Africa, dominant approaches to òrìṣà practices were silenced and hierarchies of respectable personhood subjectivities took shape through the interpersonal regulation of the law. Over time, religious practices became institutionalized; the effectiveness of the rules of the Catholic Church was in their power of internalization, as individuals became disciplined and began to self-regulate their moral behavior. The privacy of òrìṣà worship also became self-regulated, and those who continued to engage in òrìṣà worship were equally concerned with saving their souls from hell's damnation.

Similar processes took shape in the newly forming British colony in what was to become Nigeria. In the mid- to late nineteenth century, many of the old homeland connections to the family earth cults shifted as Christian conversions took place in large numbers and former slave captives returned to Yorùbáland as educated and literate Christians (Crowther 1968). These former slaves were freed by British mariners and returned to what was to become the southwestern regions of the Nigerian state. These new converts contributed to the transformation of traditional, educational, religious, political, and economic spheres of power as early as 1859. As many converts to Christianity became critics of ancestor worship, they recast the once widely held reverence for the ancestors to the realm of paganism. Taking on the moral mission of Christian Enlightenment, those of the reformed Christian fraternities participated in the transformation of West African governance.

With the ordinance of British indirect rule in Nigeria (the British Native Council Ordinance of 1901), British administrators working with various local leaders divided the region into district councils and appointed from the traditional leadership principal ruling chiefs for each district (Asiwaju 1976, 99). Although this reorganization relegated pagan cult groups to the realm of primitivism, the symbolic meanings continued to have cultural significance in people's daily lives.[24] With the massive conversion forces of Christianization in the second half of the nineteenth century, many former occult devotees formed alliances with Christian institutions. This shift resulted in the development of an underground movement of ancestor worshippers, consolidated by bonds of secrecy. Worshippers, some of whom also professed their conversion to Christianity, joined inner executives of various cult societies. And although the rituals required a certain degree of covert participation, there existed cultural manifestations of public ritual performances that were widely accepted by many Christians and Muslims alike (see Morton-Williams 1960).

As a result of these Enlightenment influences, the transformation of the Ògbóni cult and its associated rituals was propelled forward by nineteenth-century Christian conversions. Given the prestige of reorganized traditional kingships, the Ògbóni cult in Ọ̀yọ́ continued to shift from a majority pagan membership to a membership of growing numbers of educated Christians. In this light, ancestor worship and the belief in the occult became a practice of the past. Within spheres of customary power in earth òrìṣà societies, practitioners increasingly represented their Christian influence on customary practices as a need to eradicate the "old ways" and to replace them with what they saw as "civilized" leadership.

The changing membership was influenced heavily by the popular Abẹ́òkúta Reformed Ògbóni Fraternity (ROF). By the late 1800s, members of the ROF restructured it to adopt the approach used by the Protestant sects of Foresters and Free Masons. Eventually, it was the reformed movement that replaced the once non-Christian earth òrìṣà secret societies. A similar adaptation of another Yorùbáland traditional society occurred in connection with the occult òrìṣà known as Ọbàtálá, a universal force personified in the character of the Yorùbá deity Ọbàtálá, who was thought to cause severe illnesses and human deformities. The political significance of Ọbàtálá was evident historically during warfare when many people suffered losses and deformation. Ọbàtálá was represented as the people's protector and was closely associated with sentiments of high moral purity. He was placed at the town gates to ward off evil spirits. Over time, Ọbàtálá became the patron deity of many southwest Nigerian towns, known by a range of names: òrìsàlá in Ìbàdàn and Adó-Èkìtì; òrìṣàńlá at Ilé Ifẹ̀; and Ọbàtálá in places such as Ẹ̀gbá, Ìjàyè, Ìkirè, Ọ́bà, and Iwofin, as well as outside of the borders of Yorùbáland. However, the centrality of deities or òrìṣàs also waned with the rise in Christian conversion. By the mid-twentieth century, òrìṣà worshippers in various towns propitiated a patron deity for good health and fortune. However, by the twentieth century, both òrìṣà and organized ancestor worship had been relegated to the domain of cultural festivals and traditional celebrations.

In the region that would eventually be known as Cuba, slave participation in Christianity brought access to education and marriage, making possible upward mobility. In this regard, the Catholic Church developed and facilitated early inheritance and marriage rules. These rules took their inspiration from religious laws that originated in European Old Testament texts. With the increasing power of the Church's role in civil society, new regulations on sex and reproduction were legally established and over time came to constitute the moral fabric of Yoruba life. For example, with marriage as an institution, the church could forbid illicit sex, thereby regulating sexual desire in particular ways; rules of sexual conduct were rules of marriage and only under conditions of marriage was sex rendered legitimate. Interracial marriage was allowed, further exacerbating the range of status and color distinctions in the colony. Color hierarchies of scale privileged the proximity of complexion to whiteness, further contributing to heightened levels of public discrimination against dark-skinned people. Also marginalized were non-

Nigerian Christian church worship, Atlanta, Georgia.

Catholics who lived in rural areas and were seen as the "heathen" and "uncivilized" perpetrators of cult-based òrìṣà worship.

With the regulation of racial hierarchies, the disciplining of bodies through ideologies of morality, and the effectiveness of self-regulation, the state took over the central authority of the Church, putting in place colonial courts and old canon law rules which eventually formed the basis for early legal formations in the Americas. Even as the courts in Europe and its colonies began to offer injunctive relief, the colonial state absorbed old Church powers into the law and began to administer rulings in local and urban courts.

Yorùbá revivalism today continues to reflect the hierarchy of social scales of the former Spanish postcolony. The political and economic zones of cultural production, which shaped the slave trade and the institutionalization of slavery, also shaped particular ideological zones of engagement. These zones, located in the history of transatlantic slavery and complexities of mixture and hybridity, contributed to setting the terms of belonging, especially those regulating which agents in the Americas invented new meanings.

A genealogy of religious practices created a new space of private and public life with the reconfiguration of family cult organization. In its place, particular social organizations known in Spanish as *cabildos* took shape. These processes of social change are best represented by Cuba's Bishop Pedro Agustin Morel de Santa Cruz, who encouraged plantation slaves to venerate Catholic saints in religious clubs. This new social pastime involved the recreation of Spanish cabildos found in urban areas such as Havana. African-based religions in Cuba came to be known as *regla-mentos* (*reglas* or rules), and *cabildos de nacion* (mutual aid societies) were organized along ethnic lines, in distinctive groupings that emerged during the transatlantic slave trade. These included Lukumi, Carabali, Congo, and Mandingo cultural, religious, and linguistic divisions. In general terms, the establishment of Spanish cabildos was a success. The prestige of these new forms of groupings was based on the display of Christian morality as well as new networks of accountability.

Òrìṣà cult groups were indeed present in the *cabildos*; operating against state rules that regulated the presence of certain kinds of practices, cabildos became a venue in which practitioners could conceal their religious links to African cosmologies. The signs of ritual practice that once defined the Yorùbá-speaking past were imported into the colonial present and ordered in a way that indexed both the signs of ritual that had been constituted in the Spanish colony and the mixing and mobility that radically transformed the iconic symbolism of reglas (what was to become Santería). For some scholars, the most appropriate approach to explaining the invention of Santería in the Americas or the creolization or hybridity of *regla de ocha* is to refer to particular adaptations as a beginning of change and not a continuation of ongoing changes. However, it is clear that the creation of regla de ocha emerged from the Yorùbá òrìṣà pantheon and was organized around myths of the òrìṣà, which are themselves representations of ongoing changes over time.

In Cuba, as in many regions in the United States, the development of the early colonial state involved the establishment of notions of rights and citizenship by which those who belonged to the developing nation had the legal right to participate and be heard in the political community. In relation to the development of racial hierarchies of scale that developed alongside the development of capitalist property relations, within which modern political life was structured, public life, that is, citizens' access to the polity, was regulated according to status. Whether one was owned as property or owned property (slaves, a wife, a knife), the ideological center of the modern individual was measured according to racial, gendered ancestral markers and was eventually subject to the reaches of the state.

In the late nineteenth century, with the increasing institutionalization of colonial bureaucracies, new notions of religious identity, once an individual concern, became matters of the state and the law. Regulations that prohibited the exercise of all other forms of religious practices, including African-based worship, led to the transformation of Lukumi religious life into new iconic representations under the sign of Roman Catholic Christianization. As a result, Cuban reglas developed out of the need to change practices that were less relevant in the Americas. In many cases, òrìṣà cult groups died out, òrìṣà from distinct regions were joined together, and rituals were forgotten. Changes ranged from the transformation of divinatory rituals and Yorùbá incantations to the use of praise songs. Yorùbá-Lukumi phonetic and lexical structures were transposed, and what in Yorùbáland was referred to as ẹsẹ (verses that describe the life of the òrìṣà) were translated into Spanish and became *patakis* (things of importance, from Yorùbá *pàtàkì*: "important"). Many rituals were conducted with Lukumi blends, and parallel standardizations of the Spanish language revolutionized the language of Yorùbá ritual. Similarly, the pantheon of òrìṣà and ritual practices that once indexed historical meanings associated with West Africa focused instead on the hybridity of religion in relation to the history of slavery in Cuba. Òrìṣà were resignified within the iconography of Catholic saints, and the preservation of òrìṣà houses involved the merging of interconnected cells or units. Òrìṣà names were changed to represent Spanish pronunciations, and characteristics of òrìṣà types were matched with the moral features of Catholic saints. This form of superimposition of Catholic saints over òrìṣà constituted the creation of a fragmented set of practices that transformed the visible signs of African-based òrìṣà worship. In the context of the Americas, however, the syncretization of Yorùbá deities involved the visual transformation of the signs of the òrìṣà. Ṣàngó, the principal deity of Ọ̀yọ́, became the most popular òrìṣà in Cuba, signifying a macho womanizer. The Yorùbá deity Ọ̀ṣun was linked to the virgin of the Caridad del Cobre and was a symbol of racial mixture. Ọ̀ṣun was often represented as having light skin and fine features and thus represented the symbol of the mestizo nation (Ayọrinde 2000; Kutzinski 1993).

With the development of new iconic symbols and kinship configurations known as cabildos, new units of social organization were constituted conceptually through the system of *ilés* or "houses." The house, a unit of ritual practice clearly adopted from Spanish colonial ordering schemes, relied on nuclear kinship organization, in which the *madrinos* (godmothers) or *padrinos* (godfathers) trained and provided services for their "children in god," or godchildren. In this context, unlike in past practices where individuals pursued intensive training and received one patron òrìṣà with Ẹlẹ́gba, the òrìṣà of the crossroads (popularly referred to as "their road"), priests began initiating practitioners into multiple cults. These practices moved further from the rituals of Western Africa and closer to a synchronization of earlier òrìṣà ritual structures and adapted Catholic cosmologies. Yet, even with these transformations, the increasingly regimented religious and social codes imposed by the Cuban church in 1792 led to the Spanish establishment of a law that banned cabildos. The political oscillation between tolerance, participation, and repression forced the cabildos to go underground. Once again, in the late 1800s the

Spanish colonial government passed laws that prohibited the existence of the cabildos. As a result, more sophisticated secret societies took shape and soon gave way to a new generation of slaves born in Cuba (and not West Africa). The underground development of cabildos maintained some properties of òrìṣà societies. However, in response to the distinctive Lukumi identities and fraternal practices that once constituted the cabildos during the same wave of repression, other laws were introduced to promote the confiscation of drums and religious paraphernalia. Basic components of òrìṣà worship, such as individual membership in separate and distinct cult groups, evident in the cabildos, disappeared from public visibility. Slaves formed secret cults under regimented conditions, and, in the process, practitioners in Cuba incorporated Catholic iconic signs to shield the African-based cosmologies and meanings. The Ọ̀bàtálá òrìṣà (known in the Americas by white colors; characterized by metaphors such as peace, tranquility, order, and tradition; and transformed to personify the saint known as the Virgin of Mercy) was, in various Yorùbáland towns, identified by qualities of creativity, protection, and balance. Ògún, once represented by metaphors of warfare, the forest, and iron use, was resignified by the reglas as Saint Peter; Ọ̀ṣun, the òrìṣà of the river, became the Virgin of Caridad del Cobre and was characterized as the goddess of sex and marriage; Yemoja, the goddess of the sea among the òrìṣà, became the Virgin Saint of Regla (Brandon 1993, 77).

Other changes included the incorporation of Kardecan spiritualism, an adaptation of Yorùbá traditional and religious practices, and Espiritismo, a Hispanicized version of Kardecan. The eventual Christianization of African-based Lukumi practices was developed by African slaves in two forms of religious invention. The first, Spiritism, represented a diverse late-nineteenth- and early-twentieth-century adaptation of Yorùbá ancestral earth òrìṣà. With the mass standardization of Spiritism in both free and enslaved communities, a range of literature flourished in Cuba and Puerto Rico in 1856 and circulated among learned populations. To establish power and legitimacy in reincarnation, the notion of communicating with spirits was easily incorporated into Catholic cosmologies. The concept that spirits could enter a medium's body became popular among many members of the middle and upper classes. The decentralization of religion provided individuals with an alternative to Catholicism as a dominant religious institution. Justifying their practices in discourses of science and truth, Spiritism practitioners believed that direct spirit communication with the dead was possible. In contrast, Espiritismo, often seen by Lukumi practitioners as a lower form of worship, was a healing practice that provided slaves with a forum in which spirit mediums could communicate with their African ancestors, who, they believed, were on near and faraway shores. The manifestation of Yorùbá-Lukumi ritual into that which had to be disguised should be seen not simply in the objects that were produced and the signs that were transformed, but in the obscuring of that which was signified. Thus, in relation to the transformation of òrìṣà practices in Cuba, that which Santería signified was lived in the imaginary, through aesthetic omissions and the history of particular inclusions.

By the mid-nineteenth century, with the ongoing adaptations of Yorùbá practices, sentiments of home as both Africa and the Americas were reconstituted in ways that combined racial mixture with diverse origins: Spanish, African, and Indian. Where once, over the course of the late nineteenth and early twentieth century, indigenous or predominantly mixed-race Cubans had held economic power, large numbers of white male and female Spaniards, the new Spanish elite, emigrated to Cuba and through their economic power changed the terms of economic access to domestic resources. Rather than negotiating with the former mixed-race elite, they competed with the United States and other international powers for economic trade. As a consequence, African-descendant Cubans remained at the lowest economic and political levels of Cuban society.

After the emancipation of slaves in 1897 and the 1902 War of Independence, the post-Independence period in Cuba, as in the United States, was marked by a new wave of national protests against racial injustice.[25] This period was fraught with racial marginalization. Although racial discrimination was outlawed under the Cuban Constitution,[26] racial and class-based inequities continued to permeate Cuban social life. Many early intellectuals criticized Cuban institutional racism and contested the class injustices that seemed to operate through newly forming racial spheres of power.[27] As we shall see, however, Santería and òrìṣà practices transformed from a persecuted and marginalized ritual practice to a globally dynamic and economically lucrative domain for particular forms of social reproduction.

By the early twentieth century, the inclusion or exclusion of African consciousness in Latin American populations was increasingly problematic. People tended to connect notions of being African with being black, relegating cultural belonging to African racial biological belonging. However, in time it was also clear that there existed a need to represent the complexities of the racial, ethnic, and cultural mixtures particular to the historical specificities of this Spanish colony. As an extension of the newly developing black bourgeois class of the early twentieth century, interested in articulating the duality of their European and African cultural roots, a new movement developed that was influenced by the academic writings of Cuban and Puerto Rican scholars, such as the internationally renowned Don Fernando Ortiz (1912/1992; see also Moore 1997). Influenced by sociobiological evolutionary theories of human progress, Ortiz was interested in theories of transculturation in which he attempted to produce theories of racial mixture by developing anthropological explanations of the relationship between race and culture. Initially interested in explaining why black people were more prone to crime, Ortiz became one of the early Caribbean scholars to explore the workings of the particularities of cultural hybridity in Cuban racial identity. He was instrumental in planting the seeds for what would become a larger movement toward a new identity, that of Afro-Cubanism. This emphasis on "biological mixture," described as a synthesis of racial groups, was also part of an attempt to highlight the distinctive biological and cultural heritage of a new Cuban national identity. Concepts such as *mulatez* (mulattoness) and *mestizaje* (mixedness) were part of this form of consciousness.

Though Afro-Cubanism became prominent at the height of Cuba's nationalist struggle for independence from Spain, between 1912 and 1940, initially heralded by predominantly mixed-race and lighter-skinned political leaders, it grew exponentially as a national identity and eventually became both a political assertion of national struggle and a way to highlight the particularities of Cuban class, color, national, and religious alliances. Referencing both African roots and the legitimacy of Cuban nationalism, Afro-Cubanism had the effect of producing a hyphenated symbol of "mixture" and became a popular classification for the hybridity of blackness, leading to a different way of seeing race in twentieth-century Cuba.[28]

Over the next forty years, a range of governments steered the new nation.[29] The government that radically affected the shift in international relations on a world scale was the one that succeeded the corrupt Baptista government, that is, the Partido Communista de Cuba (PCC), led by Fidel Castro. Inspired by feelings of economic marginalization, racial oppression, and political injustice against the masses, in 1959 Castro and his party leaders successfully staged a military coup and took over Cuba. The Cuban Revolution enabled the development of a new socialist Cuban government. Castro nationalized private property and established alliances with the Soviet Union. However, this connection was interpreted by the Kennedy administration of the United States as a threat to national security and complicated the tense balance of the cold war. The fallout from the Cuban missile crisis between Cuba and the United States led to a reduced standard of living in Cuba, the eventual exodus of hundreds of thousands of Cuban political refugees to the United States, and the consequent movement of Afro-Cuban religious practices.[30]

With Cuban migration to the urban centers, the contact between Afro-Cuban Santería practitioners and black American Yorùbá revivalists intensified during the height of the Black Power movement. Conceptualizations of racial difference, as well as language barriers, continued to shape the politics of cultural difference from which Yorùbá revivalism developed in the United States. Many of the new immigrants were either bilingual or spoke predominantly Spanish. Of these new immigrants, a small number became leaders in the establishment of a U.S.-based Santería-Yorùbá occult underground that was part of the development of òrìṣà voodoo as a vindictivist and reclamation movement.

By the 1960s, large numbers of Cubans had emigrated to the United States, and new underground Santería institutions developed because of this migration. This, in turn, contributed to a new discourse on the secrets of Santería, not to be circulated among outsiders. It is this requirement of silence, embedded in the historical necessity of the survival of slaves, that produced the contemporary impetus for black revivalists to discuss the very mechanics of its existence in terms that signified liberation. This fervor of freedom, which was based on the rejection of the European roots of Santería and the institutionalization of an outlawed Lukumi movement, occupied the realm of the occult underground. The reclamation of Yorùbá empires by Ọ̀yọ́túnjí Village practitioners is not a miscalculation of the history of slavery, in which enslaved Yorùbás were sold to slave traders predominantly in the Caribbean and South America, and not in the United States. Their construction of Yorùbá roots is part of an attempt to resignify the shame of slavery into a form of black empowerment that will aid in the production of black redemption. With greater contact with Yorùbá West Africans, òrìṣà voodoo was transformed from its overtly Cuban Santería form to a ritual of African science in which new rituals, new systems of truth and value, were developed that corresponded to a different narrative of truth-producing discourses. The form of Santería that developed and was revolutionized by black Americans was renamed òrìṣà voodoo; it was mobilized to counter the spread of the once regulated "secrets" of Lukumi ritual.

How one approaches questions of social change depends on how one links the past to the present, thereby mapping historical inscriptions with contemporary networks. Today, the effects of the racialized regulation of slave subjectivities are what make the relevance of revivalist imaginings of black bodily attachments to Africa critical for understanding how racial ideologies that developed in Africa were fundamentally connected to the formation of plantation slavery in the Americas and the shift from slave- to Western nation–based, colonizing, capitalist economies. The meaning of the black body became the basis for the development of racial discourses concerning the degeneration of African peoples (Young 1995, 4). With the formation of nation-states and hierarchies that produced particular scales of value, biological notions of blood, race, and descent were used to define primordial sedimentations in terms that linked race to place.

Whether social practices are valued, silenced, formalized through legal or religious roles, or informally regulated through silences or person-to-person criti-

Ọba of Òyọ́túnjí doing
a welcoming dance for
his guests.

Gelede masquerades.

Ọ̀yọ́túnjí young female residents patronizing the community restaurant.

One of the wives of the king. Here she is sporting the three scarifications—known as ila—on her face. They symbolize her connection to the Ọ̀yọ́ homeland. It is believed that such forms of markings were used historically to distinguish Ọ̀yọ́-Yorùbá speakers from other Yorùbá speakers.

Ọ̀yọ́túnjí practitioner performing a ritual dance at a community event.

cism, it is important to note that there exist critical mechanisms of regulation that are historically constituted within particular orders of meaning and value.

History for Networks

The problem with analyzing the relationships between nations and their people without looking at the politics of their construction is that it fixes the illusion of homogeneity to biology in the midst of complex circulations and transformations. As a result of their conscious rejection of what many revivalists see as signs of European dominance, Yorùbá-influenced Cuban religious communities (Santería) in the United States are embedded in struggles over ownership and legitimacy, interpretation and authenticity. Òyótúnjí-based priests often foreground the imagery of Yorùbáland as an originary site for contemporary devotees in the New World. Because the historical experiences of African Americans is based on a phenomenon of transatlantic slavery in the Americas and the consequent Christianization of their communities, in the process of rearticulating the terms of the Yorùbá past, they stand at the crossroads of Yorùbá-centered desire, yet Santería-influenced genealogies. As a heritage site for the commemoration of the African past, Òyótúnjí Village became both a site for the procurement of Africanized practices and a racialized alternative to Santería.

Maurice Halbwachs (1980) has argued in *The Collective Memory* that individual and group memories are deeply embedded in public representations of the past and that both memory and identity are shaped through commemorative practices. Revivalist uses of slavery as a domain in need of rearticulation highlights the need for historical mappings of linkage rather than either race-based assumptions of origins or unlimited terrain for the work of the imaginary. It is through an understanding of these interrelated formations of slavery and racialization, the relationship between religious and legal formations, the transformation of òrìsà practices, and state formation that we can understand the politics of Afro-Cuban migration to the United States as it relates to black cultural nationalism and Yorùbá revivalism. These and related social movements have their roots in particular formations of institutional regulation that frame discourses of modern human subjectivity in particular ways. Motivated by the goal of racial emancipation, revivalists use the sign of black cultural redemption to indexically reference their practices as African. The shift from Santería to òrìsà voodoo to black national revivalism was possible with the proliferation of resignified rituals circulated by new institutions of knowledge through which Òyótúnjí was recast as a deterritorialized ideal. The modern geopolitics of race and its referential categorization of origins link the routes of trade to the geopolitics of belonging. In other words, circulating discourses of the African past as distinctly black and originally African are not simply established in Ọ̀yọ́túnjí through the imagined symbolics of shared origins between African slaves and African Americans. Rather, racial difference was produced in Ọ̀yọ́túnjí through the routinized rearticulations of African-centered rituals, and symbolic references to African authenticity were possible through public exclusions of whiteness. In these routinized enactments of racial belonging, practitioners resignified the whiteness and Catholicism in Santería and, with the Africanization of black symbolic signs, produced racially specific countermemories. The value of blackness and Africanness, as signs of African symbolic power, therefore, were developed as performative rejections of white oppression. Even as Yorùbá revivalists shaped the social meanings of black African practices as counterrepresentations to whiteness, their erasure of whiteness was necessarily incorporated in these practices through its refraction. This rejection, which, for the sake of recognizability, occurs alongside the use of the very categories of belonging that they are trying to contest, is central to the conundrum of the modernity of time and space—the strictures of temporally linear and spatially normative standards that we have inherited. It is because of the normalization of these standardizing mechanisms that, even in the midst of globalization, what persists is the strengthening, rather than the weakening, of attitudes toward territorialized origins—autochthonous attachments. I am not saying that race is the unit of analysis by which all global flows are mediated, nor am I suggesting that there is no correlation between race and culture. Rather, there is a connection between the contemporary global imagination and the meanings of bodily subjectivities in relation to the hierarchies of scale and the institutions of power that shaped the building of the modern world. In other words, roots narratives, as they are used by Yorùbá practitioners to align identity with localities of birth, reinforce particular modernities of blood and nationhood and enforce geographies of race as the basis for black American connections to Africa.

The dilemma, therefore, especially given the disjunctures in the ideological fluidity and hegemonic fixity of the spatialization of belonging, is in understanding how originary narratives, which exist alongside transnational movements, circulate and continue to be maintained within new lines of global authority, be they religious or legal, political or cultural. Patterns of meanings are constituted in particular histories of production, and sites of difference are embedded in variations between old practices and innovative rearticulations. This reclassification of culture and descent through race, while critical to the empowerment of black American contests with social domination, is also a feature of the ways that new forms of practices are being shaped and reinforced in historically inscribed ways. Understanding the relationship among ideology and historical legacies, movement, and settlement are critical, for to study globalization is to study networks of connections—past, present, and future—in time and space. Most fundamentally, the development of capitalism and the making of new imperialisms and colonies involve a necessary analytic that employs techniques that allow us to understand how people and places, though embedded in fragmented pasts, are products of larger networks of global capitalism writ large. In the context of transatlantic slavery and the development of capitalist regimes and colonial empires, the very structure of labor linked the local to the global. To study global or transnational networks today, therefore, is to conduct a different form of fieldwork. It is to adjust how we understand people's senses of time-space and how the past may already link them to a global present. Thus, the forms of globalism of late capitalism, which are producing both spaces of marginalization and spaces of opportunity, can be mapped using forms of historical ethnography. When local-global flows are studied in relation to historically constituted imaginations and to political economic connections, we see that how objects of study are seen is critical in shaping how ethnographers reach conclusions about their social world. Seen thus, though particular mappings of connection are in the realm of the imaginary, the imaginary itself is productive of material consequences. Ultimately, connecting history to ethnography involves linking movement to settlement, imagination to practice.

As I demonstrate in the next chapter, the late-twentieth-century spread and revival of deterritorialized òrìṣà practices are reflective of the denationalization of religious practices that are being driven by increasingly autonomous cultural networks. Racial biology has been surpassed by a new regime of knowledge, that of cultural heritage. The state, its institutions, and its agents are engaged in dialogic negotiations over the way the past is both remembered and forgotten. These cultural productions, routinized in the particularities of racial formations in the Americas, have been used by Yorùbá revivalist practitioners to chart symbolic connections to Africa from which particular scales of meaning have been forged and continue to frame the conditions of imaginary possibility.

2. "White Man Say They Are African":
Roots Tourism and the Industry of Race as Culture

"WELCOME TO LAGOS, NIGERIA," read the tattered white sign above the stairway encircling the terminal. It was dark and windy by the time the plane landed on the Lagos runway and we disembarked. As the Ọba of Ọ̀yọ́túnjí and the six members of his entourage walked down the plane's steel staircase, he fell to the ground to kiss the cold white concrete. Some members of his entourage helped him to stand up as he embraced himself and then raised his fists in the air to signal victory.

His facial expression changed from that of someone involved in sobering prayer to enthusiasm, as if to say, "The hardships are over. Africa, I'm home."

"I don't know, I think I'll wait for the broooown soil," muttered Adé Bíọ́lú, one of the younger members of the contingent. "This concrete isn't the real Africa," he added.

For Adé Bíọ́lú, as a first-time visitor to Nigeria, the airport runway's concrete was not satisfyingly symbolic of what constitutes appropriate "African" soil. For the venerating priest, in contrast, as he later stated, "The fact of arriving [in Nigeria] is the homecoming, not the way it's been colonized."

As the six other members of the entourage walked to the terminal building with the other passengers, I noticed Adé Bíọ́lú greeting many of the staring workers and observers. "Àlàáfíà [Peace]," he saluted them in Yorùbá, continually initiating eye contact with the native onlookers. The interaction resembled the arrival of a delegate who had just descended from a private jet and was greeting his constituency. However, most of the onlookers reacted nonverbally by either nodding or ridiculing him to nearby coworkers or companions. Most refrained from respond-

Muslim mosque in Abeokuta, Nigeria.

ing in Yorùbá, perhaps because they assumed he would not understand them or perhaps because they did not speak Yorùbá at all. They either smiled or nodded and waved back.

Adé Bíólú was the first from our group to approach the line for immigration clearance. The rest of us followed him, chatting quietly among ourselves and laughing at what we referred to privately as his bluff: the pretense of familiarity and assumption of acceptance. When it was our turn to proceed to the front of the line, Adé Bíólú greeted the officer, saying, "Àlàáfíà," this time in a more serious tone.

"Good evening," replied the official in his crisply ironed police uniform and curved hat, as if to correct him. "You are visiting," he declared without asking. "What is your country of citizenship?" he demanded, staring at Adé Bíólú with an outstretched hand signaling for our passports.

"United States," the others replied in staggering order as Adé Bíólú turned to us to collect our passports. "Canada," I chimed in.

The officer looked at them and then at me. We were dressed in traditional regalia with cowry shell jewelry and common beads around our necks.[1] A few seconds later the officer seemed to notice the *ilà* (tribal scarification designated to show tribal descent from Ọ̀yọ́) on their faces. He stared at one of the darker-complexioned people in the group whose ilà were prominently figured on his upper cheeks, and in a new turn of disbelief he asked, responding to our statement of origin, "All of you?"

Nigerian compound in Ọ̀yọ́.

A Nigerian village community in Abeokuta.

I looked at everyone in our group. Half of us had a dark brown complexion; the other half had lighter skin. Together, we were distinctly different shades of brown. We wore the traditional Nigerian clothes that Ọ̀yọ́túnjí residents are expected to wear: the women with elaborate head wraps and colorful garments, the men with their *fìlà* (a Yorùbá traditional hat) and traditional cotton pantsuits, known in Yorùbá as *aṣọ òkè*. I looked to the back of the line and observed men, women, and a few children with faces darker than ours, wearing plainly colored Western clothes. We North Americans, it seemed to me, were the only people in this section of the airport who were wearing what was seen as traditional Nigerian clothing. Twenty men with brown, black, or beige jackets or shirts, carrying briefcases and multiple large bags, and women with varying hairstyles—chemically straightened hair, loosely curled, long, braided or unbraided weaves—watched us with curiosity, amusement, and perhaps even disdain.

"Purpose of your visit?" continued the immigration officer, as he looked at our passports, eventually raising his eyes to study us.

"Educational," responded Adé Bíólú, just as seriously.

"Vacation," another one in the group said, immediately and loudly, as if to correct Adé Bíólú and hide the ritual initiation and learning goals that inspired their travel.

"What kind of education?" the officer asked, as he looked toward those standing near Adé Bíólú.

"Traditional education," Adé Bíólú replied. "I was born in America, but Africa is my home. We have all come home," he added, moving his hands slowly as if to encircle all of us in his description of a homecoming—all of us, including the unimpressed officer. The officer's serious and unwavering frown turned into an unflattering smirk, perhaps a response of disbelief, nonacceptance, or offense at Adé Bíólú's attempt at so liberally remapping us as African citizens.

"What are those marks there?" continued the officer, cutting off Adé Bíólú's "homecoming" performance, and instead pointing at the cuts on the upper cheeks of three of the lightest brown people in the entourage. As he looked at the last person's ilà, he exclaimed self-assuredly as he shook his head and smiled, "Why did you let them do that to you? These Nigerians will do anything for money."

"They're ilàs," Ìyá Sisilum responded boastfully. "And we did it. We do this in America too, you know, and . . . ," she hesitated, and speaking in Yorùbá this time, overemphasizing what should be tonal inflections with Standard American English ones, "Àwa ń lọ Abẹ́òkúta and Ọ̀yọ́ [We are now going to Abẹ́òkúta and Ọ̀yọ́]."

"O kú iṣẹ́! [Well done!] Obìnrin [Lady], you speak Yorùbá!" responded the officer approvingly and with a smile. He looked over to one of his colleagues, who had been listening to our interactions and looked amused. They both raised their eyebrows, and the officer who had been questioning us said quickly and with a chuckle, "Òyìnbó ní they are African! [White man say they are African!]."

As both of them chuckled together, Ìyá Sisilum added charmingly, as if to indicate that she understood the paradoxical subtext, "Bẹ́ẹ̀ ni, a wá kọ́ èdè Yorùbá! [Yes, and we are here to learn more Yorùbá]."

Without an attempt to request a bribe for not harassing us, clearly tourists, the officer chuckled and, as he opened each passport, looked at the picture, matched it to the correct person, and said, "Okay, *a dùpé* [thank you]," or "You can go now," each time opening a passport, looking at the photo, and scanning our faces to match the appropriate face to the photo. Ìyá Sisilum's passport, though, he put aside.

After ushering all of the men through and then me, he handed Ìyá Sisilum hers, and, with a sly smile, he said, "*Olúwa yíó pànà mọ* [The Lord will keep you safe on the trip], American Nigerian lady," and then he asked, in English, if she had anything for him.

"*A dúpẹ́ púpọ̀* [Thank you very much]," she responded, flirting with a bashful smile, as if to misunderstand his question as a request for a future meeting or date, not a bribe. As she walked away, both of the officers waved good-bye to all of us and chuckled as they watched Ìyá Sisilum's buttocks moving toward the baggage and customs area.

Rethinking Race through Ancestral Heritage

The above description of one of many heritage visits by òrìṣà revivalists to West African countries reveals key issues of diasporic belonging in relation to how we understand national rules of mobility for citizens and noncitizens in framing relations of inclusion and exclusion. Here, the interface of individuals and governmental officials is part of a larger political economy, in which Western tourists seek cultural heritage experiences from the non-West. The role of capital—cultural, economic, political—is central to historical routes of connection and, therefore, fundamental to how membership is forged and negotiated according to larger norms of belonging. For many Nigerians, for example, the terms of Yorùbá membership may be understood in relation to both norms of state citizenship and sociocultural laws of paternal descent (as the term *òyìnbó* suggests). For the Ọ̀yọ́túnjí revivalists, membership may involve historical connections that predate the formation of the Nigerian colonial state as well as racial ancestry. Thus, despite the differing claims to membership, the criteria for legitimacy are connected to particular institutional norms.

Today, as a result of the globalization of cultural heritage opportunities, claims to membership are increasingly deterritorialized and far more negotiable and manipulable than ever before. Ultimately, members of both groups seem to desire what the other group has, and the existing features of desire and belonging continue to be deeply economic in conditions of possibility and production. Nigerian òrìṣà practitioners, for example, tend to want access to the resources and connections of the West; Ọ̀yọ́túnjí revivalists, predominantly heritage travelers, as Paulla Ebron (2002) has described using parallel formations, want the knowledge of ritual to develop increasingly independent deterritorialized mechanisms for reclaiming and legitimizing their ancestral membership—what they see as their birthright.

Though the dialogue between black American heritage tourists and revivalists and African-born practitioners is embedded in relative fields of power, the contours of exchange tend to be unequal and asymmetrical. In the process of re-articulating the terms of the Yorùbá past, Ọ̀yọ́túnjí practitioners stand at the crossroads of Nigeria-centered symbolics of origins and Santería-influenced histories of slavery and survival in which the direction of the revival of òrìṣà worship is actively taking shape in the Americas. These uneven relations point to the heart of one of the unending questions concerning whose "Africa" is "Africa"? Whose "Africa" is "African"? Which patterns of cultural production are "authentic"? And who is to say, and with what authority do they speak, judge, and shape the process of cultural production and the implications it has for laying diverse claims to a "black," and African, and African American raced identity?

In the context of understanding these processes of norm formation as a form of what I refer to as "heritage economy," today we are witnessing the changing demographics of "ethnoracial" identity composition in the United States, which is contributing to a desire for both diasporic membership and ethnic controversy. Typically, commentaries have focused on the "browning of America," as statistics point to the time when those subsumed under the category "Hispanic" or "Latino" are likely to become the largest "nonwhite" segment of that composition. However, far less attention is being paid to a no less dramatic demographic shift and its ideological consequences for cultural production within the category "black" or "African American" that is presumed to be displaced as a result of new shifts in Third World urban migration. However, when people in the United States refer to the category "African Americans," for example, they often assume that it identifies persons who are descendants of U.S. slaves, for the most part, with occasional recognition that not all persons of African descent in the United States have a direct ancestral linkage to slavery—the latter, a nod to the "free" black populations. Yet little analytic attention is devoted to the current composition of global African immigration in relation to the forces of market capitalism involved in reshaping the growing numbers of black Americans who have reclassified their ethnic nationality as African, as well as what this composition might mean for contestations over the "right" to claim or to reject blackness, African Americanness, or the presumed conjunction of the two.

In pragmatic terms, issues relevant to such contestations arise in media-driven debates over the appropriateness of persons of African descent claiming affirmative action redress when they have not been subject to the history of slavery and discrimination in the United States, which such programs were intended to redress. As black studies programs and departments of African American studies come to include recent African immigrants or old African-descent immigrants that claim identities that are not "just" black or "just" African American, these debates then also give rise to mere puzzlement or divisive internal tensions. They add new life to the means of reinforcing and reproducing whiteness in varied domains of institutional racism, and they beg for a more sophisticated understanding of the cultural politics of difference in relation to the importation of race as "culture" and the production of American blackness as Africanness.

In the United States, after centuries of enforced racial segregation, two different strands of black racial consciousness coexisted in the second half of the twentieth century. One was on the level of intellectual conceptions of cultural heritage and roots. The other was shaped by hegemonies of racism and the centrality of racial biology as the basis for human difference. Though both are operative in different ways, the form of cultural race that took shape was aligned with democratic politics of the 1990s and contributed to a new structure of national membership that emphasized cultural pride about origins. Race-conscious activism against the biological segregation of blacks and the shame associated with it shifted to the notion of place of race as culture. The development of a new American rights agenda of the 1960s and 1970s, protected by state institutions, was propelled forward by global business opportunities of the post–cold war period. One such arena was the mass media, which was spurred along by a second, the advances of educational institutions. These two institutions, mass media and education, were developing area studies programs that flourished at the end of the cold war in the United States and played a profound role in the shaping of heritage programs in U.S. education.

Over time, the biological regulation of race overlapped with a cultural heritage revolution in which state policies promoted the celebration of ethnic heritage, and in popular black circles the slave narrative was supplemented with the nobility narrative. This shift from the shame of slavery to the pride of nobility produced a dueling conception that shaped what it meant to be black in the popular imagination. In the context of heightened governmental policies toward heritage categories and market interests in what is often referred to as cultural race or the ethnicization of race, there developed a dominant trope about both ethnic pride and black heritage that is today revolutionizing the ways race is increasingly taken up as a cultural commodity to be celebrated through heritage and ethnicity. Despite the roots of the meaning of being Negro or black in America and its deeply located history of enslavement and loss, a substantive shift took place that was enabled by the educational and the later commercial development of the African heritage narrative. Òyótúnjí practitioners of the late 1990s went in and out of heritage and biological concepts of race. This interplay highlights the importance of recognizing how and when different forces of ordering are operative and why. In the context of global flows, it forces us to explore how race-based distinctions are both hegemonic and modalities through which people imagine themselves beyond national borders.

The changing face of the "New American" was also affected by the new global economy; despite the continuities of race as the backdrop of U.S. politics of difference, these changes in the globalization of mass media were grounded in a social politics of a new citizenry and influenced the reorganization of capital and significant changes in new mass technologies. And despite these changes and the ways that social differences in perceptions of race continue to reference the biological body, it is the institutional conceptions of how we *see* difference—in terms of race, sex, speech, phenotype—that is changing and that is making the study of deterritorialized communities outside homelands one that demands the understanding of how agents use institutional empowerment strategies to extend alliances beyond state-based borders. What was conceived as the biologically established color line of the twentieth century became part of a larger politics of ethnic heritage in which belonging to the nation became less about biology and more about *roots*. Ultimately, there are many ways of analyzing different types of race. For our purposes, understanding the globalization of race and, more specifically, the sign of blackness is more about how people see blackness in relation to historically constituted contexts than about determining concepts about what blackness is.

Thus, although the history of slavery continues to undergird what it means to be black in the United States today, when understood in relation to revivalist and radical cultural movements in which heritage themes are incorporated within a larger state imperative, this manifestation of membership in the nation is constitutive of a new racial order. This order reflects a substantive shift from separate race categories to the production of a new citizenship movement that remapped previous struggles over civil rights and entitlements onto a new terrain of Americanness as the depths of heritage.

For example, the publication of *Roots: Saga of an American Family* by Alex Haley (1976) and its subsequent broadcast as a television miniseries was the most significant event in the ideological transformation of black American identities in the twentieth century.[2] It was the third-most-watched program in the history of television: 130 million people, representing a broad spectrum of viewers worldwide, were estimated to have seen it. Bringing to life narratives about the complexities of African American enslavement, loss, struggle, victory, and survival, the *Roots* story began with the birth in 1750 of the protagonist, Kunta Kinte, in a West African village in the Gambian River region. Detailing the trials and tribulations of seven generations of Kunta Kinte's descendants in the U.S. South, *Roots* ends in Arkansas with the life of Alex Haley. Declaring his ancestry as a narrative of African continuities and freedom, redemption and triumph, Haley's story follows the movement of Africans to slavery in the U.S. South, to freedom, and, finally, to their empowerment in mainstream America. By creating a narrative in which the cultural politics of blackness merged with the ancestral history of slavery, *Roots* brought to life a history that was not part of the personal experience of African Americans but became part of black popular social memory in the United States—a memory of the production of subservience that had relevance in their personal lives.

In 1999, some twenty-four years after *Roots* was published and televised, Henry Louis Gates Jr. produced the television documentary *Wonders of the African World*. It also represents a significant moment in the history of black studies in the United States, rattling the academy by disrupting dominant institutional representations of slavery as a product of white Europeans and Americans exclusively. Unlike *Roots*, which reinforced a predominant narrative about European and Muslim participation in the transatlantic slave trade, *Wonders* invoked the grandeur of African civilizations while pointing to the complicity of some Africans in contributing to the enslavement of other Africans. Though *Wonders* did not circulate as widely as *Roots*, it had been preceded by another significant moment—the airing, in the 1980s, of Ali Mazrui's *The Africans*, a PBS television series about colonial and contemporary African politics that also emphasized the cultural attainments of the precolonial African past. Following up on a theme set by its two most influential predecessors, *Wonders* was also about a noble African past that had been rendered invisible in Eurocentric histories. Gates's retrieval of this precolonial past as a site for the acquisition of African American heritage established a new intellectual discourse about Africa's contribution to world civilization.

Structured as Gates's pilgrimage back to the symbolic homeland, the filmic text is organized as a travelogue, a personal voyage that is also a return, in which Gates—successful Harvard professor, family man, and tourist—returns as the distinguished son of the formerly enslaved who has embarked on a leisurely trek in search of Africa's wonders. Significant at the time was the representation of African history by a scholar of African descent who was funded by elite institutions of academic knowledge in the United States and new channels of global commerce. Rather than focusing on an imaginary of shared roots, *Wonders* signaled the nobility of the African past, as well as the complexities of African and African American tensions, where Africans were seen as complicit in the enslavement of African Americans. The series foregrounded the return of the once enslaved, who now have the power to represent African and African American history. However, by highlighting the complicity of Africans in the enslavement of Africans, while, at the same time, unraveling the negative image of Africa as a dark and primitive continent that lacked "culture" and promoting an image of Africa as a place of great civilizations, *Wonders* brought to the fore the dialectic of slavery and nobility. These representations incited controversies in U.S.-based African and African American studies programs, centering around three key problems. The first was Gates's focus on the precolonial African past and not on Africa's sociopolitical and economic realities. The second was his representation of African complicity in the capture and transport of Africans into transatlantic slavery. The third was the significance of a black public intellectual setting the terms in the United States for how African history should be represented by mainstream Americans. By limiting his focus to precolonial African civilizations, Gates was accused of de-centering the importance of contemporary African concerns and sources of pride; by focusing on African participation in slavery, he was accused of placing the minor role of Africans on a par with that of the European machinery of the slave trade. However, by claiming to be the voice of Africa's *prodigal son* returned home with *riches*, Gates's success was a statement about middle-class black America's place in the new world order. Thus, despite the outrage, *Wonders*, like *Roots*, responded to an absence that addressed a social void, providing alternatives to imagining the African past.

The content of the representation in *Roots* and *Wonders* and the role of presenting alternatives to the African diasporic past have contributed to new forms of black social memories. During the 1990s, the literature on diasporas certainly explored the political and cultural politics of exile and forced movement. However, in the context of how to theorize diasporic connections, where diasporic separation and exile reflect the transportation of captives many centuries ago, the issues remain distinctly different. Instead, it is the production of the social memory of the slave past through the representations of diasporic memory that we must chart in relation to the ways those histories constitute a cultural politics of difference. It is important to recognize that assemblages of diaspora, therefore, often emerge from a reconstituted history of violence in which diaspora is called on to serve a reclamative purpose. Such is the case with the Ọ̀yọ́túnjí project: many members of Ọ̀yọ́túnjí are invested in the political project of unification, in which redemption from slavery and "the revival of racial pride" are critical to the institutionalization of a deterritorialized movement.

Traditional debates in the anthropology of the African diaspora have tended to address issues of culture in relation to an asymmetrical flow of cultural practices from Africa to the non-West. Such approaches have established the presumption that the only practices that are authentic are those from African countries and that those invented outside Africa are either appropriated or inauthentic. The other problem with the asymmetrical approach to diaspora is that it does not recognize the ways African peoples also incorporate and claim Western practices as their own. As Terrence Ranger and Eric Hobsbawm (1992) have shown, even the practices seen as the most "traditionalist" are often themselves equally dynamic and have changed over time and space. In this age of hypercapitalism, in which the development of information and technologies and capital flows from the West to Africa are increasingly unequal, there are commensurate inequities in filmic representations of African peoples. These inequities are exacerbating the asymmetrical production of knowledge on a global scale.

One of the most important issues in the anthropology of Africa of the late twentieth century has been the "invention of Africa." V. Y. Mudimbe (1988) demonstrated that, in addition to the existence of particular forms of native logics, colonial constructions of history, classifications of ethnicity, boundaries, and the imposition of European languages have informed the discourses by which Africans understand each other and themselves. As discussed earlier, this invention of Africanness has been revived by many African Americans in the United States, who, looking to Africa for ancestral roots, have reinvented themselves as *both* Africans and Americans. In the United States, these codes of meaning continue to be influenced by legacies of transatlantic slavery through which people resignify the basis on which their national identities are understood. It was the historical formation of cartographies of nationhood and descent—Africanness understood in relation to the politics of race—fueled by radical responses to racial oppression and segregation, such as the Black Power movement of the 1960s and 1970s, that propelled, through particular institutions, new commonsense notions of Africanness in the United States. Thus, how we understand these shifts in institutional power and access, intellectual and institutional fads, and diasporic social movements has everything to do with postmodern economic subversions of the modern metanarratives. The articulations of counterdiscursive and hyphenated identities are a reflection of the generative capacity of culture as fundamentally linked to market forces and the production and power of consumer desire.

To focus on changing institutions of power and how the imaginary shapes people's placement in relation to homelands and how it structures conceptions of origins is to illustrate how, through complex territorializations, particular subjective meanings are framed. If, in the production of racial meanings, signs are produced in relations of economic and political power, then the body is also a social construct which, as David Harvey (2000) has argued, cannot be understood outside of the economic and historically political forces and hierarchies of scale that construct the body or render it invisible. It is important, therefore, to highlight the production of an "African homeland imaginary" in the context of the U.S. institutional retelling of the African past, as this past is constituted within the changing political and market forces of late capitalism. Electronic technologies and African American teledramas, coupled with the rising significance of the rights movement, through their alliances with mainstream market capital since the cold war have significantly contributed to representing the African diaspora through the history of slavery, silenced by a new overemphasis on the history of Africa's nobility and grandeur.

Roots, Race, and the Transition to Nobility

It should be no surprise that two of the most powerful ideological narratives of U.S. black nationalist imaginaries that took shape in the mid-1960s and continue to circulate in the present are the slavery narrative and the African nobility-redemption narrative.[3] The slavery narrative (Martin Shaw and Clarke 1995) is based on notions of ancestral and therefore biological commonalities among black people. It narrates how Africans were torn from Africa, how they were enslaved because of racial oppression and brought to the New World. Despite the oppressive conditions under which they lived, enslaved Africans produced "diverse cultures" and maintained a fundamental connection to their African past. Through the symbolics of blood and diasporic displacement and suffering,[4] these narratives signify a connection to Africa that produces notions of ancestry as constituted by one black ancestor to another. It describes black Americans as surviving incarnations of preslavery African societies, thereby enabling a self-identification of black Americans as not simply racialized, but fundamentally embedded in genealogies of "African" heritage.

The African nobility narrative, on the other hand, legitimates the centrality of slavery as the basis for African American connections to Africa, while also eliding it as secondary to the pride of black heritage. By highlighting that African Americans are not merely victims of slavery but descendants of an African noble elite—kings, queens, and religious elites—who are, at the present time, culturally imprisoned in the racist United States, the African nobility narrative ambitiously links the noble African past with African American hopes for an institutionally empowered future. The need for redemption is due to the involuntary nature of African transportation to the Americas; black Americans are seen as having lost their traditions and culture to white America. The nobility narrative offers African Americans the promise of reclaiming their "true African selves" by embracing African traditions. This narrative incites black Americans to take control of their destiny by reclaiming their ancestral identity.

Since *Roots*, these narratives have come to represent popular commonsense and daily conceptualizations of blackness as Africanness in the late twentieth and early twenty-first century, thereby reinscribing slavery and nobility as fundamentally linked to transatlantic global circulations. Admittedly, such processes of trans-local connections and imaginings of African homelands are not new; processes of creating linkages between America and Africa have long preceded late-twentieth-century shifts in globalization. Black nationalist formations of the nineteenth and early twentieth century were constructed around counterculture hardships of racial marginalization and the cultural politics of black racial belonging to Africa and/or the Americas. However, as a result of transnational and national forms of agitation during the cold war and with the U.S. post–World War II empha-sis on democracy and integration—driven by Western market capital ambitions sympathetic to the lucrative possibilities of marketing the ideological shift toward the desire for cultural heritage—there was also an ideological shift in U.S. edu-cational, governmental, and cultural institutions that institutionalized the *Roots* phenomenon of African heritage as a legitimately American identity.

This shift in a *heritage-conscious* population began with the interest of the black middle class in restructuring the social order, to see race not simply in biologi-cal terms, but in relation to the nobility of historical ethnic origins. This process of ethnicizing racial belonging was also influenced by the institutionalization of ethnic history in higher educational settings in the United States. It had the effect of producing a black popular imaginary shaped by an articulation of prideful heri-tage and roots, captured in what Ariana Hernandez-Reguant (1999) has referred to as the ethnicization of the African diaspora. More fundamentally, then, rather than approaching questions of race and diaspora in traditional discourses, which presume an a priori articulation of identity, late-twentieth-century conceptions of racial belonging were embedded in a more aggressive form of capital institutional-ism conducive to the marketing of black Americanness as a sign of African slavery and the glorification of a preslavery past.

The development of diaspora studies in the United States contributed to place-based conceptions of race and culture. In the case of the African diaspora, it pro-vided a model for tracking the movement from Africa to the *black Atlantic*. The very term "diaspora"—a Greek word whose prefix, *dia*, means "through," and root, *speirein*, means "to scatter seeds"—refers to the scattering of people's off-spring. By the 1970s and 1980s, however, African diaspora studies not only over-determined the homogeneity of race and culture, but also created an approach to diaspora that charted migration as a unipolar link from Africa to its *elsewheres*. By positing the originary descent of black people to Africa and therefore ignoring the mutual influences between the Americas and Africa, sociology and anthropology, followed by African American studies in the United States presumed teleologies of ancestry that were unipolar and/or racially constituted. It has been well documented that the problem with this approach is that it presumes both the possibility of finding an "authentic" articulation of origins, which depends on Africanness as being produced in Africa alone, and biology as the basis of this linkage. Instead, diasporic analyses in the twenty-first century should demonstrate how, through particular complex interactions between Africa and the United States, diasporic identity and consciousness are made, and as such, how narratives of descent are constructed in historically constituted ways. Approaches to diaspora should demonstrate how agents, institutions, the state, and markets selectively set ideological roots where physical and material routes do not always exist (Scott 1991).[5]

To understand what is new about U.S. workings of race today and to understand the invocations of diasporic connections to heritage, we must recognize both the historical particularities that shape the history of black segregation and the workings of transnational capital in the production of a new heritage consumer that has played a critical role in the transformation of race in the American imaginary. One form of transformation was in the telling of the history of slavery and segregation; the other was in the liberalization of late-twentieth-century capitalism. The mercantile and transatlantic slave trade set in motion the ideological terrain for particular forms of racial mappings. The eventual globalization of transnational capital further reinforced preexisting norms by which notions of difference were demarcated. By tracing a genealogy of black popular activism over the late nineteenth through the twentieth century, the development of the politics of black Atlantic consciousness that took shape in the late twentieth century becomes clear.

First, however, we must trace a particular genealogy of antiracist protest traditions to differentiate the development of late capitalist formations of "cultural race" (such as current forms of heritage identities of the late twentieth century) from early-twentieth-century conceptions of "biological race" that grew out of centuries of plantation slavery and legal racial segregation. I begin with early black nationalist and transnational Pan-African linkages and move on to demonstrate how civil rights articulations of blackness contributed to the eventual institutionalization of particular popular approaches to talking about cultural race. Here, with underlying narratives of slavery and the nobility of the African past intertwined with the mass telemedia reporting about black disenfranchisement and struggle, we see how various global changes (such as the movement of Third World migrants to the West and the related formation of transnational political and cultural linkages with African elites) set the stage for the formation of a civil rights ethnic and closely connected corporate interests willing to exploit lucrative markets. The cultural formation of a new commercial politics of linkages between people in the Americas and those in their homelands set the stage for the establishment of a heritage category encompassing black Africa and black America.

This emphasis on diasporic interconnection overlapped with biological race with cultural race; now race meant that every human has an ethnicity—an ancestral heritage. This notion of heritage was deeply territorial, though manifest in deterritorial contexts, and reflects the ontology of race becoming historical rather than biological.

I am not suggesting that the materiality of biological concepts of race, such as phenotype, are no longer operative and cease to enforce hierarchies of racial aesthetics and value. I argue that race as a cultural and political unit of classification has come to stand for territorial heritage and the slave narrative is the modality in which particular claims of belonging are referenced. As such, the new trend toward territorial heritage does not fully supplant race, but it superimposes another layer of meaning that has a profound impact on mainstream America. Biological race, which, through modern science, authorized the terms of U.S. citizenship, has given way to a redefinition of ancestral heritage that was propelled by the rights movement, transnational migration, and the flexibility of economic markets. These patterns of change make it all the more important to reframe our diasporic area studies models in ways that are generative of social changes in the twenty-first century.

New technologies and market forces propelled new possibilities of popular racial alliance in the late twentieth century. These popular cultural conceptions of black identity enabled African American culture brokers—such as public intellectuals, religious leaders, cultural workers, and government officials—to create new kinship narratives of the African past.[6] Electronic technologies served as engines of social change and contributed to the production of increasingly autonomous modalities through which new conceptual linkages are increasingly becoming terrain for the legitimation of new practices. This has implications for how we understand people's sense of connection and difference and how we theorize an anthropology of diasporic movement in light of these late capitalist formations. Yorùbá revivalism is critical here because the predominant theories of diaspora employed here would still locate Ọ̀yọ́túnjí claims as an anomaly.

Toward a Mapping of Yorùbá Transnationalism: Black Cultural Nationalism

Many late-nineteenth-century black American leaders of African nationalist movements, such as Martin Delaney (1812–85), Edward Blyden (1832–1912), Alexander Crummel (1819–98), and Reverend Henry Highland Garnet (1815–82), responded to U.S. racism by taking it upon themselves to educate their constituency on the effects of racism.[7] They advocated black empowerment and redemption from the debilitating effects of slavery (see Bullock 1967). Despite differing approaches and concerns, these early thinkers all believed that shared racial typography is the basis for transatlantic black unity. These forms of African historical pedagogy set the stage for later developments of African American constructions of African-centered education. That is, through the development of black empowerment and nobility programs and the spread of knowledge about African history as African American history, late-twentieth-century African Americans engaged in African religious revivalist or political social movements.

After the U.S. emancipation of slaves in 1865, black minister and black nationalism advocate Bishop Henry McNeal Turner, envisioning equality for black Americans in the period prior to Reconstruction, attempted to pursue Pan-African goals by working toward the creation of an independent country in West Africa to which black Americans would emigrate (Falọla 2001, 148). However, although the idea of emigration caught the attention of poor blacks in the South, a very small number actually returned to Africa. Many early nationalists, such as black abolitionist Frederick Douglass, decided against emigration and pursued an accommodationist approach to racial equality that obscured the centrality of Africa as home and instead claimed the United States as the new and "legitimate" home of black Americans. Leaders such as "Pap" Singleton and Henry Adams contributed to these sentiments by arguing for the attainment of full citizenship for black people in the United States, the country of their birth. Such organizers developed early independent African American towns and with limited resources took control of the electoral process. Under the protection of the U.S. Constitution, they promoted black candidates and elected them to political office. Similarly, in the early twentieth century, Christian African Methodist Church movements throughout black populations in the North and South of the United States also sowed seeds of black American nationalism. Black participation was central to the survival of these organizations. It is important to note that members of these organizations did not always identify Africa as a locus of black American liberation. Rather, race and conversion to Christianity were the basis for kinship; place of birth in America was more important than territorial origins in Africa.

By 1914, however, a more radical Protestant-based movement revived themes of black self-determination and African empowerment. Led by Marcus Mosiah Garvey (1923), the "back-to-Africa" themes that had pervaded black social movements in the mid-1800s were revived. Garvey's Pan-African movement, which operated under the Universal Negro Improvement Association (UNIA), originated in Jamaica and spanned the English Caribbean, the United States, and Canada. The UNIA was the largest and most widely known black-identified political movement of its time. Heralding the political philosophy of black nationalism,

Garvey advocated the need for the cultural, political, and economic separation of African peoples from white society, and following those activists of the previous century, he advocated the physical return of "talented" black people to Africa. Locating himself as a messianic figure of the first major back-to-Africa campaigns, he set up a hierarchy of blackness, imagining himself as a ruler of a Pan-African kingdom. The growing members of UNIA contributed to the production of discourses about the importance of black self-determination in which they emphasized the need for economic self-help principles for black people as the basis for their empowerment.

During this period, black Americans with middle-class aspirations competed for educational training and attempted to assimilate neoliberal principles of economic success into a particular form of black radicalism. For Garvey, race pride was also embedded in the precolonial sanctity of the nineteenth-century Ethiopian heritage narrative, in which God was to be worshipped in the context of the greatness of Ethiopia as the site of early Christianity. With principles of Christian religiosity, he likened the acceptance of UNIA doctrine by the black masses to the acceptance of Christianity by the Roman masses. However, by the mid-1930s, with the Great Depression and the demoralization caused by the political conflicts that surrounded Garvey, the movement dwindled after his death, only to be supplanted by the Civil Rights and Black Power movements of the 1960s and 1970s.

In the midst of the struggle to deal with the fundamental issues of race inequality arose of one of the most prominent Pan-African intellectuals of the twentieth century, W. E. B. Du Bois. A graduate of Harvard University and a political activist, Du Bois played a critical role in documenting African history and connecting it to African civilizations and the contemporary sociopolitical economy in both Africa and the United States. With the goal of achieving black liberation through intellectual progress and freedom from colonial domination, Du Bois, a prolific writer and public intellectual, emphasized the need to connect socialist principles with Pan-Africanism. Inspired by goals of black uplift, his publications charted the complexities of race in relation to the history of capitalist plunder and the social constructions of cultural identity. Works such as *The Souls of Black Folk* (1903), *The Negro* (1915), and *The World and Africa: An Inquiry into the Part Which Africa Has Played in World History* (1947), among many others, documented the social conditions of black people and, though initially limited in circulation, became increasingly prominent in U.S. institutions of higher learning, especially in the later years of his life. His publications contributed to the rise of black consciousness among a black elite.

In an attempt to shift the politics of power that excluded black Africans from education, governmental power, and access to land and other resources, Du Bois convened the second Pan-African Congress in Paris in 1919, at which scholars, political activists, and public representatives agreed to finance early institutional domains of linkage to work toward a new public agenda on addressing race discrimination. This and similar early alliances provided the framework for the development of public intellectuals whose books about race and the political economy of Third World underdevelopment represented a fundamental struggle against both state enforcements of racial discrimination and individual prejudice. The development of these early transnational linkages were formative. Du Bois and his colleague George Padmore examined histories of Pan-African connections among black people transported from Africa in the British transatlantic slave trade, therefore contributing to a generation of elite scholars who set the framework for Pan-African linkages.

Similarly, in the nearby islands, Spanish colonial scholars such as Ferdinando Ortiz (1880–1969) planted the seeds of what would become a transnational discourse of black hybridity that led to the creation of Afro-Cubanism. Afro-Cubanism referenced the influences of African and Spanish racial and cultural mixture, creating the hybridity of Cubanness as a statement about racial mixture. Likewise, the Negritude movement in Francophone countries led to a range of political collaborations between African and Caribbean students, politicians, and colonial activists. The development of these connections between members of African and Caribbean colonies and black American leaders shaped the formation of horizontal linkages conjoined along racial and colonial histories of interconnection. These activists collaborated on intellectual pedagogical writings and political strategies to gain insight into European colonialism, imperialism, and racial marginalization in the Caribbean, Africa, and the United States. However, by the second half of the twentieth century, the changing World War II climate, anticolonial independence movements, the development of bipolar world powers and the eventual rise of America's lone superpower status enabled the developmental strengthening of a new international political economy. These shifts reflected a moment in which social opportunities were increasingly shaped less by racial considerations and more by postwar economic and political interests.

World Wars, the Cold War, Superpowers,
and Horizontal Alliances

During and after the First and Second World Wars, there existed a plethora of job opportunities, especially in the U.S. North, as a result of the developing war industries. New job opportunities led to the migration of large numbers of Southern blacks to Northern urban areas in the United States. After World War II, ever larger numbers of black Americans had unprecedented access to higher paying jobs as well as increasing access to unionized positions. Economic demand, coupled with socially unwelcome conditions, contributed to the politics of the struggles against enforced U.S. legal segregation that operated in relation to a range of other underlying forces. The aftereffects of Nazism and fascism, the growing political power of black people in the U.S. North, the rising economic and social integration of the nation, as well as the shifts in U.S. Southern racial attitudes—all converged with the growing tide of modern democracy. Concomitantly, desegregation struggles became embedded in legal challenges over the lack of equality in segregation laws.

Between 1945 and 1960, forty countries worldwide achieved independence. African and Caribbean political leaders and intellectuals collaborated with each other and with African American political leaders and intellectuals to forge a transatlantic Pan-African vision. Though characterized by sentiments of social protest, the early 1960s represented the apex of the cold war, a term coined by Churchill in 1953 to characterize a heightened climate of political competition and suspicion. During this period, the United States and the Soviet Union (USSR) emerged as superpowers that competed with each other for allies. As bipolar challengers with different visions about governance, both of these powers developed military and security measures to protect themselves from each other in case of nuclear attack. These measures involved furthering the development of nuclear power and missile technologies, as well as the formation of diplomatic and security relations with postcolonial states.

The existence of weapons of mass destruction further heightened political tensions between the superpowers. This was especially instructive when Asian countries, such as North Korea and China, became part of a larger socialist alliance with the USSR, as well as when socialist Fidel Castro's 1959 July Revolutionary Movement succeeded in toppling Cuba's Batista regime and formed an alliance with the USSR. The threat of communist proximity also contributed to the heightened sense of crisis in the United States.

Alongside this period of turmoil, citizens of African nations were engaged in anticolonial struggles. As these nations gained their independence from European colonial powers, U.S. and Soviet leaders vied to establish new diplomatic relations with them. Both superpowers increased their foreign relations with African and Caribbean countries in an attempt to develop new alliances with these postcolonial nations, often based on neocolonial political and economic arrangements, leading to the institutionalization of increasing webs of interdependence with the newly developing superpowers. The United States established diplomatic relations with African countries such as South Africa, Nigeria, Ghana, and Kenya.

With the use of information technologies, such as radio technologies to establish American cultural programming in newly independent states, a new tactic of horizontal alliances was developed by the United States to ensure African loyalty to the West. Throughout the 1950s and the 1960s, to foster diplomatic relations, the United States Information Service (USIS) sponsored a series of radio programs whose goals were to circulate anticolonial sentiments, disseminate anticommunist values, and extol the virtues of democratic freedoms. The 1960s was thus a period in which democratic freedom and technological advancement worked in tandem with the development of increasing linkages between newly independent African states and the U.S. government. By this process of spreading the virtues of democratic liberties to Third World countries, the United States shored up its economic alliances and established arrangements with various African nations, even after they had become independent, with the goal of leaving channels open for future trade and telecommunications activity.[8]

The development of new forms of political regulation and communication and technology networks, allowing intensified surveillance of the public, was a fundamental outcome of the cold war. When, in April 1961, the Kennedy administration made a failed attempt to overthrow Castro at the Bay of Pigs, the defeat triggered a major international crisis in which political loyalty became more important than ever.[9] Once the first satellite was launched into orbit above the earth, however, the possibilities for instantaneous communication gave rise to the rapid development of even newer forms of regulation and technology. By the 1970s, new forms of computerized communications had been developed. These technologies radicalized former approaches to telecommunications, resulting in the incorporation of computers into people's daily lives—at work, in school, and, by the 1990s, in cyber cafés.[10] The resulting possibilities of readily available knowledge contributed to the shift in the centrality of information technologies in people's lives. These new technologies required the development of new daily practices that, in turn, led to the distinctive reorganization of space and a shortening of temporal horizons: the act of time-space compression (Harvey 1989a, 147). The compression of time and space in the production and circulation of contact among people and the consequent changing technologies inscribed a new technology onto otherwise routinized daily practices. This transformation, which reflects the condition of postmodernity—that is, the post–cold war reconfigurations of new time-space horizons—emerged as a result of the shift from industrial to electronic technologies. Telemedia, via satellite, supported by the flexible accumulation of capital, provided a new way of imagining social relations and formed one of the expanding sites for the transmission of mass media knowledge into the average Western home and various sites around the world.

A range of scholars have examined the role of telemedia in shaping perceptions of transnational subjectivity (Abu-Lughod 1989, 1993; Appadurai 1996b; Larkin 1997; Mankekar 1999). The consumption of mass media, as well as its influence on shaping subjectivity, is a site for exploring the reformulation of identity in an increasingly globalized world. The spread of televised political forums, characteristic of the changing domain of the modes of communication, led to the shaping of information about shared black political struggles. The history of the rising tide of Pan-Africanism and black nationalism is linked to the role that satellite television played in shaping transnationalist fantasy and the desire for the pride of heritage.

New Technologies and Intensifications of Horizontal Collaborations

Throughout the 1950s and into the 1970s, the establishment of horizontal linkages between Western governments and members of the African elite led to the familiarization of the plight of black Americans as well as new possibilities for collaboration. One such forum for the establishment of further horizontal linkages among Third World states was the 1955 Bandung Conference in Indonesia, at which representatives from twenty-nine African and Asian countries embraced the position of nonalignment in relation to the superpowers. Instead, they voted to commit to the struggles for independence of colonized peoples worldwide. Similar political collaboration among Africans culminated in the 1963 formation of the Africa-based umbrella organization for the development of political strategies known as the Organization of African Unity (OAU).[11]

Heightening traffic among these horizontal alliances has forced many scholars to focus on a range of transnational connections. Some have involved Pan-African cooperation between African American political movements and African independence movements, especially in relation to news reporting in Ghana, Nigeria, South Africa, and Kenya on civil rights problems in the United States. At times media alliances that existed between countries and these avenues for the circulation of information prompted black American organizations to lobby the U.S. State Department on behalf of their African compatriots. These alliances also worked in reverse, and African diplomats criticized state-enforced racial segregation in the United States. In the late 1950s, for example, Ghanaian and Guinean diplomats raised questions at the United Nations about race relations in the United States, which marked the beginning of a "communication network" through which news about the West was transmitted elsewhere.

Historically, black colleges and universities and black churches were also sites of collaboration between Africans and black Americans. In the late nineteenth and early twentieth century, for example, the collaborations between the African Methodist Episcopal (AME) Church and South African independent churches brought ministers from South Africa to AME churches in the United States; in exchange, various ministers from the AME made evangelical visits to South Africa. These collaborations were funded by educational institutions and tended to be limited to the arenas of education and religion (Campbell 1995). They reflected an already established link between Africans on the continent and black Americans in the United States, in which they shared experiences of racial subalterity because of either their colonial subjectivity or their plight as victims of racial segregation. As a result of the diplomatic and nondiplomatic pressure placed on the United States for its enforcement of racial segregation (known informally as Jim Crow), there was increasing pressure in the foreign policy realm to adjust domestic inequalities between blacks and whites. These foreign policy considerations were key contributors to federal intervention in the Deep South, when, in 1954, the U.S. Supreme Court ruled, in *Brown v. Board of Education*,[12] to desegregate public schools. When desegregation was enforced in 1957, as manifested in the Little Rock, Arkansas, crisis regarding school desegregation, these issues gained importance throughout the United States.

The burgeoning mass media also played an important role in publicizing black complaints about the institutionalized racism black Americans encountered on a daily basis (Van Deburg 1992). By the mid-1960s, under the influence of civil rights leader Martin Luther King Jr., students, and political activists, the power of the Civil Rights movement reached an all-time high and culminated in the civil rights march on Washington. Activists demanded the eradication of segregation practices and worked toward the mobilization of black participation in voter registration. This led to the increase in black elected officials, a new pool of black influence connected to governmental and international politics, and the implementation of government policies aimed at race and, later, gender equity. By the early 1960s, the Kennedy administration started to implement the conditions for the passage of the Civil Rights Act of 1964. Yet, despite the political success of civil rights activism that led to the achievement of constitutional minority civil rights, U.S. social and political institutions were as politically regulated and racially divided as ever before. By the early 1970s, many activists were convinced that civil rights, as a means to an end, could not be the only goal of black self-empowerment in the United States. Given that the new legal amendments did not alter social conduct immediately, black political leaders continued to voice their disappointment with ongoing racism against black people in the United States. Televising the march on Washington nationally and internationally made American racial inequalities public; the growing reach of the media, especially telemedia and radio, captured and sensationalized the rising tide of protest throughout the United States in the 1960s.

By 1966, there was more for the media to report, as advocates for civil rights developed a more radical social movement, one that advocated Black Power as the basis for racial equality. Black Power ideologies, which extolled positive black self-esteem, social empowerment, and self-determination, were incorporated into organizing strategies to challenge racial hierarchies. This development of Black Power identities is characterized as the shift from "being a Negro" to "*becoming black*"; that is, blackness as a sign of African pride moved from the eradication of the term "Negro," associated with slavery and the biological justification of racial segregation, to the term "black," as Black Power activists described dark-skinned people in the United States. Empowerment was thus connected to black pride and, eventually, African pride. Consequently, *blackness* became a form of "consciousness" that black Americans needed to achieve. Extolling the virtues of a cultural politics of blackness, the multilayered and increasingly transnational ideological movement advocated a consciousness revolution in which black people attempted to transform the cultural tenets of European influences in their lives.[13] Black Power not only was a political movement but also had ideological goals — that of reshaping the cartographies of blackness. Many Black Power activists believed that becoming black allowed them to ground themselves in a black collective identity (Van Deburg 1992) and consequently adopted mantras to counter hegemonic assumptions of whiteness as not only the norm, but as more desirable. One of the famous slogans of black power, *Black is beautiful*, was incorporated as a challenge to dominant signs of whiteness as superior and blackness as primitive. By expressing black aesthetic virtues and solidarity against white racism, members of the growing Black Power movement self-consciously recast the centrality of Europe in their lives, rendering it marginal but curiously dialectical. They rejected their given names as residual from slavery and changed them to African names; they used African-derived kinship terms such as "brother" and "sister" as new ways of communicating racial unity; and they reeducated themselves about the existence of African civilizations, village life, and "traditionalist" lifestyles, even though Black Power had the effect of acknowledging linkages in biologically racial terms. Becoming black and conscious was a fundamentally cultural process.

Black Power sentiments became increasingly radicalized when Stokely Carmichael (later known as Kwame Ture), of the Student Nonviolent Coordinating Committee (SNCC), told reporters on the nightly news that "the greatest hypocrisy we have is the Statue of Liberty. We ought to break the young lady's legs and point her to Mississippi" (quoted in Karim 1971, 131–32). By capitalizing on controversial statements, the media played a fundamental role in not only sensationalizing racial strife, but also rendering trivial the grievances of black people in the

United States. The press often characterized black organizing and black protests as violent and militant and black claims as too radical to be taken seriously.

At the vanguard of the Black Power movement was the Black Panther Party (BPP). As an icon of militancy, headed by people such as Bobby Seal and Huey Newton, the BPP implemented revolutionary and community-based approaches to U.S. social problems. By the 1970s, membership in the BPP exceeded thousands. They promoted black health and educational programs, the Buy Black protests, the "Don't Buy Where You Can't Work" calls for economic solidarity, prison outreach and education programs, and a voter registration drive to put more black people on juries. They created welfare counseling and provided military-style protections. The Party's radicalism was a response to growing political abuses and increasing disenfranchisement in inner-city neighborhoods. Alongside it a range of other organizations proliferated: the Revolutionary Action Movement, the Black Liberation Front, and the Black Liberation Army. They followed the ideological principles of the BPP but adopted covert approaches to defending their communities against what was, at the time, a white backlash against the integration of predominantly white institutions.

Black nationalist Islamic movements also provided forums within which black people could claim self-determination based on shared racial oppression and religious convictions. The spiritual leader, Elijah Muhammad, became a prominent icon of political significance, especially in the urban U.S. North, and popularized the Nation of Islam as a political alternative to racial marginalization. The Nation of Islam extolled black personal empowerment as a tool for social change and insisted that quotidian participation in pilgrimages to either Mecca or the African continent and learning about the Koran should constitute a critical component of daily self-teaching. The range of black Islamic movements that developed in the United States, unlike that of the multiracial religious Islamic networks worldwide, was often highly racialized (B. S. Turner 1996). Black Muslim political leaders such as Malcolm X, for example, also advocated black empowerment and racial justice, inspiring thousands of black Americans to convert to Islam. Blaming white racism and the political domination of black people for the growing poverty in inner cities, Malcolm X attracted hundreds of thousands of black Americans to follow his leadership.

Islam was one of many growing religious movements that provided an alternative to Judeo-Christianity. The roots of back-to-Africa cultural movements took shape with the development of African-based religious diasporic movements such as Ashanti-Ghanaian, Haitian voodoo, Brazilian Candomblé, and Yorùbá òrìṣà revivalism, which found its most radical form in Ọ̀yọ́túnjí Village intentional religious communities in the rural South. These forms of religious awakenings became increasingly lucrative institutions from which to create a new market of social uplift with the promotion of narratives of slavery and nobility.

Genealogies of Studying the Anthropology of Black America

The late twentieth century witnessed the reconfiguration of global spaces in the wake of decolonization and the end of the cold war. The reorganization of capitalism into new institutional forms has continued to produce new networks, forms of practice, and technological means of communication. The spread of capital pushed forward by electronic technologies and changing national and international legal regimes is widening the gap between sites of production in Third World countries and sites of consumption in the West. The new millennium has seen the intensification of economic and technological development and the migration of people from rural to urban locations, from former colonized and noncolonized Third World countries to new imperial regions, and from poorer to richer regions and nation-states. Such movements, as a result of socioeconomic disparities, developments of multinational corporations, and changes in small-scale property ownership, are leading to reconceptualizations of citizenship that extend beyond the nation-state. These reconceptualizations are of considerable significance for understanding the forces of power in shaping who gets access to new forms of citizenship and who controls how new maps of cultural belonging are redrawn along particular lines of power.

Since the mid-1980s, various manifestations of transnational and multinational linkages between African nations and the West have revolutionized the way Africans from various countries have engaged in transnational interactions across large-scale capitalist economies. Yet, despite the apparent newness of these shifts, the modernity of national origins in the nineteenth and early twentieth century, which fixed nomadic movement to settlement and *biologized* citizenship, has continued to inform the ways people link notions of belonging to origins. Even as governments and social scientists attempt to establish analytic standards by which to measure the qualitative and quantitative meanings of these social changes, there is a growing academic and intellectual schism between emphasizing the globally new while also recognizing the extent to which historical classifications continue to constitute new formations of deterritorialized linkages along lines of race and lineage.

The development of anthropology in the late nineteenth century took shape with the formalization of biology as the basis for human difference. Anthropology's village studies of the early twentieth century contributed to conceptualizations of territorially and biologically distinctive peoples and cultures in relation to territorial conceptualizations of belonging. It is also no surprise that racial biology, as the science of empire, was fundamental to the founding of the circum-Atlantic world. As such, traditional debates in the anthropology of the African diaspora have employed biological notions of race as the basis for connection and continuity. The institutionalization of anthropological science led to the classification of racial groups.

Anthropology in the United States had its roots in intervening in the institutionalization of hierarchies of Aryan supremacy as the basis of the eugenics movement. Franz Boas, for example, the forefather of U.S. anthropology, writing in the early twentieth century initiated discussions about the relationship between race and culture by examining how intergenerational change occurred. Boas (1932) outlined the development of the American concept of culture by developing a way to discuss changes in identity in time and space through approaches of acculturation. Notions of intergenerational transfers of cultural practices marked the unidirectional socialization of these practices that led to the transfer of knowledge and continuity, and acculturation referred to the bidirectional process of socialization. Building on Boas's articulation of intergenerational change, described by Robert Park (1931, 1938, 1949, 1950; Park and Miller 1921) and the anthropologists Ralph Linton (1936) and Robert Redfield (1953) as cultural transmissions, Melville Herskovits (1941) developed a study of acculturation that was methodologically scientific and highlighted essential units of human psychology central to shared traits and their related sources/origins. They opened new frontiers concerned with relations and continuities—the authentic traits embedded in individual practices—and charted a theory of cultural survivals to account for the cultural continuities of black people from Africa to the Americas.

Herskovits, a student of Boas, was specifically concerned with understanding the relationship between race and culture. In *The Myth of the Negro Past* (1941), Herskovits argued against long-standing Africanist assertions about black inferiority as well as arguments that Africans on the African continent were distinct from black people in the Americas. First debunking the myth that Africa did not have sophisticated civilizations, Herskovits then demonstrated that African practices and beliefs were fundamentally implied in black American practices. Arguing against the assertion that the system of plantation slavery in the United States was so brutal that all remnants of African culture were lost and had been replaced with new cultural forms (Frazier 1963), Herskovits contended that the assumption that culture could be lost was not only misleading but historically incorrect. Instead, asserting that culture was dynamic and could be intergenerationally preserved, he explored the ways individuals reproduced culture in new social settings.

Herskovits's contributions pushed forward larger analytical shifts from structure to process, that is, what analytic weight to give to patterns, practices, and social reproduction. His critical contribution, however, was the development of theories of cultural survivals, which revolutionized the apparent fixity of black Africans as separate from black people in the Americas.

This popularization of the concept of survivals was taken up by later generations of anthropologists and sociologists such as Robert Farris Thompson (1983), Roger Bastide (1971, 1978), and William Bascom (1969a, 1969b, 1980), who charted the complexities of survivals alongside theories of racial biology, memory, and loss. The relationship between racial biology and cultural influences was debated over many decades in the mid- to late-twentieth-century, and various assumptions about human subjectivity that shaped late-twentieth-century traditional ideas of belonging—along lines of race, ethnicity, gender, class, and sexuality—were increasingly being called into question. It was not until the early 1970s, with the publication of works by John Szwed (1970), Sidney Mintz and Richard Price (1976), and Roger Abrahams (1964), that anthropology began to recast the survivals concept as the processes by which people construct racial categories. Laying the groundwork for the development of *an anthropology of black America*, which led to the development of new ways of understanding relationships between race and culture, these anthropologists demonstrated how cultural behavior was socially acquired over time and in and across different geographic spaces.

Such approaches to race and diaspora have relied on narratives of racial connections in which sameness is privileged over difference. However, despite the claims of activists as well as scholars to assume sameness as fundamental to African American relationships to African landscapes, the genealogical reality is that this relationship of linkage is often idyllic and connected to the larger politics of modern classification joined to the retelling of migratory enslavement. And though narratives of slavery and redemption are used to invoke historical themes of struggle, reflections on the cultural politics of difference such as in Gates's *Wonders of the African World* can be seen as a foil for unraveling the ways that diasporic relations, as metaphors of historical connection, are invoked as narratives of sameness. Instead, foregrounding assumptions about difference through a rethinking of how communities of people discursively and institutionally construct these relations of similarity, we can use as a starting point the assertion that what is at stake in the intellectual project, as Tina Campt (2003) has argued, is a "less celebratory, less comfortable, more problematic element of this discourse as well as their implications for our attempts to make sense of the histories, cultural formations, and expressions of black communities elsewhere." Indeed, we are seeing the rise in the conflation between race and heritage identities—in this case, blackness as Africanness; however, this is not because of an absence of a complex politics of difference. For this relationship of black Americans to Africa is not as comfortable as early diaspora theorists presumed. Theirs was a different project with political interventions and analytic stakes (see Herskovits 1941).

Even as stories about the production of cultural linkages and Pan-Africanness are often experienced by people as a homecoming, they can also be stories of marginality, and in some cases the hostile rejection of their claims to African identity. In the study presented here, although the interactions highlight that both groups of Yorùbá practitioners needed each other and celebrated that collaboration, the data suggest that those interactions were fraught with discomfort and, more fundamentally, a mutual disregard for the forms of changes that the different grounds endured. At this moment, in which transatlantic travel and travelers' desires to reclaim "their" heritage are the popular lingua franca, scholars of the African American politics of diaspora must recognize how the referent "Africa" in the term "African American" is as much about a political claim and a form of symbolic and historical recognition as it is a site of difference. Further, in this period it is being catapulted along as an institutional and economic enterprise. Seen thus, diaspora is a complex form of displacement that is always being articulated in relation to movement, marginalization, the articulation of narratives of loss and redemption, and a late-twentieth-century political economy of heritage. The key issues to parse in the mapping of diasporic belonging are: What kinds of relations emerge from a field that draws its meanings from "heritage of roots" as fundamental to membership? In relation to analytic approaches to diaspora, how are the events of slavery and dispersals constitutive of the resultant inequalities being redeemed? And how does that provide a transnational language in which to interrogate the making, excluding, and legitimation of alliances? How does attention to the salience of difference and disjuncture undermine this project?

Building on a framework of racial linkage to Africa, scholars such as Elliott Skinner (1992; Skinner and Chu 1965; Skinner and Robinson 1983), Joseph Harris (1982), St. Claire Drake (1987), and Roger Bastide (1971, 1978) charted the cultural practices of various groups of black communities in relation to how, in varying locations and differing conditions of constraint, they represented, on the one hand, the extreme of disconnection and, on the other, varying degrees of connections.[14] These works set the stage for new approaches to race, culture, and diasporic commonalities to black people around the globe. By the 1970s and 1980s, diaspora studies had become the popular basis for an understanding of blackness as Africanness. Nevertheless, the problem with such approaches to race and diaspora was that they posited blackness and African descent as a priori foundations of history and experience. Since then, the foundations of racial sameness have changed significantly over time, and so have the geopolitics of race through which commonalities are seen.

Not only was the production of Third World subjectivities and their representations under analytic scrutiny in the 1980s and 1990s, but anthropology's original focus on local communities as isolated microcosms failed to capture social worlds that were increasingly becoming complexly interconnected. Paul Gilroy's (1993a) exploration of diaspora addressed some of these concerns by producing an alternative mechanism for articulating what constituted blackness in the circum-Atlantic region. Signaling a critical shift in studies of blackness as spatially contingent, Gilroy identified the black Atlantic not simply in relation to race or residence in the territory of the African continent, but as a product of modernity in which the history of modern capitalism shaped the development of the modern nation-state, which, through the history of slavery and mobility, constituted formations of blackness as we in the United States know it today. This conceptualization of seeing race through ways of making race is useful for highlighting how late-twentieth-century formations of black cultural networks have created alternative relations of belonging that are at once embedded in difference and diversity and also constituted by a black Atlantic geography. Thus, even diaspora as a political project must begin analytically to contend with the politics of difference and the institutions that people call on to reconstruct belonging. In the case of religious nationalist back-to-Africa groups, such as Ọ̀yọ́túnjí Village, in which the charge is to promote the reclamation of African nobility through invocations of struggle and loss, there is a critical political project at work that is driven by political economic possibilities. Analytically, however, we need to be able both to understand the nature of cultural desire that inspires such politics and to chart the processes by which this enabled the resources that are called on to make it possible: How is the past invoked physically and discursively? What institutions are both operative and called on to legitimate these claims? Why do particular concepts such as roots, race, and heritage continue to resonate even in their postmodern manifestations? How are the forces that created continuities in racial nomenclature, yet discontinuities in material conditions, operative in the making of national identities into transnational identities?

Given the postsegregation shift in framing race—from legislation to markets— we need to understand the way narratives about the origins of people's past are remembered in landscapes of power: How do agents actively reclassify their national identities, and what might that tell us about the production of diaspora in its sociopolitical and economic contexts? To understand how such institutions propelled legislative enforcements of race, moving race from biology to concep-

Table 1. Geographical Scale of Òrìṣà Voodoo Genealogy

Development of Modern Capitalist Nation-State(1870–1930)
    Post–Civil War—Postslavery—Reconstruction
    Early Black Nationalist Formations
    Racial Segregation–Jim Crow

Development of Modern Welfare State (1930–50)
    World War II
    Racial Segregation–Jim Crow

Development of Horizontal Institutions/International Community (1950–70)
    African and Third World Independence Struggles
    Postcolonial State Formation
    1959–Ọba of Ọ̀yọ́túnjí Is Initiated in Cuba
    1960–70:
    Spread of Santería throughout U.S. Urban Centers
        Civil Rights Movement
        Height of Black Power
        Racial Divisions in Santería Communities

Vertical Reconfiguration of Racial Rights/Civil Liberties (1970–80)
    1970s–Ọ̀yọ́túnjí Formation–Segregation Politics
    Beginning of Early Ọ̀yọ́túnjí Travels to Nigeria/Benin
    Black Cultural Politics–Self-Determination
    Airing of *Roots* Movie
    Racial Integration in U.S. Urban Centers
    Outward Migration of Ọ̀yọ́túnjí Residents to Urban Centers—Early Development of
        Stage I of Network
    Development of Ọ̀yọ́túnjí Roots Readings

Post–Cold War—1980–90
    Institutionalization of Deterritorial Yorùbá Practices
    Development of University and Community Heritage Programs
    Institutionalization of Affirmative Action Hiring and Admissions
    Ọ̀yọ́túnjí–Institutionalization of Deterritorialized Practices
    New Wave of Electronic Technologies
    Accessibility of Air Travel
    Development of World Theme Park Concept
    Development of Linkages between African *Babalawo* and Ọ̀yọ́túnjí Initiates

Table 1. Continued

Global Market Expansionism of the Rights Movement (1990–2000)
Global Market Capitalism
    Post-1989 New World Democratic Movements
    Fundraising for World Theme Park Concept
    New Internet Technologies/Urban U.S. Computer Access
    Popularization of Kwanzaa Movement
    Commodification of African-Centrism
    Black Cultural Nationalism and New Market Heritage Alliances

tualizations of heritage, we must examine this genealogy of the present. This shift from early-twentieth-century forms of antiracist organizing led to the creation of a rights movement that, through market participation, reconfigured race as heritage and thus the basis of American educational entitlements. These shifts from the state-enforced biological science of race to the ancestral heritage of subjectivity suggest that what was presumed to be the basis of "natural" unity was shaped just as much by institutional ideologies of seeing racial sameness as by the materiality of classifying distinctions.[15] The genealogical shift from African to Negro, as biological conceptions, to black and African American, as forms of social heritage is incomplete without an examination of the ways that new institutional and capital forces in the late twentieth and early twenty-first century are contributing to a global revival of territorial heritage in the establishment of new norms of ancestry.

I call for an end to the word "diaspora" as noun. Instead, and in light of these formations of power and politics, it is the process of making, legitimating, erecting, and dismantling the national that we need to mark. The categories that were employed in the early twentieth century are motivated today by different objects of scrutiny, different forces of production; thus, it is the process and not the state of being that we must examine. Even the utterance of diaspora is itself a rearticulation of an object that does not exist.

Vertical Alliances and "Rights to Heritage" Norms in a Post-Fordist Moment

By the early 1970s, the convergences between revolutionary Pan-African movements that accompanied the achievement of African independence were replaced by problems of economic development in many Caribbean and African independent nations. The end of the cold war marked the United States as a world leader; technologies that were once used for transportation and national security became available for American consumption. In line with the rise of U.S. economic power,

African leaders, in search of economic opportunities and political alliances, began to drop the centrality of race, which had previously occupied earlier transatlantic black and Third World alliances. They shifted their focus to new strategies for political and economic survival.[16] Some of these political alliances involved the development of trading partners, the export of African products to the West, and the development of slave castles, safaris, great ancient ruins, and the like for the African tourist industries. Changing institutional policies, which were once shaped by the biology of racial alliances, led to the creation of "rights-centered" entitlements to heritage in which narratives of slavery were invoked and the mobility of African empires celebrated. These entitlements were shaped by an increasingly opportunistic transnational market that propelled forward the vertical integration of new civil rights norms. Ultimately, historical contexts, political consciousness, and economic possibilities mobilized a different form of modern subjectivity that imagined race in politically relevant terms.

With the increased political power of American activists fighting for social change, brought about by the urban unrest of the 1960s social movements, the rights movement, buttressed by extrajudicial and legislative mechanisms, led to the push for civil liberties. Legislative programs that mandated affirmative action and equal pay for equal work took shape and established mechanisms for the inclusion of minorities. By the 1980s, the mechanisms by which ethnic heritage categories were introduced and employed were just as important as the institutionalization of the concept itself. With the production of a new moment in U.S. national culture in which civil rights and democracy became the sociopolitical context, a new shift in heritage consciousness occurred that conformed to new forms of post–cold war national consciousness. The scholarly shift to ethnic heritage categories as a recasting of derogatory racial categories, such as Negro, emerged at a specific historical moment and has had the effect of producing new units of classification and institutional study. Equally, African diaspora studies, as a unit of analysis, spread as a popular conception for classifying people during a time when politicians, culture brokers, and activists, as well as academics and public and private donors, were willing to participate in the creation of new forms of classification for the development of a new national consciousness.

Educational institutions responded by developing new hiring and admissions practices as well as affirmative action institutional initiatives. With the end of the Civil Rights movement and the establishment of basic civil rights norms, a new "educational rights" movement took shape that was redrawn along new lines. The assertion of the right to learn about one's heritage became increasingly accepted over time. These initiatives, as well as the growing national and international protest movements, contributed to the transformation of American higher education to include a right-to-heritage agenda on the basis of human equality and individual rights. Interestingly, something new had taken shape in fundamentally mediated forms. It is important to establish that fact with a historical overview that highlights this transformation of the racial imagination and the way the meanings of racial roots reattached people to particular places. What emerged was a new mechanism of reinforcement, that of the production of new forms of cultural race; the invention of "heritage" and the results of these transformations of rights included the development of black people's rights to learn about their ancestral roots in Africa. Opposing presumptions of racial and cultural sameness around the United States, students lobbied for the formation of black studies departments and demanded that university administrations provide African studies courses with tenure-track jobs for black faculty. They demanded diverse educational heritage curricula and advocated for the recruitment of black students and faculty into predominantly white universities.

The eventual proliferation of African and African American studies in universities and community colleges throughout the United States overlapped with the curriculum of already established disciplines such as anthropology, sociology, and political science. In response, activists demanded separate programs to further promote racial and national origins and gender studies, thereby leading to the establishment of Africana (African and African American) studies and ethnic and women's studies programs. The institutionalization of these special programs marked the beginning of a significant shift in new approaches to origins and heritage as the basis for the widespread importance of roots as central to learning and teaching about human civilizations.

At the same time, a multicultural curriculum was integrated into schools around the country, and African American subjectivities as ethnically African took on a new meaning. Alongside the institutionalization of heritage there was a critical shift from racial notions of primordial territorial attachments to Africa. Biological race became cultural race and inscribed a different set of institutional frameworks onto a new sector of black nationalism—that of cultural nationalism. Race further concretized a particular form of black global cultural belonging and, in the United States, was catapulted forward by the roots revolution of the late twentieth century. Where race as the basis for African and black American unity had its place in earlier social movements, blackness came to stand for African heritage and the right of black Americans to reclaim the heritage taken from them as a result of transatlantic slavery.

Agents of the Black Power movement succeeded in further concretizing a particular invention of blackness as a basis for unity. Its contemporary by-product, the black cultural nationalism of the 1980s, which was propelled by new forms of global capital accumulation, contributed to the production of ideologies of blackness as Africanness. What changed in the period following the early 1980s? It was the formation of new institutions of power within which difference was classified along ethnic lines. The governmental institutions that regulated laws; the cultural and religious intermediaries that interpreted religious knowledge; the international organizations that convened conferences; the shopkeepers, traders, and manufacturers who sold ritual and cultural commodities; the groups of corporations that looked for commodity possibilities; as well as academics and amateur historians, music companies, and jazz and rap artists became conduits for a new expression of subjectivity. With the already developing global demands for these heritage artifacts, the commodification of African heritage gave rise to markets of transnational travelers.

The TV miniseries *Roots* was critical to these new imaginings, for it contributed to the production of collective memory of an already marginalized American community; as time progressed, the nobility of the African past featured prominently in the development of cultural blackness as a heritage identity. The *Roots* theme and the theme of nobility central to Gates's *Wonders of the African World* bring to light how the institutional power of African heritage, as a form of dignity and black pride, took shape with the rise of African American institutions of higher learning. Similarly, the eventual proliferation of heritage literature, market products, heritage days, popular public artists and celebrities, and public intellectuals such as Ali Mazrui and Henry Louis Gates were possible as a result of the creation of a population willing to consume the productions of a growing heritage market.

Heritage and the Popular Reclassifications of Racial Biology

Locating *Roots* as a key force in the shift in black Americans' imaginings of their connection to an African heritage is critical for understanding the establishment of a new commonsense notion of racial categories in heritage terms. The early twentieth-century dominant textual narratives of slavery were reconfigured with what became a different public discourse about black American connections to African kingdoms. In the late twentieth century, these new constructions of the incorporation of the nobility of the ethnic past did more for the development of a widespread commonsense notion of the African roots of black American identities than any other back-to-Africa social movement in the United States. Ultimately, these nobility narratives contributed to the establishment of ideological terms for ongoing black American genealogical roots of African nobility.

In addition to foregrounding the centrality of slavery in transporting African captives to the Americas, *Roots* contributed to a narrative shift from what was popularly represented in schools as black Americans being victims of slavery who were *saved* by Abraham Lincoln, to blacks as noble survivors and agents of their own freedom. Blackness became a popular signifier of cultural heritage and ethnicity emblematic of multicultural principles of a post–Jim Crow, post–Black Power "American society" and signaled a classificatory shift in categories of U.S. citizenship. For, unlike past Pan-African and black nationalist movements of earlier centuries, the mass circulation of *Roots* contributed to the widespread invention of an African ethnic identity constituted as a derivative of African-Atlantic heritage. It followed a wave of wide-scale demands for civil rights that reconceptualized black America's inclusion in a larger pantheon of U.S. ethnic histories.

After *Roots* genealogies of ancestry became a popular activity among Americans in general and African Americans in particular; assertions of the African heritage of African Americans began to overdetermine race as culture. Given that African Americans could not draw on the experiential memory of transatlantic slavery, in the collective experience of a nation watching the story of slavery unfold *Roots* brought to life the remaking of a collective memory of subordination that gained its experiential power through the power of association and rearticulation. As a result of the production of a community of black cultural nationalists willing to claim a different narrative about Africa and slavery, new consumer demands for an African heritage industry took shape. Like the proliferation of black participation in the political arena, the collective production of these counternarratives led to mainstream discourses about white barbarism and black survival. By providing knowledge about the "secrets of the African past," black public intellectuals contributed to setting new terms for the ways that commonsense notions about slavery and the African American past were to be understood. By highlighting the connections between Africans and African Americans as a result of slavery, they not only began to highlight the complicity of African and European slavery, but they also left an opening for rethinking African enslavement as an experience of a long and sophisticated African heritage of empires and rulers.

Filling the demand for knowledge about the transatlantic slave trade and the precolonial African history that preceded it, the circulation of black heritage products and books expanded in size and number with the proliferation of black bookshops in U.S. cities.[17] Given this shift in training and interest, not only were books about African history readily available for purchase outside of African countries, but in the mid- to late 1980s, with increasing numbers of literate and educated populations and a wider range of black university-trained graduates, a new middle-class black American consumer developed.[18] Some public intellectuals, self-trained or recently trained in urban college programs, contributed to the development of new networks of African knowledge and of a black history industry.[19]

To satisfy the demands of this new market of heritage-conscious consumers, black-owned publishing houses used newly emerging computer technologies to either reinvigorate or create new African-centered black and Third World publishing houses, such as Africa World Press (AWP), Third World Press, and Black Classic Press.[20] The late 1980s was a period of corporate mergers, during which small mainstream American publishing houses were subsumed by larger national and international corporations; in some cases, mainstream publishing houses negotiated contracts with smaller presses to reprint key bestsellers based most critically on market demands and quality of scholarship and not as much on racial politics. For example, in line with the consolidation of publishing companies, Grove Press, through Vintage Company, sold the rights to publish *Malcolm X Speaks* (1965) to its new corporate parent, Grove-Weidenfeld, then a subsidiary of Getty Corporation. The reissue of *The Black Jacobins* by C. L. R. James, first published in 1938 and reprinted in 1963, was another example of both changing public interests and a business response to new market demands.

The development of a black history industry led to a growing tide of black cultural nationalism, starting with the celebration of black American history. A special day in February, called Black Heritage Day, was set aside to commemorate black history. By the early 1980s, Black Heritage Day was officially renamed Black Heritage Week, and eventually the week developed into a full-fledged month-long celebration supported by educational and governmental institutions. Cultural nationalists began to participate in the celebration of black American and African history, arts, literature, and music. The concept of heritage months spread throughout American social institutions in the 1980s, and African American History Month was vertically incorporated into educational programming. Now, it was not just African Americans who celebrated African American history; rather, the creation of African American History Month coincided with increasing numbers of educational and governmental institutions internalizing these practices into their own institutional structure. The shift from biological race to cultural race was shaped by the rise of a new character of roots.

The development of multiculturalism in U.S. colleges was accompanied by a critical legislative shift. In 1980, the U.S. census for the first time used ancestral heritage as the official unit of difference for classifying Americans. Where once the census had organized identity according to racial groups ("Whites, Orientals, Negroes, Amerindians, and Non-Whites"), the census now shifted the terms of classification to ethnicity (Hernandez-Reguant 1999). Ancestry, such as country of parental birth, became the form of classification by which Americans were asked to identify themselves. This led to a shift from a bureaucratic politics of racial biology to a way of incorporating new heritage standards by which American belonging was increasingly institutionally framed. Of course, although notions of biological race overlapped with cultural race, the standardization of hyphenated identity categories—such conceptions as Native American, Chinese American, and Polish American identity—was incorporated into the new census classifications. Thus, notions of cultural race became the lingua franca of U.S. governmental institutions.

Similarly, the category "African American" was used by the Reverend Jesse Jackson in his 1988 presidential campaign to recast the centrality of slavery in the lives of black people by laying claim to the noble African "origins" of black Americans. African American as a middle-class household term came to represent the mixing of primordial origins with U.S. citizenship. Further, Jackson's Rainbow Coalition linked African Americanness to other hyphenated identities that were simultaneously entering the American mainstream. These relations of belonging—though inscribed in modern notions of race, biology, descent, and nationhood—cultivated the virtues of ancestry that it valorized.

Corporations and small-business investors participated in the production of African linkages to American blackness through the marketing of the symbolic nobility of black history. African trading corporations worked with small and large U.S. corporations to export increasing numbers of African-related commodities. Some of these included Ghanaian *kente* cloth and prints,[21] African jewelry, artifacts, food, and accessories. By the mid-1980s, U.S. corporations such as McDonalds, K-Mart, J.C. Penney, and a range of other urban department chains began to sell what many store managers referred to as an "Africa-friendly image" to mostly middle-class black Americans. Their consumers were black middle-class women and men interested in African-centered images, self-help books, fabrics, artifacts, and tourist packages, and they were willing to wear African clothes and embrace African history. The wearing of African fabrics, such as kente cloth, was initially limited to formal dress for weddings and graduation ceremonies; however, from the mid-1980s to the mid-1990s, African garb became increasingly integrated into casual wear and increasingly popular, especially among sectors of the black middle class. With the greater affordability of air travel in the 1980s, more and more corporations marketed heritage tourism to a range of regions: West and Central Africa in search of slave castles and heritage lessons; East and South Africa in search of game safaris, ancient ruins, and unspoiled wildlife; and North Africa, especially Egypt, in search of noble civilizations and the cradle of humanity. The expansion of heritage tourism and the development of commemorative events further propelled the institutionalization of African American heritage identities.

Another arena for participation in the creation of African heritage was the development of religious communities for African-based rituals. Producing what came

Chief of Ṣàngó preparing to present gifts to the Ṣàngó òrìṣà at festival.

A Nigerian priestess interpreting her divinatory cowries known as eerindilogun.

to be seen as the experience of Africa was just as important as the embodiment of Africa through clothes and practices. Those who were able to afford transnational travel to various African regions did so; otherwise, the U.S. production of the experience of African rituals through manhood training programs and cultural rituals further propelled the institutionalization of the narratives of African slavery and African nobility. One such social ritual that had a wide-scale impact was Kwanzaa, a black nationalist ritual holiday that symbolizes the resistance and survival of African Americans as well as the ancestral past.[22] This invented holiday is based on the celebration of seven principles: unity, self-determination, collective world and responsibility, cooperative economics, purpose, creativity, and faith.[23] Using Swahili language names and invented rituals that outline moral principles, Kwanzaa represents a 1960s heritage movement that memorializes the history of transatlantic slavery and celebrates the nobility of black history in Africa. Formerly a marginalized black nationalist celebration, over time its influence spread throughout the United States when, in the late 1980s, President Bill Clinton endorsed it along with Hanukkah, Christmas, and Ramadan as an American heritage holiday.

Kwanzaa's power resides in its ability to provide parallel alternatives for African Americans to celebrating Christmas with Christians, Hanukkah with Jews, and Ramadan with members of the Nation of Islam. As it involves the giving of gifts,

Kwanzaa's power also lies in its ability to align itself with already-existing forms of economic gift giving in America. Ultimately, Kwanzaa represents expressions of convergence between African American and African cultural heritage, thereby establishing another form of practice that is identifiably African American.

With the growth of the mainstream holiday movement, new cultural icons, and a new commitment to African pride, a new group emerged as participants in the heritage trend: black people who were not leaders, not activists, not necessarily middle or upper class, but rather post–affirmative action citizens recasting their place in and entitlement to all that the United States could offer. On the whole, black cultural nationalism was an extension of the rights revolution. It produced an African heritage movement that, through the workings of market mechanisms, went from occupying a marginal place of radical black power to a multimillion-dollar industry in mainstream America. Ọ̀yọ́túnjí Village, with its rise from a separatist community to a network of òrìṣà voodoo practices, is yet another example of the denationalized heritage movement in action.

Ọ̀yọ́túnjí Yorùbá Revivalism and the Spread of Cultural Markets

With the gradual development of Africanized òrìṣà voodoo cultural institutions over the course of the development of black nationalist movements of the 1960s, a network of Yorùbá chiefs, priests, leaders, and clients developed to produce Yorùbá religious practices in such U.S. cities as Beaufort, New York, Chicago, Columbus, Houston, and Washington, D.C., as well as London and elsewhere. These people also sponsored heritage visits to West African cities, with the goals of participating in cultural rituals and reestablishing networks with Nigerian practitioners. With the growing availability of electronic technologies they could obtain religious counsel, ritual services, and knowledge, as well as market products, such as books, pamphlets, ritual objects, and medicinal products (which could be ordered over the phone or by Internet), thus developing new economic and political institutions of knowledge for the formation of deterritorialized practices in the United States. Using these new electronic technologies to represent their African roots and to develop ritual services and theme park communities as sites for tourism, members of the growing Yorùbá cultural network interested in expanding their knowledge about Yorùbá and òrìṣà religious practices participated in the creation of new network forums, services, and travel opportunities.[24] Ọ̀yọ́túnjí and Yorùbá revivalists in the Ọ̀yọ́túnjí network regularly traveled to West Africa; they continued to build political alliances with West African òrìṣà priests and established trade markets for the buying of African clothing. Over time, and with increasing

Chief of Egbaland in Nigeria outside the Alake of Abeokuta's palace.

fluency with Nigerian Yorùbá cultural practices, they incorporated histories of the Yorùbá in southwestern Nigeria into stories about their own ancestral dispersal to the Americas as slaves. As such, the production of linkages to Africa constituted a production of master tropes about African nobility.

After going through a phase of building and instituting Africancentric traditional practices that reflected the empires of days past, the once separatist ideologies that distinguished òrìṣà voodoo from its Santería predecessor shifted to an integrationist economy of tourism and expansionism that attracted mainstream black Americans (as well as Christians and white American tourists) and became critical to the Ọ̀yọ́túnjí mission. Of particular significance in the progression of black nationalism, therefore, was the shift from the separatism of the 1970s to the formation of divinatory ritual institutions and wide-scale tourism in the 1980s and early 1990s. It is important to note here that while this religious movement had its antecedents in the history of the civil rights struggle, black cultural nationalism was also a product of new market forces and developed in connection with the rise of the United States as the center of the world economy. Indeed, these religious movements, with their roots in sociopolitical and racial protest, are reflective of the shift from Black Power nationalism to African American cultural consumerism of *things African*. This phase is reflective of the increasing need in Ọ̀yọ́túnjí to withstand the Reagan-era budget cuts by building self-sustaining economic institutions.

Like many cultural and religious movements that arose in the late 1970s, therefore, Yorùbá activists adapted their practices to the demands of a changing and dynamic social movement. By the 1980s, the tourist market in Ọ̀yọ́túnjí grew in importance, and ritual practices, for example, became heavily commodified (see chapters 4 and 5). In the 1990s, ritual commodities were available on demand and provided practitioners and tourists with a heritage product. For some practitioners in Ọ̀yọ́túnjí Village, this meant adapting ancient divinatory practices to the "changing needs of their people": as therapy for people with marital and financial problems; as consultancies for legal and health problems; and as advice for lotteries. For others, it meant supplementing their income by working on the popular Psychic Line, accepting nonblack clients, or joining the Afrocentric lecture circuit and being paid the same amount for a single lecture that they might regularly make during a month of ritual work.

In the realm of ritual, an initiation in Ọ̀yọ́túnjí Village or in the larger Yorùbá network that was once characterized by modest cost and an arduous six-month to one-year period of isolation, initiation, and prayer, by the late 1980s cost over $5,000 and an on-site time commitment of one long weekend. Thus, by the late 1980s, interested initiates with an urban lifestyle and demanding careers did not have to travel to West Africa or Cuba to become initiated in the prestige of a more traditional venue, nor did they have to move to Ọ̀yọ́túnjí for a three- to twelve-month period. Instead, urban practitioners could undergo the principle phase of an Ọ̀yọ́túnjí initiation over a four-day weekend and pursue the other components of the postinitiation process from the comfort of their urban homes.[25] Despite these ritual and cultural transformations of earlier initiation models, born-again requirements such as the shaving of hair, the wearing of postinitiation white clothes, and the sworn induction into cult groups were maintained. However, throughout the mid- to late 1990s, new technological means, such as affordable telephone communications, cassette recordings, and, later, electronic mail easily facilitated by the Internet, led to new adaptations of the former period of Jim Crow segregation which required the physical presence of practitioners. Though they maintained the ideal of traditionalism, most priests and residents modified their ritual practices to accommodate the changing needs of their diverse clients.

In 1986, tourism contributed to over 60 percent of the community's gross income. The growing rate of practitioner participation and the tourist market was increasingly fueled by visitors' search for the unusual and the exotic. In search of divinatory services and fees for bus tours and dining services, Ọ̀yọ́túnjí began increasingly to cater to outside demands rather than the black segregationist politics that characterized its first decade of existence. In the early 1990s, the development of a business plan for the Òyótúnjí Big Continent African Theme Park represented the epitome of the merger between black nationalism and cultural marketing. The theme park idea is still pending and business partnerships are being developed, but envisioning sponsorships from multinational corporations represents a pattern of larger alliances already established with major transnational corporations, such as McDonald's Black History Heritage, Time-Warner's collaboration with American Black Cinema Corporation, the Public Broadcasting Service's collaboration with black projects, and so forth. The African theme park is the brainchild of the king of Òyótúnjí and his chiefs, who are working with practitioners and nonpractitioners interested in developing a general tourist attraction comparable to Disney World. Such a project would represent the postmodern ideal, a deterritorialized Africa situated in new categories of identity and belonging that Americans can consume at will.

As designed, the project would be developed in two phases. In the first phase, the theme park would be divided into ten village regions, each featuring live entertainment, gift shops with handicrafts and African attire and cloth, and a central campus or parade ground for the display of grand pageants. The development of an area with mechanical rides and aquatic excursions in a human-made Nile River characterizes the second phase. This phase would involve the design of gardens and courtyards to reflect the grandeur of African kingdoms and royal palaces. The surroundings would be embellished with life-size posters and video/filmic illustrations to impart the visual and cultural experience of Africa to visitors. Factories for the production of a range of African arts and artifacts—plastic, wood, ceramic, and brass artwork—would also be available. The Big Continent African Theme Park would offer recreational, cultural, and educational experiences for the whole family. In addition, the park would provide a practical purpose, that is, revenues for Yorùbá revivalists so that they can ensure their survival and manage to provide their youth with jobs in their community.[26] What distinguishes it from other mainstream enterprises is its celebration of African aesthetic cultural expressions and the articulation of linkages between black Americans and Africans.

The business plan describes both phases as being designed with the input of "carefully researched and constructed diverse African 'Villages' set to ethnic music and sound." It would be one of many tourist sites in South Carolina.[27] The figures in the business plan—a proposed investment of over $20 million in 1990, with a $15 to $45 admission fee and projected gross revenues of over $62 million for a 100-acre site—are accompanied by images of African landscapes the tourist is invited to explore in an "authentic African experience." Such a project represents a heightened rendering of place secondary to the experience of a deterritorialized Africa,

African World Theme Park
advertisements.

as the recurring caption on the document aptly states: "This is an Idea Whose Time Has Come!" This literature emphasizes the need for capitalizing on new technological innovations: "Each 'Village' will permit the tourist to walk through its interiors embellished by art and [furnished with] electronic information devices." By using the technological innovations available to them, the developers of The Big Continent are attempting to produce an Africanized tourist commodity to compete with currently existing theme parks such as Carowinds, Dollywood, Busch Gardens, Disney, Six Flags, Kings Dominion, and South of the Border. As described in the literature, it would reproduce the architecture, dress, cuisine, arts, and ceremonies of Africa.

Cultural Heritage, African Pride, and Global Capital

In the larger U.S. black communities, the late 1980s was also a period marked by the rise of the black teen rap music counterculture. The 1990s were marked by the height of the technology revolution. In the realm of artistic culture, the development of an Africancentric protest movement of artists was best represented by Queen Latifah, a young female rap artist with a message of African nobility and urban American pride. Queen Latifah incorporated the themes of black pride from the earlier decade; however, her music was a response to American racism and the female derogation that was marketed by the largest recording industries in the United States. Following this lead, other artists, such as reggae musicians, formed alliances with American rap and rhythm-and-blues artists to produce a new generation of Caribbean reggae. By the 1990s, protest artists such as Wyclef Jean and Lauryn Hill of the Fugees were fully integrated into the U.S. mainstream. Further, the middle-class appeal of the developing cultural nationalist movement broke down as the youth embraced an African symbolic counterculture of pride and protest. With the proliferation of films, events, music, consumer goods, institutions, and black academic production, the creation of territorial heritage featured a fundamental rethinking and reworking of the racial imaginary at the end of the twentieth century that was unlike earlier forms of black nationalism.[28] These shifts in the development of cultural race were allied with transnational corporate power, setting the stage for new ideologies of seeing race and deterritorialized linkage through different domains of belonging in the twenty-first century.

New conceptions of race have not supplanted biological conceptions, but through the development of a post–cold war democratic polity, the politics of rights and the shifts in market technologies occurred alongside economic and political institutions to produce new institutional mechanisms to reconstitute race through the commodification of cultural heritage and development of notions of heritage groups as constitutive of the American people, descendents from a vast array of cultural traditions. This shift in subjectivity has implications for how we think about the utility of theories of the African diaspora in a post–civil rights, (post)modern era. It focuses our search on understanding the selective processes that shape diasporic formations and highlights the need for studies to be far less focused on prescribed attributes of race and commonalities in specific geographic spaces and far more attuned to changes in relations of global power. Ultimately, it has implications for how we think about diaspora as a process in the making rather than as a state of authentic loss.

Clearly the story of globalization requires a shift in how we understand affiliation and access. Conceptualizations of race were reconfigured with a broad-based diasporic reformulation of blackness as ethnically African in the popular imagination. This development suggests that, given the ways that diasporic connections have been made and remade through time, scholars need to go beyond the mere charting of diasporic claims to homelands. We need to focus on the making of diasporic connections and the ways that diasporic formations have been and continue to be embedded in hegemonic institutions of power. Thus, in the making of African diasporic linkages, it is the creation of slavery and nobility narratives through the prestige and privilege of ancestral heritage, the role of institutional alliances, and the forces of the market that shaped what forms of ethnic heritage came to be seen as appropriately legitimate and therefore part of a larger regime of hyphenated American identities. These formations are distinct from the earlier racial classifications that were regulated through governmental racial policies and legitimated through science. This shift from race to culture and ethnicity became a statement both of how conceptualizations of race have been facilitated by the fusion of market capitalism and new technologies and of how they were intensified by the rights movement, which displaced racial subordination and reconfigured it as ethnic history and the privileges of belonging to the human species.

In the preface to this book, I reflected on my own situation to demonstrate how the development of a particular local history of racial logics is situated differently. In twentieth-century Canadian contexts, hierarchies of race relations, specifically the cultural politics of blackness, were not situated in relation to whiteness in the same way that blackness was situated in relation to whiteness in the United States. As outlined in chapter 1, one of the ways racial formation in U.S. contexts was inscribed was in relation to accessing white privilege; however, in mid- to late-twentieth-century urban Canada, the majority of whose relatively small black population were immigrants from elsewhere, the cultural politics of blackness produced different forms of subjects. In Cuba it was shaped in relation to *mesjahe* (mixture); for Yorùbá practitioners in Nigerian contexts, the politics of membership are variously located and driven by different historical and institutional regimes. As illustrated in the arrival story introducing this chapter, blackness certainly is not the basis for Nigerian belonging.

The next chapter demonstrates that the interface with whiteness was shaped by a different bodily logic, a different politics of seeing. West African encounters with Europe tended to be related to hierarchies for classifying civilization and modernity as they played out through the cultural politics of daily practice, such as differences in religious and ethnic categories. Yorùbá òrìṣà practitioners use particular tropes of racial linkage and techniques of time-space mappings to legitimate their claims to African membership. This form of mapping is relevant in particular historically significant and locally relevant contexts.

PART TWO
The Making of Transnational Networks

3. Micropower and Ọ̀yọ́ Hegemony in Yorùbá Transnational Revivalism

RED BLOOD SPLATTERED THROUGHOUT the oval-shaped room. Robed in his best traditional clothes and pulling the trigger of a borrowed shotgun, one of Ọ̀yọ́túnjí's young men had fallen to his death. The news of the suicide rang throughout the community. His last words, inscribed on paper, expressed how much he tried and wanted them to be proud of him, how much he hurt and how much he could not deal with the addictions that haunted him, how much he continued to fail those he loved the most. His solution saddened the residents as they scrambled to explain how it could have happened, wishing they had paid more attention to the signs. If only they had tried harder. The lack of experience dealing with death in Ọ̀yọ́túnjí, a three-generation-old community, left residents with a numbing powerlessness and malevolent curiosity about how the leaders would deal with a life taken in this way.

The emotional inclination of many, regardless of the cause of death, was to honor with a special ritual the life of their friend and "brother in the religion." During the first few hours, members of the Ọ̀yọ́túnjí community researched the appropriate ritual protocols. They alerted the authorities of the City of Beaufort, used divinatory rituals to consult the ancestors, telephoned knowledgeable practitioners outside of Ọ̀yọ́túnjí, and read a range of historical texts from which to establish the appropriate Yorùbá traditions. An examination of the various sources confirmed that, indeed, there is a hierarchy of knowledge to be employed in various contexts and not all diviners command the same interpretive respect and authority. The advice of their ancestors was sought collaboratively by the high priest and a few chiefs; the literary research for information on how to proceed with traditional burial practices for suicide victims among the Yorùbá of southwestern Nigeria was derived from Samuel Johnson's (1921) *History of the Yorùbás* and not more contemporary texts. Most of the texts that document Yorùbá traditional practices and are used in Òyótúnjí today were published by early anthropologists and sociologists. These include various early-twentieth-century Yorùbá revivalist classics such as Johnson's *History*, N. A. Fadipe's (1970) *Sociology of the Yorùbá*, William Bascom's (1969a) *Ifa Divinations*, Robert Smith's (1969) *Kingdoms of the Yorùbá*, and A. B. Ellis's (1894) *Yorùbá-Speaking People of the Slave Coast*. These texts form the source of knowledge for African American ancestral history, and, despite the apparent stability of these written historical forms, Yorùbá revivalists participate in shaping norms of acceptability by basing their terms of practice on renditions of these accounts.

These hierarchies of knowledge and differential relations of power among practitioners are critical for establishing what forms of Yorùbá knowledge have circulated transnationally; who, within those transnational arenas, are the central agents of change and influence; and why. Over the course of the development of the black cultural nationalist movement, as it moved from Harlem to South Carolina, African Americans disillusioned with Christianity converted to Yorùbá practices in an attempt to revive their African past. Òyótúnjí Village was built on a commitment to revering traditional values, hierarchies of kingship, and religious ritual. The structure of community governance is often described by tour guides as "emulating the structures of governance in their homeland."

At the beginning of biweekly town meetings and other formal events, in an attempt to enact the social, religious, and political life of Yorùbá ancestors, Òyótúnjí revivalists educate themselves about Yorùbá history and cultural practices. They often pursue ritual apprenticeships through which they can become worshippers, learn the divinatory corpus, and study texts about the history of African peoples. Their goal is for black Americans to be redeemed from the aftereffects of transatlantic slavery, when detailed documentation of the transport of captives from various parts of Africa—their names, ages, clans—was never made. Rather, slaves were categorized as chattel, not worthy of name recognition, requiring only the numeric codification of property. Much of the remaining evidence about those Africans consists of ship records with ports of slave embarkation and disembarkation that numerically list the enslaved bodies for transatlantic trade, auctioneer records of slave advertisements, and bills of sale. This erasure of African identities and connections to African American family genealogies led to the dependence of revivalists on textual knowledge. Despite this absence of historical specificity, members of Òyótúnjí Village–aligned communities actively reconstruct African roots using the solidarity of racial membership and the prestige of institutionally legitimized knowledge such as historical canons and divinatory mechanisms.

Three days after the death of the young man, the eight chiefs, all members of the Òyótúnjí governing council, known as the Ògbóni Society, voted on the final rule of action. Claiming directives from the ancestors who prevailed over the society meeting, Ọba Adéfúnmi announced the results. Prefacing his statement with a declaration that Yorùbá traditions were based on ancient practices and that it was his job, as supreme ruler, to ensure that ancestral directives are followed, the Ọba ruled that "the deceased man's body was neither to be honored by the Yorùbá family and friends, nor were village practitioners to attend any rites offered on his behalf." He made clear that "Òyótúnjí did not have and could not invent a space for dishonorable death." Instead, identifying other places where the body should be disposed, the Ọba made clear that the body was not to remain in Òyótúnjí and that it should be sent to the family of the deceased in either Atlantic City, New Jersey or Philadelphia, Pennsylvania. "We must see beyond our emotional reactions and human desires," he insisted. "He [the deceased] allowed the spirits of evil to win his soul, and honoring his life would be like honoring the spirits of evil, and that would only cause his spirit further turmoil in the next life."

The popular villager response, however, was contrary. Given that where there is power, contestations of power are always present, the friends and relatives of the deceased who lived in Òyótúnjí mourned the loss of their compatriot. Disappointed in the traditionalist prohibitions against suicide, they reacted by arguing that Yorùbá American practitioners who are victims of the extremes of poverty and oppression should be honored with new and different rituals relevant to African Americans. This position was dismissed by the Ọba as not in keeping with traditional Yorùbá approaches.[1] In reaction, they attempted to lobby for the application of the textual funeral rites relevant to contemporary circumstances.

Even with personalized sorrow and objections to the application of canonical traditions as recorded and published in historical texts, the existence of written documentation, as proof of traditional authenticity, prevailed as the basis for identifying archaic Yorùbá practices. It is important to note that if practitioners disagreed with a given divinatory interpretation, they tended not to contest it publicly. However, debates concerning which textually informed aspects of "tradition" should be fully adopted and which should not be applied to their daily regimen took place highly structured in political forums, in small talk during work duties, and in between ritual activities. With the absence of Yorùbá funeral rites, by the eighth day the fallen man's estranged family in New Jersey received and entombed his body and held a Christian burial for him.

Òyótúnjí practitioners confront problems resulting from hegemony, agency, and interpretation using divinatory directives that reconfigure histories. The leader of Òyótúnjí Village had to undermine the villagers' desire to revere the deceased body as a disavowal of his power. He took the opportunity to emphasize pre-existing normative, legitimate ritual acts and to punish other acts as deviant, as unacceptable. Underlying the fundamental tenets of Yorùbá traditionalism is the belief that practitioners should dispose of their worldly possessions to protect the integrity of their African community and their racial group, thus propitiating the ancestors through ritual and sacrificial acts. With this underlying principle, the human body is not simply an extension of the individual: the body belongs to the spiritual and human triad—the community, ancestors, and the individual. Suicide is not only not a sacrifice, but is a desecration of power, a mockery of the chains of succession within which the body lives. These rules shape the types of knowledges and histories that constitute different types of subjectivities under which those in power govern. To disobey the rule is to disobey the power of the leader. Therefore, the basis for selecting who or what social practices will be revered or forgotten is embedded in particular rules of social conduct that are extensions of these normative practices. The criteria are connected to hierarchies of governance and operate in particular hierarchies of scale by which acts are evaluated. Within these hierarchies of power, practitioners and the governing elite negotiate daily the life of the community, maintain a differentiated hierarchy of traditional rules and history, and give meaning and substance to what constitutes history in the modern present.

To understand the various ways the symbols of Africa and slavery are employed by Yorùbá revivalists to make sense of anthropological renditions of the Yorùbá past, it is necessary to highlight the local networks of power and knowledge within which agents actively cultivate relationships between the past, present, and future, the here and the there, and within the simultaneous conflation of the temporal and the spatial. These complexities of locating an originary historical narrative complicate the capacity of the imaginary by shaping the micropolitics of belonging in particular ways. What I refer to as geotemporality reflects this self-conscious assertion of distinctly different chronotopic experiences posited against modernist standards of constructing reality. Operating in deterritorialized modes of contact, resignifying origins in both nationalistic and counternational terms, geotemporality is a process of redistributive enactments through which particular individuals recast time and space in a different form of chronological succession and use the power of vindication to assert different types of moral subjectivities. This process of articulation points to the limitations of European modernity as just one terrain in which particular linkages are drawn in relation to European formations. In different contexts, however, especially in which there exists a moral force that motivates different forms of classifications geotemporality is productive of the suspension of order and the creation of spaces of exception in which innovations occur.

These transformations are possible with the mobilization of different chronologies and spatialities that produce new mechanisms for charting counternormative approaches to measuring reality. By demonstrating how particular agents aligned with normative practices gain the power to operate in domains outside of particular normative geographies, my goal is to demonstrate the institutional means by which temporally and spatially contingent rules of conduct are differently established within the territoriality of the nation and circulate outside of it. Such an inquiry brings to the fore the dubious role of literary institutions in facilitating the standardization of identity, and therefore in shaping the criteria for the transformation of governmentality from regimes of slavery, to precolonial orality, to modern forms of nationalism. Within these changing domains, the determinants for which practices are constituted as legitimate are directly connected to the ways that domains of knowledge are authorized as foundations of social practices.

The development of Yorùbá cultural revivalism was one such effect of new commonsense notions of Africanness as African Americanness. Revivalist claims to an African past, a village as a site of traditionalism, were connected to scholarly treatments of localized villages. Yorùbá revivalism in the United States can be usefully explored by examining how, with the modernity of print capitalism, particular standardizations of group homogeneity were produced out of the management of a body of discourses that aided in the documentation of African and African American culture and history. Thus, the use of this textual knowledge and of successive publications to set the terms for traditional prescriptives for the present is reflective of genealogies of power that framed ideologies of national and ethnic subjectivity. By exploring the emergence of discourses about transatlantic Yorùbá slavery among Yorùbá revivalists, we see how the circulation and spread of early European literary institutions and their role in shaping the canonical authority of Yorùbá revivalism has been critical for understanding why particular versions of the Yorùbá past have become dominant features of transatlantic historical cartographies. Studying the relationships between the intellectual production of data on Africa and the ways it has been used by those within and outside of the African "homeland" points to another circuit of cultural production reflective of the complexities of globalization today. For while most scholars agree that race and diasporic origins may shape practices conducted by dispersed populations, they also argue that these factors neither fully constitute the practices, nor do they define the totality of their subjectivity (Martin Shaw 1995; Rofel 1999; Gilroy 1993a, 2000). With so much of the popular twentieth-century African diaspora literature privileging race-based origins and not the ideological work engaged in constructing ways of reading race and descent, scholars often locate identity as embedded within the individual. However, it is becoming increasingly important to recognize the institutional formations that form ideologies and shape how identities are seen. These formations of knowledge have the effect of shaping identity in relation to the institutions through which people work to make meanings legible.

This chapter has three parts. In the first, I begin by asking how a new zone of Yorùbá cultural production emerged in Nigeria as a consequence of British colonization and Christianity. I look briefly at the standardization of a particular type of Yorùbá nationalism as an ideological and political force in which European colonial forces deployed particular forms of modernity which had the effect of contributing to the already developing formations of a sense of Nigerian national identity as a formal identity. This nationalist project, which was set in motion by Christian missionaries, had its greatest impact in the ideological (and not simply economic) domain.

The next two sections unfold with two key examples of how early ethnic and national identities were shaped by large communities of liberated slaves in Brazil, Cuba, and Sierra Leone who resettled in Yorùbáland. The first example demonstrates the politics of constructing a particular Yorùbá canon from which New World practitioners incorporate notions of authentic practice. To understand the role of various literary institutions in facilitating Yorùbá transnational linkages in the late twentieth century, and to understand how individuals use them to facilitate dominant forms of revivalist governmentality, the second section explores another form of change: the contemporary politics of changing the Yorùbá canon through the retelling of transatlantic slavery. Written texts, like oral narratives, which circulate through acts of interpretation, not only undergo significant historical variation, but also incorporate particular temporally linear forms of hegemonic symbolic capital. Such formats, mediated by the very modern codes of legitimacy that shape their intelligibility, create the colonial subject as a participant in the documentation of his or her past. By using two ethnographic examples that demonstrate how new temporalities and spatial readings are used by Yorùbá practitioners to incorporate while also violating British colonial written codes, we see how geotemporality works; new institutional histories of Yorùbá ancestral linkage are reconceptualized by revivalist priests and clients who produce variation from written histories using particular temporal and spatial invocations in order to vindicate and redeem. Even as Òyótúnjí practitioners' use of the Nigerian historical classics represents their search for an ancestral past, their adaptations are just as strategic as they are symbolic and highlight their alliances within institutions of hegemonic power. Yet although these innovations are not always in keeping with dominant norms of print capital, they hold power through the commutation of disenfranchisement from slavery to redemptive formations. These shifts, represented through reconfigurations of modern temporal and spatial codes as the basis for shared historical origins, take shape in abstractions of governmental power. These transnational reconfigurations of citizenship are culturally and historically embedded. The critical distinctions are among the incorporation of written narratives, the use of orality to narrate redemption as the centerpiece incremental change, and the traditional forms of state governance and management as they compare to the forms of rule that Foucault referred to as governmentality, or modern regimes of power where people are citizens of a state and respond to state domination but where the operative form of domination reflects people's contact with knowledge technologies—in this case a "history" through which to shape individual practice.

Colonial inscriptions of Nigerian Yorùbá history have played a critical role in promoting some narratives of the past over others. Approaching the production of knowledge in terms of the hegemony of Nigerian state building alone will only demonstrate how some discourses carry the force of institutional power. Instead I situate all histories as representations of innovations on multiple levels over time—highlighting what constitutes history, what is disregarded as history, what people reproduce as their history, and what elements are borrowed from historical canons and must be recognized as deeply enmeshed in the politics of capitalist modernity, governmental management, and self-regulation. For if history is useful insofar as it provides us with a point of reference for understanding long-standing social relationships, then exploring the complexities of reinventing history and its uses is equally critical. In contemporary revivalist communities such as Òyótúnjí, the leaders have similarly prescribed an "authentic" history of the Yorùbá, one of the early histories written over a hundred years ago. But rather than focus on a sustained search for the authentic past, we need to examine the relationship between written histories and those created by historians, local elite, and individuals in their particular contexts. This is the task that modern scholarship on the Yorùbá has traditionally set for itself, following Hayden White's (1973) suggestion that "history is not a matter of 'truth,' but of the choice of a particular expository style that is itself determined historically."

The benefit of treating written texts in the same way we approach oral tellings is that it allows us to recast our conception of written texts as objects to explore the production of authenticity within changing historical forms. By examining the forces of legitimacy that shape what gets to count as traditional Òyó history, we can see how the Òyó nation in the eighteenth century was propelled by social, colonial, and literary institutions that brought together individuals who shared similar sociopolitical and linguistic capital. As such, the formation of the category of people subsumed under Òyó dominance came to be known as Yorùbá. Nevertheless, as an ancestral sign of both political prestige and a place from which captives of war originated, the concept of Yorùbá identity changed over time. British colonial literary institutions, as they worked in alliance with early Nigerian scholars, played a major role in the standardization of these conceptual organizations in written historical texts. This development of modern literacy was a means of assembling knowledge in particular ways. It contributed to interrelationships between European regimes of knowledge and power and various assemblages of local knowledge.

In this vein, I turn to two sites of Yorùbá cultural production to demonstrate how power operates internally by inducing people to aim for what Foucault (1988) referred to as "self-improvement," which may seem to be voluntary. The first is the history of the demise of the Ọ̀yọ́ Empire that led to nation building in colonial Nigeria; the second is the development of a Yorùbá community in Ọ̀yọ́túnjí Village that uses nineteenth-century colonial history to reconstruct its ancestral past. I highlight these two cases to examine the way that the same written history has been used differently in two locales and has been shaped by convergent and divergent relations of symbolic and material power. The power relations embedded in each community have given rise, out of the same texts, to inventions of belonging that have markedly different spatial and temporal contours and that demonstrate how history making is inextricably bound to institutional domains of power. The following is an exploration into the historical formation of institutional mechanisms that shaped and legitimated global Yorùbá linkages. That the vision of the Ọ̀yọ́ Empire has transmuted into a concept of African American heritage and has legitimated the management of new leaders is a statement of the production and uses of particular mythic conceptions of nobility in relation to connections of racial order. Seen thus, we see how the transformations in management and governing play out with the changing forms of interaction among state authorities, exports, practitioners, and private agents.

Literacy, Enlightenment, and European Modernity

In northern West African cities such as Katsina, recorded history extended as far back as A.D. 1000; however, what little has been recorded about the Yorùbá of southwestern Nigeria prior to the nineteenth century exists only in the eyewitness accounts of early missionaries and travelers who wrote cataclysmic descriptions of warfare and empire rule. In villages along the West African coast, as in other early societies prior to the eighteenth century, when writing was unknown or where only a minority of people—clerks, bishops, the wealthy classes—were engaged in the reading and writing of texts, the art of oratory flourished (Barber 1991; Akínnasọ 1981, 1982, 1992). The nucleus of daily knowledge emerged from the ritual authority of the local chiefs, and social values were reproduced and encoded in the form and content of oral genres such as songs, divinatory verses, mythic tales, and adages (Goody 1975). Embedded in a complex system of multilayered rule, members of the quotidian class gained knowledge through collaborations with diviners, elders, and governing councils.

By 1838 European missionaries, explorers, traders, settlers, and government officials of the colonial regime stationed in Yorùbáland worked on stabilizing preexisting treaties for commercial and political alliances.[2] These inquisitors documented preexisting social spheres with the goal of gaining dominance over political and economic resources as well as religious moral orders. Conversion to Christianity and the development of individual relationships with missionaries involved the substitution of indigenous superstitions with the grandeur of various technologies, including clocks, books, and compasses. Many relied on parallels with indigenous occult or magical beliefs to employ what seemed to be comparable magical technologies of knowledge for the sake of achieving political influence.

The Ẹ̀gbá and Ifẹ̀ chiefs, representing prominent Yorùbá-speaking clans in the southwestern region of Yorùbáland, were known to have welcomed missionaries and incorporated new techniques of knowledge forms to achieve victorious political ends. Among those who attended Christian educational institutions during the mid-nineteenth century and eventually converted to Christianity, most adopted Christian principles through the force of new technologies of institutional knowledge. These technologies of literary knowledge were used to establish the moral grounds on which particular types of modern subjects were produced. Notions of liberty, justice, and individual accountability to society and the nation were shaped with the development of Nigerian civil society. People working in Christian missions planted seeds of nationalism as a way to transform the region; early converts to Christianity were introduced to the goals of nation building in Europe, first by Christian missionaries and then by British officials.[3] However, many envisioned black self-government independent from colonial rule, arguing that they were fit to represent themselves in the international arena.

Despite African participation in Christian missions, there was considerable disagreement among missionaries about whether it would be more effective to teach Christianity to those often classified as "uncivilized" people, or whether it would be best to "civilize" them first. If the latter, many felt that with the acquisition of European civility Africans would evolve in such a way that they would "naturally" become Christians — something the Europeans thought they could not learn without this training (see Samuel Annear, 1844, "Journal of a Visit to the Encampment," Badagry, Methodist Archives, London). With discourses of civility as a central component of Christian conversion, both British missionaries and African converts proselytized with the goal of eradicating native traditional ways and implementing new moral practices. These practices formed the basis for the development of legal codes by which both converts to Christianity and nonconverts were expected to abide.

Yorùbá missionaries contributed centrally to the widespread understandings of Yorùbá life through their participation in transforming modern Nigerian nationhood. By the late 1800s, Christian missions were key revolutionizing institutions that further propelled the formation of the Nigerian colonial state in newly forming regions. Among the Yorùbá, the once prominent gods known as the òrìṣà and organized around ideas of ancestral continuity and reincarnation gave way to a mass movement of Christian conversion in the non-Muslim areas of what was to become the southwestern region of Nigeria.[4] In the south, the transformation was slower and the reaction of òrìṣà practitioners and royal monarchs to missionaries often depended on personal and political incentives that in some cases were achieved by building alliances with British colonial forces. As a result, Africans exposed to literacy adopted various forms of knowledge, thereby participating in spreading literacy throughout parts of Yorùbáland.

To participate in what was increasingly seen as a Christian civilizing mission, more Christian missionaries migrated from Europe to the newly developing British colonial nation. The changes, though propelled by Christian missionaries and later by British colonial institutions, contributed to the processes of nation building. The eventual penetration of late-nineteenth-century Christianization was facilitated by nation-state building and print capitalism. For although the spread of literacy was facilitated by the expansion of Christian missions, the role of colonialism in the development of Nigerian statehood served as one of the key facilitators of the colonization of the Yorùbá.

In southwestern Nigeria, where the historical trajectories emerged out of various forms of British colonization, the symbolic and violent dominance of that relationship was distinct from the conditions of European expansionism that produced plantation slavery in the Americas. The regimes of appropriation, constituted by hierarchies of governance, were differently situated in relation to borders, boundaries, and possibilities of return. The cartographies of diaspora that persist today, although cloaked with narratives of transatlantic slavery, are those of intra-African dispersals in which new imperial maps were drawn to reflect different political patterns of European governance. Confronted with the political violence of the African colonial and postcolonial state, the standardizing logics of modernity and globalization shaped a political machinery in parts of Africa that contributed to the idea of Africa outside of itself, in relation to the West (Mbembe 1992). As such, contemporary reformulations of Nigerian national boundaries and overlapping spatial demarcations that merge difference and sameness are both local and global, deterritorialized and hybrid, overlapping and divergent.

These new processes of production were deployed through a range of social, economic, and legal-political institutions. As Fabian (1986) demonstrated in *Language and Colonial Power*, Swahili, the language of trade in East Africa, was imported to the Congo region and imposed as a national language on its subjects. In that example we saw that language is not just a signifier of cultural internal meanings. What circulates through new forms of language are ideological structures of power marked not simply by internal systems of signs and meanings, but by the hierarchies of power as they demonstrate the relationships among intended meanings, available language choices, and the degree to which the symbolics of speech are conjunct with the geopolitics of place.

Under indirect rule, the British annexed coastal towns and subdivided kingdoms to promote colonial governance. Nigerian chiefs, working under new forms of governance, assisted in the enforcement and imposition of governing regulations, the collection of taxes, and the documentation of social life. The political economy of the growing British regime along the coastal areas eventually penetrated formerly dominant Yorùbá administrative districts. This included the establishment of Nigerian civil society that, in theory, separated the state from religious rule and led to the eventual British takeover of the region now known as Nigeria. Nevertheless, British direct rule in the early twentieth century reduced the authority of the former chiefs and undermined indirect colonial governance by replacing it with indirect mechanisms of governmentality. This turn of governance was maintained by British economic control of resources and land and played a central role in the development of the new governing institutions that shaped Nigerian civil society.

With the growing development of national colonial institutions, print capital served as a useful technique of governance. It involved the circulation of particular notions of civil society that were enmeshed in principles of Protestant Christianity: the institutionalization of particular ideas about the redeemable individual in relation to society that presumed human life as embedded in linear properties of succession. This development of notions of subjectivity in relation to civility set new standards for a critical arena of knowledge acquisition that involved the training, governance, and accountability of the subject and had the consequence of circulating certain forms of European bourgeois moral codes.

Scholars such as A. B. Ellis (1894) and Leo Frobenius (1913) were among the first Western social scientists instrumental in writing comprehensively about the Yorùbá people. In their attempt to trace the origins of the Yorùbá to migration patterns from ancient Egypt, they set the framework for a genealogy of Yorùbá descent that persists in both formal and informal origin stories today. With the circulation of knowledge, spread through these developing secular and nonsecular literary institutions, populations were enumerated and classified and racial codes were legitimized as constituting fundamental differences. The shift from indigenous approaches of governmentality to principles of civil society involved the replacement of clan accountability with individual accountability to both God and the law. Despotic rulers were given new jurisdiction over populations, and new moral standards were used to police their subjects. Individual actions were legally constituted in the language of individualism, choice, justice, and accountability. Notions of life and death, and their related rituals, were taken from the domain of the community, becoming matters of the state and the law. Practices such as human sacrifice and suicide were outlawed; instead, particularly in southern Nigeria, new notions of the individual and society were recast in the formation of a secular state that rested on Christian temporalities and Protestant moral codes.

In the process of establishing a secular nation, Nigerian colonial government officials eventually adopted new codes for defining national ethnic identities that conflated preexisting linguistic, ethnic, and religious affiliations. The regions invested in nonsecular governmental rule, such as that of the Muslims in the north, eschewed the idea of a secular non-Muslim government. This exclusion of the presence of Islam in Nigerian state building is a critical example of the way Protestant webs of power are established along ideological governmental alliances.

Recent approaches to theorizing modernity in Nigeria have highlighted modernity's role not only in contributing to the production of standardizing mechanisms, but also in pointing to the production of human evolutionary differences through the use of scientific approaches to racial subjectivity. British colonial nation building, fueled along racial lines, involved the creation of distinctions between African subjects and British citizens.

In local contexts, stratifications in identity distinctions grew out of the 1914 amalgamation of the three British colonial districts constituting the new Nigerian nation. This new entity, a country with over four hundred indigenous languages among 110 million people (Akínnasọ 1989, 134; see also the study by Hansford, Bendor-Samuel, and Stanford 1976), dealt with the challenges of defining a contemporary Nigerian nation. This 1914 amalgamation was also met with a range of stratification differences by religious faith, precolonial communities, alliances according to ancestral cities, and òrìṣà patron gods and family totems (Laitin 1986, 16). Attempts were made to foster the expansion of the three major languages: Hausa (22 million speakers), Yorùbá (20 million), and Igbo (17 million). These language groups represented 53 percent of the population (Akínnasọ 1989, 135). The

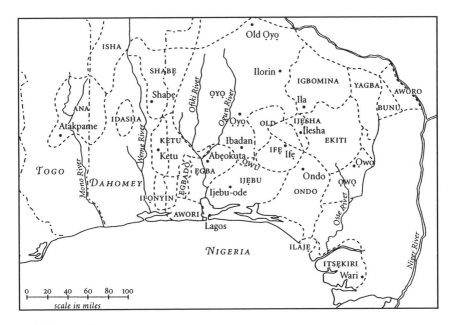

Archaic map of Nigeria.

1979 post-Independence Constitution emphasized the learning of English in addition to one of those major languages and in addition to the individual's "mother tongue" (138).

The goals of linguistic pluralism and of English as the official language of government created conflicting models of language emphasis. Throughout the colonial and postcolonial nation-building process, English became the language of mobility, and the use of other indigenous languages declined in educational contexts. For example, even though the 1987 Nigerian federal electoral literature was published in all three of the official languages, the vast majority of daily federal business at the time was conducted in English. Ultimately, the dominance of English and the secondary status of the indigenous languages led to social language hierarchies; the consequence was that the government promotion of colonial world languages as the language of politics relegated to the educational system the teaching of Old World "official" languages. The stratification of these languages had profound effects on the symbolic use of the Yorùbá language and on social status in Nigeria. The data suggest that English fluency was seen by the Ọ̀yọ́ traditionalists as "modern" and "progressive," and that indigenous languages such as Yorùbá were seen as reflecting an older, more "primitive" tradition. The consequent use of language to mark social status was also abetted by international pressures resulting from British colonialism and the predominance of state and federal legislature and administration in English. Today, the prevalence of English in Nigeria reflects the standardization of English as an international language of trade and commerce.

These forms of differentiation and reorganization have implications for how we understand the role of literary institutions as facilitators of governance and accountability. For such distinctions in the production of national identity were germinal, not so much to the way that Samuel Johnson was to circumscribe the Yorùbá as unified, but to forging the basis for racial difference and establishing the virtues of honorable behavior for the communities of the diaspora in the twentieth century. Yorùbá returnees reproduced Ọ̀yọ́-dominant histories that led to the normalization of particular practices. These, in turn, shaped the ways that Yorùbá revivalists, in an attempt to institutionalize placement in displacement, adopted colonial grand narratives about the Yorùbá past from which they generalized about Nigerian society as a whole. This construction of a Yorùbá ethnic identity was a process brought about in large measure by the development of various institutions of state power that shaped the basis for ethnic difference.

Missionary Returnees, Print Capital, and the Circulation of Moral Subjectivities

Prior to the nineteenth century, neither a unified national identity nor a linguistic identity known as Yorùbá existed under such a name.[5] Nineteenth-century linguistic categories that were subsumed under either Yorùbá or Hausa governmental enclaves were eventually subsumed under the domain of twentieth-century categories of Nigerian nationhood. By the mid-1800s, many former enslaved captives returned as freemen to their countries of birth from locations such as Sierra Leone and Brazil. Much of the impetus toward the formalization of written Yorùbá, as well as the translation of Yorùbá oral texts into English written texts, and English into Yorùbá, was driven by the involvement of returnees who participated in developing national institutions (Matory 1999). With the temporal and conceptual ordering that Christianity offered and after many years of British training, these early Yorùbá missionaries, once sold to white European traders, were schooled abroad and converted to Christianity. One such missionary was Samuel Crowther (1968). Freed by a British intercepting ship in 1822, he, along with thousands of other captives, was taken to Sierra Leone, where he became an Anglican missionary. Upon returning to his homeland, he participated in building early literary institutions by publishing the first history of Yorùbáland. In 1843, Crowther was instrumental in the development of a Yorùbá orthography, setting the roots for a writing system that continues to be used in Nigeria today and has led to the

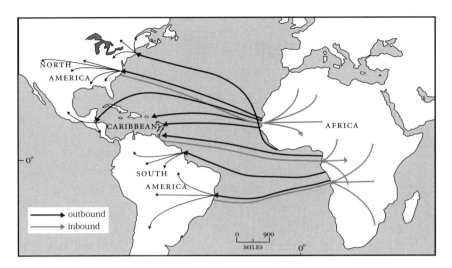

Slave trade and return travel routes. This highlights the back and forth movement between Africa and its sites of dispersal.

standardization of Yorùbá as a language. The process of standardizing Yorùbá as a written and translatable language involved the merger of the Ẹ̀gbá lexicon with a predominantly Ọ̀yọ́ morphology and syntax (Ajayi and Crowder 1972, 1973; Matory 1999). The result was the formation of an official language that resembled the dialect used by a range of men from the Lagos ex-captive returnee communities to the Ọ̀yọ́ political elite. There is significant evidence to suggest that most Yorùbá speakers who were once under the rule of the Ọ̀yọ́ Empire of the early nineteenth century saw themselves as distinctly Ẹ̀gbá, Ìjèbú, Èkìtì, or Ọ̀yọ́; thus, most subjects of the British Crown claimed to belong not to the newly developing colonial state but to a standardized ethnic category under which Nigerian national identity was constituted.[6] With the formalization of the Yorùbá language, Crowther greatly influenced the ways members of the Church Missionary Society used Yorùbá and therefore legitimized it in British colonial spheres of power. Other projects on which Crowther and his colleagues embarked included the formation of Christian educational institutions, training institutes, and venues of higher learning, such as colleges, which added to the hierarchies of knowledge and separated the learned scholars from the nonliterate classes.

Though it is Samuel Crowther who is credited with popularizing the name Yorùbá, many Yorùbá returnees and freed slaves played critical roles in standardizing Yorùbá ethnicity and developing the infrastructure for various institutions of knowledge. They formalized land deeds, produced taxation papers, translated the Bible, and adopted British historical formats using budding scholars who documented and incorporated local lore and myth in modern scientific investigations, creating innovative approaches to producing historical knowledge.[7]

Two early English publications included a list of the kings of Lagos since the late eighteenth century, documented by Reverend C. A. Gollmer in 1877 under the title *Historical Notices of Lagos, West Africa*. Another, prepared by Reverend J. B. Wood and published in 1879, charted the history of Lagos from its origins to the 1861 British annexation. These publications, written by a small pioneering elite, circulated as authorial documents about Nigerian history. One of the first publications by an African writer was Olaudah Equiano's *Interesting Narrative of the Life of Olaudah Equiano, or Gustavus Vassa, the African*, published in England in 1793. This work reflects on the cruelty of slavery as well as the perpetuation of it as a system of capital accumulation, yet it holds in tension both an ironic defense of slavery as well as an account of the horrors of Equiano's experiences of it. The text highlights his experience first as the owner of a domestic slave in Africa, and then as a captive transported in a slave ship to the Americas.

Nigerian returnees also included such people as John Ọlawunmi George (1897), John Augustus Payne, and Samuel Johnson, who played key roles in revering the history of what would become southwestern Nigeria and the cultural politics of Enlightenment and Christianity, critical forces in the transformation of the Nigerian colonial state (Matory 1999; Falọla 1993; De Moraes Farias and Barber 1990) and the early development of ideological principles of civil society. To document early nationalist history, they became teachers and linguists, contributing to the newly forming Nigerian literary community.

John Augustus Payne, an Ìjẹ̀bú native and former captive who was exiled in Sierra Leone, returned to Yorùbáland and produced a comprehensive study published in the 1890s. In the years following his return to Yorùbáland, he served in the British administration in Lagos, where in 1893 he published *Table of Principal Events in Yorùbá History*, and, from 1874, published annually the *Lagos and West African Almanac and Diary*. Similarly, as a member of one of the early societies of educated young men, John Ọlawunmi George, also a returnee who had been exiled in Sierra Leone, lectured locally, eventually becoming a prominent Lagos-based Christian merchant. In 1897, he authored a short book about the history of the Yorùbá from their origins to the Yorùbáland wars of the 1800s. His work described the Yorùbá ethnic groups—the Ẹ̀gbás, Ketu, and Ọ̀yọ́—as homogeneous, "of one stock" (18), and described the Yorùbá Empire as a kingdom that incorporated many tribes and countries and was destroyed by invasions by Fulani Muslim groups. Although George's historiography attempts to generalize about Yorùbá history, it is regionally shaped and based on the power and uniformity of the Ọ̀yọ́ Empire and not the differences within it.

Reverend Samuel Johnson, a native of Ọ̀yọ́ and also a former captive freed in Sierra Leone, was educated in missionary schools facilitated by the Christian Missionary Society (CMS). His *History of the Yorùbás* (1921) became one of the most authoritative publications written about the Yorùbá of southwestern Nigeria. Inspired by his interest in highlighting the role of Christianity in promoting changes in traditional practices, it was a story about Christian redemption and served to formalize popular knowledge about Yorùbá traditions. It is no surprise that the historical and intellectual canon to which global practitioners, tourists, and a range of historians in the Americas refer includes his works alongside those of his contemporaries, sociologist N. A. Fadipe (1970) and American anthropologist William Bascom (1969a, 1969b, 1980).

Along with other literate Yorùbá returnees and members of the late-nineteenth- and early-twentieth-century intellectual classes, Johnson participated in the shaping of the burgeoning historical canon that came to be characterized as Yorùbá history. But it was through the influence of various institutions, such as publishing houses, schools, and missionary establishments, that there developed ethnic categories within which distinct forms of differentiation prevailed. With the shift in the economy from mercantile to early capitalist monetary systems of exchange and with the rise of print capital, the determinants for what was published and by whom were connected to a highly selective political and economic process governed both within and outside of the colony. Additionally, because of the magnitude of racial discrimination that fueled the conceptual apparatus within which Johnson and his colleagues worked, they were both within and outside of colonial institutions.

Johnson's (1921) *History of the Yorùbás* presents examples of how new and differentiated fields of knowledge were legitimated under conditions of British governmental influence and within the specificities of local Yorùbá politics. It was with the displacement of older forms of indigenous governmentality with the influx of British colonial institutional power, emphatically coded in racial difference, that new forms of knowledge merged with international power. Notions of racial difference in colonial Nigeria were not free from Protestant institutional moral injunctions and global codes of ordering. By reproducing these Christian injunctions, Nigerian nationalists superimposed their goals onto preexisting kinship and linguistic alliances. And because race did not supplant these alliances, the axes onto which racial distinctions were forged converged in the newly shaped religious-ethnic relations.[8] In transforming oral histories into literary texts and translating English literary texts into Yorùbá, these elite classes of scribes and missionary returnees adopted British epistemological approaches to initiate changes in various forms of indigenous knowledge. This, in turn, contributed to significant changes in the lives of village societies along the West African coast in which traditional conceptions of ethnic and religious identity shifted into differentiated identities. Such differentiated subjectivities were constructed with distinctive values and performed different purposes, as evidenced in the publication of Johnson's groundbreaking work. An analysis of the Christianization of Yorùbá history, as reconstituted by early Yorùbá scholars, moves us away from the overt politics of ethnicity, race, and nation. Instead, as *The History of the Yorùbás* illustrates, looking at this past through the lens of British imperialism produced the illusion of Yorùbá homogeneity in the context of heterogeneity. Yet, by privileging black solidarity, and thus demarcating racial difference, revivalist practitioners reconstruct the temporal geography of the Nigerian past as they create new distinctions within it. These politics take shape through the strategic uses of historical texts and have great import for understanding not only the site of variability in textual documents, but also the ways that institutions of power shape the mechanisms that legitimate knowledge. For if the mechanisms of power that, through written texts, led to the symbolic production of a unified concept of the Yorùbá people were facilitated by the development of international print capital, then the twentieth-century development of literary institutions was also influenced by the absence of literary regional differentiation and the temporal underpinnings characteristic of the modern liberal subject. At the core of this Yorùbá literary canon used by African American practitioners is a politics of difference, even as they depend on the symbolism of black homogeneity.

Slavery, Colonialism, and Institutions of Power

In the shift from predominantly oral forms of communication to colonial governance, where writing was central to the authority of knowledge, the structure of technologies of print capital contributed to the production of literary institutions. The development of these institutions of modern knowledge fueled the massive processes of social change in modern Nigeria. These institutions set organizational standards for documenting truth and knowledge, thereby leading to the legitimation of Nigerian history as textually documented and temporally specific. This, in turn, played a critical role in establishing the forms of knowledge that were necessary for the legitimacy of Yorùbá revivalist communities outside of Nigeria. Communities of revivalist practitioners interested in reclaiming Yorùbá practices as their own and establishing rules of Yorùbá governmentality outside of African contexts adapted this work within accepted discourses of historical science and truth. They borrowed from the institutional symbolic power of British colonial governance, which played a critical role in ordering, standardizing, and ultimately circulating knowledge about particular types of colonial subjects. This form of subject formation was not only constituted from a diverse African past but was prominently resituated in the transition from orality to written texts and through a colonial governmental apparatus organized around the science of objective inquiry, intensive documentation, and the possibility of uncovering a knowable subject. Ultimately, these processes of defining new subjectivities across geographic space and time were regulated by particular dictates of nation building that shaped both temporal and spatial determinants for classifying belonging and determining appropriate behavior in relation to it.

The central issue is that the factors for determining which practices and histories are worthy of historical endorsement constituted the basis on which revivalist norms were shaped in institutions of power. By incorporating modern techniques of science and knowledge from which modern subject formations were developed, Yorùbá revivalists in the United States actively shaped the basis for producing new identities. But this process of invention is not a new phenomenon. The influence of transnational forms of knowledge in Nigeria—the shift from indigenous oral forms to accessible circulating literary writings—facilitated the generative locus of power and led to the privileging of Ọ̀yọ́-Yorùbá ancestry as the popular literary icon of African American revivalism. Embracing the growing significance of late-nineteenth-century scientific inquiries deployed by native-born Africans, Nigerians participated in the documenting of human sciences and thereby contributed to the invention of a particular type of "Yorùbá history." The production of these histories took shape with the participation of large numbers of formerly enslaved Yorùbá-speaking men and women from various parts of southwestern Nigeria, especially the Old Ọ̀yọ́ region. The newly developing Yorùbá elite, who, in documenting Nigerian history, were themselves inserted into British colonial regimes, challenged not only the politics of historical representation but also the preexisting formations of values and principles that rested in Ọ̀yọ́-Yorùbá relations of power and knowledge. This process, mediated by the temporalities of modern subjectivities, led to the standardization of "the Yorùbá" as we know them and was allied with the development of the Nigerian nation. These subjectivities, intellectually framed in relation to an Ọ̀yọ́-Yorùbá historical imaginary, were recorded, published, standardized, and ultimately circulated from literary texts to new oral forms and continue to form the basis for black American Yorùbá revivalist populations.

In examining changes in social meanings over time, it is important to locate the sites of variability and to question why they exist as such. What changes must take place and which canonical tenets must remain the same for new meanings to be seen as legitimate? In identifying transnational mobility and the consequent mixing that emerges, we must necessarily distinguish the ways emergent identities are facilitated by various techniques of governance that allow for particular forms of cultural production and delimit others. For to understand how some national or ethnic reclassifications or forms of citizenship are accepted as legitimate, we must understand how, based on contemporary codes of classification, they are already allied within particular fields of power. These fields are embedded in historically complex webs that code geographic and temporal meanings in particular ways.

Anthropologist Jack Goody (1977) has speculated that the shift from orality to written language engendered a shift from the creative fluidity of oral knowledge to a recorded canon of stored and linear information within which incremental knowledge could be added. He argued that orality led to more variability than is permitted by literary texts. The debates concerning the extent to which written texts lend themselves to new interpretations, and variability within them, are not new to anthropological studies of culture and power, but they have significance for understanding the role of literary institutions in the production and maintenance of transnational cultural citizenship. Goody's explorations have great import for theorizing transnational negotiations of cultural belonging as facilitators of new forms of knowledge. However, it has long been demonstrated that he overestimates the degree to which literacy is linked to learning (Akínnaso 1992). For even as interpretations of oral traditions that circulate locally may give analysts the impression that orality provides the intellectual ease with which new histories can be forged, written texts are extensions of the interplay between written and oral knowledge and often accommodate the circulation of global meanings, even as they are in tension with them. But these articulations are not just narratives without consequences; they are mechanisms for producing the conditions of relations between people. Therefore, the reinterpretation or restructuring of narratives leads to the production of competing narratives that also contribute to the production of collective memory. Where there are competing narratives and consequent social crises, we see most explicitly how both the uses and the value of orality and textual documentation have critical social consequences. Thus, in the next section I focus on another omission that has long pervaded anthropological work: that of the influences of global circulations of knowledge classifications in shaping both oral and written production in ways that reconstruct different taxonomies for deriving membership and rendering it legitimate. The ways we think of citizenship and membership is one such example.[9]

The Making of Historical Institutions and the
Politics of Difference

Several centuries ago, Ọ̀yọ́ managed a splendid political system which was remarkable for the way it balanced power between the Aláàfin, the King of Ọ̀yọ́, and representative assemblies, the Ọ̀yọ́ Mèsì. Ọ̀yọ́'s political system has especially appealed to students of the political sociology of ancient Africa because it achieved an uncanny system of accountability in which noblemen of the Ògbóni Chamber as well as the King of Ọ̀yọ́, the Aláàfin, were fully answerable for their public behaviors. Such a tradition was manifest in the famous institution of royal suicides by which the King of Ọ̀yọ́ was compelled to take his life if his acts of governance were gravely abusive of the public interest or if he were defeated by an enemy. It was the ultimate expression of the norm of accountability in ancient Africa.

All these remarkable achievements were ruined when Ọ̀yọ́ plunged itself into the Atlantic slave trade, becoming a major source of supply of captives for the evil trade. Slave raids into neighboring ethnic groups could not satisfy the demands for captives; it was a matter of time before the violence of the slave raids turned inwards, as members of many non-royal groups became victims of the slave trade. As violence begot violence, Ọ̀yọ́ imploded in a fierce civil war in the early part of the nineteenth century.

The story that I wish to share with you was set in these circumstances. Soldiers from an Ọ̀yọ́ satellite town, ruled by a Bale, a feudal lord, were pressed by their leader into the civil war. They lost. Rather than being taken as prisoners of war, as it would be the case in [these] times, they were now sold into the slave trade. Six of these soldiers—all grades of them: general, horsemen, foot soldiers, and of different ages—found themselves as slaves in a Caribbean sugar plantation. One afternoon, as they labored in the field, three new slaves were brought in to join them. One of the ex-soldiers looked up to observe these new labor recruits. He then cried out: "Oh no, oh no, oh my God: It is the Bale himself." The others joined him in this emotional recognition of their ruler back home in Yorùbáland and Ọ̀yọ́ nobility and commoner, all now slaves, wept together at the fate of their fallen ruler and their fallen civilization. None of them knew of the fate that had befallen their wives and children and relatives at home. But each of them had paid a heavy price for the mismanagement of Ọ̀yọ́'s public affairs.

Ọ̀yọ́'s misfortunes in the nineteenth century should provide us with a parable from which to examine Nigeria's current predicament. Ọ̀yọ́ was not conquered from outside its realm. It collapsed under the weight of its own mismanagement. It had a lot going for it. It could have resolved its problems internally through dialogue and its own tested institutions. Instead it chose the violence of the slave trade. And it destroyed itself.—Peter Ekeh, "A Case for Dialogue on Nigerian Federalism," keynote address to the Wilberforce Conference on Nigerian Federalism

This excerpt was part of an introductory speech delivered at a meeting on Nigerian federalism and represents a popular narrative explaining the demise of the Ọ̀yọ́ Empire and the forces that led to the enslavement of Ọ̀yọ́ people by European traders. The narrative emerges from a dominant historical account of Ọ̀yọ́-Yorùbá history that articulates the birth and demise of Ọ̀yọ́ greatness central to òrìṣà voodoo reclamations of Yorùbá practices in the West. Using parallel renditions of the Ọ̀yọ́ past, Yorùbá revivalists locate their originary moment both in the creation of Ifẹ̀ and in the particularities of their deterritorialized condition in the transportation of captives of war to the West. Ọ̀yọ́túnjí revivalists tend to reproduce this past as their own using the textual words from Samuel Johnson's (1921) *History of the Yorùbás*. Its narratives of origins, demise, and dispersal serve to legitimatize their linkage to Ọ̀yọ́ royalty and to explain their condition outside of Africa.

The historical range of Johnson's book spans a period that exceeds four hundred years. Using mythic tales and historical documentation, his account of preeighteenth-century wars and successions, practices, and customs was based on the lore of the Yorùbá people. Submitted to a publisher in 1899, Johnson's manuscript was neither published nor acknowledged as received. After Johnson's death in 1901, his brother reconstructed the lost manuscript using the notes left behind. Not only does the correspondence between Yorùbá intellectuals suggest that gaining access to publishing resources was extremely difficult, but the mysterious disappearance of Johnson's manuscript suggests that there may have been attempts to subvert the publication of a text focused on specific details of Yorùbá life.

Johnson's process of recording Yorùbá history was to systematically document information in relation to scientific approaches to causation and consequence. His intellectual effort was in alignment with both Protestant aspirations for humanity and the principles of Western Enlightenment.[10] Identifying ancestor reincarnation as based on the primitivism of the old ways, he relegated Yorùbá deities to the category of myths and lore. With the eventual publication of *The History of the Yorùbás*, along with historical analyses of earlier writers, the emergent Yorùbá canon formalized the institutional terms by which Ọ̀yọ́-Yorùbá history would be consolidated as Yorùbá history for an increasingly interested international audience.

Johnson charted the story of the decline of the Ọ̀yọ́ Empire as taking place prior to the British takeover of western Nigeria. He detailed the Ọ̀yọ́ Empire as being at its height from the early eighteenth to the early nineteenth century. The empire was ruled by, as he described it, "a ruthless *Aláàfin*" (king) who collected tribute from the kingdoms that he annexed (including groups such as the Ẹ̀gbá, Ẹ̀gbádò, Nàgó, Aja, Ewe, Adangbe and the Gã). Johnson's reproduction of this history is an attempt to clarify the concentric circles of Yorùbá lore by recasting the history of the Yorùbá through the lens of historical objectivity, and it is central to his struggle for representation in the burgeoning British colonial state.[11] The passage that I will analyze is an attempt to explore how the history of what was to be the Nigerian nation was shaped not simply by members of excluded and marginalized groups. Rather, the historiography of the Yorùbá, which formed the foundation for the historical canon that circulates today, emerged from individuals who belonged to a developing ethnic group whose narratives of the past expressed the characteristics of Protestant liberal values central to British colonial governance. In Johnson's account, the dishonorable acts of jealousy by the Ọ̀yọ́ prince, Abíọdún, led to Abíọdún's alliance with "outsiders." This alliance, Johnson explains, eventually led to the weakening of the Ọ̀yọ́-Yorùbá political and military apparatus, governed by King Aolè.

Charting a historical trajectory of flaws in the execution of Ọ̀yọ́-Yorùbá ancestral succession, Johnson explained that the region known today as Nigeria dates back to a period more than two thousand years ago. This was a time when Nok cultural practices flourished and where, in A.D. 1000, the Hausa kingdoms and the Bomu Empire prospered as centers of trade between North African Berbers and the local forest dwellers. The Dahomean kingdom was established two hundred years later, and the Ọ̀yọ́ and Benin kingdoms four hundred years after that. Subsuming both the Benin and Dahomey kingdoms between the seventeenth and the nineteenth century, the Ọ̀yọ́ kingdom rose to its heights during the eighteenth century, becoming the Ọ̀yọ́ Empire, thereby achieving high levels of political government.

The demise of the Ọ̀yọ́ Empire ruled by the Ọ̀yọ́ monarch, King Aolè, began in 1796, and the last Yorùbá empires finally toppled with the 1821 conflict that led to the Òwu Civil War and the Fulani Muslim takeover of the region known as Old Ọ̀yọ́. The southward migration of Yorùbá refugees to Ìbàdàn, Abẹ̀òkúta, and surrounding regions resulted from internal slavery and warfare and was later followed by British colonial and missionary penetration along the coasts and cities. Marking the tragic end of the Ọ̀yọ́ Empire as beginning with quarrels concerning kinship succession and the loss of honor, Johnson linked the rise in the Islamic crusade of the nineteenth century (which led to the formation of an Islamic center of governance in the Nigerian northern city of Sokoto) to the internal problems of egocentrism and the loss of noble honor among Yorùbá subjects. Explaining the succession with metaphors that described the rise and fall of the Ọ̀yọ́ Empire in linear terms, he detailed how the revolt at Ìlọrin was the manifestation of Àfọ̀njá's success at mobilizing local and foreign (read: Muslim) armies to overthrow the Aláàfin of Ọ̀yọ́.[12] Arguing that it was the problems with succession that led to the downfall of the Ọ̀yọ́ Empire, Johnson demonstrated that none of King Abíọ́dún's sons succeeded him on the throne. Instead, it was King Abíọ́dún's cousin, Prince Aolẹ̀, who was elected as Aláàfin rather than King Abíọ́dún's eldest son, Àfọ̀njá. King Abíọ́dún's son was given the title Baṣọ̀run, but as a prince (through his mother's line) the new title was below the rank that he had already achieved. Therefore, he rejected his given title and demanded the highest military title, Kakanfò the Àfọ̀njá of Ìlọrin, which he claimed by force.[13]

For Johnson, it was Àfọ̀njá alone who was depicted as the king's enemy. Johnson explained that King Aolẹ̀'s actions were intelligently calculated because to have mishandled the situation would have led to an even more destructive situation — and probably civil war. In the passage that follows, Johnson represents the death of Kakanfò Ọyabi as the beginning of the end of Ọ̀yọ́ governance.[14] Explaining that the Ọ̀yọ́ Empire was under siege by insubordinate forces, he states:

> Several weeks passed and they were still encamped before Ọ̀yọ́ irresolute as to what they should do next. At last an empty covered calabash was sent to the King—for his head! A plain indication that he was rejected. He had suspected this all along and was not unprepared for it. There being no alternative, His Majesty set his house in order; but before he committed suicide, he stepped out on the palace quadrangle with face stern and resolute, carrying in his hands an earthenware dish and three arrows. He shot one to the North, one to the South, and one to the West uttering those ever-memorable imprecations "My curse be on yea for your disloyalty and disobedience, so let your children disobey you. If you send them on an errand, let them never return to bring you word again. To all the points I shot my arrows will yea be carried as slaves. My curse will carry you to the sea and beyond the seas, slaves will rule over you, and you, their masters will become slaves.

The trope of the fracturing and dispersal of slaves represents the symbolic splintering of the Yorùbá people due to their lack of honor and their consequent display of greed and egocentrism. The calabash is thus symbolic of the popular perception of the homogeneity of the Yorùbá, and the dispersal of its pieces is a reflection of their enslavement and disenfranchisement. The rise and fall of the Ọ̀yọ́ Empire reflects dominant renditions of the ways the Yorùbá have come to be seen popularly: as a homogeneous group that was "invaded by strangers." Johnson's narrative of Yorùbá sameness was shaped by his deployment of Yorùbá unity and Muslim difference, for his classification of Muslims as invaders further reproduced a meta-narrative about Yorùbá homogeneity that located the concept of Yorùbá Muslims as a contradiction in terms, reinscribing particular tropes of Ọ̀yọ́-Christian inclusion and Islamic marginalization. However, there were five modern-day Nigerian provinces—Ìbàdàn, Ọ̀yọ́, Abẹ̀òkúta, Ìjẹ̀bú, and Òndó—that were home to multicultural subgroups of Yorùbá-speaking people. The residents of these subgroups had related, though at times distinctly different, dialects.

Shifting the Literary Terms of Yorùbá Origins

Despite the fact that Ilé-Ifẹ̀ is the city popularly represented by most scholars as the birthplace of the Yorùbá, Samuel Johnson (1921) enacted his version of the origins of the Yorùbá people through a number of literary constructions that charted Ọ̀yọ́ as the force of Yorùbá greatness and noble honor. Many late-nineteenth-century historians and early-twentieth-century sociologists tended to adopt one of the following versions of Ọ̀yọ́- or Ilé-Ifẹ̀-centered prominence narratives.[15] Not only does this approach make secondary the symbolism of Ilé-Ifẹ̀ as the birthplace of modern Yorùbá, but it further reinforces age-old rivalries between Ọ̀yọ́ and Ilé-Ifẹ̀.

One narrative posits that the mythic god Odùduwà settled in Ilé-Ifẹ̀, having arrived from the Far East. Odùduwà's children and grandchildren dispersed throughout Yorùbáland; over centuries, they became the rulers of the many Yorùbá kingdoms. Johnson is among those who decried this history and instead argued that the origins of Yorùbá culture began at Ilé-Ifẹ̀, where humankind was created, and that the Ọ̀yọ́ Empire was the site of Yorùbá prestige. The second narrative places Ọ̀yọ́, and not Ilé-Ifẹ̀, as the site of Yorùbá prestige and reign. Although by recasting the birth of Ilé-Ifẹ̀ as a home place for the Yorùbá, and Ọ̀yọ́ as the place where the Yorùbá exercised power and flourished, both narratives maintain that Ilé-Ifẹ̀ was the place where the Yorùbá people came to see themselves as a unified people.[16] What distinguishes the two narratives is that the first posits Ilé-Ifẹ̀'s prestige as a product of the colonization of the Yorùbá by "outsiders": Muslims. In the first version, Johnson decentered the mythic personage of Ilé-Ifẹ̀ onto Mọrèmi, the mythic wife of one of the ancient heroes of Ilé-Ifẹ̀, and Odùduwà. Thus, instead of endowing Ifẹ̀ with the prestige of origins and, therefore, a more prominent martyrdom, Johnson contributed to the construction of the symbolic imagery of Old Ọ̀yọ́, and not Ifẹ̀, as the place of Yorùbá greatness. Johnson claimed that the figures of Mọrèmi and Odùduwà, respectively, were actually Jephtha and Ọ́rànyàn, the deified mother and father of Ọ̀yọ́, whose two sons, Àjàká and Ṣàngó, succeeded them and became famous in the history of the Ọ̀yọ́-Yorùbá people. By making animal sacrifices to the gods of Ifẹ̀ and sacrificing her only son, Ṣàngó, Johnson shows that Mọrèmi protected the people of her town from the repeated raids of competing outsiders, such as the Igbo tribes. This act made her a heroine of the Ilé-Ifẹ̀ nation. By decentering the importance of Mọrèmi, Johnson is able to foreground the deification of Ṣàngó, the patron òrìṣà of Ọ̀yọ́, and highlight the centrality of Ọ̀yọ́, and not Ilé-Ifẹ̀, as an icon of the Yorùbá past.

Second, Johnson's description of the spatial and political organization of Ilé-Ifẹ̀ contrasts with his description of the grandeur of the king of Ọ̀yọ́, the Aláàfin, and renders Ilé-Ifẹ̀ secondary in grandeur to Ọ̀yọ́. According to Johnson, the Aláàfin of Ọ̀yọ́ lived in an exquisite palace surrounded by his administrators and nonroyal servant residents. The government and social structure were based on a hierarchy of political officials, an Ògbóni cult, diviners, and a chief priest of Ifá. This is not true of his description of Ilé-Ifẹ̀.

Third, although other historical accounts attribute the downfall of the Ọ̀yọ́ Empire to a range of factors, Johnson indicts Àfọ̀njá for causing the Òwu War which led to the eventual invasion of Old Ọ̀yọ́ by the Fulani. Ultimately, it is Àfọ̀njá's ruthless egotism that Johnson sees as the primary cause. In Johnson's account, Àfọ̀njá's greed and recklessness led him to do almost anything, including inviting Muslim Fúlàní and Hausa foreigners from the north to join forces with him to wage a war against King Aolẹ̀. For Johnson, not even the symbolism of King Aolẹ̀'s metaphoric curse, a symbol of the enslavement and dispersal of the Yorùbá people, was a dishonorable form of retaliation. Rather, he blamed Aolẹ̀'s actions on Àfọ̀njá, for, according to Johnson, the homogeneity of the Ọ̀yọ́-Yorùbá government was wrongly dismantled as a result of the 1810 revolt at Ìlọrin.

Finally, Johnson not only construed Àfọ̀njá as the main cause of the Òwu War, but he identified the events surrounding the war itself as the leading cause of the Ọ̀yọ́ Empire's downfall. In depicting the Òwu War as the source of the fragmentation of the Yorùbá people, Johnson upheld Ọ̀yọ́ as the primary hub of both Yorùbá origins and demise. Àfọ̀njá's actions, such as joining forces with external Islamic powers at the beginning of the Òwu War, were represented by Johnson as indicators of greed and disrespect for empire, while he describes King Aolẹ̀'s deliverance of the deadly curse and act of suicide as heroic martyrdom.

Contemporary Yorùbá historians have noted that a range of factors, such as shifts in mercantile consumption, British colonialism, and the growing power of the Hausa states in the north, contributed to the demise of the empire. This history is not without contemporary importance beyond the claims of Yorùbá historians and Ọ̀yọ́túnjí practitioners, for these origin narratives of both Ifẹ̀ and Ọ̀yọ́ reflect the residual consequences of the demise of the Ọ̀yọ́ Empire over the past 150 years and are connected to the most recent Ifẹ̀-Modákẹ́kẹ́ crisis of the 1990s in Nigeria.[17]

As the explanation goes, despite their birth in Ifẹ̀, the Modákẹ́kẹ́ people neither belong as legitimate Ifẹ̀ people, nor do they see themselves as Ifẹ̀. They continue to claim Ọ̀yọ́ as their originary home, and to Ọ̀yọ́ they should return. These ongoing contestations over belonging are connected to the meanings of people's claims to membership in relation to perceptions of the legitimacy of the power to authorize those claims.

The existence of different regimes of power highlights the distinctions between the spheres of power that coexisted with the writing of late-eighteenth- and nineteenth-century histories, British interventions into Yorùbá governance, and the role of social narratives that seek to explain the legitimacy of placement and displacement. The intersection of these regimes of power define the parameters within which individuals determine relations of belonging. The symbolism of emphasizing the "once homogeneous, ever powerful Yorùbá Empire" and the consequent dispersal and/or enslavement of Ọ̀yọ́ men and women form the nexus of Yorùbá strength and power, rather than the alternative narrative of Ifẹ̀ power, and emphasize the centrality of Ọ̀yọ́ as a form of empowerment for those otherwise seen as having marginal claims to various regions: Modákẹ́kẹ́s and Yorùbá revivalists. Johnson's motive for placing Ọ̀yọ́ at the site of prestige might stem from his own status as the grandson of King Abíọ́dún.

The Ifẹ̀-Modákẹ́kẹ́ crisis in late-twentieth-century Nigeria continues to highlight the originary homeland of the Ọ̀yọ́-Modákẹ́kẹ́s and their migration as refugees from Ọ̀yọ́ as a result of their defeat in nineteenth-century warfare. For Ọ̀yọ́túnjí practitioners, claiming Ọ̀yọ́ provided an opportunity for legitimating their connection through their slave dispersal and, therefore, their nobility based on their connection to King Aolẹ̀ and his royalty. Unlike Johnson, however, Ọ̀yọ́túnjí uses of Ọ̀yọ́-centered Yorùbá history has produced an insistent desire for redemption by which individuals realign themselves with the West African past. The prevailing discourse, as is often the case in oral narratives, describes a narrative of anteriority in which, before the demise of West African empires, Africans were once noble kings and queens. These discourses provide possibilities for reconceptualizing the literary production of Yorùbá origins and its transnational metaphors of dispersal as constitutive of the ways that slavery and histories of dispersal can be detached from geographical space and symbolically rerouted to different places. These metaphors are articulated through temporal and spatial convergences, and for the purposes of legitimizing their connection to the honor and prestige of the past, Òyótúnjí practitioners lay claim to Òyó ancestry, therefore repositioning black Americans (and not simply white European slave traders) as complicit in their own enslavement.

In "Forms of Time and of the Chronotope in the Novel," Mikhail Bakhtin (1981) examined how time and space fold into each other in specific literary genres. He explored the diversity of chronotopes (literally, the simultaneity of time/space) and their varied representations and especially discussed chronotopes in relation to the hegemony of form. One component of the chronotope, time, takes on diverse forms: cyclical time and linear time. Cyclical time is reoccurring and locates events outside of the standards of human mortality as we know it. Linear time, on the other hand, lacks cyclicity and ties perceived reality to the human scale. Space, the other component of the chronotope, is changed with the movement of time and is used to define place in terms connected to the perceived relative stability of the written form. Such chronotopes, although reversible and interchangeable, carry with them a degree of cultural specificity that limits the ways new social rules order interpretive logic (Stewart 1996, 11; Irvine 1996, 258; Gilroy 1993a, 199; Bakhtin 1981, 84). These specificities of form and structure influence the cultural codes that individuals use and thereby explain as well as legitimate their states of "being." However, even as forms of time change from linear to cyclical and space to particular meanings of place, both the written and spoken word are characterized by an intrinsic connection, albeit abstract, between spatial and temporal narrative techniques. It is the chronotope that Johnson and other Yorùbá returnees transformed to shape new perceptions of Yorùbá history. This chronotopic incorporation of modern British peculiarities of linear time and abstract space produced not only new codes with which to interpret social norms but also what I refer to as a geo-temporality for the innovations, by which new measurements of belonging were established and vindicated.

Ultimately, the codes of modernity that took shape in Nigeria involved the drive for nationalist fervor, an ideological separation of linear time from cyclical time, and a three-dimensional responsiveness of space to the recognizability of place. But it is not simply orality that was subjected to this form of variation; rather the opposite. The ideological reconfiguration of state-based civil society, shaped by the peculiarities of modern life, transformed precolonial African governance into an international bourgeois order secured within the capitalist relations that shaped it. The scope of civil society and the developing nation-state shaped its legal, political, economic, and educational orders, among others, on the fixity of modern chronotopes. The contemporary manifestation of this invention has become so abstract that the chronotopic variables that in the past century radically remade the "real" did so in such a way that they achieved the homogenization of time as linear time. Written texts gained meanings from the standardization of distinctive expectations of stability and virtues of truth through the structure of textual authority. As a result, narratives of civility, morality, and honor, as they were embedded in the written histories of the Yorùbá, were, even with their Africanized resonance, structural extensions of European modernity.

The goal of unifying analytically the global importation of modern European organizational principles with local social and political action is to demonstrate how everyday practices follow the same spatial and temporal conjunctures of the past and how the specificities of local history shape the particularities of interpretive variation. These chronotopic variations, which ultimately set the terms for different relations of belonging, are geotemporal. They represent people's processes of employing chronotopic connections to reconfigure "reality," against which they recast European modern chronotopes and reuse them in order to rework them. These complex practices, dialogic and dialectical, have implications for governmentality, that is, for the forces of power that shape the determinants for how people's lives should be lived on a daily basis. Although individuals engaged in related geotemporal processes are intentionally participating in distinctive acts of normative reconfigurations, they do so by building on the very principles and forms that they are undermining in the first place.

The Ọba of Ọ̀yọ́túnjí Village and his constituents in South Carolina and throughout the United States are no different. In an attempt to recast their membership in Africa, they also employ chronotopic techniques that are interwoven with modern rules and order. These chronotopic strategies shape their world through the incorporation of the familiar of everyday life into a world partially unfamiliar to them. Despite these disjunctures, they use particular concepts of identity and racial subjectivity that not only emerged out of the history of European modern nation building, but also structure their everyday life. These concepts are interwoven with contemporary rules of order in ways that blur the binary of "real world" and "imaginary."

By employing taxonomies of racial difference to claim black homogeneity across national boundaries, Yorùbá revivalists reconstruct Yorùbá territorial attachments to a particular historical teleology through the reorientation of institutional mechanisms. These new identities tie chronotopes of modern human life to the temporality and spatiality of an ancestrally detached world as a mechanism by which the basis for black American reclamation of their "homeland" was established.

Revivalist Governmentality:
Conduct and Spatial and Temporal Linkages

One summer day, an open-air town meeting (known as an Ọbanjòkó) was announced.[18] The beating of the drums accentuated the imminent appearance of the main speaker, the Ọba of Ọ̀yọ́túnjí Village. Dressed in white and pastel colors with traditional *lapas* (cloth that women wear around the bottom of their bodies) and head wraps, with Ọ̀yọ́ tribal inscriptions etched on their faces, giggling girls and chattering young women gathered chairs for the impending event. The evening air thickened with the smell of the oncoming rain. As the rain started to fall people quickly entered a nearby building, known as the community leisurely hangout, the Ọ̀yọ́-Horseman.

The low chattering stopped as the community members gathered into the main courtyard and the Ọba entered the room. A senior chief opened the session, commanding loudly in Yorùbá, "*Dìde* [All rise]!" Everyone in the room stood up as His Majesty, Ọba Adéfúnmi I, the Ọba of Ọ̀yọ́túnjí, walked into the room. A relatively small, light-brown-skinned man, accompanied by his right-hand chief and royal wives, dressed in cloth of royalty, walked in proudly. He sat on an elevated chair in the front of the room and faced his community members. The session began with the pouring of libation followed by vows to the leader and the Yorùbá nation. The members declared their allegiance to the king, with fists outstretched and bodies erect. They shouted a series of words in unison, first in Yorùbá and then in English, lagging behind others, each one looking sternly at the Ọba and the display of artifacts at the front of the room. At the conclusion of the pledge, the Ọba's right-hand chief commanded that the audience take their seats. He addressed the audience, reviewing the order of events and using formal language, sometimes struggling with Yorùbá, sometimes in formal English.

Once the introductory rituals were completed and the relations of power and allegiance established, the leader prefaced his opening message by announcing the results of the divinatory "reading of the week" conducted a day earlier and posted on the side of the building: "So our reading this week indicated that we suffer from uncontrollable egomania. That in essence we could wind up destroying the very thing we are trying to build because of ego. Ego is that characteristic which all human beings have, unless of course it can be weeded out of them through cultural habits and forms. But ego is that thing that makes you think that you are really hot stuff. Ego is that thing that makes you think you are too big, too great, to endure any kind of rebuke or refusal, or that people will not pay you maximum attention and honor."

Upon establishing his legitimacy through the symbolic power of ancestral communication, the Ọba proceeded with his speech by linking the problems of greed among the elite in Ọ̀yọ́túnjí to Samuel Johnson's textual description of the greed and egocentrism that led to the fall of Old Ọ̀yọ́. To demonstrate how Johnson's account of King Aolè's death, and therefore the downfall of the Ọ̀yọ́ Empire, had prophetic consequences that were directly linked to their American community, he recounted Johnson's tale of King Aolè relinquishing his power: "So the result of it was that King Aolè went out and took with him a huge vase—a ceramic vase. He took with him a huge ceramic vase and he took four arrows. He went out and he pronounced his famous curse to the Yorùbá people. He shot one arrow to the north, to the south, to the east, and to the west, and then he took the vase and held it up and smashed it to the ground. And he said, 'As a broken calabash can be mended, but never a broken vase, can never be mended, it is smashed into thousands of fragments.'"

Demonstrating how the dispersal of Yorùbá slaves was central to the linkages between the enslavement and dispersal of the prisoners of war of the Ọ̀yọ́ Empire and black Americans whose ancestors were sold into transatlantic slavery, he continued: "'To the directions in which I have shot my arrows, to the north, to the west, to the east, to the south, may the Yorùbá people be carried as slaves. May they send their children out on errands and never hear from them again. May slaves rule over them and they become slaves.' And then having pronounced his famous curse, as the high priest of the nation, which is what the Ọba is, this was like the servant of all of the Gods denouncing the people whom the Gods were supposed to protect, or who is to guide people to find ways of protection from the Gods. After he had smashed his vase and shot his arrows he went into his chambers and took poison and died, never retracting his words."

These excerpts demonstrate how the leader of Ọ̀yọ́túnjí used geotemporal approaches to transform the codes of modern subjectivity. This approach to recasting belonging outside of the temporal distinctions of Nigerian citizenship involves a reconfiguration of transnational symbolic linkages between Africa and the Americas, the past and the present. Though this innovation was legitimized using both divinatory oral and written sociological texts, laying claim to the authority of literary institutions, the orator used modern codes to produce interpretive variations. These codes—slavery as the basis for connection, techniques of orality for community, and literary and divinatory sources as geotemporal domains of governance—demonstrate how another generation of individuals whose ancestors were formerly enslaved in the Americas may, although differently situated in relation to the Ọ̀yọ́ Empire, substitute their identities with different chronotopic sequences with which to establish recognizable codes of belonging.

Slavery and Race as the Basis for Connection

Among some black Americans interested in claiming Yorùbá ancestry, Johnson's descriptions of the dispersal of slaves is a modality through which the links between Ọ̀yọ́-Yorùbá and Yorùbá revivalists in the United States are shaped. Motivated by an attempt to claim membership in relations of power, Ọ̀yọ́túnjí revivalists actively embraced Samuel Johnson's history of the Yorùbá as their own. They often extrapolated from Johnson's work not simply because his text is one of the foremost to detail the history of the Yorùbá, but because it serves as a prestigious articulation of the principles of Yorùbá nobility that enrich that history. Nevertheless, the carryover is far from invariable, for while Johnson distanced himself from the insubordinate actions and excessive pride of Àfọ̀njá the Kakanfò, thereby blaming him for forcing King Aolẹ̀ to deliver the vengeful symbolic curse of enslavement, the Ọba of Ọ̀yọ́túnjí linked its residents to both Aolẹ̀ and Àfọ̀njá.

Significantly, the Ọba's use of Johnson's text encodes racial commonalities as the basis of shared origins. This renarrativizing of Yorùbá history was connected to the Ọba's use of the symbolism of race as biology, thus shared ancestral heritage. Using a symbolism of blood, he incorporated a language of unity, emphasizing the history of Yorùbá dispersal in the Americas. In contrast, it is clear that Johnson's self-conscious racial analysis is absent in the text. He was more concerned with ethnicity and nationality as units of analysis—that is, similarities and differences of Yorùbá and European civilizations (Law 1991). At the heart of Johnson's articulations of Yorùbá membership are highly regionalized histories of Ọ̀yọ́-Yorùbá codes of behavior from which the hegemonic criteria of membership were shaped. On the other hand, the Ọba superimposed the notion of racial kinship onto the cultural, enlisting individuals to monitor themselves according to new alliances. His message demonstrated how race, thus kinship, figures prominently in the linkages between Nigerian Yorùbá and American Yorùbá revivalists. His use of the symbols of the dispersal of black people creates a racially homogeneous imaginary in the midst of a clearly heterogeneous context.

Johnson's work is interpreted for local purposes. His classification of Yorùbá identity suggests that the cultural practices of the Yorùbá of southwestern Nigeria were not reducible to shared racial or ethnic commonalities. Yorùbá were organized in units that cut across lines of ethnicity, kinship, and religious practices. The effect of Johnson's typography was to cast those who were not members of the newly developing ethnic group as outsiders. However, the Ọba's incorporation of race as kinship replaced these regional codes with a deployment of a new politics of nationhood and place. This difference in historical expression represents differences in narrative intention. It also suggests that while, on the one hand, Johnson's history details the rise and fall of the Yorùbá people in relation to the downfall of the Ọ̀yọ́ Empire and the enslavement of Yorùbá captives of war, on the other hand, it provides the chronotopic opening by which Yorùbá revivalists can claim strategic complicity in their own enslavement. That is to say, they believe that they were the hegemonic Ọ̀yọ́ leaders defeated at the hands of the Fulani. As such, the precarious mechanisms of modern values that enable the conflation of race with shared ancestral heritage are allied with a moral authority in which causality and historical consequences can be conflated and strategically substituted with grand narratives of blood and statehood.

Through the biological imagery of race, the precolonial history of the Yorùbá and the largely undocumented history of transatlantic slavery are imbued with alliances that extend beyond the imagination of the nation-state. During the early stage of his lecture, the Ọba emphasized the link between Americans and Africans in which he identified contemporary Ọ̀yọ́túnjí royalty as former Yorùbá nobility.[19] By making central Ọ̀yọ́ origin narratives and tropes of slavery the basis of their racial ancestry, the leader established and further reproduced particular types of Yorùbá subjects. He employed a narrative that connected recursive temporalities of African greed and egotism with transnational connections to African American complicity. With a profound sense of duty and charismatic presence, he connected the people of Ọ̀yọ́túnjí to those great cultures of antiquity.

In using Johnson's history, the Ọba highlighted the demise of the Ọ̀yọ́ Empire as transcendence of power—the abuse of power that ultimately led to the victory of British and Muslim colonial interests. He also blamed "outsiders" for contributing to the forces that led to the "civilization of the Yorùbá."[20] For the Ọba, vices in the Ọ̀yọ́ governing elite did not produce long-term ideological gains. His narration of Johnson's history did, however, highlight other effects of that earlier period of disruption on the current Ọ̀yọ́túnjí community. For in his talk, people in the present who "descended" from those who suffered the consequences of disagreements among royal kin were told that they were embodiments of the long-term consequences of those disagreements.

In examining the codes of governance in relation to the connections between spiritual and textual knowledge, the Ọba often called on books or ancestral designations to legitimate his assertions. By claiming divine ancestral teachings, the Ọba performed his duty within a system of authority, similar to what is mythologized in the histories of the Yorùbá Empire. With his implicit references to canonical sources, the Ọba's political authority was evident during his introductory remarks, in which he cited the established canon of Yorùbá literature and asserted it through his authority as a king. For the Ọba to adopt and produce doctrine that his membership had to follow, it was important for him to establish boundaries within which his constituency would exercise choice. This opening for how to deal with choices is connected to the second issue: personal accountability. Clearly, in the Ọba's case, Ọ̀yọ́-based nobility also extends beyond his person. His speech, like everyday oratory, was governed by codes of interpretive legitimacy that he used to modify the types of subjects and actions that he felt needed to be studied. However, to maintain his own authority to interpret history, his message was assumed to be informed by ancestral channels and historical sources. Thus, his identity was not that of a small-framed, American-born man from Detroit, Michigan. Rather, as a female resident mentioned to me in an interview, "The Ọba is a transmitter of royal Yorùbá knowledge."

Oral Techniques for Unity

Speech acts are the social practices that enable individuals to develop certain types of knowledge that, in particular contexts, overtly reference modern regimes of "truth" that shape individual subjectivity. Speech acts are embedded in referential indexical practices and are formed in relation to particular regimes of knowledge (Silverstein 1976). These regimes provide frameworks with which individuals produce particular rhetorical and historical genres of knowing that correspond to the temporal and spatial particularities of the actor in question. By shifting the temporal and spatial terrain, that is, "becoming" Yorùbá and therefore reclaiming the history of Ọ̀yọ́ nobility, the Ọba used a grammar of plurality to invoke the relevance of slavery and redemption to African Americans as critical components of Ọ̀yọ́ ancestry.

Various Nigerian Ọ̀yọ́-Yorùbá narratives of historical greatness represent people's desire for a particular type of national history. It is history that rests on the antiquity of the soil, on past lessons learned, on the wars fought and won, and on homogeneity in the midst of heterogeneity (Williams 1990). Those narratives describe how omnipotent forces from the heavens protected the people against human suffering. While they obscure the ruthlessness and eventual defeat that accompanied the transformation of both cities, these stories link the Yorùbá people to great victories of warfare and empire, conveying the power of place in designating historical belonging. They render the antiquity of its people as an intrinsic component of what constitutes national belonging. Though the Ọba's representations of shared ancestral origins among black Ọ̀yọ́ practitioners and black Americans in Ọ̀yọ́túnjí marked both a linguistic and a racial connection between the Ọ̀yọ́ Empire and the U.S. Ọ̀yọ́túnjí Village, his use of linguistic markers such as "we" and "our" instead of "I" and "my," the selection of possessive markers to convey the link between the archaic Yorùbá of the Ọ̀yọ́ Empire and the community assembled in the room, was a critical geotemporal technique.

Further, the Ọba used Johnson's imagery of King Aọlẹ̀'s arrows dispersed in many directions to signify the scattering of the Yorùbá people to the four corners of the earth. This metaphoric dispersal posits the existence of their Yorùbá homeland as a shared homeland from which Ọ̀yọ́túnjí practitioners believe they were expelled and which they have symbolically reclaimed. Such a notion of diaspora and home is a dominant paradigm in the lives of many African Americans in this movement. Ọ̀yọ́túnjí villagers often refer to places in Africa as home and identify phenotypically black people in America as Africans; as such, the notion of a physical return to Africa is not essential. Instead, the ritualization of transnational identity provides Ọ̀yọ́túnjí practitioners with a sense of belonging.

Despite Yorùbá revivalist claims to African belonging, however, many Ọ̀yọ́ Nigerians employ narratives of slavery as a means to distinguish black Americans as ancestrally similar but culturally different. An example of this is reflected in the following speech made by a Yorùbá man from southwestern Nigeria as he introduces the king of Ọ̀yọ́túnjí Village to his Yorùbá compatriots. Here, he qualifies the basis on which membership as African is granted by marking particular elements of ritual engagement that have created the conditions in which Ọ̀yọ́túnjí membership and royalty should be seen as legitimate. The passage describes the king of Ọ̀yọ́túnjí as a legitimate member of Yorùbá royalty:

—Ladies and gentlemen. . . . The West African coast was named by the Europeans according to what they got there. You have the Grain Coast, Ivory Coast, Gold Coast, Slave Coast. It was the Slave Coast that was off shore that you have the people called the Yorùbás. It is a symbol of aspirations and loss and I won't get into the whole history that caused the loss and shipment of thousands of Yorùbá across the Atlantic. Instead, I am gratified to have the honor of introducing His Royal Highness Ọba Oseijeman Adéfúnmi I.

—He was born James Knight on October 5, 1928 in Detroit, Michigan, USA. He graduated from Cass Technical High School. He began African studies at the age of fourteen. He withdrew from Christianity at the age of sixteen to explore his quest of the gods of Africa. His first exposure to African religion was during a brief association with Catherine Dunham Dance School at the age of twenty. He traveled to Haiti the same year and founded the Damballah Wedo ancestral temple in Harlem.

—In August 26, 1959, he became the first African American in American history to become initiated into the òrìṣà voodoo African priesthood with

Afro-Cubans at Matanzas, Cuba. This marked the beginning of the spread of Yorùbá religion and culture among African Americans.

—After the dissolution of the temple of Damballah Wedo he founded the Ṣàngó temple, which was relocated and renamed "Yorùbá Temple" the same year. He introduced the *dashikí* and began a small-scale manufacture of African attire in the summer of 1960. He founded the Yorùbá Academy for the academic study of Yorùbá history, religion, and language in 1961. He published *The Yorùbá Religion, The Yorùbá State*, and *The Yorùbá Origins*. He participated in black nationalist rallies throughout the 1960s.

—He was interested in establishing an African state in America by 1972. In the fall of 1970 he founded the Yorùbá Village of Ọ̀yọ́túnjí in Beaufort County, South Carolina and began the careful reorganization of the òrìṣà voodoo priesthood, along traditional Yorùbá lines.

—He was initiated into the Ifá priesthood by the Oluwa X at Abẹ́òkúta. In August 1972 he was proclaimed "*AlÀSE Ọbà*," and made the King of Ọ̀yọ́túnjí in October 1972. He started an official Ògbóni parliament [a council of land owners] in 1973. And later that year he founded the Ìgbìmọ̀lóṣà, the priestly council, to organize laws and rules and to adjudicate disputes among Yorùbá priests. Also in 1972, he commenced the construction of the Osaginyan Palace. He has been called the father of the African Restoration Movement.

—In June of 1981 he was sponsored by the Caribbean Visual Arts and Research Center of New York to present a paper at a conference of òrìṣà voodoo priests at the University of Ifẹ in Nigeria.

—He was presented to his Very Royal Majesty, King Opode . . . I, the Ọ̀ọni of Ilé Ifẹ who ordered the Ifẹ chiefs to perform initiation rites on him. Ọba Oseijeman Adéfúnmi I became the first of a line of New World Yorùbá kings consecrated at and to the Ọ̀ọni. He was presented with a special ceremonial sword of steel. In fact, the name of his leopard totem is the emblem and right to speak in the name of the king of Ifẹ.

—In the fall of 1993, he became the Arába of Ija Ọrúnmìlà, the African American Ifá society. He became the only official representative of 100 years of the history of Africans.

—Ọba Adéfúnmi is presently married to four queens. He has fathered twenty-six children. He has designated and contributed the major finances to most of the public buildings. He is responsible for the establishment of Yorùbá temples in New York, Chicago, Los Angeles, Philadelphia, Milwaukee, Indiana, Georgia, North Carolina, and South Carolina. He has initiated

300 priests into the òrìṣà voodoo, Ifá Eshu, Ọbàtálá, Yemọja, Ṣàngó, Ọṣun, Ògún, Ọya, Balógun.

—He has restored with African Americans the ancient rights of *gèlèdé*, voodoo, and the ancestor worship.

—Audience: *Kábíyèsí!*

—His coat of arms is the rampant golden leopard with an ankh in one paw and a sword in the other. The leopard is an emblem of African royalty. In time you feel you belong to the shepherd.

—Ladies and Gentlemen, it is my privilege to introduce to you Ọba Adéfúnmi I. (Everyone in the room rises and claps as the drummers begin to drum and the master of ceremonies leads them in a four-line song.)

This speech highlights how the legitimacy of the Ọba of Ọyọ́túnjí is reflected through invocations of history of transatlantic slavery and the recognition of on-going acts of ritual that constitute the remembering and forgetting of the slave past. The details of transatlantic slavery and the ritual practices are described to symbolically attach the Ọba to West Africa. The validity of his royalty, however spatially American, is ritually contingent.

Institutions and Governance

Contestations over belonging, membership, truth, and knowledge are central to the geotemporal processes by which governance is shaped. People engage in processes of reinforcing new norms through the usage and reproduction of particular meanings; of course, these process of making, though equal in structure, are embedded in different domains of power and authority. There are critical parallels between the deceased man described in the opening pages of this chapter and Samuel Johnson's description of King Aolè's suicide. In the retelling of King Aolè's death, the Ọba of Ọyọ́túnjí articulated the determinants of what constitutes honorable death. The distinction between justifiable deaths and unjustifiable suicides may be difficult to establish morally; however, the articulation of taxonomies for evaluating the morality and virtue of some acts is deeply entrenched in particular codes of governance and individual accountability.

First, the social hierarchies of nobility and kingship as distinct from followers in Ọyọ́túnjí and in the Yorùbá Empire were narrowly defined by Ọbas and rulers. As an absolute monarch, the Ọba of Ọyọ́túnjí defined personhood by decentering individual ownership of subjectivity. As he stated, "The ego of a nation should be contained within the Ọba. He should have an ego, nothing should be denied him, and he should be above the common law." In other words, it is different for a noble king to exercise the choice to take his own life; because of the politics of hierarchy and governance, everyday citizens are not expected to exercise absolute power by committing suicide. Their actions are expected to maintain standard codes of order. Max Weber (1958, 1963) calls such authority of character and conviction charismatic authority. For Weber, in contrast to traditional authority (which relies on inherited characteristics such as birth order) and legal authority (which derives from characteristics of office), charismatic authority rests on the intrinsic attributes of a leader. Such leaders often draw their authority from different kinds of sources, such as social memory, critical historical evidence, and religious institutions, but at the heart of these institutions is their profound power to influence and reformulate people's internal logics in such a way that the structure of the life of institutions is voluntarily circulated, even as the process itself is far from voluntary. Because the Ọyọ́túnjí nework's success is shaped by the Ọba's institutional leadership, the remainder of the chapter explores the making of Yorùbá-Atlantic òrìṣà communities in relation to charismatic leaders as the foil by which to understand successful social movements such as òrìṣà revivalism. These movements, though dependent on people's participation, owe their success to the uses of particular institutional strategies by those occupying leadership roles. Ọba Adéfúnmi of Ọyọ́túnjí Village is one such figure in the North American òrìṣà movement.

Being highly stratified, Ọyọ́túnjí's social hierarchy is divided into levels that range from the charismatic leader to the chiefs, the head priest, and then the nonpriest practitioners, and finally general clients. Ọyọ́túnjí's political sphere is represented publicly as a democratic dictatorship in which the political leader, the Ọba, ultimately has symbolic as well as physical decision-making power. The Ọba, sophisticated and traditionally learned, is more commonly known by his followers both in and outside of Ọyọ́túnjí as the Yorùbá father of dispersed Africans. He claims a constituency of thousands of African Americans in the United States, hundreds of whom lived and trained in Ọyọ́túnjí and continue to be linked to the Yorùbá network. It is the Ọba who appoints all of the chiefs. As wards of the state, the chiefs must serve the Ọba and Ọyọ́túnjí kingdom. They are divided into two basic groups: those who are on his inner executive council and are voting members of the Ògbóni society, and those on the outer executive council who are not voting members of the Ògbóni society: the Ààfin chief, the town chief, and the honorary or ancilliary chief. Although not all chiefs sit on the Ògbóni, all of the members of the Ọba's inner executive, the Ààfin and town chiefs, constitute the Ògbóni.

The Ògbóni is organized around a religious-political system of governance. Unlike in nineteenth-century Nigeria, Ògbóni, a Yorùbá word referring to land-holders who participate in the central ruling council, was constructed using his-

Ọba of Ọ̀yọ́túnjí giving a speech in Washington, D.C., at a function organized by a Nigerian Yorùbá association, and in state and parading at an official event.

Chiefs of Ọ̀yọ́túnjí performing their oath to the king.

torical records. As reproduced in Ọ̀yọ́túnjí, the council is based on a form of representation in which member chiefs meet to consider and rule on issues and disputes that cannot be dealt with in smaller religious or interest-based councils. Instituted as the Ọ̀yọ́túnjí governing board of the community, the council of the Ògbóni makes all governing decisions, religious, legislative, judicial, legal, and executive. In general terms, most residents see it as serving the ancestors and their families. With the force of democratic input, each member of the council has one vote, and the Ọba, as the chief priest of the òrìṣàs and of the Ògbóni society, has the final word on all decisions. He also has the power to appoint his chiefs and to dismiss them from office, but is expected to serve his administration with the goals and well-being of all of his members in mind. The various societies in Ọ̀yọ́túnjí implement the goals of the Ògbóni on a daily basis and are answerable not only to the king, but to all of the members of the Ògbóni.

The Ààfin chiefs govern the well-being of the Ààfin or palace and oversee the affairs of the town. Their duties may involve collecting taxes and documenting the monetary affairs of the Crown. The town/district chiefs, who are also on the inner executive council, govern specific districts in the town. There are a total of eight Ààfin and town chiefs in Ọ̀yọ́túnjí, and these chiefs must be priests of an òrìṣà. Their titles reflect political positions of importance and are always described in Yorùbá: Chief Ajétunka (town chief and tax collector), Chief Ẹlẹ́ṣin (the right-hand

man of the king), the Chief Alàgbà (the head of the men's society), and Chief Oní-
Ṣàngó (head of the Ṣàngó temple). The other members include the chief priest,
who is the head of the society of priests (Ìgbìmọ́lóòṣà), the head of the women's
society (Ẹ̀gbẹ́ Mọrèmi) and the head of the men's society (Akíkanjú), the Ìyálóde
(mother of the town), the Dowpe gan (head of the work force), the Ìyá Orñtẹ́
(mother of protocol), the principal of the Yorùbá Theological Archministry, the
head of tourism, and the head of the militia.

To date, the lack of many transnational studies that examine the specificities
of cultural processes as they travel from country to country, borrowing and im-
porting and inventing new social institutions over time, highlights the desperate
need for such examinations of transnational institutions and forms of historical
knowledge that are changed and that serve to legitimize what forms of knowledge, what leadership techniques or charismatic qualities, do and do not travel and
why. Yet, these links in the study of social change should neither be posited as exceptions nor be relegated to the margins. Rather, such analyses are central to the
ways that European colonial history is fundamental to the geopolitics of making
and unmaking transnational alliances in the midst of social contestations. This is
so especially in relation to the ways individuals use competing notions of history
to produce forms of governmentality that are atypical of traditional definitions
of sovereignty. Instead, the sovereignty of state power is a myth, and it is critical to examine innovations in knowledge production as those forms of meaning
that are propelled by decentered institutions of power. Though the new histories,
especially those that structure deterritorialized networks, are influenced by older
hegemonies, they also intervene using new lines of logic.

I opened with a discussion of the community's effort to respond to the tragic
death of a young man who committed suicide because he was unable to overcome
his drug addictions. I followed with a detailed analysis of the production of canonical texts and the interpretation of those texts to return to the tragedy as a way
to demonstrate how and why, in the context of hierarchies of types of persons
and their relation to transatlantic enslavement and dispersal, Ọyọ́túnjí authorities
rejected responses to his death by suicide that would have allowed his burial with
honor and compassion in the village. Returning to the opening passage, we see
that individuals are able to use canonical histories and themes to incorporate old
forms, at the same time reproducing those forms to create new forms and innovations. Even as the Ọba entreated his followers to form a way of life intended
to reclaim a morality contrary to the egotism and shame of suicide (which sealed
the demise of the Ọ̀yọ́ Empire), he used the symbolism of suicide to discuss the
parameters of appropriate behavioral practices—that of the honor and nobility of
redemption. The differences in the exercise of King Aolẹ̀'s power and the expecta-

tions of revivalist followers are not in the contradictions. The contradictions make the differing power relations and shape the criteria for who should be revered after death. They are connected to the changing mechanisms of value, different lines of logic, that are based on the differential politics of power and the institutions of knowledge that legitimize some forms of knowledge and not others. To come full circle, therefore, we see that the Ọba does not critique King Aolẹ̀'s suicide because it is in keeping with the legitimacy of canonical authority and hierarchy. As he explained, "There is a lesson which we here have never forgotten, and that is why we try to teach royals to restrain their obstreperous egos—because we have never forgotten what happened to [Baṣọ̀run Gáhà]."[21] The Ọba referenced the historical royal figure to show how the lessons of Gáhà were relevant to members of the Ọ̀yọ́túnjí's own nobility, implying that their descent followed that of ancestral royalty.

Legitimating his lesson, the Ọba linked historical and divinatory knowledge with textual histories. In relation to the task of creating homogeneity in the midst of spatial and temporal heterogeneity, he drew on two beliefs central to the Yorùbá revivalist canon: that black Americans are intimately linked to the antiquity of the Yorùbá people, and that they carry noble blood. Through this connection, he adopted King Aolẹ̀'s curse of enslavement as a necessary consequence of Àfọnjá's dishonorable transgressions.

The authoritative sources that support Ọba Adéfúnmi I's narration of identity and history are critical for understanding the determinants of what constitutes history, how these are charted, and to what extent disjunctures and conjunctures are significant to the overall reformulation of the past. Today, contestations over the standardization of modern temporal and spatial configurations have profound implications for the ways Yorùbá experiences are conceptualized, "authenticated," and claimed by those who see themselves as the offspring of enslaved Africans and who "became Yorùbá." The interpretations of traditional Yorùbá practices and histories are numerous. Some aspects of making history are flexible; popular knowledge can be incorporated into dominant canonical ideologies and vice versa. Yet, whatever the historical norms, the processes by which individuals achieve are of utmost importance. In the case of Yorùbá revivalist practitioners in the United States, geotemporal analysis is critical for the reconfiguration of transnational subjecthood and highlight which institutions and which practices, using which moral convictions, are relevant in legitimizing the establishment of norms.

What are the authoritative sources that shape everyday meaning? In American communities where geographic rupture is fundamental to òrìṣà imagery and homeland claims, the systematic knowledge that constitutes the Yorùbá canon is mutually tied to the modern processes of shaping categoric distinctions between blackness and whiteness, life and death, civilization and heathenism, in relation to other possible approaches to ordering. And although the ordering of normative meanings is critical to the authorization of knowledge, here we see how the perceived "authentic" form is idealized and the "inauthentic" is remade into another form. The package of values present in Samuel Johnson's history is not challenged. Instead, revivalists, in this case represented by the leader of Òyótúnjí networks, use the form of the perceived authentic structure of the original to produce rectified forms that produce a new logic, a deterritorialized logic of vindication and reclamation. After the narrative is incorporated it loses its perceived flexibility through its ritualization of the making of religious knowledge. How much of Johnson's history of Òyó is relevant to Òyótúnjí practitioners and how much is part of an unrelated past is critical for understanding the role of the vindication of slavery in the reformulation of new institutional formations. The reproduction of both oral and written texts depends on the regulated unity of a shared classificatory universe. Ultimately, variation is possible under the authority of particular institutions. In this regard, the notion of Yorùbá belonging has taken on different spatial and temporal dimensions in different sites within relations of historical and contemporary power.

This process of making and remaking Yorùbá history speaks to the ways that subjectivity is reconceptualized and narrated across transnational borders and the mechanisms by which individuals form alliances with domains of power are employed. Though many members of Òyótúnjí base the authority of their worldview on the same texts whose writing was constituted at a different historical moment, the differences in relevance reflect the ways power is negotiated in different circumstances, with different criteria, and for different processes of recapitulation. The institutionalization of various normative practices used by leaders of Òyótúnjí to enforce particular articulations of modern subjectivities is connected to the referential values embedded within them that circulate within relations of power. Thus, any analysis of the intellectual production of Yorùbá nationhood in the South Carolina Òyótúnjí enclave necessarily connects to the standardization of normative parameters of the past with the interpretive politics of governance and legitimacy in the present. It pushes us to go beyond a focus on the standardization processes of colonialism and the development of state governance and to expand our focus on the ways that individuals act within, outside, and through spheres of power. It also provides us with ethnographic insights for theorizing the means and conditions under which new historical narratives are produced, reproduced, and realigned along vectors of power, thereby shaping the ideological frameworks that legitimate religious knowledge.

In keeping with the production of historical knowledge, the next two chapters explore another form of institutional power, religious ordering, in which the routinization of ritual mechanisms produces knowledge. Defining religion as a set of ideological frameworks by which people shape reality in multiple or varied temporalities, I explore the ways that diviners and charismatic leaders use religious ritual to structure normative rules. In the case of how diasporic slavery and nobility narratives are incorporated into ritual, people incorporate a moral economy of suffering to innovate narratives of the past in particular spheres of power. Here, in the process of imagining and in the execution of acts of agency, hegemonic forms are stabilized for the purposes of legitimation. This focus on the processes of institutionalizing new norms allows us to examine how variation is possible through the production of contextually relevant adaptations. It also enables us to answer the question, Why is it possible for revivalists to see racial continuities rather than discontinuities in time and space? And, in relation to the replication of culture and the production of links to the ancient and the old, it explores how, through attention to the spatial order and temporal movement of "culture" through the world, alternate ways of conceiving subjectivity are called on to produce new boundaries of òrìṣà transnationalism. As we explore these replication processes, we see that "culture" and cultural conceptions of life and death are interchangeable and, therefore, do not move along a linear trajectory from the past to the future. Rather, conceptions of the past are overlapping and, therefore, remembered, revered, and/or simultaneously linked to present and future forms of cultural production in socially relevant terms. This approach to cultural production is what I refer to as geotemporality. It is through this conception of culture and power that new conceptions of identity are produced and stabilized and take shape in complexly spatial and temporal terms.

4. "Many Were Taken, but Some Were Sent": The Remembering and Forgetting of Yorùbá Group Membership

THE END OF MAY MARKED the close of yet another monthly festival in Òyótúnjí Village. This one, the Egúngún Festival, which is usually held on the U.S. Memorial Day, is organized to remember and pay homage to the ancestors, the personal dead of practitioners as well as the unknown dead of one of the most revered cults, that of *Damballah Wedo*, which symbolizes Africans enslaved during the transatlantic slave trade and brought to the Americas. In celebrating the ancestors during the same weekend as the U.S. Memorial Day holiday, practitioners see the Egúngún Festival as a time to celebrate themselves and their survival.[1]

The festivities always involve ongoing libations, prayers, testimonials, and rituals in which practitioners dress in multicolored ritual clothes, conduct animal sacrifices, initiate newcomers into the principal cult of the ancestors, and parade their ancestral line by wearing certain masks and gowns. At the end of the inland festivities, practitioners and their families pack up their cars and drive twenty miles to the Atlantic coast to complete their ritual offerings.

The celebration attracts a range of participants: African American children, elders, male and female residents, former residents of Òyótúnjí Village who return to participate in the celebration of what some refer to as the "ancestors of their race," and potential converts. On this particular day in 1995, practitioners dressed in colorful African prints climbed out of old station wagons, Jeeps, a posh convertible, and a Mercedes Benz. The children, laden with fruits, candles, preserves, powders, and flowers, dressed in common African fabric with broad abstract designs wrapped over brightly colored bathing suits, ran from the parking lot to the edge of the water. After setting these offerings on a table in the sand, the children spent the first part of the morning swimming and playing in the warm ocean. Most

End of Ọ̀yọ́túnjí festival at the Atlantic Ocean, where practitioners make offerings to the ancestors.

of the men drank beer and played cards under the shade of trees. Different groups of women talked among themselves until it was time to distribute the potato salad and fried chicken they had brought. Five hours later, as the sun began to set, a tall gray-haired elder put on his large *aṣọ òkè* and walked toward the water. He stopped at the water's edge and bellowed a ritual invocation in Yorùbá, "*Àgò, Òdùmàrè A júbà*," as he looked toward the horizon. "We pay homage to you our god," he translated, and the practitioners around him responded with "*Gbogbo ikú*."[2] As he poured a libation, he continued the remainder of his incantation in Yorùbá:

SECTION I
Tí ń gbé lẹ́sẹ̀ Olódùmarè
Who upholds the feet of god

Response: *Ìbà ará t'ọ̀run*
Salute to the bodies of heaven.

SECTION II
Mo júbà gbogbo òkú ti ọdún láéláé
I pay homage to all of the ancestors from heaven.

Mo júbà gbogbo òkú tí ń gbé lóde Ifẹ̀
I pay homage to all the dead outside the gate of Ifẹ̀.

Mo júbà damballah Wedo
I pay homage to all the unknown dead of the race.

Mo júbà gbogbo òkú tí ó kú ní Africa
I pay homage to all of the ancestors that died in Africa.

Mo júbà gbogbo òkú tí ó kú ní òkun
I pay homage to all the ancestors that died in the ocean.

Mo júbà gbogbo òkú tí ó kú ní ayé tuntun
I pay homage to all of the ancestors that died in the New World.

Mo júbà gbogbo òkú ìdílé Adéfúnmi
I pay homage to all of the ancestors of the Adéfúnmi.

Mo júbà gbogbo ti òkú ti ìdílé Aladahunnu àti Adéfúnmi
I pay homage to all of the ancestors of Aladahunnu and Adéfúnmi.

Mo júbà gbogbo òkú ti ìdílé Òyótúnjí
I pay homage to all of the ancestors of the families in Òyótúnjí.

Mo júbà Àsàbí
I pay homage to Àsàbí.

Mo júbà Oyábádé
I pay homage to Oyábádé.

Mo júbà Péláyò Koriente
I pay homage to Péláyò Koriente.

Mo júbà Fereako Amamas
I pay homage to Fereako Amamas.

Mo júbà Itowa
I pay homage to Itowa.

Mo júbà Ògúnjobí
I pay homage to Ògúnjòbí.

Mo júbà Sanagba
I pay homage to Sanagba.

Mo júbà Òsúnbùnmi
I pay homage to Ósúnbùnmi.

Mo júbà Masemi
I pay homage to Masemi.

Mo júbà Fedi Ososi
I pay homage to Fedi Ososi.

Mo júbà Omítònàdé
I pay homage to Omítònàdé.

Mo júbà Ọbáméjì
I pay homage to Ọbáméjì.

Mo júbà Òṣúndélé
I pay homage to Òṣúndélé.

Mo júbà Omíyẹyè
I pay homage to Omíyẹyè.

Mo júbà Orìṣàtòwáṣẹ̀ Ifẹ̀
I pay homage to Orìṣàtòwáṣẹ̀ Ifẹ̀.

Mo júbà Orìṣàmòla
I pay homage to Orìṣàmòla.

Mo júbà Èṣù Zangbeto
I pay homage to Èṣù Zangbeto.

Mo júbà Ṣàngófẹ́mi
I pay homage to Ṣàngófẹ́mi.

Mo júbà Ṣàngókúnmi
I pay homage to Ṣàngókúnmi.

Mo júbà Ṣàngógùnmí
I pay homage to Ṣàngógùnmí.

Mo júbà Omítònàdé
I pay homage to Omítònàdé.

Mo júbà Nana Dinizulu
I pay homage to Nana Dinizulu.

Mo júbà Ifá Morótì
I pay homage to Ifá Morótì.

Mo júbà Adélétí
I pay homage to Adélétí.

Mo júbà Ọbálùmí Oyèyànà
I pay homage to Ọbálùmí Oyèyànà.

Mo júbà Felepe Zulueto
I pay homage to Felepe Zulueto.

Response*: Ìbà ará tòrun*
Salute the bodies of heaven.

SECTION III
Kí nnkan má ṣe Ọ̀ọ̀ni ti Ifẹ̀
May no evil happen to the king of Ifẹ̀.

Kí nnkan má ṣe Aláàfin ti Ọ̀yọ́
May no evil happen to the king of Ọ̀yọ́.

Kí nnkan má ṣe Aláṣẹ Ọ̀yọ́túnjí
May no evil happen to the power (ruler) of Ọ̀yọ́túnjí.

Kí nnkan má ṣe Babalóòṣà mi
May no evil happen to my father of òrìṣà.

Kí nnkan má ṣe Iyálóòṣà mi
May no evil happen to my mother of òrìṣà.

Kí nnkan má ṣe Baba Ifá mi
May no evil happen to my father of Ifá.

Kí nnkan má ṣe Ajubona
May no evil happen to my witness of Baba Ifá.

Kí nnkan má ṣe gbogbo àwòrò ti ilé òòṣà Ọbàtálá
May no evil happen to the priest of the temple of Ọbàtálá.

Kí nnkan má ṣe gbogbo àwòrò ti gbogbo ilé òòṣà Ọ̀yọ́túnjí
May no evil happen to all the priests of all the temples of Ọ̀yọ́túnjí.

Kí nnkan má ṣe gbogbo àwòrò tí ń fọ̀ sí wa lẹ́nu
May no evil happen to the priests who have the ability of incantation in their mouth.

Kí nnkan má ṣe gbogbo àwòrò tí í ṣe ìsẹ̀dálẹ̀ Yorùbá tí kò sí nílé
May no evil happen to all those who are working for the Yorùbá nation who are outside their homeland.

Kí nnkan má ṣe
May no evil happen to

Kí nǹkan má ṣe
May no evil happen to

Response*: Àṣẹ!*
So be it.

Jọ̀wọ́ jẹ́ kí ire
Please give us good luck.

Jọ̀wọ́ jẹ́ kí agbára
Please give us strength.

Jọ̀wọ́ jẹ́ kí orí dáadáa
Please give us a good head.

Jọ̀wọ́ jẹ́ kí ìmọ̀
Please give us knowledge.

Jọ̀wọ́ kó má rí osobo
[Let there be] no bad luck.

Kò sí ikú
[Let there be] no death.

Kò sí sí àrùn
[Let there be] no sickness.

Kò sí ejọ́
[Let there be] no unjust punishment.

Kò sí ọ̀nà burúkú
[Let there be] no bad road.

Kò sí ọlọ́pàá
Let no one have trouble with the law.

Response*: Kò sí*
No more!

A dúpẹ́ fun ohun gbogbo
Thank you for all of the good things.

"They went to meet their creator for they would not comply with their bondage," he followed in English. "And to our Santería brothers and sisters, we say thank you for preserving our heritage during slavery, but today is our rightful time for the African to reclaim his practices from you, too."

In the midst of the preliminary libation, several men and women carried additional offerings to the front of the ocean's shore. Boys and men ranging in age from two to twenty-two accompanied the proceedings with rhythmic drumbeats. As the sound of drums called the sleeping dead to rise up, the refrain "We are children of the sacrificed" echoed through the salt-laden air. The visitors swayed side to side, looking ahead of them, singing chants to their ancestors. Twenty men and women walked toward the water's edge, looking deep into the horizon, as if they were searching for the West African shores on the other side.

"Our ancestors were from those shores," another elder added as he pointed toward the eastern horizon. "Many were taken, but some were sent. The ones who survived gave birth to us, the children, Africans in America."

With this addition, he located black Africans as direct descendants of the enslaved, but signaled that some of the enslaved—select African priests, soothsayers, and revolutionaries—were chosen by the gods to join the enslaved to guide and protect them. Immediately following his last words, a visitor's child ran along the shore, yelling and pointing, "Africa is there! Africa is there!" He was quieted by his mother, who apprehended him and replied coarsely, "Yes, this water separates us from your brothers in Africa."

"My brothers . . . from Africa?" the young child asked with a puzzled and disturbed frown, not understanding the diasporic reference but questioning his mother's suggestion that he had siblings in Africa. Seemingly in reaction to the visiting boy's question, the first priest made his point clearer: "Today we pay tribute to our sisters and brothers that we never knew, the kings and queens, princes and commoners who bear no name in our history books. Our ancestors were enslaved because they were black and posed a threat to the white man. They destroyed our great empires and used us to build theirs. Today we pay homage to our enslaved ancestors. We praise them so that they can bless us."

The evening continued with themes of praise and regret. Jubilant prayer echoed in ritual serenity as the reddening sun announced its last moments in the slowly darkening sky. Six men gathered the gifts from the table and set them on a wide piece of white cloth. With the waves lapping against their wet clothes they treaded toward the evening horizon laden with offerings. The songs grew louder and filled the air with testimonial wailing. When the men could not go into the deepening water any further, they offered the gifts to the roaring waves.

Ọ̀yọ́túnjí drummers playing the bàtá drums.

The repetitive *djimbe* beat and Yorùbá chant became a trance-like refrain that filled the evening quiet with short rhythmic accents. As the groove intensified, the dancing became more elaborate. Gestures and chants symbolizing the pain and sorrow of centuries past were continually invoked in the evening's speeches, but the mood was not one of sadness. Incantations were recited and the ancestors were celebrated. The day's ceremony concluded with the setting of the sun.

How should we analyze the role of ritual language and performance in everyday life? How should we approach an understanding of ritual change when it seems that hegemonic forms are ritually constructed in performative forms that reproduce authorial practices? What is the interplay between the uses of performative ritual language and the kinds of conditions of social relation that lead people to make particular choices in the production and variation of rituals? What is the role of linguistic techniques of dislocation in deterritorialized contexts?

Both the above ritual incantations and the articulations of subjectivity in time and space highlight the referential functions of language for transnational religious and racial reproduction. The use of nontensed performative phrases such as "Today we pay homage" take us out of the present and into the past and the future, calibrating the act into a world outside the present world. The indexical prophetic interaction invoked in phrases such as "we are the children of the sacrificed," "those shores," and "We/us, the children, Africans in America" highlight what linguists refer to as indexicality, or the co-reference of things or persons who draw relationships to other things or persons. The major challenge of transnational studies, therefore, is understanding the relative value of these indexical and referential techniques as they relate to language resources in time and space, especially in relation to people's capacity to operate adequately in given spoken contexts in a range of spaces. As such, the uses of language forms across different geographic domains highlight the need for understanding shifts in uses of signs and meanings as well as the reallocation of the uses of language as agents move in space. Ultimately, in charting the relative value of language in mobilizing new meanings in deterritorial movements, we see how both ritual language is deployed to produce new orientations and in so doing produce new spatial indexicalities (Silverstein and Urban 1996). When new language forms are incorporated into socially different contexts and places, the focus must necessarily shift from the "origins" of linguistic systems to the ways that language works in new contexts. As scholars of language have shown us, the ways that language is performed in ritual contexts and the purpose it serves are linked (Hanks 1990). As I demonstrate, once we establish the different functions of specific language resources among Yorùbá revivalists in American contexts, we can examine how the language articulation and language resources that are available to people are mobilized toward the production of relevant social logics. In the end, the incorporation and replacement of particular words, the changing value they have, and the consequent gaps in meaning ("my brother is in Africa?") point to the need for an engagement concerning how transnational institutions are performatively mobilized.

By analyzing the ritual incantation earlier invoked in the course of a series of venerations to their African ancestors and building on earlier explorations into the role of the past in shaping how people imagine the present (chapter 1), we can examine how particular Ọ̀yọ́túnjí priests adapt ritual practices using indexical techniques while also maintaining the hegemonic structure and form of the original text. The ability of the practitioner to produce incremental change while also maintaining the stability and authority of the ritual act lies in the ability of the priest to make the context and utterance relevant to those involved. Fundamentally, in African-centered Yorùbá revivalist contexts, it is the memory of the immorality of suffering endured during the transatlantic slave trade and the intrinsic and experiential value of ritual spiritual engagements that is at the heart of deterritorialized Yorùbá ritual. For practitioners to see these rituals as authentic, they must be reflective of a persuasive doctrine that is seen as "fixed" in its originary form, while also being variable enough to reflect amendments that are continuous and, therefore, in keeping with the larger hierarchies of spiritually legitimate ritual.

Over the nineteenth and twentieth centuries, analytic attention on power traditionally focused on the role of the nation-state in the international sphere. However, increasingly there is a shift toward considering the power of institutions with religious and historical purposes. Therefore, understanding how religious innovations are linguistically sustained is as important as charting the ways these appearances of continuities are naturalized. The role of knowledge and the uses of religious ritual help us explain how variations in structure and form lead to both transformations of meaning and integrity of practice. The changing forms of Yorùbá practices are more connected with the historical particularities of the migration of African captives under specific conditions of exploitation than with an unmediated imaginary that shapes the formation of Yorùbá revivalist aesthetic and spatial relations. In other words, social relationships are structured according to how particular hierarchies are valued. By exploring the alterations of the structure of rituals that Ọ̀yọ́túnjí practitioners derived from their Santería counterparts, examining the performative representation and changes in the meanings of rituals and how they relate to the social conditions in which òrìṣà voodoo devotees find themselves, and exploring how these changes provide an idiom with which Ọ̀yọ́túnjí òrìṣà voodooists structure their relationships with other groups of people that they identify as ritually important and less important, we see the ritual production of these social relationships and their role in shaping the authority of òrìṣà social relationships by way of representing personal and group identities. Ancestral ritual, thus produced, is fundamentally about the enactment of divine knowledge, by which deriving the *right answer*, which is communicated from god (Olódùmarè) and through the òrìṣàs, is prioritized. However, in relation to understanding the ways social hierarchies are reproduced, much depends on how people understand Olódùmarè's originary narrative in relation to people's ideological values. The contestations over Santería, òrìṣà voodoo, and Nigerian Yorùbá authenticity are contestations over the standards of legitimacy. It is a fight over deriving the right answer from the sacred texts. Therefore, understanding how people structure social importance is about understanding how, through hierarchies of authority, the word of Olódùmarè is made legible in relation to the power of the originary. The differences in forms of legitimacy can be tested with questions concerning compliance with an originary moment, thereby making possible particular forms of variation. The toleration of variation, therefore, is connected to the perceived legitimacy of the originary moment. Thus, even with variation, the text is still perceived as being intact; it is not seen as being unrelated to the legitimacy of the origins of variations. However, where the origins of the variations that follow are perceived to be antithetical to the originary moment, the variations are seen either as illegitimate or excluded from narrative.

The play of the imaginary and innovations related to it take place on two levels of interaction. The first begins with the individual and is connected to techniques of spiritual transformations through which many black Americans involved in these ritual practices believe they are making direct spiritual connections with their African ancestors. How do these micro levels of personal ritual enable people to imagine themselves as part of a community culturally different from their own?

On a broader level of analysis, people employ these religious techniques performatively and, in conjunction with social conceptions about the rules of religious practices, their perceived function and origins, practitioners create gods relevant to their daily lives. In exploring these practices as acts of agency under particular conditions of possibility, we can examine the uses of the imaginary both as a site of unmediated invention and a locus of historical routes of interaction. It is fundamentally about the role of knowledge and power in local and global spheres of interaction in which people mobilize dominant meanings to renarrativize new forms of practice.

The first sphere of power central to the hegemonic reproduction of religious meanings and its related forms of intervention exists within a particular ideological power with which agents code everyday life. It reflects an *always* unfinished articulation of subject formation that exists in relation to regimes of modernity. Within this sphere, individuals enforce a logic of practice where the organizing principles of national citizenship circulate within modern regimes of knowledge and power. Analyzing these processes through the lens of governmentality, which extends beyond state institutions, is partly a matter of decentering macro forces to examine the interplay with microspiritual practices that constitute subjectivity.

The second sphere is connected to the first but interacts with the ways individuals both incorporate and contest hegemonic meanings through disjunctive acts of contestation and gain intrinsic spiritual meanings. It characterizes individual agency in relation to globalizing forces. Here, agents of change are at once historical and contemporary, global and local, both setting the terms for regimes of knowledge that authorize national belonging and explaining experiences of spirituality in both innovative and preconceived ways. Keeping in mind the symbolism of the Atlantic Ocean as the geographical site of African captives drowned during the transatlantic slave trade, I now move to one of the most foundational ritual incantations performed on a daily basis publicly and privately by òrìṣà voodoo practitioners paying homage to their ancestral leaders. Particular texts, though hegemonically structured in form and content, are also sites for the application of spiritual techniques and moral and historical yearnings. Here I refer to acts of agency as the use of moral fortitude to incorporate histories of ancestral suffering and loss; Michael Shapiro (1994) refers to moral geographies as narratives of deterritorial belonging to an anterior past that is made socially significant.

Performative Acts of Ancestral Loss: Language as Symbolic Power

Throughout the 1960s and 1970s, Americans, especially African Americans, claimed and adapted African-based religious practices for their own consumption. Likewise, Ọ̀yọ́túnjí practitioners place high value on claiming Yorùbáland as their originary home and Yorùbá as their traditional language, and they tend to use the language of Yorùbá religion to commune with the spiritual authority of Olódùmarè, the Yorùbá god. Knowledge of Yorùbá words, songs, rituals, and mechanics of divination made it possible for Ọ̀yọ́túnjí residents to organize religious and cultural events for their growing constituency.

Over the first few years of the formation of Ọ̀yọ́túnjí, the Yorùbá language was used only in greetings and in repetitive phrases, such as in prayers and ritual recitations. Up until the institutionalization of household speech codes, most residents in the village spoke Standard American English in casual contexts. After the

Yorùbá-language-only edict in the late 1970s, Yorùbá cultural revivalists integrated Yorùbá words into their daily speech. They institutionalized intensive Yorùbá language classes for elementary and high school students and required that adults take Yorùbá evening classes. This involved the regulation of Yorùbá-only conversations, and these techniques of linguistic discipline led to the elaboration of a hybridized speech community that found its fullest expression in the performance of Yorùbá traditional cultural life outside of Yorùbáland. Òyótúnjí practitioners substituted Spanish influences on spelling, pronunciation, and iconic images with Yorùbá words and objects, accentuating different pronunciations and meanings. These significations also included conducting rituals in Yorùbá and wearing what is popularly termed "African clothes," such as the African dashikis and *bùbás*. The Òyótúnjí leadership thus recast Santería influences on U.S. Yorùbá practices and rearticulated ritual practices by accentuating particular acts and debunking others.

Given the existence of established networks of Santería practitioners in the United States, whose knowledge about Yorùbá practices was integrally connected to Catholicism, some African American attempts to pronounce Santería's Christian iconography and rituals illegitimate and to authenticate African-centered approaches became politically charged. It was in this political context of reclamation, rejection, authentication, and innovation that a new form of Yorùbá performative language became the basis for the formation of òrìsà voodoo.

With the desire to claim a new identity based on their slave trade histories, the leadership, both male and female, developed new forms of signifying Yorùbá traditions and rendering illegitimate dominant Santería signs in a range of ways. For example, the Yorùbá-Santería word used in some contexts to refer to power, ACHE, was pronounced by Òyótúnjí practitioners as *Àse*; the "ch" sound was replaced by a "sh" sound. The Yorùbá deity, Òsun or Òshun, whom Santería speakers would refer to as (read phonetically) OCHUN, was always pronounced to emphasize the "sh" instead of the hard "ch." Similarly, the soft "j" sound in *Mo júbà* (prayerfully, "I thank you") was emphasized instead of the phonetic *Mo yuba* used among Santeros. These attempts to resignify ancestry through Yorùbá revivalism often result in an indexical icon of difference in which a gap in understanding may occur as the result of the mispronunciation of standard Yorùbá. Because Yorùbá fluency has not yet been attained by anyone in Òyótúnjí, it is important to recognize the indexical strategies that are reflective of the play of power. In other words, Yorùbá language choice in Òyótúnjí is more about the resistance of Spanish hegemonies in Santería than it is about Yorùbá competence.

In the 1990s in Òyótúnjí, Yorùbá language classes continued to be integrated into both lessons taught in the school system and weekly and monthly cult meetings. The leadership always began their public speeches by pouring libation to the ancestors, invoking the Yorùbá ancestral empires, and reciting accompanying prayers in the Yorùbá language. Today, members of the community employ Yorùbá words as an indexical gesture, as a form of cultural reclamation without the necessity of literal comprehension. Having lost some of the radical fervor of the Black Power charge, when Ọ̀yọ́túnjí residents speak with each other in Yorùbá they actively integrate Yorùbá nouns with English verbs and syntax with the goal of indexing their membership in Africa as grounded in linguistic competence, at the same time forfeiting details. In general terms, practitioners invent linkages between semantic codes and their social relationships, thus recreating themselves in relation to Nigerian Yorùbá and employing the very hegemonic signifiers of Yorùbá membership that because of their own spoken "incompetence" may also lead to their marginalization. The performative techniques used by members of the Ọ̀yọ́túnjí elite demonstrate that the use of Yorùbá language by revivalists in public ritual performances is embedded in racially complex forms of alliance in which they link linguistic codes with social contexts to communicate blackness as the sign of Africanness.

Donald Brenneis (Brenneis and MacCaulay 1996, 69) has discussed the symbolic role of comprehension and public performance in social relationships, arguing that religious speech and meaning production "deal ostensibly with sacred topics, but speakers often convey a second political message as well. The political meanings are quite opaque and not all members of the audience will understand them." Brenneis argued that political discourses are used indirectly as a form of mediation that might not be fully understood in available and accessible speech genres, but, in the process of political arbitration, they signal important relationships. The performance of Yorùbá language by "noncompetent" Yorùbá speakers in the United States is as much about producing the sign of the Yorùbá ancestral past as it is about signaling political meanings. Yorùbá language use, interpretation, and competence are evaluated by Yorùbá speakers and listeners to signal national belonging.

The challenge for African-identified Yorùbá practitioners who live in the United States, therefore, is to signal Yorùbá belonging in relation to the geopolitics of place—that is, to claim membership in Nigerian citizenship. In both Old (indigenous Yorùbá) and African-centered New World Yorùbà communities (Yorùbá revivalists in the Americas), there is a negotiation between uses of English and Yorùbá and the standards of competence by which we must measure the speaker's intention. The Ọ̀yọ́túnjí emphasis on using Yorùbá in different speech communities is different and holds different levels of social value. Following Brenneis's articulation of language and performance, which emerges and departs from a tradition of Chomskian (1965) explorations of the relationship between linguistic competence and intended meaning, I have classified two varieties of linguistic cultural performances: New World symbolic performances and Old World symbolic performances. The former refers to speech practices where the use of Yorùbá is symbolic and where communicative competence is secondary. In the latter, Old World speech communities tend to base their rhetorical strategies among other native Yorùbá speakers on presumed competence (in the language), using the Yorùbá language to signify social relations and to communicate ideas. Although the two speech situations are not mutually exclusive, the indexical/iconic use of language to mark Yorùbá "traditionalism" is critical for thinking through the role of language, the meaning of usage, and assumptions about comprehension in actively shaping transatlantic alliances.

John Mason, a prominent Yorùbá scholar and practitioner who has written extensively about òrìṣà traditions in the Americas, examines the problem of "devotee ignorance" of ritual language by discussing the use of fragmented Yorùbá and Lukumi language song. Mason's 1992 book, primarily a text for devotees, contains the words and literal translations to an impressive list of Yorùbá religious songs. Each section introduces the social context for the particular god that the songs venerate and illustrates each song's form and history. His work addresses his concern with the uses of Yorùbá in the absence of verbal comprehension: "I come to this work not as a language specialist but as a follower and student of òrìṣà who is totally amazed by the fact that for the last hundred years in Cuba and other parts of the Americas where Yorùbá culture has been transplanted and taken root, the overwhelming majority of devotees, lay and priest alike, sing songs and perform ritual without knowing the meaning of most of the words they are saying. My own ignorance prompted my involvement in this work before you. It is much like driving a car, one doesn't have to be a mechanic, who knows every minute part and its function, to get the car where you want it to go."

For Mason, ignorance of literal translation is compensated for by intended meaning. The intended meaning is often indexed through various performative codes that are "still governed by the ritual colors, numbers, familiars, paraphernalia and abodes of the òrìṣà" (Mason 1992). In performances of cultural knowledge (Fabian 1991) one can see how hegemonic frameworks reproduce themselves, and how agents might possibly resist and reshape them in their own local contexts, in some cases based on lack of literal understanding. Thus, practitioners' struggles with language are not simply about language as such. They are about the resignification of deterritorialized practices whose referents originated in precolonial West Africa but have relevance for black Americans. Through Yorùbá utterances, ritual invocations of the historical dispersal of their ancestors provided them with the possibility of recharting their descent patterns to Africa. As language, ritual, and the spread of other technologies of Yorùbá knowledge contribute to connecting Ọ̀yọ́túnjí practitioners to their Yorùbáland alliances, revivalists no longer have to travel to Africa to acquire Yorùbá òrìṣà knowledge.

Words and Sociohistorical Relations

The ritualization of divinatory prayers in the Yorùbá language to the Yorùbá god Orunmila and by the divining bablawo is an important component for not only routing deterritorialized ancestry, but for charting complex racial and territorial alliances. In carrying out all five sections of the invocation above, as well as performing the divinatory process, Yorùbá priests engage in specific requisite forms of delivery such as rapid recitations and ritualistic movements in which ritual technologies are engaged in a form identifiable as traditional. Among Ọ̀yọ́túnjí practitioners, kinship relations are mediated by these complex performances. The history of African enslavement in the Caribbean and South America shapes social notions of lineage patterns and raises concerns about who and what is constituted in these relations of belonging and what are the enforcement mechanisms that are used not only to pay homage to the ancestors, but also to demonstrate the cultural and ancestral maps to which the deliberating priest belongs. Yorùbá revivalist kinship relations are connected to discourses that invoke transnational slavery, the politics of dispersal, and the racialization of Yorùbá belonging. These webs of inclusion are historically contingent and frame the basis by which groups are granted privileges to claim particular roots and not others, to redefine some cultural alliances and not others. In understanding Ọ̀yọ́túnjí practitioners and their transnational networks, the important questions are, How are new transnational linkages that are without historical empirical documentation not only formed and maintained but also legitimized? What signs and symbols govern membership, and how is membership expressed and realigned through ritual practice? What privileges does membership grant, and what does it take to transform hierarchies of membership? The ability to create traditional Yorùbá imaginaries is evident in the ways that individuals in institutional settings use various modes of cultural production to turn attention from the popular conceptualization of American life to ideals about the exotic West African past. Thus, the articulation of spatial links to Africa highlights the ways that practitioners use dominant structures of African-based ritual forms to mark important alliances and omit others. The incantation uttered by the priest engaging in the celebration of African ancestry demonstrates how articulating Yorùbá ancestry follows a selective process of inclusion and exclusion from which racialized narratives of African membership are shaped.

Understanding Ritual and Sites of Incremental Change

At the highest level of analysis, the Ọ̀yọ́túnjí priest's incantation follows a four-part structure, consisting of an opening salute, a kinship narrative (from Africa to the New World), requests, and the epilogue. I have divided this four-part structure into five sections. The first section represents the offering of the highest respect to Olódùmarè, the Yorùbá high god. The second section is concerned with paying homage to the unknown ancestors, the known ancestors, and those in the religious lineage through which the presiding priest has developed. The third section represents requests in which practitioners ask to be protected from supernatural forces. The fourth section marks the priest's attempt to petition the spirits to protect the client against unwanted circumstances. Finally, the fifth section ends with a prayer in which the priest pays tribute to the ancestral forces. Each of these five sections has a recognizable presentation format and invokes, first, transnational ties to Africa; second, the middle passage; and third, national and local ancestral remembrances.

The incantation, ritualized and performatively delivered, has a recognizable format that is dominant in Yorùbá ritual. It is almost always delivered in the Yorùbá language and begins with a tribute of thanks to the highest and most general form, that of god and the ancestors "who uphold the feet of god." The main function of section 2 is to pay homage to the ancestors. There is variation in length and content, but two basic patterns are used: one offers reverence and the other is for ancestral remembrance. The organization of incantations in each sentence is structured as a mnemonic device in which repetition assists both in memorizing the phrase and in emphasizing the performance. In relation to the types of articulation that produce responses conducive to the acceptance of the authenticity of the ritual utterance, sections 1, 4, and 5 are the most conceptually fixed. Yet, even as particular inscriptions of historical power are hierarchically reinforced, ritual innovations are possible in other domains of ritual practice. The two sections on which I focus my analysis of variation in social ordering, therefore the realm of agency, are 2 and 3, where some forms of improvisation often occur. They are also the best example of the ways that popular knowledge of the history of African slavery is used to enforce particular cultural practices and in so doing highlight the moral geographies by which these ritual practices are empowered.

The sections of the incantation are organized hierarchically; that is, ancestral entities are listed in progressively declining generality, and African-based entities are listed before those existing in the Americas. Similarly, the organization of temporality follows the same sequencing as the spatial order; the most historically ancient entities (usually unnamed beings) are prioritized, and the most recently deceased individuals are listed toward the end of the incantation. The groupings of individuals include (1) groups of unnamed ancestors whose relevance is signified by their location: from heaven to Africa, the Atlantic Ocean, the New World including the Caribbean; the ancestors of Ọ̀yọ́túnjí residents through the line of Àṣàbí; the senior priestess of the Ọ̀yọ́túnjí line; and the ancestors of Ògúnjọbí, the Cuban godfather of the Ọba and therefore the first in the line from which the hundreds of priests initiated by Ọ̀yọ́túnjí affiliates trace their descent; (2) the names of known priests in the New World, listed in order of date deceased, who are the predecessors of Ọ̀yọ́túnjí residents; and (3) the names of the known priests and chiefs, listed in order of the earliest deceased to the more recently deceased, who were initiates of the Ọba of Ọ̀yọ́túnjí or personal and religious kin in his "lived world" experience.

To further enhance the participatory agreement, most sections maintain a call-response refrain. Although the call-response pattern structures each full sentence, for the purpose of clarity, I have listed the pattern at the end of each section, For example, *Ìbà ará t'ọ̀run*, "Salute the bodies of heaven"; *KÒ SÍ*, "No more"; and *ÀṢẸ*, "So be it" are all predictable responses, and an "appropriate" response follows each sentence.

Sites of Innovation

This chapter breaks from theorizing ritual as an extension of religious social order or as merely constructed categories within which agents create meanings. Instead, I now move to examine the historical and institutional logic of inclusion and the moral force of redemption by which agents use particular typologies to perform the task of alliance and erasure and shape ideological forms of forgetting. Even while categories are constructed and their meanings change incrementally over time, their alliances with larger institutional forces of power are essential to the institutional regimes that maintain them. What is most striking about the interplay between ritual constructivism and the categories and forms that are called on to reproduce particular forms of meanings is that they work within particular institutional spheres that are constituted by boundary-making processes that pervade theoretically critical questions about how social relations are both remembered and reconstituted. In the case of transatlantic slavery, the desire for redemption and the moral geographies of inclusion serve as sites for the resignification of different forms of belonging. Through referential alliances with dominant categories and language and performative forms, which frame the basis for innovation, ritualists produce new interpretations. By asking how people use religious rituals to

Chief Awolowo's body revered in state.

both remember and forget the past, we see that not only does religion do critical ideological work, but it also reflects the historical and political conditions from which it emerged. Through the performance of Yorùbá ancestral rituals, practitioners often transform ritual structures to resignify particular social conditions as the basis for racial alliances.

In *How Societies Remember*, Paul Connerton (1989) suggested that distinctions between social memory and historical reconstruction must be made to identify the evidence of the interpretive legitimacy of social acts. He argued that though narratives of the past serve to legitimize the contemporary social order, these narratives are insufficient if they are not conveyed and sustained through routinized practices, what he called performative acts. In the routinization of ritual as a form of performativity, ritual practices serve to structure social relationships and reproduce others. I approach the questions of constructing memory as productive of questions about the social politics of remembering and forgetting (see also Appadurai 1981; Rappaport 1990; Tonkin 1992).

Performative Acts as Means for Structuring Social Relationships

Extensive variability in content exists across religious and national lines in this incantation. However, when I compared it with ten other Ọ̀yọ́túnjí incantations in terms of the frequency of the repetition of each segment, I found that compared to section 3, section 2 was repeated with the greatest accuracy and very little variation. This repetition represents a common and observable phenomenon in incantations in which each section either pays homage to Olódùmarè or signals tribute to significant forces that contributed to the practitioner's development. As demonstrated by the priest's incantation, after the invocation of generic high ancestors, specific names of individuals from the Santería Cuban priestly line followed. Because the Ọba of Ọ̀yọ́túnjí was initiated into one of the religious cults of Matanzas, Cuba, he and his followers tend to list the names of the Cuban priests who initiated him as well as those from whom the incanting priest descended. In section 2, the deceased maternal and paternal religious parents (Ọ̀ṣungbadé, Ọyábádé, Péláyọ̀ Koriente) of the first recognized Ọ̀yọ́túnjí priest, Àṣàbí, are called on. This is followed by a parallel logic: the first recognized male ancestor from the Cuban line, Ògún Jọbí, is also revered. Most important, however, there are clear exclusions of significant Cuban/Santería priests, and this is indicative of Ọ̀yọ́túnjí revivalists asserting their transnational claims to Yorùbá sameness. By charting new formulations of descent relevant to practitioner social realities, these ritualizations of Yorùbá past are differently constituted. But this phenomenon of establishing racialized kinship is a highly contested process, and the forces that shape what constitutes Yorùbá authenticity and, more specifically, who will belong to the legitimizing groups, are shaped by the ways that local agents author and contest dominant versions of descent. The articulation of ritual incantations further reifies who is included in the process of imagining belonging and how diasporic connections are authorized. Just as Afro-Cuban ritual configurations were shaped by particular histories and practices and not others, Ọ̀yọ́túnjí Village priests regulate community inclusion against determinants of what their notions of blackness are not. In this case, Ọ̀yọ́túnjí Village-based Yorùbá kinship invocations represent ideals of the Yorùbá family ancestry in which the priorities of the somewhat variable sections 2, 3, and 4 are demonstrated in public manifestations of ritual practices.

The national allocation and invention of authentic traditional identities instigates a cycle of subjectivity that doubles in the end as "natural." Therefore, in charting social change, we need to understand how people's imaginaries are made into realities and how what may be seen in larger terms as inauthentic forms of unreality are means by which new exclusions are enforced. These processes of resignification push us to ask, What politics come from racial exclusions? and What politics are generated from the erecting of boundaries that are productive of other forms of inclusions? Yorùbá ritual utterances are deeply embedded in historical meanings, which are cyclical and dialogic, and racial classificatory ordering. Future possibilities for variation are crafted through moral geographies of suffering as sites of intrinsic value. Here, the social memory of slavery is emblematic of new forms of innovation. These adaptations of the structure of a recognized hegemonic form are examples of the ways that globalization is leading to the production of increasingly autonomous spatial practices. The creation of new institutions within which these new forms of practice are adapted highlights why it is critical to explore questions of flexibility and instability underlying the apparent stability of Yorùbá identity. Particular Yorùbá practices circulate as well as serve to guard the terms of authentic traditional knowledge because the boundaries of membership are sites of historically embedded relations. Part of understanding these processes of social change is identifying the disjunctures between agency and institutional regimes as locations of ideological power, as they contribute to reshaping the institutional spheres within which agents are actively engaged.

As linguistic theory has shown, the presumed semantic referential meanings of an object do not contain independent value outside of its use. Although the meanings of objects are arbitrary and do not, in and of themselves, contain specific referential meanings (Silverstein 1976), sign values of objects are communicated with referential indexes (also referred to as shifters), and through the context of people's use of them, they take on different meanings (Silverstein 1976; Dominguez 1989; Caton 1985, 1990). Hence, it is only through the production of referential meanings that objects take on indexical values. Even as these codes are sometimes contingent and produce new meanings, these values are always interpolated within larger codes that are at once historical and contextual. Ways of seeing change are about understanding ways of both producing knowledge and reordering socially

Wooden carvings of Egúngún
in chairs, and three wooden
carvings.

Wooden carvings of captives.

important relationships. In the process of resignifying meaning—using measurements that may not be empirical but spiritual—individuals combine preexisting ideological forms with new forms of ritual practices. These practices, sometimes leading to spiritual empowerment, are productive of particular forms of religious reproduction which, coupled with material social relations, can be mobilized to reinforce or reorder what might otherwise be seen as purely ancestral practices.

Charting the spirituality of ritual, the moral geography of suffering, and the structuring of social relationships in relation to what people do, I approach an understanding of ritual performance akin to Nietzsche's (1967) notion of subjectivity. Thus seen, there is no "being beyond doing."[3] Ultimately, in the process of "doing" or enacting a notion of "identity," individuals effectively become particular types of subjects in larger webs of hierarchies and meanings. If we understand identity as the ongoing performance of social typologies that shape individual categories, then identity is constituted through the act of doing in particular regulations and innovations. As such, individuals form alliances through which to create new meanings and, to this end, maintain, reinforce, and sometimes subvert the categories that compel and shape them. Such patterns, as they are constituted in time and space, are recursive and transformative. Seen in this way, mixture and change can be mapped in relation to the temporal and spatial basis onto which the past, present, and future, the here and the there, are understood. This is so because agents cultivate what constitutes reality in terms of modern values of scale. These forms of classifying difference and sameness are constituted in the ideological terrain where agents interpret and change meanings.

Time and Space in the Reclassification of National Attachments

By highlighting the semantic workings of space and time in this incantation, we see how notions of historical descent coupled with perceptions of racial, thus cultural, alliance are modalities that signify African diasporic connections. In addition to understanding how people reconfigure time and space, it is critical to understand how, in these approaches, culture becomes marked as a moral and therefore redemptive process. Thus, these reclassifications of spatial origins from Africa to the Americas and circular chronologies of ancestral time are complexly embedded in historical articulations of the modern capitalist past.

Ọ̀yọ́túnjí practitioners produce "formulations of descent" that exclude significant Cuban/Santería priests as a manifestation of racial locality. With these formulations Ọ̀yọ́túnjí revivalists also assert their transnational claims to Yorùbá authenticity to shape new renditions of the Yorùbá past. Thus, though specifically American in the production of metaphors of race as culture and of histories of racial suffering as constitutive of a particular moral geography of African descent, spatiotemporal notions of identity are structured to represent personal and group identity in relation to spatial connections. It is here that the intrinsic value of moral geographies—the intrinsic value of suffering—comes alive with spiritual utterances that deterritorialize Africa and Africans as simultaneously black Americans. Through the routinization of new practices, practices that index African origins, and the production of the necessary ideologies for legitimizing new meanings, deterritorialized senses of place, complexly territorialized in particular ways, are produced by ritualists within and outside of sites traditionally identified as indigenous. Though they are outside of Africa, members of the community rendered irrelevant the spatiotemporal distance between the African past and the American present. They reconfigured the parameters of identity and, in so doing, reshaped, along lines of racial membership and Africanized iconic signification, who was qualified to claim African ancestry. With the formation of new technologies of knowledge, the spatiotemporal distance between the creation of a new imaginary and the site being replicated has produced notions of Africanness that are racialized by particular ways of seeing transnational linkage in the United States. Thus seen, features of the "racial injustice" of transatlantic slavery and the possibilities for redemption must integrate the symbolic links between historical events and contemporary circumstances. However, seen in relation to larger definitions of citizenship, membership in contemporary Nigerian social life is constituted through birthplace and territorial affiliation and not racial biology mapped through color. Thus, in terms of the globalization of African cultural production, what circulates is not national identity as such; rather, it is ideological discourses of membership by which cultural belonging is shaped, authorized, and contested.

In ritual terms, the chanting priest must move from the invocation of religious kin to marking the religious hierarchy and political affiliation—from Africa to black America. By exploring how ritual genealogies are conducted within the structure of normative ritual incantations, revivalists engage in discursive innovations from which to recast old canonical structures and produce new social relations. These incantations serve to resignify African and Santería kinship within complex territorialized relations.

Paying attention to specific sites of innovation, and under what circumstances variations are possible, we see that revivalist practitioners use ancestrally focused social rituals to remap their ancestry. Performative acts link words to sociohistorical relations; in so doing, people establish the basis by which new geographic mappings can take place. It is by the establishment of ritual legitimacy through the production of ritual fixity (the ritual structure appears intact) and mechanisms for ensuring the legitimacy of interpretations that disjunctures in meanings are possible and contingencies incorporated. In section 3 of the incantation, where the possibility of variation is the highest, the inclusion of people and relationships is not based on popular notions of historical ancestry but on ideological alliances. Here the elision of Santería and whiteness as passage points of cultural adaptations is forged. With the complexities of a history that globalized humans as commodities and left scant record of names and no detailed histories, these Òyótúnjí nationalist interventions make more allowances for generalities. These generalities, enabled through the symbolic assertion of moral suffering, articulate acceptable ways of classifying human losses in relation to the unknown dead. However, it is also here where spaces for improvisation and reclassification are critically possible. It is the moment of contingent possibility enabled through the ritual as a form of redemption from the bondage of ancestral slavery. As seen in line 1 of section 3, the priest began his invocation by calling for protection for the king of Ifè in Nigeria, popularly represented by members of Òyótúnjí as the chief commander of Yorùbá in the world. Here we see Yorùbá political/religious officials, such as the king of Òyó, listed in descending order. This pattern of recognizing leadership is followed by a call for protection of those in the priest's maternal and paternal godparent lists and ends with a call for priests who are working for the betterment of the Yorùbá nation. These calls for alliances as a form of black social uplift are also spaces for the incorporation of others who might be called on for redemption or to offer spiritual support.

By extension, the regulation of who is included within the network of the Yorùbá òrìsà practitioners is produced in the context of complex negotiations of historical and political relationships. Therefore, not only is the materiality of the Òyó Yorùbá homeland, for example, deeply embedded in competing conceptions of membership that are temporally connected to modern conceptualizations of the present, but òrìsà voodoo claims of Òyó ancestry are deterritorialized outside of the geographical boundaries of the nation. These homelands are produced outside of Nigeria through the routinization of ritual practices that index African origins. People's performative claims to particular meanings of rituals are often used to index the territory of Òyó and Africa and are fundamental to what constitutes Òyótúnjí claims of proximity to West African òrìsà practitioners. Such forms of referentiality to the African homeland work because they reference particular values that draw from the prestige of the past. However, without micro and macro institutions and the sociocultural and spiritually derived ideologies that inform how places and boundaries are to be read and classified, these imagined signs have no significance in and of themselves. Here, I refer to a form of imaginative construction that is self-conscious but reflects differences in relation to the ways that these imaginations are embedded in divergent ideologies. While Òyótúnjí practitioners use racial categories to draw linkages to modern territorialized spaces seen as originary, they also produce the ideological terms by which new forms of governance are legitimized in new locales. This production of spatial territories is linked to popular black American notions of racial ancestry, thereby distinguishing Yorùbá revivalism as ideologically American. Thus, the reproduction of deterritorialized spaces is as much about the routinization of practices that produce meanings as it is about the construction of an ideology of deterritorialized belonging that produces and resignifies new understandings of spatial boundaries.

Social Change in Transatlantic Perspectives

The social processes for determining Yorùbá inclusion in Òyótúnjí Village are connected to the political economy of plunder in Africa and the enslavement of Africans in the Americas. They are also highly selective in reconstituting the meaning of the Yorùbá nation through racialized formations. These relations of kinship call on different conceptions of relatedness that crosscut the conceptual frame of nationhood. They consist of ex-communities and nongroup members who are otherwise excluded. The way to understand these social movements is to understand how naturalizing kinship is embedded in historical meanings of relatedness as they are performatively ritualized. Such approaches to kinship demonstrate the need for a theory of ritual change that highlights the interplay between innovation and regulation. Ultimately, rituals represent another symbolic system of value by which to observe the ways that particular meanings are carried into the present. If we understand these articulations of reclassifying social order as attempts to create intelligible structures and norms, we can see that what is at stake is the maintenance of norms, be they national, gendered, or scientific, for they are articulations of authority and legibility. Thus, challenges to racial orders through the reclassification of national or ethnic identity and the reformulation of Santería are challenges to the modernity of subjectivity. Moving to the ways early modern subject formations are tied to uneven zones of global penetration and alliance, we see that religious revivalism represents another example of the imaginary that is regulated, fought over, struggled through, negotiated, and historically constituted in particular ways.

Given the importance of using interrelated micro- and macroanalyses, we need to go beyond models that assume unilateral schemata of state power or politics of agency that disregard the historical specificities of how and why people classify what they see in the first place. How we respond to questions concerning how signs referentially index objects and how state regulations and economic exchanges contribute to new forms of aesthetic value depends on how we see and interpret change, as well as the kinds of practices and the forms of institutions in which agents operate. We need to relocate the theoretical assumptions about the discursive fields through which to translate the past by pointing to the ways that the semiotic codes of subjecthood are at once historically constituted and ritually agentive.

Agents use incantations to engage in the legitimate process of ancestral invocation; the relationship between the performative use of works and socially significant relationships highlights what Web Keane (1994) has referred to as the manifestation of words to create relations between things, and what Roland Barthes (1982) has referred to as the conjunction of words and things as an indication of their value. The symbolic role of language lies not in the process of changing meanings but in the ways that performative acts are exercised through institutions of power to inscribe social relations (Butler 1993). The historical disenfranchisement of enslaved Africans brought to the Americas, the legacy of racism that developed with the transatlantic slave trade, and the consequent colonial regimes that politicized racial differences continue to figure prominently in the ways that residents of Ọ̀yọ́túnjí Village contest and reclassify historical relations through routinized performative utterances. The invocation of these histories provides the terrain for variation in interpretation, and it is in the performance of ritual utterances that variations in meaning are possible. Furthermore, it is through their alliances with the institutional prestige of canon forms that particular changes are rendered legitimate and therefore moral. As such, even as we attempt to understand the relationship between the West and the rest, especially in relation to the circulation of their various hegemonies, the connections between what is taken as knowledge and the production of the possibility of new knowledge domains need to be rethought. A theoretical recasting of the processes involved in transnational identities is instructive as a means of unpacking the rhetorical and ideological interpretations that surround the basis for group alliances. It is clear that hegemonic logics of belonging have their rules, just as local forms of logic are embedded in rules of inclusion and exclusion. How we conceive of and classify meanings, why we rationalize their utility, and the force with which alterations are made are just as much products of classification, in this case of race and territoriality, by which we establish those truths as they are about the mechanisms by which we align ourselves.

Understanding the globalization of the Yorùbá imaginary calls for microanalysis of how agents borrow from the dominant meanings of the past while also resignifying them. Similar to the dispute described in chapter 1, in which the leader-to-be of Ọ̀yọ́túnjí Village diverted his attention from Santería networks, a new mechanism for the circulation of new òrìṣà practices led to the development of hybrid forms of Nigerian and Santería òrìṣà voodoo, ultimately establishing the formation of Ọ̀yọ́túnjí Village and post-1980s networks of Yorùbá revivalism in the English-speaking circum-Atlantic region. Within Ọ̀yọ́túnjí networks, disputes arise when people overstep their socially perceived roles, take more than or give less than expected, commit an offensive attack, or are seen as misinterpreting, disregarding, or abusing an informally accepted social truth. However, unlike scholars who may see the negotiation of diasporic imaginings as unlimited in its imaginative capacity, by demonstrating the mechanisms of historical knowledge production (chapters 1 and 2) and the use of ritual structure as a mechanism of norm enunciation, I demonstrate that these proof systems are shaped by deeply constituted sociohistorical values used to shape conditions of ritual legitimacy in deterritorialized networks.

There are ideological limits to imagination that must be acknowledged if we are to understand the production and persistence of racial distinctions as historically specific sets of classificatory codes that people use to shape social and individual distinctions. These codes are historically contingent and are of critical importance in understanding the relationship between ideologies and the cultural practices that inscribe meanings. Three factors are critical for detailing the zones that shape the intelligibility of particular forms of alliances and interpretations: territorialized meanings of particular places, the uses of ritual as a form of routinized practice, and the working of the moral imaginary through which the resignification of symbolic codes is legitimatized. These features of transnational ritual are symbolic of how, in the midst of global deterritorialized formations, the past and the processes of shaping the imaginary are themselves highly mediated by hegemonic and personally innovative mechanisms.

We cannot analyze the continuities and shifts in Yorùbá religious institutions from Nigeria to Cuba to the United States, the shifts in ritual meanings, and the shifts in the aesthetic significance of race without understanding how people link complex historical meanings to institutions of power. Ultimately, it points to the impossibility of power to totalize that which it shapes. The forces of accumulation that drove the triangular slave trade, the regulation of African religious practices, the migration of Spanish-speaking òrìṣà practitioners to the United States, and the routinization of ritual inventions all contributed to the development of a triangular node of Yorùbá cultural production that shaped the racialized and spatialized meanings of Yorùbá transnationalism. And alongside these continuities are discontinuities in the development of Yorùbá practices in the Americas. Although southwestern Nigeria is the referential index of Ọ̀yọ́ grandeur, conditions of slavery in Cuba set the terms of territoriality from which Yorùbá revivalists claim their power. Even as Ọ̀yọ́túnjí, as a site of deterritorialized Yorùbá production, is an example of the reorganization of national and religious meanings, it also depends on the tools of modern state formation—that of primordial attachments—to map new aesthetic meanings.

The question, differently articulated, is: What are the bodies of knowledge that produce these commonsense notions of race and its power of enforcement and legitimacy? For Cuban practitioners dominant symbolic codes served as critical measuring devices for how the past, present, and future were to be remembered and reproduced. The politics of regulation that shaped the parameters of religious practice employed critical codes with which to imagine the boundaries of belonging and membership. Such interpretations were performed in sites of struggle within which meanings are reworked and reclassified and new performative determinants carved out.

Ritual practices are both sites for reproducing social order and sites for the reconfiguration of social relationships. This chapter has been an attempt to explore the sites of change within which new forms of variation are possible. Instead of thinking of objects or forces of hegemonic power as productive of change, I am interested in asking what practices are generative of new forms of institutions. In this case, it is the formation of ritual incantation that is productive of particular moral geographies through which certain types of performative practices are producing certain types of alliances. These ritual practices are as linguistic as they are performative, and the sites of variability are at the intersection of both the performative structure of ritual authority and the social relations that produce particular values of inclusion. This practice in the òrìṣà voodoo context is racially historicized and provides an idiom in which Ọ̀yọ́túnjí practitioners both represent and structure their relationships with other groups.

If anthropology is to come to terms with the cultural politics of globalization in relation to the ways that meanings are transformed and made intelligible across time and space, scholars must chart the ways linguistic performances of inclusion are negotiated through moral geographies of loss, using redemptive techniques for social ordering. As this book demonstrates, there are three qualifiers of membership that are used by U.S. Yorùbá revivalists to frame claims to Africanness: tropes of slavery and the uses of historical institutions (chapter 3), semiotically driven ritual institutions (chapter 4), and legal institutions (chapter 6) by which to legitimate linkages. I now turn to an exploration of divination as a form of institutional knowledge and power to explore further how religious ritual is used to authorize particular norms of descent and membership in Yorùbá transnational networks. As we shall see, diviners as well as clients actively engage in patrolling the borders of Yorùbá membership.

5. Ritual Change and the Changing Canon:
Divinatory Legitimation of Yorùbá Ancestral Roots

DURING MY YEARS OF FIELDWORK in Òyótúnjí and in a few communities in the network—New York, Abeokuta, and Òyó, I recorded more than one hundred divinatory interpretations, known informally as readings, performed for different clients by particular priests. I also collected forty roots readings performed by the Oba of Òyótúnjí. The following description of divination readings in Òyótúnjí resembled a regular day in which visitors, mostly black Americans in search of divinatory advice or new religious possibilities from various parts of the United States, England, and the Caribbean, visited the community for one of its monthly festivals.

Case Study: Roots Reading 1.
The Recanonization of Ifá Divination

On this particular day, like most, the overwhelming majority of visitors wore African-derived "traditional" clothes, and having either converted to Yorùbá practices or having made the voyage to Òyótúnjí for purposes of spiritual exploration, four determined voyagers waited for one particular divinatory interpretation known as a *roots reading*. One awaiting his reading, in describing his need for a divination reading, claimed that he had converted because they "couldn't live like a good Christian in racist America"; most, however, discussed their need for support and guidance during periods of personal difficulty or overemphasized their desire for spiritual transformation. Another client, whom I will refer to as Adé Tọlá, a young dreadlocked man in his twenties, told me, "Any kind of help will do in this hellhole called Amerika." Discussing other reasons for converting to Yorùbá traditions, a small minority revealed that they were in search of clarity or "answers to explain the reasons for the enslavement of black people." An essential element of their conversion often involved a predisposition to reject Christianity and believe in something "African." Of the vast majority of individuals who consulted Ọ̀yọ́túnjí practitioners from March 1995 to March 1996, 69 percent (N=111) eventually adopted or had already adopted Yorùbá "traditional" beliefs because they were disillusioned with what they identified as the Eurocentricity of Christianity.

As I sat and waited outside the gates of the palace of the king of Ọ̀yọ́túnjí for another client to begin her divination session, I was struck by how long we had to wait for each divinatory reading, and I was intrigued by the seriousness with which clients incorporated the new information. My new acquaintances did not appear to be bothered by the passing of time. Both Adé Ṭọlá and the second client, whom I refer to as Ọ̀ṣúngbèmí, were prepared for a full weekend of ritual, communion, and personal transformation. After her divinatory ritual, Ọ̀ṣúngbèmí was proud that, according to the priest, her new Yorùbá name identified the Yorùbáland town in which her ancestors had lived over six hundred years ago. So proud was she that when I introduced myself to her, she was determined to remember the pronunciation of her new name and introduced herself by integrating the new name.

"Ọ̀ṣúngbèmí Àjàyí," she said as she contorted her face and nodded her head to the right on every syllable.[1]

"Nice to meet you," she continued with an outstretched hand and a big smile. Quickly incorporating such "traditional" practices—new names, clothes, and greetings—is common among many of the African American visitors I met during my year in Ọ̀yọ́túnjí. For new practitioners the divinatory roots reading references the nostalgia of the past and provides them with guidance for the future. "If you know where you came from, then you'll know where you're going," Adé Ṭọlá said to me a few days later. On this particular day the "where you're going" portion of his statement was answered with a divinatory directive for him to reclaim traditional practices to redeem himself, a call he had already begun to incorporate into his new Africancentric lifestyle. His statement is particularly appropriate because it is in keeping with popular metaphors that form the basis for Ọ̀yọ́túnjí roots readings.

The first client, Adé Ṭọlá, took his place on the mat, then remembered that the standard protocol involved saluting the priest by lying in front of him. As he lay there, the priest responded, "Dìde," and motioned for him to rise up.

"Thank you," replied Adé Ṭọlá, inappropriately responding in English.[2]

"Ẹ káàbọ̀ [You are welcome]," responded the priest in Yorùbá. After this preliminary exchange, the priest resumed his place on the divining mat and the client sat across from him. The priest began with a melodious incantation with which he beckoned the gods and the ancestors to join them. As he spoke, he repeatedly dangled his *òpèlè* (divining chain) over the beaded cowry in front of him. He then asked Adé Ṭọlá to place his money on the mat. The priest's voice cracked as he spoke. The money became the object with which the divining chain made contact.

The priest was dressed in a white cotton *agbádá* (traditional top) with matching pants. Necklaces embellished his neck and rings decorated his fingers. His hair, with its white streaks, was combed back and braided at the end. His head was covered with a distinguished and flashy Yorùbá "traditional" hat known as a *fìlà*. As he chanted quickly in Yorùbá, offering invocations to the various Yorùbá deities, he continued to touch the money with the divining chain. This part of the ritual incantation was similar to the incantation outlined in the previous chapter and is generally followed by a sequence in which the divining priest pays homage to religious and ancestral kin. As the priest methodologically lowered and elevated the divining chain, he chanted a meticulously constructed incantation. Even after he finished recalling all of the names, revering a genealogy of gods, ancestors, Ọ̀yọ́túnjí, Cuban, and Nigerian priests, and places imbued with diasporic nostalgia, he continued to look at his diving chain, an *òpèlè*, posing questions in Yorùbá as he gazed at it. It is important to note that responses arrive in the form of particular configurations of the *òpèlè*, known as the odù, which the priest then interprets. There are 256 odù configurations, and as the priest cast his chain down continuously, as if to throw dice and await the numeric configuration before him, he called out each odù, interpreting them as responses to each question posed.

The priest's assistant recorded all of them on a sheet of paper, and upon the establishment of the initial four odù, the priest studied the written configurations one after the other, occasionally muttering in English the story of a proverb (*ẹsẹ* or verse) associated with one of the four odù before him. After careful consideration of the proverbs and their meanings, he began the interpretation, translating the information for the client into English, prefacing each interpretation of the *ẹsẹ* with the slow and pensive authorial claim, "Ifá says."

The diviner began by claiming the sanctity of the interpretation as ordained by the gods. He carefully selected his words, often combining his English sentences with Yorùbá, and declared, "Ifá says that your family was from a lineage of Yorùbá royalty who practiced Ifá worship during their reign. . . . These clans folk," he declared, as if he had an insightful revelation, "lived in Ọ̀yọ́ and ruled there for centuries before evil individuals, commoners from a nearby town, deceived them and sold your family into transatlantic slavery. . . . Ifá says that the redemption of the offspring of this kinship clan could be realized through the worship of the Yorùbá deities, Ifá, and Ọ̀bàtálá," he added. The odù in the positive, or *ire*, as illustrated by the odù *Ogbè ṣé + mo jalè*, is the component of the canon that the diviner referenced to designate Adé Ṭọlá's family as emerging from a royal clan.[3] In this case, the reading is an ire, or positive reading, and an "ire blessing from the ancestors."

The diviner, who is usually highly trained, is endowed with the license to interpret the divinatory apparatus for clients (Akínnasọ 1995) and to narrativize solutions. In this first divinatory example, to establish a connection between New World identities and precolonial Yorùbá societies and to reference the institutional domain of Yorùbá power, the divining priest ritualized the incantations in Yorùbá. The bodily movements performed by the priest also flagged repetitious mechanical rituals common among Yorùbá priests throughout southwestern Nigeria. Through the routinization of repetitive bodily movements and speech acts, acts that Foucault referred to as *techniques of the self*, the priest reinforced particular inscriptions of power and knowledge by which truth emerged in a structure of rules communicated according to a range of discursive forms. Using technologies of the self, agents deploy particular ritual acts to cultivate particular practices with which subjects constitute themselves as worshipers, as well as to reinforce contextual frameworks that produce the particularities of truth.

Given the differential status and authority of diviners, certain types of knowledge are employed in particular hierarchies of institutional power by particular types of agents. The age structure of the community, combined with the economic conditions that make ritual specialization a financially desirable opportunity, and the rules regulating qualifications are among the key factors that shape who can become apprentices and who can perform certain types of divinatory rituals. Outcomes of involvement in divination enhance the hierarchy of priestly diviners.

The production of legitimate narratives from which a sacred, ancient, and fixed source must be referenced is the duty of the diviner alone, and in this process the diviner is in command of diagnosing the problem and narrativizing the solution. The diviner's ability to enact a ritual environment and to link the odù to relevant interpretations of the past forms the basis for the production of divinatory authority. When I looked into the eyes of the diviner as he spoke his slow and pensive mantra, I surmised that he saw himself as involved in a legitimate process of interpretation. To interpret the odù he was not only employing his training, but he believed he was in a trance that enabled him to communicate with the ancestors. In addition to his enactment of the divinatory ritual, the slow delivery of speech and his glazed eyes were important indicators that the interpretation of the odù emerged from an altered state. Anthropologists have long written about the authenticating dynamics that ritual-induced possession, often illustrated with altered speech (slow and pensive), has on the perceived legitimacy of ritual performances. When I attempted to interject my interests into the course of the interaction, I was cut off and forced to return to my role as listener, earlier designated by the divining priest. This further reinforced the uneven relationship between the diviner and the client. Nevertheless, through active reception, the client too participates in the making and legitimation of divinatory knowledge. These productions, shaped by determinations of truth as "natural" or as emergent from the heavens and therefore divine, are inextricably linked to the social, historical, and geographical worlds in which their meanings were constituted.

Thus far, I have examined the various zones of connection within which Yorùbá ancestral connections are forged. As we have seen, narratives of slavery and nobility are fundamental to the geopolitical basis for racial alliance. Here I now move to asking what are the various spiritual mechanisms within which the particularities of Yorùbá transnational connections are embedded and through which new meanings are spatially and temporally legitimized? How are ritual practices fashioned and refined to render a useable past to those who travel there seeking assistance? What are the interpretative constructions of ancestral connections with West Africa? With linkages established, the power of ritual often lies in the personal authority generated by the subject who is revered—as one would revere a prophet or a saint.

Explorations of divinatory ritual have demonstrated how Yorùbá religion provides the ideology by which people can understand their world and a means to interpret their role in it (Bascom 1969a, 1969b, 1980; Abímbọ́lá 1976, 1977; Akínnasọ 1995). Like the use of race as a way to interpret identity, and history as a way to understand the past, divination in Ọ̀yọ́túnjí Village and in larger Yorùbá networks is a domain for the revitalization of African nobility and a means for the actualization of legitimate meaning. A range of anthropologists has studied the centrality of divinatory knowledge in the lives of individuals and demonstrated that divination provides a means by which individuals can understand their world and interpret their role in it (Bascom 1969a, 1969b, 1980; Abímbọ́lá 1976, 1977; Akínnasọ 1995). It has also been demonstrated to be a mechanism by which agents interpret, consult, and hold symbolic power (Clarke 1997). Yet, even as divination involves the repetition of formal acts and utterances through which sacred knowledge is derived, it is also a highly interpretive act, embedded in particular relations of power. Contemporary studies of the processes of interpretation have placed attention on the value and power of divination as a ritual property, as well as on the role that ritual processes play in making the past and present coterminous (Herzfeld 1992; Maddox 1993). They have paid less attention to the specific processes by which changing divinatory interpretations are incorporated into the divinatory canon, thereby changing the canon itself. As I demonstrated in chapter 4, even as ritual incantations are used by practitioners to render ritual practices legitimate, the sites of change from which meanings are produced emerge not from discontinuities in meaning but from the production of apparent continuities in the status of the ritual form. I argue that the processes of enacting divinatory performances do not differ substantially from those of the Ifá canon characteristic of Nigerian Yorùbá religious traditions. As Niyi Akinnaso has shown us (see *Bourdieu and the Diviner*; 1995), Nigerian diviners also engage in the invention of divinatory forms and interpretations. Similarly, the invention of a new form of divinatory ritual reading, the roots reading, enables practitioners to incorporate the form and structure of Ifá divination and the history of slavery and women's insubordination into new institutional forms. For if religious ritual is useful, its value is in its ability to create relevant information consistent with both the past and changing daily circumstances—a fundamental feature of all divinatory acts.

Toward the Institutionalization of Yorùbá Tradition: Divination and Social Change

Divination is represented by practitioners as an application of sacred knowledge. It operates as a mechanism whose canonical divinatory structures enable priests to transport information through the temporal past to detached spaces. For divinatory communication to be seen as efficacious, however, the process must involve the systematic repetition of ritual protocol. The specialized knowledge that is derived is enacted in the daily life of Òyọ́túnjí Village residents and is characterized by both a performative language and a discourse of legitimation engaging both the diviner and the client in creating the ritual process, for ritual practices are central to Yorùbá revivalist life. Not only do they offer practitioners the ability to control their fate and therefore empower themselves with transformative acts, but they also allow practitioners to promote an underground economy in which like-minded believers can form economic alliances.

When practitioners are initiated into òrìṣà cult groups, divinatory readings are conducted to communicate with both the òrìṣà gods and Olódùmarè. This process of communion with the gods is at the center of practitioner obligations to a higher authority, and the odù (verses) that are derived and interpreted form the basis for a personalized law of conduct. Revivalist practitioners derive meanings from divinatory interpretations of ritual practices, constantly producing new divinatory "packages" of knowledge rules known as readings. These readings are performed within the particularities of those ritual codes deemed legitimate. These interpretations are written, sometimes tape-recorded, and revisited as a reminder of personal rules of conduct. These rules shape personal obligations that bind practitioners and provide the path to divinity (often referred to as a "road") and a type of specialized ritual knowledge based on the philosophies, training, and epistemologies of religious specialists.

One of the highest forms of Yorùbá ritual initiation is the marriage of a worshipper to one of the gods. This ritual process produces qualifications of priesthood into the world of òrìṣà worshippers and marks a reconnection to the ancestors below and above the earth.[4] It involves committing one's life to god forces, thereby entering the òrìṣà priesthood, and undergoing a series of ritual cleansings in which the old body must die for the new body to emerge. The strength of these ceremonies lies in their ability to link the past to the authority of god and to present contemporary social contexts.

In many religious traditions, the nature of interpretive narratives makes extreme diversity of interpretation problematic. Yet, unlike highly textualized religions that depend on one sacred text from which social codes are shaped, the power of prophetic messages in Yorùbá divination is in the social insights and relevant social advice that are transmitted through them. To look at essential forms of authority to understand how interpretive determinants change and how they are legitimized is to begin with the assumption that the recognition of knowledge as legitimate always involves critical processes of declaring the basis of authority.

In the case of Yorùbá divination, it is believed that through the course of a given ritual, priests channel the ancestors and therefore receive insights about the past and guidance for the future. Through the transmission of oral predictions, the priest is thought to engage in symbolic processes, and as a qualified intermediary derives from divinatory acts ancestral messages with which to link relevant social values to relevant social conditions. The act of spiritual channeling, therefore, results in the production of the prophetic message that is seen as being in the realm of the transcendental. Seen thus, the relationship between the symbolic and the social produces the conditions for structuring variations that are regenerative and paradoxical.

Victor Turner's (1967) work on ritual, borrowing from Arnold Van Gennep's (1960) theory of rites of passage, led to a philosophy of change which was simultaneously about the dialectics of structure and antistructure, producing a theory of ritual freedom within conditions of constraint. By developing liminality as a passage of transmission—from one social status to another, one condition to another (Apter 1992), Turner developed a modality through which to locate how ritual may provide a space for the articulation of ambiguity in which regeneration and renewal was possible within conditions of structural regulation. This dialectic of structure and antistructure marked the paradox in Turner's work and is fruitful for thinking about the production of spaces of variation, their limits, and their exceptions. In the case of Òyótúnjí divinatory mechanisms, it is national identities, temporal ordering of ancestral continuities, and racial meanings that are being ritually remapped. In divinatory terms, new narratives are being legitimatized in the context of superhuman power. As we shall see, when a divinatory ritual is performed and an interpretive analysis embarked upon, ties between hegemonic ritual structures are established and reproduced, and taxonomies in violation of particular forms of order are born. Thus, it is in the moment of religious trance— the embarkation of what Catherine Bell (1992) refers to as ritualization—that the divinity of the suprahuman produces the site of exception, the site of difference, that of erasure where momentary change is possible. Ultimately, I build on Turner to demonstrate that liminality, predicated on what Andrew Apter (1992) referred to as a "negative dialectic" can be pushed further to characterize particular forms of social power—that of Giorgio Agamben's (1998) conception of *states of exception*—an articulation of bare life, an existence that is included in democratic life through its exclusion. This realm of exclusion, this polluted state in need of redemption, is the sphere in which Yorùbá revivalists are engaged. And if we see the reordering of exclusion as the realm of the prophet, the taking up of the slavery of Africans, the people without history now marginalized and impoverished in the Americas, is productive because the diviner is operating outside of the legibility confines of not only the law, but the nation-state, thereby engaging in a form of transcendence that both reinforces and overturns the social order.

Using the example of the Yoruba prophet in the person of the Ọba of Ọ̀yọ́túnjí who claims to be able to use Ífa divination to trace the ancestry of all black Americans, we see that by attempting to address those outside of the reach of the sovereign, in the realm of exception, he engages in the power to suspend the reaches of sovereign pronouncements of citizenship and instead recast forms of knowing the past with alternate knowledge technologies. As the ultimate authority, the Ọba uses ritual mechanisms to engage in the suspension of particular norms of knowing by which to produce exceptions. This suspension of the law through the empowerment of the exception and the negation of the intelligible is a site of agency where variation is possible and a site of power mobilized to produce new routinized forms of practice within different fields of logic. Seen thus, the exception may become the norm within particular fields of power not just because he is already in command of community power, but because the discourses of redemption which are engaging the moral authority of subversion of the racial hierarchy of scale that marginalized blackness in the first place, was only able to achieve this through the ordering of whiteness in paradoxical distinction between blackness and whiteness. The national and racial order being subverted in Ọ̀yọ́túnjí divinatory discourses is only possible through the suspension of the forms of institutionalization that created black marginalization in the first place. When this is done, the divinatory order and supernatural logics are called upon to produce a reordering. In this context, what circulates is a threshold of chaos, a domain of disorder in which new spatiotemporal limits are assigned and racially derived ancestral mappings are produced according to race and not citizenship. Agamben, speaking through Schmitt in *Das Nomos*, has explained that this is made possible

> through the creation of a zone of indistinction between outside and inside, chaos and the normal situation—the state of exception. To refer to something, a rule must both presuppose and yet still establish a relation with what is outside relation (the nonrelational). The relation of exception thus simply expresses the originary formal structure of the juridicial relation. In this sense, the sovereign decision on the exception is the originary juridico-political structure on the basis of which what is included in the juridicial order and what is excluded from it acquire their meaning. . . . As such, the state of exception itself is thus, essentially unlocalizable (even if definite spatialtemporal limits can be assigned to it from time to time). (1998)

This articulation demonstrates that if the rule of determining citizenship and ancestral roots can be understood only in relation to a particular regime of authority, then the production of a new regime of logic, whether a supranatural regime or a regime that uses useful knowledge techniques, emerges outside of the authorial regime. It is the moral authority of Òyótúnjí divinatory reclassification that carries human redemptive goals that make explicit the ways the exception—the racial Other—is intimately tied to the fundamental ordering of race. Therefore, the production of the two categories of extreme difference—whiteness and blackness—are already included in the whole. Where Agamben concludes that sovereignty is precisely that which applies to the exception, the space of exception—that which seems to appear outside of social order—is able to mobilize change precisely because it constitutes the antimony of that order. Divinatory ritual, as a technique of redemption, can produce variation if the structures of legitimacy are in place, and the moral order can be mobilized to remap new inclusions, even if within different domains of knowledge.

Producing Spaces of Exception in Yoruba Divination

There are six principal methods of Yorùbá divination in Nigeria (Akínnasọ 1995, 237) that range from Ifá to *obì* divination. Among New World Yorùbá, four standard divinatory techniques and approaches are used. Despite these differing techniques, the objectives of both involve communication with a higher power. Not everyone in Òyótúnjí is a diviner, and not everyone has equal participation in all divinatory rituals. There is a clear distinction between those individuals who are initiated into the priesthood and those who are not. Priestly initiates gain access to sophisticated divinatory practices, and their status in the community is imbued with secrecy.[5] Uninitiated practitioners interested in divinatory knowledge either consult a priestly initiate for divinatory knowledge or perform their own divinatory methods with a four-piece divinatory apparatus known as an *obì*.

The obì approach allows noninitiates to pursue questions for which a yes-no response is adequate. It is the most basic form of Yorùbá divination (for more, see González-Wippler 1992, 3; Mason 1992, 26–35). The *Èrìndínlógún* and Ifá forms of divination are performed only by initiated priests; they are considered more accurate and so have a higher knowledge-producing status. It is not by accident, therefore, that in Òyòtúnjí Village, the Qba was for many years the central figure for performing exclusive rituals and producing the authoritative word on various divinatory interpretations. Between 1972 and 1988, the Qba of Òyòtúnjí was the only performing Ifá divinatory readings in Òyòtúnjí.[6] The rarity and complexity of stages of Ifá initiation and divinatory training contributed to its prominent status in Òyòtúnjí. One could not easily become a babaláwo in Òyòtúnjí because initiations into the Ifá cult were not conducted in the village until 1997. They were scarcely available in the United States in the 1990s and only became more accessible in the early 2000s.

Òyòtúnjí revivalist practitioners are not hierarchy-neutral. Diviners are valued according to their status as priests. Social boundaries are deeply embedded in status and rank rather than conventional class distinctions. Their particular forms of specialized knowledge, their sex, access to archaic technology, political standing in the community and reputation from general gossip, and client feedback all contribute to their rank. Throughout the 1970s to the late 1980s, the unique status of the Qba as the only babaláwo to conduct Ifá divination contributed to a situation in which his services were always necessary components of all priest initiations in Òyòtúnjí. By the late 1980s and early 1990s, as more Òyòtúnjí priests traveled to Nigeria and Benin to pursue *Igbó odù* (the initiation procedure of obtaining a primary divinatory odù for Ifá), increasing numbers of residents became equipped to conduct the highest form of Yorùbá divination. It was not until the late 1990s, when a mass of five priests had traveled to Benin and Nigeria and pursued their own Ifá initiations, that the Qba's involvement could be replaced by high-ranking chiefs.

Ifá divination is represented in Òyòtúnjí Village as the most sophisticated and ancient form of divinatory knowledge. It is believed to have sustained its ancient and traditional form over longer periods than the other system, Èrìndínlógún (Brandon 1993, 142). Èrìndínlógún is the most common form of divination among recently initiated priests in Ọ̀yọ́túnjí and throughout U.S.-affiliated and Santería communities. This approach is more inclusive in its potential for participation, for both women and men can function equally as Ẹ̀rìndínlógún priests. This is not true for Ifá divination; although both women and men can undergo the preliminary stages of initiation, granting them tools to legitimately conduct Ifá divination, only men are permitted to pursue the secondary, more complex level in which they are said to go to Igbó odù and become babaláwos, the highest rank of priesthood. Because the majority of prominent priests in Ọ̀yọ́túnjí are now babaláwo, much of the following is based on my observations of Ifá divination, the most prestigious divinatory form.

The main sources of income for residents in Ọ̀yọ́túnjí range from ritual services such as divination and counseling to tourism tours and sales. The priests who are called on to provide services during religious ceremonies are paid. Those hired to perform ritual work are engaged if they are already ideologically and politically allied with a priest's particular system of interpretation. Most practitioners who join the community strive to undergo the necessary ritual procedures so that they can become initiated in an òrìṣà cult and train to be a diviner. By asking how race and religion shape the ideologies necessary to enact particular forms of divinatory knowledge production, I follow genealogies of scholarship that connect Max Weber (1947, 1958, 1963) and his contemporaries to Pierre Bourdieu (1990) and his contemporaries. I also explore the role of status in the formation of divination as a system of prestige and power. Most of the new clients who visited Ọ̀yọ́túnjí tended to be from lower-middle- to working-class families and ranged in age from their late twenties to their late forties, but class distinctions are complex and do not always fit neatly into traditional approaches to power, access, and privilege. I establish particular material measurements of wealth and access that shape the relations of possibility by which status is measured, and use class as a category in relation to its intersections with not only income level, occupational skill, and education, but also consumption practices and social value—insofar as they cross-cut status and prestige, gender and patriarchy in particular fields of power. For the ability of practitioners to enforce different meanings depends not only on the basis on which claims are legitimated, but also on the status of the agents making those claims. As we will see, the diviner is often seen as a spiritual medium through which divine information is communicated and some diviners, those with more years of practice, are seen as more precise and gifted than those who are younger both in priestly years and physical age.

Praise-laced gossip and the differential size of clientele, along with monetary gain, also create order and status among the differentially successful diviners, who are already hierarchically structured in terms of age and, to some extent, sex. To develop a clientele priests must provide a variety of services; thus, networks of experts are created. For example, follow-up ritual work that results from divination readings often generates additional income-producing possibilities, and the products that must be purchased to carry out this work are often bought from aligned supporters.

The local economies of Yorùbá traditions in the United States are also shaped by material and historical forces that involve ritual sharing and are significantly affected by religious and political alliances. In the context of the network of Ọ̀yọ́túnjí-affiliated communities in the U.S., diviners in Ọ̀yọ́túnjí tend to be the highest-paid workers because of their specialized knowledge and power of interpretation. Both initiated and uninitiated Yorùbá practitioners solicit the work of priests and priestesses to perform divinatory rituals.

Institutionalizing Readings: Types of Divination Readings

I have classified divination readings into two categories: the standard individual reading (which incorporates the ancestral family), and the civic society reading (which incorporates cult groups known as *Ẹgbẹ́s*). If a divinatory interpretation is performed for an individual client, the priest's task is to pose a question or request and to interpret the encoded message. If the message is negative, it is the priest's duty to ascertain the type of sacrifice that must be made to remedy the client's problem. If the divinatory reading is employed to serve a public purpose, broader questions might be asked and more variables investigated. During such processes, after the invocations and opening questions are completed, the actual consultation through divination can begin. Different divinatory methods involving both Ẹ̀rìndínlógún and Ifá are used for the standard individual reading; however, only Ifá readings are used for readings that have civic purposes.

Individual readings are the most common in both Yorùbáland and the Americas and are conducted between a client and a diviner. In Nigeria, they tend to take place in the presence of the client. In the United States, although in most cases the presence of the client is necessary, there are new innovations allowing absentee divinatory readings that can be communicated by telephone (otherwise known as divination by phone) or by Internet. Nevertheless, the standard interaction is organized as a private consultation in which the priest functions as a conduit through which messages from the ancestors and òrìṣàs are transmitted and communicated to the client in person. In the pursuit of ritual interpretation, the priest is said to "read" the configuration of the divinatory tools and is then expected to verbalize these interpretations for a client in the form of a message. Individual divination readings can also be a necessary part of social activities. Two examples of the creative incorporation of standard readings in U.S. revivalist movements are the river reading, designed to ritualize the process of initiation of new Ọ̀yọ́túnjí residents, and the family reading, *orò ìdílé*, otherwise known as the roots reading.[7]

Divinatory roots readings follow the same logic and format as both standard and civic readings, but their goal is to recover client ancestral histories. By tracing family lineage, determining kin occupations, and endowing the client with new Yorùbá names, the reading has a transformative purpose. It reproduces a canon of Yorùbá divinatory structure while reshaping the terms in which Yorùbá history is resignified in new locations. With the goal of obtaining knowledge about Yorùbá or West African ancestors, the exchange of knowledge between client and diviner is made possible through the ritualization of the Ifá canon.

Both forms of divinatory processes share the same methods but serve different functions. The most necessary form of divination for establishing a personal ancestral connection to West Africa is the roots reading. The highly individualized standard reading can be contrasted with the civic society reading, which, although structurally similar to the individual reading, is conducted for the purpose of group instruction. In both Nigeria and Ọ̀yọ́túnjí Village, chief priests conduct civic readings to alert the leadership, the community, or the nation of the oracle's predictions. The types of civic readings popular in Ọ̀yọ́túnjí include the reading of the week, the reading of the month, the reading of the year, and the annual òrìṣà cult (Ẹgbé) readings.[8] Often, civic readings are performed by two or more priests from a designated cult group and occur in incrementally consistent periods.

The reading of the year is one such civic divinatory ritual and represents a set of predictions for the New Year.[9] Similarly, the readings of the week are conducted on a weekly basis in Ọ̀yọ́túnjí and represent practitioner attempts to collect and document authoritative translations of the Yorùbá past. Although traditionally delivered orally and committed to memory, in the late twentieth and early twenty-first century the production of these divination readings has shifted from the oral transmission of narratives to the translation of oral narratives to the written documentation of these predictions and postings on electronic mail and the Internet.

The priests who are called on to provide services are always compensated for their labor. But most of the income earned from divination comes from nonresident nonpriests who call or visit Ọ̀yọ́túnjí for mandatory follow-up ritual work deemed necessary by the gods. If an uninitiated nonpractitioner or a practitioner resident expresses interest in further exploring the remedies to conditions raised during the divination reading, he or she may establish a work relationship with a priestly intermediary who can serve as a consultant or *olórìṣà* (òrìṣà guide or trainer).[10]

Until the mid- to late 1960s, in New York City Santería-based divinatory techniques were incorporated by many òrìṣà voodoo Yorùbá revivalists and provided adherents with the necessary tools to produce Yorùbá ritual knowledge about the past and to predict the future. Over time, Ọ̀yọ́túnjí-centered revivalists radically adapted their divinatory rituals to produce a new mechanism through which the ancestral past could be known. These ritual acts incorporated the historical narrative of slavery and were made to perform the changing face of òrìṣà voodoo. Through the development of ritual institutions, various rituals, such as divination readings, circulate as a form of knowledge production about the past and future.[11]

With the increased centralization of authoritative divinatory texts and the emergence of a centralized authority, divination became less personal and individual and more bureaucratic. This transformation led to the routinization of particular forms of authority through which religious movements and their constituents create ways of arranging, structuring, and resolving disputes connected to dealing with other, competing claims to authority. That is, with the establishment of normative values and bundles of divinatory types, transnational Yorùbá revivalists tend to reproduce the social values in their world. Challenges to these norms, whether from external political institutions such as states or superior authorities, are often either incorporated and routinized in the social norms of the everyday, or they are rejected. In the case of Yorùbá revivalism, the symbolics of whiteness, Santería, and slavery are distinguished from signs of blackness and Africanness. The rules regarding who can belong and why, how rituals should be performed, and how people can redeem themselves or claim privileges of ritual action are connected to the routinization of authority for the purpose of self-preservation.

Case Study: Roots Reading 2

As seen in chapter 3 academic texts describing divination practices during the colonial period in West Africa also provide a critical canon for the interpretative process. Although the canons that otherwise direct and shape the authenticity, stability, and, hence, legitimacy of the ritual are critical, the authority of the diviner—one in command of diagnosing and narrativizing the solutions—is as central to the formation of the legitimacy of the ritual process as is the authority of the canonical history. The process of performance allows Ọ̀yọ́túnjí practitioners the means of narrating selected ancestral lineages; differentially affixing blame to past ancestors of those lineages is consistent with the gender and behavioral characteristics the diviner attributes to particular persons seeking their assistance.

Like all the others, the priest's reading of my ancestral genealogy began with a standard incantation to the gods. As I sat on the mat across from the diviner,

I began to tell him about my project and why I was there, but I quickly realized that my unsolicited comments had no place in the diviner-client exchange. The priest's incantations and technique of identifying my family lineage were based on his consultation of the oracle in Yorùbá—not me. Once I had paid the requested amount, the diviner continued with his invocation.[12]

A presumption of authority on the part of the diviner is negotiated in the process of client-diviner interaction and is an important component of the ritual. Although clients may question or challenge the interpretation offered to them and doubt the efficacy of the ritual or the qualifications of the diviner to exact his or her interpretations, the ritual is often measured by clients according to the extent to which the form and content of the ritual is in alignment with a dominant canonical structure (Akínnaṣọ 1995, 244).

In a U.S. Yorùbá dialect, the diviner posed to the gods the necessary questions about my ancestral heredity. To obtain the answers he cast the ọ̀pẹ̀lẹ̀, each time deriving a new odù configuration. As he cast the chain he called out the name of the odù and his assistant recorded it on a piece of paper. Once completed, the diviner read the paper and took a few minutes to think about the interpretation. Puzzled by the meaning of the first configuration in relation to the last, the diviner instructed his assistant priest to open the large text, entitled *Ifá Divination: Communication between Gods and Men in West Africa* (Bascom, 1969a), that had been on the floor next to the divining tray. After thinking about the meaning of the first odù, in a slow and thoughtful, almost trance-like state he interpreted the oracle, always looking at the paper before him:

> Ifá says this was a brilliant society of enormously psychic babaláwo. The rule and respect of Ifá was predominant in this clan that lived in the environs of the capital city of Ọ̀yọ́. Ifá says this was a clan that had produced numerous individuals of outstanding citizenship. They were the pride of their community. On the negative side, there were many females who tended to become very proud, arrogant, and out of control despite numerous warnings from their babaláwo husbands. Ifá says domineering women persisted in following their own minds, which ultimately brought a perversion in the destiny of the clan. Much ẹbọ was done, and though everyone of half adult years held membership in some cult, tragedy befell the clan in the form of numerous deaths and losses. The massive ẹbọ included the sacrifice of youthful members into the transatlantic slave trade.[13] While these cruel sacrifices did redeem the clan's fortunes, they brought greater discipline to its female membership. Those sacrificed in their ocean-bound prisons sailed out of sight and were never to be heard from again.

The lesson from my ancestral lineage was that the women of the clan needed to exercise greater self-discipline. I was told that I could finalize the punishment of enslavement by resuming my family's ancestral worship and, as Ifá had instructed, "revert back to a Yorùbá way of life."

Insubordination is often highlighted by Ọ̀yọ́túnjí priests as a central cause of the enslavement of both men and women from Ọ̀yọ́ to the Americas. Its relevance is most profound in relation to the ways that women's roles are heavily regulated in accordance with what it means to be traditional, subordinate, and harmonious. In the majority of the roots readings, the priest identified that a wrong deed was committed either by a female, an egocentric individual, or an unruly kin member of either sex, and as a consequence a tragedy befell the entire community. Regardless of whether the client's family was the victim or the perpetrator of enslavement, priests often foreground enslavement as a curse that insubordinate ancestors, especially females, brought upon their community members.

As seen in the diviner's interpretation of my odù, the occupation of my ancestral clan is similar to my current occupation. The Ọ̀yọ́túnjí divinatory interpretations that emerged from divinatory ritual sessions were informed by wider social and historical concerns specific to local responses of racism and attempts to reach a deeper understanding of how the past can be rectified in the present.

Indeed, anthropological and historical texts play an important role in shaping and authorizing the diasporic interpretations of the canon. The referential use of William Bascom's text, for example, continues to provide practitioners with literate documentation of the standard interpretations for odù Ifá. Many African Americans who were initiated by Cuban practitioners in the 1950s and 1960s relied on these English textual explanations of the practices in which they were initiated (see Bascom 1969a, 26–119). These texts provided both the translation and the explanation for how to conduct Ifá divination as well as how to procure ritual sacrifices, interpret proverbs, and construct incantations for Yorùbá ritual. To legitimize their contemporary knowledge of Yorùbá ritual, Ọ̀yọ́túnjí priests continue to rely on the academic works of Nigerian cultural practices, the priesthood, initiation and divination rites, and the results of their own divinatory innovations. Nevertheless, because the divinatory canon, thus recovered, exists without long histories of New World precedents, Ọ̀yọ́túnjí villagers have a substantial degree of leverage with which to narrativize the past.

Ritualists, as intellectual producers, chart historical narratives and predict the future. They perform divination for clients and connect dislocated histories with U.S. realities. Understanding the politics of Yorùbá divinatory training and interpretation and the transmission of knowledge about the Yorùbá canon is critical to understanding the complexities of status and authority that shape how innovations are possible even as sites of exception. An example of the processes of creative change can be seen in the way the diviner incorporated the canon into a new interpretation of my ancestral past. His interpretation began with a linear progression of my kinship origins, traceable along both paternal and maternal lines of racial descent. Through the standard ritual mechanism that located race as a biological feature that passed from generation to generation in a linear pattern, from one *black* ancestor to the next, he determined that it was my maternal ancestors who contributed to the tragedy of the enslavement of my ancestral kin. Here we see that dispossession is discussed in relation to the enslavement of family members, and the hierarchical orders of race are called on to locate my phenotypic membership to blackness in those terms. It may seem that defining state power in relation to its structure of citizenship may be reflective of sovereign power at work. However, it is the form of *exception*, the capturing of the exclusive inclusion of slave ancestors from which to make redemption possible that the power of the diviner is enforced.

Another level of dispossession was evident in my reading. Implicit in such narratives was the complicity of not just African kin in the enslavement of African Americans, but the complicity of women in the enslavement of the family. As the divinatory discourses demonstrate, because of their wrongdoing African women were the central agents perpetuating the enslavement of their kin. Here, the gender of the blameworthy captive is located in the place of women as insubordinate, and therefore, guilty of disrupting the normative order of gender relations. It is the gendered order of blame as it played out in redemptive sphere. As such, the diviner explained that because of the evils of such ancestors, mine and others, contemporary black Americans still suffer from racism, poverty, and social marginalization—all consequences of the slave past. This inversion of slave suffering as intentional punishment for wrongdoing inverts the social order in such a way that is only possible with the suspension of social order through the liminality of ritual.

Divination conducted in communities such as Ọ̀yọ́túnjí Village provides the believer with the means of enacting personal prestige and power through which to undermine particular tenets of the order of things. Practitioner determinations for which rituals are appropriate and which interpretations are accurate raise concerns about the grounds on which knowledge production is shaped. Although Nigerian diviners do not conduct roots readings as such, Bascom (1969a, 37–39), in his examination of Yorùbá Ifá priests in Nigeria, documented more than sixty divinatory incantations and interpretations offered to the African gods by Nigerian Yorùbá diviners. These prayers also followed a standard sequence seen in New World divinatory performances but invoked the "gods from the heavens, fields, and trees" to join them, never making reference to transatlantic slavery. Even with the variability of New World revivalist concerns, the improvised structure of divination is maintained as credible because it incorporates Yorùbá divinatory ritual structure and language, assumes communication with the gods and ancestors, and pulls from interpretive structures known to informed practitioners.

To divine using Ifá, the key to interpretation is in matching the divining chain configuration to one of the 256 odù that exist. Their importance and authorizing power exists because each odù is a sacred message from the Yorùbá high god known as Òrúnmìlà. Ultimately, odù represent the ancient wisdom from the heavens. Each odù is identified by a two-word name that symbolizes specific characteristics, marking it as unique and enabling the diviner to connect to it a parable or verse, the ẹsẹ. The matching of the odù with a characteristic and applying its meaning to the social life of the client are what enable variation to emerge as adaptations and not deviations from the Yorùbá canon.

The challenge of charting the production of new institutional forms of divinatory knowledge is in understanding the tenets of legitimacy on which new narratives are imported into seemingly fixed forms. That is, canonical legitimacy depends on the perception of the reproduction of an authorial canon. Even as texts may appear fixed, priests incorporate new interpretations into fundamental tenets of the divinatory canon. For indeed, in Òyótúnjí, as in many Yorùbá divinatory settings, both performative language and ritual acts play a central role in ensuring the authority of the priest's ritual interpretations.

Case Study: Roots Reading 3

The next client was Òṣúngbèmí. Her roots reading followed the same pattern of noble beginnings, trauma, and redemption. The priest described her family as people who provided "initiates into the cult of Ifá," a noble and esteemed position. They were intelligent and talented. However, the factors that led to the demise of her ancestors were different from the previous two examples. In her case, the sin was far more severe. The family's arrogance and their neglect of religious practices led to their tragedy, and issues of jealousy and disagreements led to "serious calamities in their households." Yet, the priest consoled her by suggesting that the transatlantic slave trade provided her with opportunities to make sacrifices to the gods on behalf of the female members of the household. He raised another concern about the existence of sexual promiscuity. "Females are advised to proceed with care into polygamous households and to worship Ifá," he warned.

This example again emphasizes Africans' responsibility for sending their families into slavery. Interestingly, all of those involved were in a clan of diviners and were not themselves actively involved in selling African bodies into slavery; they but encountered situations in which they were victimized by slave sellers. Again, slavery was represented by the diviner as a punishment, the result of West Africans' wrongdoing.

The slavery narrative highlights the same dynamic, in which African historical figures were seen as agents and genitors of the transatlantic slave trade. Here again, only redemption can bring about social change. In other words, Yorùbá Nigerians and, by extension, Ọṣúngbèmí, as agents of wrongdoing, are able to correct past infractions through their reclamation of ancient traditions. According to the narratives circulated by Ọ̀yọ́túnjí diviners and practitioners, it was their "fall" from these traditions that led to their destruction.

The diviner located the roots of this young female client, a first-year college student of Native American and black American parentage, in southwestern Nigeria. He did not identify her ancestral lineage as coming from her Cherokee grandmother's line, but from her African American father's line. In this case, she was told that her ancestors might have been Ìjẹ̀bú, Ẹ̀gbá, or Nàgó. As I sat and listened to the way her lineage was identified, I tried to ascertain whether Ọṣúngbèmí was disturbed that her Native American ancestry was not included. I studied her facial expressions as the priest continued to talk about the confusion of the African women in her past. No mention was ever made of her Cherokee grandmother, and it did not seem to matter to her. As the priest relayed his interpretation of her past, Ọṣúngbèmí sat on the mat with her tape recorder running and her eyes closed, arms apart and up with her palms cupped to the ceiling. Occasionally, she took notes, but she seemed to be more interested in experiencing the moment by helping the priest channel this information.

When Ọṣúngbèmí and I were in Beaufort's Applebee's Bar and Grill later that afternoon, a middle-age African American woman who noticed us in our traditional clothes approached us to ask if "we were from that village" and if it was true that "the Ọ̀yọ́túnjí king is a fake light-skinned man from Detroit." In the king's defense, Ọṣúngbèmí responded angrily that it didn't matter that the Ọba was "born in Detroit, and who cares what shade his skin is? He's black, isn't he?" she added.

I eventually understood the transformative meaning that the divinatory ritual had for her. As we returned to the car, she revisited the topic by telling me that it really bothered her that people "judge the authenticity of their ancestral practices based on skin color and shade. . . . This light-skinned/dark-skinned thing is messed up," she added, insisting that when the priest was conducting her roots reading, it did not matter to her that he had been born and raised in Detroit. What mattered to her was that he knew how to channel Ifá through the gods of Africa.

For Ọṣúngbèmí, the performance of ritual was real and the obvious changes of descent patterning and New World adaptations were fine so long as the priest was acting through the guidance of Ifá. When I asked her how she knew that the diviner successfully used Ifá to contact the ancestors, she told me that she "felt the vibration," and that was why she kept her hands outstretched. Her sense of the authenticity of the ritual was based on both the feeling she encountered from being engaged in the ritual and the priest's ability to create a credible, moving environment of ritual performance. The priest's responsibilities for the environment included chants in Yorùbá, the divinatory equipment, the establishment of the odù, his references to those odù, and the use of slow, pensive speech in his delivery. But also, Òṣúngbèmí entered the situation with a willingness to believe and a need to make changes in her life. Although disappointed with the news of her family's historical turmoil, so pleased was she with the follow-up redemptive strategies to engage in "intense worship of Ifá" that she paid not only the standard $100 fee, but included an extra $10 in the bundle. I asked her why she paid more money than she was asked to. "He helped me explain my true African identity," she responded. "No more slave master's name and no more shame. That's all I wanted and that's what I got. One hundred dollars isn't enough [money] for that kind of satisfaction."

Redemption from the shame of a history associated with enslavement is indeed an important aspect of the process of reclaiming preslavery African traditions. A range of prescriptive, redemptive follow-up rituals provides clients with the possibility of redemption and often involves additional rituals at prices from $100 (head cleaning and sacrifices) and to $4,500 (initiation into the priesthood). The readings themselves, however, cost a basic fee of $40 to $100. In general, monetary exchange is a significant component of the ritual, but, according to many of the clients I interviewed, money was not a satisfying way to reward someone with "psychic powers." Nonetheless, most agreed that diviners should be paid for their services.

Because individuals new to these traditional practices choose freely to engage in divination readings to elicit answers to questions beyond the ordinary range of human comprehension, it seemed clear that they already had a desire to accept the possibility that the divination can bear redemptive and transformative results. These clients are often willing to engage in the follow-up rituals. For Òṣúngbèmí, the follow-up rituals would give her a chance to redeem her family's destiny. In her words, the family's wrongdoing regarding slavery "could be dealt with once and for all with Yorùbá initiation."

There remain three similarities among the Ọ̀yọ́túnjí diviner's roots readings. First, using the symbolics of race as the basis for sameness, all three establish an ancestral connection with West Africa. Although relatively little has been written on Yorùbá history prior to the nineteenth century, a period that lacked literate documentation, various mythic representations of the Yorùbá past have been transmitted through divinatory verses and oral histories.

A second shared feature is thematic. They all developed out of an underlying concern about the tragedy (Akínnaso 1995, 253) of transatlantic slavery, thus reinforcing the capacity of the divinatory oracle to interpret the past and prophecy the future. All three clients were told about the historical components of the transatlantic slave trade. The diviner linked their contemporary social concerns with agreed-upon historical "facts" and strategies for redemption that put the diviner in the position of providing insights and relieving social suffering. The manipulation of genealogies of ancestry as expressed through ritual serves this purpose. For divinations become *readings*, in both the ritual sense (i.e., a roots reading) and the literary, interpretive sense, where enslavement is no longer an event that "happens to" Africans as a consequence of eternal forces; it is the product of the internal, morally inappropriate actions of specific ancestors. These actions, when properly understood by those who see themselves as the now differentially embodied continuities of these ancestors, can be corrected by a proper alignment with Yorùbá tradition as defined and practiced in Òyótúnjí. In relation to the success of what might otherwise be classified by outsiders as a "ludicrous derivation of the slave past," divination and the processes of incremental change that follow highlight the ways that new narratives are incorporated into otherwise "fixed" texts. Despite being identified as the descendants of more or less egregiously blameworthy ancestors, clients often leave divining sessions grateful for both the knowledge that connects them to their previously unknown pasts and the knowledge about how to go on in the future. Òyótúnjí residents' articulations of their slave past both intersect with models of knowledge transmission and push us to ask not new but different questions about the criteria by which we chart the processes of change in Yorùbá divination.

The third similarity among the divinatory narratives is the degree to which the priest, engaged in the ritual process, adapted a traditional Yorùbá rhetorical structure of the divinatory text. This stylistic adaptation is symbolic of the process by which themes, ideas, and events are adapted into divinatory texts and how the texts are in turn recontextualized to suit particular circumstances in space and time (Akínnaso 1995, 253). Many contemporary approaches to understanding how traditions are changed and how those changes are structured around authorial components of rituals demonstrate how, even as traditions change in structure and form, they are not always identified by those who live in them as having changed at all (Bell 1992, 118; Akínnaso 1995). The notion of traditional practices sometimes persists as fixed and unchanging, yet even some anthropologists who recognize

Ifá òrìṣà pot after ritual sacrifice.

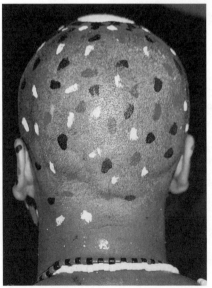

Ritual head paint/Ẹlégbá initiation.

Òrìṣà warriors; ritual sacrifice of a dog.

that change exists still miss the ways authorial ritual institutions and figures in positions of power play prominent roles in suspending particular structures of order and, instead, produce new alliances in transnational spheres of power.

In thinking of the national transformation of Yorùbá religious ritual, it is significant to understand these shifts in the context of hierarchies of relevant social relations and their reconfigurations in particular spaces. However, the relationship between structure, change, and power highlights that although identity is continually enacted through ritual, ritual is a site not only of identity formation, but of the reproduction, reformulation and regulation of local practices in particular ideological economies. The relationship between the racial regulation Africanness and the uses of Yorùbá ritual raises additional questions concerning what space diasporic producers of Yorùbá divinatory knowledge take up in their appeal for inclusion in the Yorùbá canon, and what are the consequences of those new alliances. While divinatory roots readings function as a form of social redemption for Òyótúnjí practitioners, the mechanics of producing divinatory change depend on the incorporation of innovations into preexisting authoritative structures. It is through this form that new and appropriate meanings can emerge (Akínnaṣọ

Ritual sacrifice prior to festival.

Ritual sacrifice of a goat during Egúngún festival.

1995), and as such the divinatory reading, like the incantation, become a map of particular religious alliances.

Despite the methodological role of the different forms of divinatory ritual and its changing nature, most Yorùbá diviners are intent on locating the efficacy of the ritual as ancient and therefore authentic. The relevance of thinking about change and innovation as a study about power and prestige in the diviner's interpretations is that his or her authority is not a given prior to the divination session; rather, it is created in the process (Akínnasǫ 1995, 254), and the status of the diviner, the basis for his or her knowledge, and the sites of variation are dependent on how changes are incorporated into Ifá divination by both incorporating and changing the canon itself. The Ifá canon can be changed only if practitioners recognize the form, structure, and meaning of the rituals as remaining intact. Therefore, for creative variability to take place among Yorùbá revivalists in the United States, specific conditions for ritual authenticity are necessary.

More is known about the role of religious ritual as a making of conditions for spiritual legitimacy when we move beyond the strictly ritual function to how rituals incorporate contemporary diasporic concerns to create new transnational alliances. Social rules set ideals for behavior, establish norms of belonging, and reinforce power relations through which spiritual transmissions are possible. These work through religious institutions and enable people to establish entitlements based on the experiences of both spiritual and redemptive logics of ritual norms and performative acts. In the absence of a state hegemony that is able to effectively structure the inner workings of Yorùbá revivalism, we see instead how the development of deterritorialized norms are shaped by new institutional mechanisms that gain legitimacy in particular fields of racial logics. Seen as such, the suspension of the external power of legal norms enable the interpretive power through which prophet—diviners, sacred interpreters—provide roadmaps for future action. Yes, despite the hegemony of racial categories in the U.S. as a form of exclusion, designations of the uses of ancestral categories still reinforce racial ideologies. This is not because they are so powerful that state articulations of racial order are reflections of the sovereignty of the law. Rather, it is because modern social order operates with requisite institutions that structure qualifications of participation according to classifications that make some concepts intelligible and therefore necessary for the establishment of legitimacy, and other concepts disposable if necessary. Some of those categories—birth status, origins, sex, race, and so forth—are always negotiable; however, what is critical is recognizing how and why the stability of certain categories or institutions are necessary, and when and why others are not. As I demonstrated in chapter 1 and established in chapter 2, with the development of modern capitalism, individual distinctions were shaped by human differences through a discourse of state-enforced racial biology. The shift from biological difference to individual-centered narratives about roots, though a response to the intensification of global migration and an attempt to territorialize displacement, was also reflected in the work of markets—literary and divinatory—in capitalizing on the shift to territorial heritage. Roots readings are fundamentally about the redemption of the bare life status of slaves, and therefore, in the context of the black Atlantic, they are about the suspension of whiteness or the de-centering of light skin through which to engage the exclusions of slavery and produce formulas of empowerment. As such, new conditions of possibility are shaped in relation to the modernity of racial difference as they play out in gendered and family-oriented forms. Such forms of difference provide the backdrop by which to articulate the ways in which subjectivity is reproduced in institutions of power.

The next chapter moves us to the realm of formal and informal regulation through the use of historical and legal knowledge forms. I begin with an example of informal regulation of subject codes and end with an example of formal regulation. Unlike the first part of the book, where I was interested in the history of the colonial state and early legal regulations connected to the entrenchment of ideological hierarchies, the next chapter explores legal regulations as they are imported by Yorùbá revivalists interested in recouping precolonial West African law. Here, the prestige of the past has symbolic power, but, as we will see, what constitutes the precolonial past for contemporary transnational mappings of Yorùbá traditionalism is shaped by particular colonial inscriptions (Martin Shaw 1995) that underlie the contours of those framings in everyday life.

6. Recasting Gender: Family, Status, and Legal Institutionalism

W HEN I ENTERED ÒYÓTÚNJÍ VILLAGE to begin my fifteen-month stretch of fieldwork, I wore a bright yellow, patterned blouse made out of a cotton fabric from Senegal with a pair of casual white cotton pants. I was greeted by the head of the women's society, a female chief, who had remembered me from my visit a summer earlier.[1] After we exchanged niceties in Yorùbá and I bowed to acknowledge her ancestral membership and priesthood status, she took me aside to both complement and scold me.

"You wore such nice clothes the last time," she said as she looked down at my pants with a smile. "But if you plan to live with us here you will have to wear a lapa [a skirt-like wrap]," she continued. "Òyótúnjí is a traditional village and women don't wear pants." She then insisted that the proper way to be an "African woman" was to wear traditional women's wraps around the bottom half of my body. She graciously offered to sell me clothes from her market stall.

Still, thinking that I could be excused from the standards to which all practitioners are expected to comply, I resisted by thanking her but explaining how comfortable I felt when I wore what I was accustomed to wearing. Alluding to my purpose for being there, she showed me Samuel Johnson's (1921) *History of the Yorùbás* and told me I should study it if I really wanted to understand Yorùbá traditions and the place of women in those traditions. Having read Johnson's work, I could not plead ignorance; I confessed that I simply did not bring my lapas with me. To that she responded that my attire was neither traditional nor family-oriented and that I should never return with "those men's clothes." She directed me to her market stall and told me that I was in the "right place." Pointing to the clothes in her stall (as if in an infomercial), she told me to "forget those American

Queen's market stall.

clothes, show your true traditional identity; buy African clothes." In response, we both laughed, but for different reasons.

In the evening, reflecting on the morning's interaction, the chief explained to me that her laughter was in part to relieve the tension between us. She told me that she could not believe that I would stand there so blatantly wearing the "wrong clothes," arguing with her about something that was so obviously "wrong." My laughter was inspired by my realization of the irony of my resistance. For regardless of the fact that I was a researcher studying practitioner reconstructions and contestations of Yorùbá traditions, I was a woman and therefore subject to the gendered dress codes enforced by the network of both married and unmarried women.

The chief's insistence on gendered dress codes and the familiar historical structure of proof, discussed in earlier chapters and in this case used to enforce kinship protocol, was her attempt to situate gender distinctions in the context of the revitalization of Yorùbá nationhood in the Americas. She invoked a standard model for a Yorùbá family, which insisted on distinct male and female practices. It was through my experiences of women's rebuke that I came to understand that Yorùbá revivalism in the United States is highly gendered and the Yorùbá family is the bedrock of Yorùbá tradition. In response to a question regarding the correct procedure for renting or building a compound on Ọ̀yọ́túnjí property, the chief insisted that because I was not married and did not have a male child over the age of twenty-five with whom I could live, I could neither rent nor build a house and live in it

Ọ̀yọ́túnjí marketplace.

alone. According to the rules, I had to either be married to a male resident and live in his compound or I had to live in the king's palace under his accountability. This, she explained, had to do with Ọ̀yọ́túnjí's antifraternization laws, which expected men and women to socialize separately. These laws were meant to regulate people like me: an unmarried woman and therefore a *potential wife*, who, according to Ọ̀yọ́túnjí laws, was not yet accountable to an Ọ̀yọ́túnjí family.

Ọ̀yọ́túnjí Village is a traditional community in which the symbolic order is modeled on a distinctly gendered family that is reinforced through the sanctity of the "traditional past." These approaches to Yorùbá traditionalism raise questions about the organization of male and female power, about what aspects of a given traditional practice are to be emphasized in the process of reconstructing the Yorùbá past, and under what conditions and why those aspects are to be enforced. Just as any domestic system of social order requires mechanisms whereby disputes are solved and truth established, Ọ̀yọ́túnjí social laws are composed out of comprehensive bodies of practices and rules that direct and control social behavior. The chief who met me at the front gate attempted to teach me the rules of gendered dress codes, and in that process she engaged in further producing a subject willing to comply with family and community rules. For ultimately, the basis of gendered legal rules is in the preservation of the family and the hierarchy of power. These rules are used to regulate internal relations of the family and, by extension, cult practices in the community and throughout the network.

In the process of establishing the formal and informal boundaries of social norms, social distinctions such as gender and hierarchical relations are shaped and reaffirmed. Thus, gender distinctions are not static. Processes of interpreting and negotiating rules of conduct are central to the negotiation of power and order in social life. Women are expected to act in particular ways, and young and unmarried women are often more regulated than others. However, women too participate in parodying and enforcing particular types of reconfigurations of gendered structures as well as maneuvering new meanings within them. To the chief, I was a prospective wife for one of the Ọyọtúnjí men, and she felt it critical to enforce rules of dress, protocol, and marriage, lest I pose a threat to the village's social organization. And although on that day she did not explain the dangers, the data suggest that my compliance was a signal to other women in the community that I was willingly conforming to their rules of antifraternization, thus respecting the sanctity of family.

The aim of this chapter is to explore the particularities of the gendered ideological order in the maintenance of a polygamous family institution that must, for its reproduction, closely regulate the sanctity of family. Although such an openly polygamous structure may seem to have an absence of regulation, on the contrary, both informal—through friendly reprimand and gossip–and formal rules and procedures are active in the regulation of family life. Like the sources used by practitioners to legitimize Yorùbá traditionalism in the production and innovation of individual and civic knowledge, the particularities of Yorùbá gender are embedded in the order of hierarchies: from fathers, to chiefs, to the ruling king. An individual's status comes from his or her place in the family. The family has rights and its own religion and is a metaphor for both the status and the lineage of Ọyọtúnjí order. The difficulty of reviving Yorùbá practices for revivalists in deterritorialized contexts is that the authority on which this family ideal is shaped must be seen as both legitimate and just: women must feel that they are not unjustly subservient, and there must be multiple domains of governance in which they are also empowered. Thus, the rules and laws must be seen as mirroring the Yorùbá ideal, thereby rendering the perception of fairness. For the survival of this deterritorialized network of practitioners outside of Africa is not just embedded in people's compliance with power and status hierarchies that order the place of the king in relation to the chiefs and the priests; these hierarchies are critical elements of the perceived fairness of this system and people's compliance with the core unit of the family.

The multiple layers of fairness, therefore, are central to Ọyọtúnjí core assumptions: that they are a community of their ancestors and that redemption from slavery and the reclamation of nobility form the basis for the return to precolonial

Yorùbá practices. These are central to determining why social distinctions between men and women matter and why class distinctions are secondary to status. The constant reformulation of Yorùbá tradition depends not merely on the individualistic component of gender performance as constructivism. Gendered distinctions and their accompanying practices in Òyótúnjí Village are not only constructed in keeping with dominant renditions of what it means to be traditional, but even as they are taught, regulated, and enforced, they are contradictorily accepted in people's daily lives. Both men and women enforce social rules to protect the sanctity of the family, and do so using formal and informal means. Yet even in the process of enforcing rules, maintaining social status is central to the system of value and hierarchy because social position is also relevant to legal norms: ultimately, it is not simply the enforcement of black letter rules that matter, it is also the gendered order of power and the sanctity of social hierarchies that propel the order of daily life. Formal and informal punishment, therefore, serves to enforce particular values and bonds of social solidarity and in so doing regulates and reinforces sentiments of a collective majority. Yorùbá womanhood is a signifier of norms of the past and is both learned and taught through the enforcement of the Yorùbá polygamous social organization. Revivalist notions of tradition are necessarily gendered and operate within institutional regimes that teach men and women to experience African repatriation in distinctly gendered terms. In the process, these norms construct moral subjects whose practices are in alignment with notions of the traditional woman. In other words, diasporic traditionalism is created, and in the process of production women learn how to employ the techniques of empowered subjugation to claim belonging to Yorùbá traditional membership.

The foregoing chapters have been engaged in the charting of space, place, language, religious ritual, and the informal rules that are invoked to constitute deterritorialized communities. This chapter is less about the informal rules of social relations and more about what happens when informal rules are invoked where formal rules already exist. In other words, when social regulations are explicit and people transcend them for a greater good, how is power played out when the structure of power is already very fluid? How are the modes of forgetting that are part of how community is constituted in the first place called on to impose institutional regulations through which power is recognizable, traditionally justified, and in alliance with modern imaginings of governance? In this way the work of imagining homelands in radically different spaces is about the production of alliance and power. What we see in this chapter is an example of how people live their lives in relation to the multiple layers of legal assessment determined by the politics of morality and hierarchy.

Understanding the workings of power is critical to determining the informal mechanisms of regulation and formal social forces operative in the formation of gender distinctions in the black Atlantic world. Based on their genealogical efforts, Ọ̀yọ́túnjí men and women assert Yorùbá marital laws and kinship organization. Women use rhetorical strategies to represent "ancient traditions" and regulate premarital and marital life and all Yorùbá revivalists use their local laws to enforce gender segregation to protect the sanctity of family. These laws regulate the ways boys and girls become traditional so long as they ensure the reproduction of a particular hierarchical order. Analysis of an Ọ̀yọ́túnjí court trial demonstrates that the enforcement of black letter rules is secondary to the hierarchy of order; to offend this is to offend the order of hierarchical power.

The Ideal of the Yorùbá Family: Purity, Polygamy, and Antifraternization

I entered Ọ̀yọ́túnjí soon after the death of two significant chiefs. One, a polygamous family man, died and was buried in May 1990. After his death, he was celebrated as a founding father of Ọ̀yọ́túnjí and an example of Yorùbá traditionalism. The other chief was polygamous but homosexual; before moving to New York and becoming an auxiliary Ọ̀yọ́túnjí chief, he had lived in the village in the 1970s. He died on September 22, 1993 of complications resulting from AIDS. The Ọ̀yọ́túnjí leadership saw the death of the latter chief as a consequence of his not maintaining "traditional mores." Many felt that his decision to engage in homosexual acts reflected his willingness to participate in "white male homosexual deviance." Unlike the former chief, whose life represented a traditional Yorùbá lifestyle, the latter chief was neither revered nor remembered in the pantheon of chiefs to be venerated after death. Such forms of embracing tradition have their power in the example of exclusion, thus discipline. For the message that polygamous heterosexuality is to be celebrated continues to permeate Ọ̀yọ́túnjí social life.

From the village's founding in the 1970s and through to the mid-1980s heterosexual polygamy has served as the foundation for restructuring Ọ̀yọ́túnjí family configurations. The adoption of polygamy as a form of traditional practice involves the necessary production of gender differentiation, for which marriage laws already circumscribe the terms of heterosexual unions and male patriarchy.[2] The idea that homosexual alliances have been imported into African American life and that homosexuality "pollutes" the traditional black family is pervasive among many Ọ̀yọ́túnjí practitioners. Therefore, Ọ̀yọ́túnjí practitioners abide by South Carolina laws regarding homosexuality and adapt their practices in an attempt to replicate Yorùbá traditional social structures.

With the exception of their stance on homosexuality, Yorùbá revivalists, especially the Ọ̀yọ́túnjí leader, are considered symbols of countercultural rejection of U.S. social laws and a return to African social life. Practicing polygamy openly protests the U.S. Supreme Court's ban on polygamy in 1879 (1878 *Reynolds v. United States*, 98 U.S. 145) and represents revivalists' adherence to precolonial Yorùbá ancient law. It is an example of the complex relationship of religious social norms and larger laws of the society in which they live.

The logic of the Ọ̀yọ́túnjí heterosexual family centers on principles of accountability and lineage. Each compound houses its own ancestral cult; the maintenance of the family cult is critical for the well-being of family members, for people's sense of self centers on the status of the family. The family compound is the focal point of òrìṣà religion and is in a hierarchical relationship to cult groups, town societies, and kingship relations. The father is said to be accountable to his line of ancestors as well as the council of landowners known as the Ògbóni society. Unlike Roman or common law that developed with a shift from the centrality of family to the centrality of the state, separating ritual from secular law, among many societies of precolonial Yorùbá of southwestern Nigeria, whose laws were replicated in Ọ̀yọ́túnjí networks, family rituals shape the social rules that regulate the totality of political and family life. In Ọ̀yọ́túnjí, ritual shapes family rules and permeates both nonsecular and secular life. Accordingly, Ọ̀yọ́túnjí's social organization follows an agnatic system of rules in which descent is traced according to paternity. The names of children in the family follow the father's ancestral cult, and first names are used to identify their place in the family. In all, status is regulated in Yorùbá law according to paternity. Thus, order is established with the moral sanctity of political and household rituals used to frame the rights of respect and dictate how one is supposed to comport oneself.

The symbolic imagery of traditionalism is highly gendered and structured as heterosexual. The marriage dowry is paid by the husband to the bride's family and represents compensation for the loss of their daughter. These payments augment the status and wealth of the family. A woman's status, therefore, is derived from marriage, and her access to property is through the head of the household, the husband. The marital relationship in Ọ̀yọ́túnjí is based on social contract between the individual, the ancestors, and the Ọba. The basis for marriage is not necessarily love; status and fulfilling social obligations to the ancestors, the òrìṣà, and the ruler take precedent.

Women are often classified as being responsible for duties in the home, and men in the political arena. In adherence to modern laws, Ọ̀yọ́túnjí laws depart from precolonial Yorùbá structures, in which the father had the power of life and death over the family; however, the father remains the sovereign power within the compound. By extension, the father has the obligation of accountability to the Ògbóni society, the landholder/chiefs have a responsibility to the members of the town, and the Ọba is the sovereign power and the leader of the kingdom. Practitioners often believe that it is god's will that he is the ruler and that his decisions are communicated through him by god; as such, the Ọba is a symbol of not only the authority of god, but also the prestige of past nobility.

Social Divisions: Royalty, Purity, and Social Status

Class analysis in the United States has traditionally been a tool for understanding power. Indeed, class is a critical factor for understanding who has access to material resources and who does not, and who is more mobile than whom. However, in relation to the making of daily life in Ọ̀yọ́túnjí, the politics of status and honor and the establishment of protocol to determine rank order play a critical role in establishing fundamental hierarchies of practice to reinforce social norms. Thus, even if middle-class standing is what enables practitioner travel to Ọ̀yọ́túnjí and beyond, and even if class is relevant in shaping one's ability to climb the ranks, fit in, exploit social capital, and attract clients, class standing alone is not helpful for negotiating status rank. Rather, it is the politics of class and gender, connected to prestige and status, that are relevant to the establishment of what relations of power are mobilized and why. The majority of this book has examined how agents make meanings outside of and in relation to hegemonic power, but status, prestige, honor, and other forms of cultural capital in particular fields of power also line up with the dominant values of patriarchy and Ọ̀yọ́túnjí's legal regulations.

Understanding how members of a self-regulating deterritorialized community negotiate moral standards, status hierarchies, and social rules is critical for determining how core assumptions about retributive fairness are negotiated and how those assumptions perpetuate gendered hierarchies in transnational settings. For ultimately, if power is the ability to make and mobilize meanings, it is critical to highlight the interplay between agency and hegemony, the relevance of individual free will to the ways social orders are reproduced within histories of institutional reinforcements of particular social logics.

In *Colonial Inscriptions: Race, Sex and Class in Kenya* Carolyn Martin Shaw (1995) argues that marriage in Kenya is shaped by larger issues of inequality in which young females are used by members of their family as a form of political mobility. She discusses the rules of sexual codes in colonial Kenya by examining the ways that the representation of Kikuyu sexual morality had a profound effect on how female sexuality was imagined. She argues that virginity is an indexical sign that marks a woman's physical or intact state; it is an iconic sign, referring to the intactness of the group the virgin represents. It signifies the credibility of a woman's assertion of wholeness, the lack of penetration by the Other. It is about hetero-sexual intercourse, or rather, its absence. At another level of abstraction, the virginity of daughters and sisters represents in many societies the integrity of the family group or the group concerned with female fertility (83). Likewise, social mobility in Òyótúnjí Village is possible through sexual purity: virgins are more likely to gain upward mobility by engaging in a Yorùbá traditional marriage. Girls can become traditionalists, and women cooperate and enforce laws that also oppress other women for many of the same reasons that men enforce those norms: to gain control of the political and social resources through which status and power can be achieved. Therefore, for traditionalism to be indexed as authentic, sexual purity as a mediating practice is inextricably linked to the categoric distinctions between Òyótúnjí men and women, girls and boys.

If the relations of power by which older women become traditional and enforce these laws are also connected to status distinctions and mobility, then young girls function as agents through which individual and family social status is negotiated. One such social practice instituted by the Ògbóni of Òyótúnjí and enforced by many female chiefs is codified in the antifraternization law of the 1970s. This law was instituted to enforce female premarital virginity and was intended to regulate sex by regulating socialization, and therefore marriage.

By maintaining the distinction between sexes, whereby the role of Yorùbá American boys and men is not dependent on maintaining sexual purity, the mythic Yorùbá female image can be constructed as legitimately traditional, as legitimately Yorùbá, by imposing standards for socialization. Òyótúnjí residents reference notions of virginity as purity, and through these determinants of value social norms are played out. To ensure that the young girls remain virgins until they marry, and to protect royal structures in which members of a status group marry partners from the same group, Òyótúnjí leaders organized their community according to social divisions. Females can learn to be socially acceptable by following specific gender practices. As such, their purity is sustained when they are seen as virgins and therefore pure. Women learn to act *pure*, and through their exercising of this impulse, men are protected from the *wrong* of premarital sex. If we see the symbolic value of being pure as something that one attains, then sexual codes, with their gendered distinctions, secure the workings of Yorùbá symbolic order. This regulation of sex through the symbolism of purity continues to be maintained through practices that uphold the sanctity of female virginity prior to marriage. These divisions are regulated by residents, especially middle-age women, who are responsible for institutionalizing Yorùbá-based traditional practices and assisting girls in becoming upstanding Yorùbá women.

In *The King's Two Bodies: A Study in Mediaeval Political Theology*, E. H. Kantorowicz (1957) discussed the process of legitimizing social hierarchies by examining the idea of the transmission of a "royal race." He examined the ways that specific forms of science invoke notions of pure bloodlines, authenticating the electoral succession of a king. This treatment of royal birth as constituted through "blood" reiterates that notions of royalty and procreation are intricately linked to social status and the ability to become royalty through kinship. Nevertheless, enforcing heterogeneous interpretations of female traditionalism while maintaining the appearance of gendered distinctiveness presents challenges for standardizing notions about what constitutes the traditional Yorùbá family. For, although gender is regulated in particular ways, tradition is a site of contestation.

"Tradition" among many Yorùbá revivalists is often used to describe the authenticity of historical dress, historical language, rituals, and social practices. Ọ̀yọ́túnjí revivalists make adaptations to histories and practices in a way that reflects the dominant textual interpretations of Yorùbá traditions. Indeed, much of what is identified as traditional and embedded in the customs of ancestral practices, such as clothing, has also been inscribed onto hegemonic alliances, originating in the particular cultural traditions from which changes were incorporated, claimed, and articulated into new cultural forms. Interestingly, it is uncommon to see Yorùbá practitioners talk about changes in practices as changes in tradition. Nevertheless, daily changes among revivalist practices are often performed as a relevant adaptation of traditional forms.

This desire for gendered traditionalism is central to the ways patriarchal alliances of descent and power are engaged but also incrementally transformed. Women's involvement in reinforcing the basis of women's subordination can also be seen as a contradictory yet critical site of power. The interpretative component of the process of "becoming traditional" is marked by a contested terrain of meaning production. On one hand, women grapple with the problem of affirming Yorùbá traditionalism in their lives; on the other hand, they struggle with the ambiguities concerning what constitutes traditional womanhood in the first place and who has the right to determine and enforce its changing features. Although in larger terms distinct structures of inequality pervade the value of traditional gendered roles, the micropolitics within the politics of domination are both multifaceted and transformative.

Just as particular notions of Africa as a homeland are driven by representations of Pan-African black unity and the history of transatlantic slavery, the image of Yorùbá traditionalism mutually constructs itself against the ideal of the black heterosexual polygamous family. Women's place in the home as wife and keeper of children is the cornerstone of Yorùbá tradition, and revivalists identify polygamous arrangements and motherhood as signs of the ancient past. Nevertheless, these forms of traditionalism are no more ancient than the invention of feminism. The sign of traditional gender roles is a production of a particular kind of identity that says more about the forms of diasporic regulation that constitutes revivalist movements than about women's subjugation. By recasting the role of the family and community from that of Western practices to that of ancient Yorùbá social organization, revivalists both reproduce the symbolic and material structures of patriarchy and produce mechanisms to enforce distinctions between Yorùbá men and women.

To teach the young girls to be traditional and to invoke their practices as authentic, women in Òyótúnjí Village are often engaged in a contradictory process of both maintaining the organization of community and teaching women to be keepers of the home. This compares with their image of their men as patriarchs committed to the enforcement of town rules. However, during the period in which I began fieldwork, in the early 1990s, Òyótúnjí traditional practices continued to change. Indeed, change is not uncommon. Yorùbá revivalism is dynamic and exists alongside contravening rules of the state. Further, hundreds of thousands of practitioners are U.S. revivalists and continually engaged in active processes of becoming Yorùbá traditionalists.[3] It is not unusual for people's values to clash with community rules.

Social Disputes and the Status of Resolutions

In one of many Òyótúnjí court trial hearings that I observed in 1995, the defendant, a middle-age female chief and mother of three (whom I refer to as Her Royal Grace Ìyá Sisilum),[4] was called up on charges of slander for allegedly criticizing the mothering practices of the plaintiff, whom I call Ìyá Olayindo, a nonpriest and also a mother of three. Ìyá Olayindo was popularly known by many of the townswomen as "loose"; they described her as lacking disciplinary skills and therefore void of the tools to teach her girls how to become traditional Yorùbá women. HRG Ìyá Sisilum made public allegations about Ìyá Olayindo and her daughters' loss of "sexual purity," justifying her actions by articulating the basis of traditional female behavior, for which young girls should strive. She felt that her allegations were justifiable because they were in keeping with traditionally documented descriptions of Yorùbá families from southwestern Nigeria and therefore a model for the production of the New World Yorùbá families. In so doing, HRG Ìyá Sisilum demonstrated that traditional womanhood is something that girls must learn and ultimately achieve. One becomes gendered in particular ways.

The initial trial arguments were followed by a series of witness testimonies and an important cross-examination of the defendant by the judge (the king of the village). Not only did the defendant maintain that she was not guilty, but she argued quite eloquently that as a traditional Yorùbá woman, a mother, and a village resident, she acted out of traditionalist obligation. HRG Ìyá Sisilum defended herself by appealing to values of female purity, which, she argued, formed the basis of Yorùbá traditions in the New World. As a rhetorical strategy, she repeatedly claimed that it was Yorùbá laws that had been broken by Ìyá Olayindo and her girls. She argued that "Ìyá Olayindo ignored her advice that their behavior was not socially acceptable among the Yorùbás. . . . These remarks were not stated to defame the family," she added. "These remarks were stated to uplift the family and to present a traditional model for Yorùbá women."

HRG Ìyá Sisilum's referencing of traditional models of Yorùbá female behavior during the trial not only represented her effort in asserting her beliefs and justifying her actions but also served to shape and enforce patriarchal standards — standards that she felt were the responsibility of women and girls to learn, a necessary component of becoming a traditional woman. During an early stage of the trial she described her own family's attempt to defend themselves against accusations that her young daughter was not a virgin. Knowing that there were also oppressive possibilities for the misuse of traditionalism, she argued that females had to protect themselves from unfounded accusations and should attend their womanhood initiation training to learn the necessary preconditions to become a responsible female traditionalist.

The irony of using traditionalism as a form of contemporary revivalism is that just as colonial constructions of Africanness have been selectively used to posit Africa as primitive, so too are notions of African traditions and histories selectively gendered by the postcolonial elite in the international arena (Williams 1990, 1991). As in the process of using signifiers of tradition to mark the past, women and men in Ọ̀yọ́túnjí Village use tradition to construct gendered notions of purity. The use of tradition, seen as a product of the mutual construction between and among women and men and their notions of the past, sheds light on the complexities of interpretation that regulate Yorùbá gender and power relations.

Another production of gendered traditions was demonstrated by Audrey Wipper (1972) in her analysis of the selective recuperation by postcolonial East and West African leaders of some African traditions in the shift to postcolonial regimes. Wipper argues that African leaders claimed superiority for their traditions over Western European traditions introduced during the colonial era. They publicly advocated their desire to reclaim traditional ways and openly dismissed the denigrating influences of colonialism. Yet there exist contradictions of selectively reclaiming certain aspects of traditionalism and not others. She states that "many of these men [wear] three-piece suits, [are] clean shaven, with [the] use of the latest

Members of the Ọ̀yọ́túnjí Women's Society awaiting the end of the Yemọja festival tribute to women.

Western cosmetics and shaving equipment, [and vie] for power in the bureaucracies and parliamentary government institutions left over from the colonial era. The end to aping Western ways meant that women were to return to the home, lower their hemlines, remove their makeup and stop straightening their hair, wearing wigs and using complexion lighteners" (1972).

Recognizing that communities and individuals are constantly engaged in negotiating and contesting meaning is critical for rethinking the complexities of reclaiming African cultural practices, not simply as uniform, but as gendered tropes through which Africanness is played out. The processes of reinterpretation and enforcement are measured according to the specificities of relevant local dynamics and transnational frameworks. Yet these specificities, as they are situated, form the basis for traditional codes and rules in contemporary life. That is, those who produce and are marginalized by hegemonic determinants of culture on a local level are actively involved in a larger process of reformulation and creative improvisation. While Ọ̀yọ́túnjí women use global colonial histories to inform local meanings, they also shape new meanings within them. In the process of becoming Yorùbá women, they exercise agency while also employing tools of domination.

Contestations over what behaviors constitute Yorùbá female traditionalism were central to everyday life in Ọ̀yọ́túnjí Village. The plaintiff, Ìyá Olayindo, had different interpretations for appropriate enactments of traditionalism. For her, traditional motherhood was based not just on ancient culturally specific laws, but on universal notions of a mother's relationship with her daughter and the daughter's obligations to her mother. She justified this by alluding to good deeds and reciprocity in the American tradition in which she was raised. On the contrary, HRG Ìyá Sisilum's actions attempted to enforce a different conceptualization of transnational traditionalism. For her, invocation of tradition accompanied the suggestion of the links between Yorùbá polygamous marriage and teenage virginity. HRG Ìyá Sisilum referred to the value of policing young girls so that they could retain their bridal value by remaining virgins, referencing the standard Òyótúnjí Village model of family that emphasizes the premarital mythic virgin. And with the rare exceptions of Òyótúnjí women's gender distinctions, which highlight the existence of dominant African female rulers such as Queen Njinga and the great and powerful female deities and goddesses, dominant Òyótúnjí Village narratives of traditional female roles do indeed focus on the centrality of female purity as an authentic trope of Yorùbá traditionalism. With this mission, HRG Ìyá Sisilum insisted on the centrality of mediating practices such as premarriage norms, women's dress, and polygamy in order to maintain their traditions as legitimate. These processes of traditional revivalism are at particular times adequately situated as traditional, and at other times are repudiated.

HRG Ìyá Sisilum attempted to win the support of the jury and audience with her continual references to traditional codes of behavior. Her evocative prefiguration of returning to traditional roots by upholding women's traditions can be seen as the enforcement of patriarchal rules previously established by the community's elite. For HRG Ìyá Sisilum, the differential expectations of male and female behavior were based on the fundamental teachings of traditional doctrines for the institutionalization of traditional marriage. That is, ideas of Yorùbá traditional families are not just enforced by a state apparatus or legal institution forcing people in its jurisdiction to concede power against their conscious will; instead, they are enforced by the agents of institutions, the elite who produce and regulate cultural knowledge—in this case, priests, diviners, chiefs, authors. Because some articulations of tradition are already in keeping with preexisting patriarchal alliances, they incorporate more easily definitions of Yorùbá traditions that are already in keeping with dominant meanings.[5]

Women, Men, and Ògbóni Religious Law: Rethinking Power and Agency

Given that the council of the Ògbóni is also responsible for administering judicial, legal, and executive matters, the chiefs who sit on the council constitute a

Ògbóni meeting chairs.

jury; each chief has one vote, and the Ọba, as the chief priest of the òrìṣà and of the Ògbóni society, also has one vote and veto power. The various societies in Ọ̀yọ́túnjí implement the goals of the Ògbóni on a daily basis and are not only answerable to the Ọba, but also to all of the members of the Ògbóni.

Like Old World Ògbóni members, many of whom take their membership in the earth cult seriously, Ọ̀yọ́túnjí Ògbóni members are also dedicated cult participants. To claim membership, residents must undergo a solemn induction into the secret society. This induction takes the form of ritual sacrifices, prayers, and bodily inscriptions, as well as private and public utterances of sacred oaths. It is popularly believed by residents that secretive ritual initiation into public office provides practitioners with the ancestral power with which to reclaim Yorùbá cultural and political life as their own. The ritualization of Ògbóni membership is ongoing, and because of the importance of the decision-making processes, oaths are pledged to the ancestors, the Crown, and the nation at the commencement of every meeting; this ensures honesty and commitment. The ritual oaths to the ancestors prior to every Ògbóni meeting also reinforce the connection of members to the ancestors of Old Ọ̀yọ́. Before each meeting, each chief is called on to declare allegiance by presenting the oath by rote.[6] This is performed in Yorùbá and then in English. Both the practice of using Yorùbá to ritualize relations of belonging and the pouring of libation serve as symbolic reminders of spatial links between the ancestral homeland and the New World; they are critical to the reformulation of Yorùbá diasporic identities. The Yorùbá incantations that

Nigerian chiefs at an Ògbóni meeting.

accompany libation illustrate this ongoing reformulation of transnational Yorùbá identity.

In keeping with the dominant history and social imaginary of black Ọ̀yọ́ hierarchies of rule that affirm the Ọba as paramount, the chiefs, through the Ògbóni society as group decision makers, and the traditional polygamous family as formally answerable to male husbandly power first and royal power second, complaints issued by òrìṣà worshippers in the Ọ̀yọ́túnjí network are initially brought before the male secretary of state, the Apena. His is the most formally powerful position after the Ọba. Although the Apena is not normally seen as a person with tremendous power, but instead as the Ọba's public attaché, he has the power to determine the classification of charges and make recommendations for the type of audience that complaints should receive. He is central in the filing of claims, evaluating evidence, and establishing the legitimacy of just cause to determine whether a charge will be issued and, if so, where. The Apena has the religious and legal authority to determine the specific offense as well as to widen and narrow the range of offenses.

The Ọba, as judge, however, has the absolute power to receive the reported facts and declare, with the consultation of the oracle, guilt or innocence. He has the power to appoint his chiefs and to dismiss them from office, but he is expected to serve his administration with the goals and well-being of all of his members in mind. The Ọba has the power to veto chief jury decisions, to produce guilty verdicts, and to authorize leniency. Once the Ọba rules on a case, the formal charge is final and cannot be appealed.

The power differentials involved in creating and sustaining these institutions raise questions about the totality of power insofar as mobility and contestations to traditions are concerned. One way to think about the totality of power is to identify its formal and informal regulation mechanisms. In addition to informal mechanisms for regulating informal behavior, such as embarrassment and shaming, Òyótúnjí also has formal preventative services, such as a militia, known as the *dowpe*, and formal punishment systems.

In terms of preventative mechanisms to avoid excessive abuses of force or violence, Òyótúnjí's dowpe is always on guard and ready to protect the community against attack. The members of the militia are visible (they wear army uniforms) and carry guns. A militia defense team and a religious law system, seen by the community as a form of *natural law*, are critical components of regulating behavior. Cases such as community theft, molestation, and rape committed in the community are within the jurisdiction of the Òyótúnjí court. However, because Òyótúnjí has neither a prison system nor a formal mechanism for holding people charged with a crime worthy of a prison sentence, such as homicide, those suspects are turned over to the South Carolina Department of Corrections.

The system of punishment in Òyótúnjí has five categories, and punishment is determined by the Ọba in consultation with the chiefs. Forms of punishment are: (1) formal public condemnation of the accused through a jury trial in which the defendant is declared guilty; (2) informal evaluation through circuits of gossip and disapproval; (3) the issuance of fines, ranging from $1 to $100, as a result of the determination of wrongdoing; (4) forced ritual cleansing; and (5) ejection from participation in the community.

In relation to this outline of Òyótúnjí legal institutions, the case in question involved the Ògbóni society's determining the appropriateness of the defendant, HRG Ìyá Sisilum, taking the law into her own hands by regulating traditional gender laws, a role that should have been deferred to the judge. Despite her attempt to justify her actions according to particular dominant traditional practices, upholding tradition proved secondary to the hierarchies of power. As such, the trial in question was not simply about two women vying for power. It was also a reflection of the complexities of HRG Ìyá Sisilum's status in relation to the judge's, the Ọba's, disapproval with her attempt to enforce the law—something outside the norms of their social organization and therefore suspect because it involved her enactment of a socially inappropriate procedural role. HRG Ìyá Sisilum's insistence on privileging the enforcement of tradition regardless of procedural rules was not acceptable to the judge. She argued that her actions in enforcing traditionalism justified her means. In her attempt to enforce gender laws she not only publicly un-covered the political contradictions between substantive law and procedural rules, but she violated the fundamental tenet of Ọ̀yọ́túnjí social organization—that of male governance over particular public disciplinary functions.

In the end, HRG Ìyá Sisilum was declared not guilty by the courts and appeared to have had the support of various members of the women's society for her role in standing up for tradition. A central twist that is critical to understanding the institutionalization of Yorùbá transnationalism is that despite the public victory, the judge's public rebuke signaled a more powerful disavowel of her acts. Along-side the not guilty verdict was a public opinion verdict—and herein lies the cen-trality of theorizing social logics in relation to the ways that knowledge circulates in transnational institutions and institutions of power. The Ọba's rebuke signaled an acceptance of informal punishment. Thus, HRG Ìyá Sisilum still endured social rebuke long after the trial ended.

Many residents and nonresidents with whom I spoke felt the trial was based on personal vendettas and HRG Ìyá Sisilum's manipulation and abuse of truth and fairness. Their perception of the abuse of traditions by the defendant led them to declare that instead, she should have been placed under scrutiny. Others, how-ever, especially the women who attended the trial, aligned themselves with the defendant and argued that the plaintiff, Ìyá Olayindo, was guilty and should have been tried for the abuse of traditional laws. Here, we see how public opinion is also relevant and significant, for it provides an outlet for expressive values, thereby figuring significantly into the ways social norms are shaped. The dualities are re-flections of the relationship between social order and the pragmatics of practice. While HRG Ìyá Sisilum recognized that she broke the law as well as transgressed social norms, she also felt that her moral duty to follow protocol should take precedence over those laws and norms. In the end, the not guilty verdict and the judge's chastisement shifted the issue from the legitimacy of the law and order of the courtroom to that which stands outside their local court: principles of proce-dure and practices. In this case, both formal and informal mechanisms were used by the Ọba to signal fairness as well as to establish punitive informal judgments. Both mechanisms are effective because despite the legal apparatus and the attempt by the defendant to informally publicize the plaintiff's wrong, the conclusion of the trial was marked by the judge's final reprimand of the defendant, in which he also warned the community as he counted the votes and announced the verdict: "All members of Ọ̀yọ́túnjí are of course to be very, very careful of what you say, where you say it, and of course how you say it because you do not have unlimited license to go about making statements which you cannot substantiate or which you cannot in any way make complete sense of. This court then finds Her Grace not guilty and stands in adjournment." Not only did the judge discipline HRG Ìyá Sisilum publicly, he also criticized her for usurping his power.

One way to analyze the Ọba's decision is in relation to the preservation of his supreme authority. He punished the defendant both to provide a remedy for her past actions and also to warn her that, if she fails to comply in the future, she will suffer the consequences of insubordination. This form of formal social control enforced through an institutional legal mechanism both offers entitlements and informal damages to plaintiffs and enforces norms.

Some women are able to articulate and enforce particular notions of traditionalism in public and legal spaces because their interpretations are aligned with dominant interpretations for becoming traditional. Other women are not as successful in influencing the meanings and signifiers of tradition. Clearly, formal and informal legal mechanisms are operative here, and to understand the use of Ọ̀yọ́túnjí òrìṣà voodoo customary law we have to understand how the system works to maintain hierarchies of power. HRG Ìyá Sisilum claimed that her interpretation of traditional gender codes was based on the "good of tradition," therefore, the good of the community. However, her actions must be seen in relation to the ultimate procedures and hierarchies of power. As Ọ̀yọ́túnjí imaginings of Yorùbá traditionalism are imported to new social geographies to create laws and norms—whether to reinstitute traditional practices, social hierarchy and political power (Martin Shaw 1995; Ortner and Whitehead 1981; Schneider 1971), economic inheritance, or new forms of legitimacy through the production of diasporic identity—how the past is incorporated to contest and shape social norms is the key to how gender is inextricably linked to what it means to be traditional. That is, rules of gendered practices are fundamentally secondary to the prestige of paternal kingship.

Indeed, contestations over meanings exist in the execution of transnational rules and norms because differential relations of power and differences in interpretations exist. The uses of traditionalism as a manipulable form of cultural reclamation in Ọ̀yọ́túnjí Village are bound to produce differing opinions and assertions of traditionalism. Many informal remedies are seen by social scientists as secondary, however, when applied to an analysis of social order. The Ọba's and the defendant's actions reside in unequal domains of power, but also in relation to the hierarchies of gender and roles that are part of a larger hegemonic order not only inherited via traditional Ọ̀yọ́ social organization but further accentuated through the history of British colonialism.

More is known about gender relations in Ọ̀yọ́túnjí Village when we study the discursive articulation of how, in their efforts to establish traditions and become traditional, women incorporate different forms of patriarchal authority into their lives. The duality of traditional authority and the way it is regulated demonstrate that the participation of feminists in Ọ̀yọ́túnjí Village is structured in relation to historical forms of inequities arranged in relation to male and colonial authority. The revivalism of Yorùbá traditionalism in South Carolina highlights the ways that, as agents of change, girls and women are complicit in their reiteration of patriarchal power.

Women in Ọ̀yọ́túnjí Village accept precolonial West African identity as their own through the active reproduction of "things Yorùbá." Although the concluding determinations are never based on a homogeneous agreement of what constitutes Yorùbá traditionalism in the Americas, the complexities of redefining local meanings in the context of globally shaped norms are precisely what makes connections between gender and power significant to the production of Yorùbá revivalism outside of Yorùbáland.

And yet, there are also limits to agency, for despite the various ways women participate in their own uplift, they are also subject to the hegemony of unequal social values of women's place in the work domain. The relationship between the power of institutions and the articulations of tradition in Ọ̀yọ́túnjí lies within the inscriptions of nineteenth- and early-twentieth-century histories of the formation of the Yorùbá as the basis for Ọ̀yọ́túnjí articulations of traditional family. These articulations of gender difference reproduce themselves through the formal teaching and enforcement of Yorùbá traditions as well as the informal regulation of gendered distinctiveness in dress, codes of behavior, and expressions of favorable "value" of punishable and unpunishable behavior. Understanding the play of power in relation to the institutional development of rules about what types of family configurations are legitimate is central to clarifying when certain forms of enforcement and certain forms of punishments may be suitable or unsuitable. The determinants are related to particular levels of authority that are enunciated both hegemonically and through acts of agency on the level of the individual not only in relation to the state (chapter 1), to the community and global institutions (chapters 2 and 3), and to institutional practices (chapters 4 and 5), but also in relation to the regulation of family status hierarchies and the norms that surround them. Given that the symbolic production of male governance of public venues is at its core, traditionalism crosscuts political and moral entitlements and must, therefore, always represent an expression of the favorable value of the authority of its governance. Ultimately, enforcement of the social organization of family is critical, for at the core of the deterritorialization of Yorùbá transnational networks are historically contingent conceptions of the patriarchal family. These forms of deterritorialized practices transmitted transnationally as a bundle of ancient norms accentuate the autonomy of Yorùbá in North American contexts.

Ọ̀yọ́túnjí legal institutions work alongside, in relation to, and distinct from the laws of South Carolina. It is a community of practitioners engaged in building a buffer from the reach of the state and establishing the reclassification of national identities. Thus, it helps us see that the role of the state is secondary in the making of transnational communities. Specifically, the relation of Ọ̀yọ́túnjí practitioners to the structure of the United States or the Nigerian state is secondary to the sources of legitimacy that practitioners use to gain authority. Their claims of belonging stand outside state-recognized forms of classification and therefore call on us to understand how social institutions that reflect different cultural interpretations of governance may, through the creation of different forms of legitimacy, evade state principles. Understanding power and agency outside the state and in transnational contexts involves understanding the sources of legitimacy from which social actors draw authority. It also highlights the ways that agents of change use historical traditions and sacred texts to legitimatize extranational powers and in so doing provide a mechanism by which religion, and not law, can be a vehicle for transnational linkage.

In the development of Ọ̀yọ́túnjí Village, the relations between the state, the leader/priests, and Yorùbá religious cosmologies are complex and embedded in assumptions about divine claims and human roles in them. Processes of transnational community formation in Ọ̀yọ́túnjí Village networks involve the cultural logics of personhood and their related practices. In the journey that we have taken, the nation-state has stood in for the forces of humanity: their laws, their boundaries, and those things mutable and material. Yorùbá religious cosmologies reflect the forces of the ancestral divine. Priests and leaders function as intermediaries of the gods and erect sacred conceptions of human hierarchies that produce distinctions between men and women and between priests and practitioner-followers. As such, the moral project of Yorùbá revivalism follows patterns of hierarchical ordering that are critical for the establishment of legitimate forums. However, it is also a means for African American redemption from slavery, racism, and colonization and thus an attempt by practitioners to manage injustice by rendering the invisible visible. It is an attempt to bring to the fore human beliefs in ancestors, a force the state and its laws cannot recognize in deliberations with political consequences. It is an attempt to struggle against social injustice using strategies that predate the existence of the modern state.

Thus, if it is true that meaning making involves the production of formal and informal social institutions by which legitimacy can be understood, then it is also true that understanding the differences between knowledge producers and consumers and between intermediaries and leaders involves establishing that social distinctions—the differences that make a difference—hold power because they draw from both the domain of the moral-sacred as well as the political. In the end, understanding power and agency involves understanding the cultural, historical, and religious contexts within which agents intervene. And in the end, what is important is to examine why and when tradition and the law are deployed and what histories and differences are called on to enforce particular relations over others.

Epilogue: Multisited Ethnographies
in an Age of Globalization

MAPPING TRANSNATIONAL NETWORKS is a project about the spatial geographies by which people imagine themselves, their ancestry, and their origins in historically constituted terms. For this book, it is also a temporal and ideological project, in which I chart the ways people create linkages that are at once temporally spiritual and ideological. It is a story about the mapping and regulation of linkages across and against modern concepts of time and space, across social ideological categories, and in relation to them. In this book, my interest has been to chart what complex circulations of knowledge might tell us about ways of making place and the mechanisms that authorize these productions. I have explored not just how modern concepts of religious institutions themselves are serving to authorize hegemonic *knowledge*, but, how, specifically, knowledge of these authorities flow, why they flow, and for what purposes. I answered central questions: How are these institutional mechanisms constructed—vertically, horizontally—to create social networks? and What are the conditions—historical and practical—that make possible recognizable social realities? I thus moved us out of current anthropological inquiries that remain only in traditional field sites and explored the institutionalization of particular practices in relation to the underlying forces of movement and knowledge that work on multiple levels to inform complex maps of knowledge networks today. Indeed, charting these circulations in relation to local sites is important, for it enables us to understand where and why some bundles of practice and meaning are taken up and others are relegated to the margins.

I ended the first part of the book by demonstrating that the nation-state and nationalism are not being reorganized by new institutions. Agents—religious and ritual experts—working through international networks of knowledge and authority are contributing to the reconfiguration of local and national spheres of power and governance, civil and national. By exploring the particularities of historical colonial alliances and contemporary global hegemonies in the religious and legal ordering of an increasingly globalizing world, I focused on how different bundles of practice contravene diversities in religious values. In the second part of the book I demonstrated how these historical inscriptions play out to create particular social logics.

Thus, the book was written with three objectives in mind. The first was to explore the role of institutions—historical, legal, and religious—in shaping the institutional autonomy of Yorùbá òrìṣà voodoo practices in the Americas, and, in so doing, to establish a methodological mapping of various geographical scales in which transnational connections are available. By examining the sociological and anthropological discourse on traditional Yorùbá society and the role of colonialism in West Africa in restructuring posttransatlantic slave trade customs and practices in Nigeria and the United States, I interrogated the problematic character of Yorùbá traditions and identity as units of analysis. I did so not only to interrogate the constructed nature of these cultural processes, but also to demonstrate how the production of *tradition, authenticity, blackness*, and *homeland*, for example, although historically contingent, can be studied in geopolitical terms. In this post-1989 period, culture continues to be further propelled by market capital, and so to examine these institutions in relation to the encroachment of the commodification of cultural production is to demonstrate that the forces that shape meaning, whether fueled by global capitalism or traditional institutions, continue to shape how values are constituted, in complex transnational terms.

My second objective was to illustrate the way that a community, characterized by political theorists as marginalized, actively engages in the processes of constructing redemptive strategies and reproducing hegemonic determinants of Yorùbá traditionalism, even as it subverts those classifications characteristic of European modernity, colonialism, and racism. As a form of postslavery political redemption, Ọ̀yọ́túnjí Village practitioners created a revitalization movement in South Carolina where the criteria for traditional practices are based on an archaic Yorùbá past. By examining the techniques of producing religious authority by which members of the community legitimized geographical place, this book charted the drama of cyclical and seasonal rituals and the rhythms of everyday life. In addition to exploring how understandings of cultural production and ethnography can be usefully put into practice, I tracked the effects of transforming religious practices, such as ritual forms of divination, in daily life and their relevance for asking what kinds of knowledge agents produce, through what institutions, and how that knowledge has been and continues to be used by agents themselves. These embodied practices are generative of a Yorùbá community that goes beyond Africa to include a Yorùbá village in the United States. Though outside of Africa, Òyótúnjí African Village is a geographic imaginary, and, as such, it has been erected by its religious adherents as a site of Yorùbá religious practice.

My third objective was to illustrate how uses of the idea of race do not excuse people from the reinforcement of racial hegemony. Òyótúnjí Village residents are part of a larger historical network of òrìsà practices and are educated participants in the formation of a racial politics of African heritage in the United States. However, they employ and reproduce the very hegemonic classifications of race that their new identities were intended to revoke. I conclude that it is the idea and not the mechanisms that circulate, and the idea of race is itself a construct that, to be legible, takes on particular canonical assumptions of usage that are in keeping with the geopolitics of racial meaning. However, increasingly, when one looks outside of U.S. particularities of racial classification, it becomes clearer how different histories have produced different conceptions of racial difference and how the basis for sameness and alliances takes on different forms in different places. That said, it is important to recognize how concepts of race, religion, and law change and how U.S. conceptions are influencing the ways that new concepts circulate.

These three objectives form the inspiration for studying the normative making of Òyótúnjí Village. The critical point, however, is not that Òyótúnjí Village is an intentional community invented alongside dominant norms, but that Òyótúnjí Village, like the making of daily life, exists as an ideal that must be understood in relation to larger networks, institutions, and processes of making mechanisms of legitimacy. It is the making of daily norms that produces our lives as our conception of reality. The paradox at the heart of religious and racial reproduction, however, is that the spheres of authority that enable people to create normative logics are themselves organized around a hierarchy of knowledge and power that is embedded in forms of violence that lead to exclusions and devaluations. In other words, people's exercise of religious logics and their production of a conception of community in its likeness obscures the ontological sphere in which power is negotiated. That is why identity alone—religious or racial identity—cannot be the sole object of study in the study of agency and power. Instead, in recognizing the product of religious nationalism, for example, we need to examine both the redemptive form and inherent violence of institutions and the way that people produce and call on particular institutions to engage in the production and reproduction of power and alternate possibilities. Future work on this topic needs to examine how other forms of institutions and other historical forms produce various conditions of possibility and how, in transnational contexts, it is the form of the institution that needs to be interrogated in relation to what and why particular conditions of possibility produce particular forms of practices. Ultimately, for social theory today, Ọ̀yọ́túnjí Village and its related network is a deterritorialized community developing institutional mechanisms that produce parallel formations for religious reproduction in the West.

Today, institutions, communities, and forms of identity classification are taking on new meanings with the new force of market capital. In earlier periods of the making of the modern world, the global circulation of labor and commodities produced interconnections; today, the intensification of connections is compressed temporally and spatially and people's inversions of knowledge institutions are enabling reformulations of the communities that people in the West interpret. The changes in the non-West, therefore, are also about the production of information about the non-West in the West. Therefore, to produce ethnographies of local sites is to produce ethnographies of circulations of flows that are historically contingent and complexly transnational.

Criticisms of anthropology's culture concept and the ways fieldwork methodology have been conducted raise critical questions about how we understand the field and how various fields, no matter how varied and urban, can be part of the ethnographic enterprise. Ultimately, however the field is constituted, the type of knowledge is circulated and the histories of regulation that have constituted those areas are questions for understanding global mappings today. In today's war-torn regions of the Third World, ongoing democratic upheaval and challenges to federalism in the West, questions about the significance of royal monarchies in relation to democratization movements, shifts in socialist and Islamic regimes to new forms of democracy, and the restructuring of state institutions and increasing significance of nongovernmental organizations are forcing us to reflect on how regions are shaped by each other. These upheavals ask us to consider what forms of methodological innovation might be necessary to capture these interrelationships and how older ethnographic encounters may or may not resemble newer ones.

This book is both a departure from and a reflection of the old. While the findings get to the heart of ethnographic inquiry, the methods involve a necessary crosscutting of traditional geographically bounded areas to track influences in cultural exchange and so produce different methodological priorities that explain the politics of cultural production in time and space in the making of Yorùbá communities in Nigeria and its *elsewheres* (Mbembe 2001).

If anthropological as well as social science area studies models have not been adequate for addressing the complex circuits of transnational life, then that which is studied—its logics, evidential criteria, and forms of embodiment—also needs to be reexamined. The mappings that I have provided explored how different senses of communities are produced, lived, and elaborated. Those at the helm of transnational networks use particular techniques—alternative and hegemonic, spiritual and historical—to shape and reshape their world. The question then becomes how to document these forms and contours that are at times unrecognizable yet, for their originators, generative of diasporic origins. I explored the ways transnational mappings can be used to open up not only particular forms of exploration but also forms of collaborations that can be developed over time. What is needed are discussions on how to understand complex social networks that are at once local and transnational. We need to pursue mappings with an eye to history and an understanding of what is at stake in the forms of variation that emerge from different interventions. Students can engage in the project of mapping by both documenting local practices in time and place and then following one strand of a network to adopt an analytic approach that captures the making and remaking of communities in time and place. The methodological issues raised in this book are motivated by critical pedagogical and theoretical questions. The challenge in the end is an analytic one: How do we determine the legitimacy of claims to nationhood and alternative social contracts? Where do we draw the line? At what point and after how many generations does a historical linkage to an ancestral homeland cease to be relevant? In this world of increasing migration, what role should the state play concerning which claims to citizenship and membership in other homelands are relevant and which claims are secondary? These are the challenges of understanding the power of governmental authority in relation to understanding how people create alternative norms. For, as we have seen, territorialized communities do not have a monopoly on the ways that social norms about their practices are established and circulated. State-making apparatuses are party to the legitimation of membership. Yet, I am not arguing that a general theory of transnational social change can be developed without an analysis of the state and its laws. The data have shown us that people create practices in relation to larger hegemonic norms. However, it is the institutional mechanisms that work to produce socially acceptable norms, critical in the creation of conditions of possibility, within which things happen. What is socially acceptable changes over time: the trade of slaves was once legal, then outlawed and rendered illegal, and then was followed by the legal establishment and enforcement of plantation slavery, justified by particular hierarchies of humanness. Accordingly, with the outlawing of slavery, taxonomies for the classification of black people in the Americas shifted from slaves as Negro property to the establishment of sophisticated biological justifications for race-based enslavement. Segregation laws reinforced these distinctions and these various hierarchies of value. During these periods of extreme regulation, enslaved Africans reconstructed religious and social practices in relation to and in spite of laws of the colonial state. Indeed, the role of the law and the state was present in the articulation of social value and the pronouncement of relations of belonging. Nevertheless, even as people employ normative values to reproduce social values, there are critical components of the structure of norms that represent sites of variability from which they usurp dominant meanings and instead renegotiate the terms according to alternative possibilities. For outside of the authority of the state, the capacity of individuals to build alternative institutions with which to enforce new norms and build like-minded networks is profound. The latter is often the basis for countercultural movements. Although the sites of change are historically circumscribed, they operate within informal rules of acceptability, and it is here that agency lies, under the conditions of historical possibility, not unlimited but a product of hybrid and overlapping relations of power and influence.

Given these complexities of influence and movement, the next question raised by the book is How do we take account of anthropological field sites in multiple locations? Given the historical breadth, macroprocesses of internationalization, and fine-tuned interpretations and detailing that are necessary to achieve adequate understandings of the fields of cultural production and religious adherence in an increasingly globalizing world, do we need to locate a network and follow it spatially? How do we use ethnography to represent global revivalist networks? Is it still ethnography? My analytic challenge was to chart the networks of influence and interaction that constituted the linkages of Yorùbá practitioners affiliated with Òyótúnjí. My interpretive challenge was to understand how those in parallel and convergent networks worked through institutions to create daily aesthetics. Just as this research requires emergent *analytics* for understanding the context of global change, so, too, does it entail novel *methodologies* only now becoming more acceptable in the anthropology of the twenty-first century. Scholars have struggled to achieve methodological innovation in the study of globalization by calling for additional forms of training and of collegial cooperation (longitudinal designs, teamwork on a single site, restudies at different times by different anthropologists working alone, etc.). Though I will not offer a systematized archetypal mandate of four-field interrelatedness or nation-bound field studies in which students of anthropology should be competently trained, I, like others, call on scholars to be conscientious of their own assumptions of the underlying tenets of what constitutes *the field* and why those configurations have endowed us with a sanctity of nationhood. The history of the modern nation-state was shaped by the centrality of empire, race, and cultural difference; these are therefore at the foundation of what we have come to see as the modern world. In the case of the black Atlantic world, understanding the interconnections between Africa and the Americas involves charting the ways that histories of slavery, colonial imperialisms, and capitalist participation have established particular conditions of intelligibility through which the modern black Atlantic world took shape. As such, in the face of the globalizing formation of particular post–cold war institutions, racial discourses and territorial conceptions of origins and ethnic belonging continue to be critical to our understanding of this age of globalizing institutionalization. Thus, to understand processes of globalization in the early twenty-first century we need to understand how, through histories of producing social distinctions, difference has become the companion of empire. Recognizing the global workings of political, economic, cultural, and legal institutions thus should involve the recognition of the regulatory formation of subjectivities and the ways those subjectivities get internalized and therefore reformulated by agents allied with transnational and regional institutions.

Indeed, since the cold war, the migration of people from rural to urban locations and from former colonial territories to imperialist nations is changing the nature of citizenship, religious linkages, and geographic imaginaries. Given these shifts, we need to foreground the role of religion as a form of ideological linkage that reaches beyond the nation-state and forms alliances according to other forms of connections. Such approaches to theorizing globalization posits the existence of connections understood within regional axes along institutional mechanisms. It makes necessary the rethinking of area studies in relation to how we understand the contingency of colonial formations on contemporary transnational religious movements. We need to chart the particularities of how and where new regimes of religious governance are being formed and are being used by people to subvert other forms of cultural logics. For international agents are working outside of their countries of citizenship to participate in civil societies elsewhere, and, like earlier periods of missionization in colonies, the nature of these alliances is leading to the transformation of social practices. In this light, this work demonstrates how various bundles of truth regimes, as they are intrinsically combined with cultural morals, are leading to shifts in how agents produce, contest, and transform their understanding of normative truths in various contexts.

I am calling for an ongoing inquiry that charts the terrain of networks in this period of global hypercapitalism. I take a critical approach to different forms of knowledge that we all bring to our encounters and ask how people use authorial forms of interpretation to organize and analyze our social world as well as the forms of morality people employ to make, subvert, and remake that which represents them.

Typically, studies of globalization and religious and legal institutions have been organized around such areas as culture, politics, and social organization. Now, after more than a decade of expansive research on late capitalist transnational flows and globalization, we have moved to a realm in which we must recognize how former empires and nation-states are being reconfigured and how international organizations are radically transforming local practices. We need to understand not just how the past has been articulated through imperial modernities of the present, but also how present subversions of modern categories are connected to particular carryovers that, though in different forms, continue to shape and inform even the most revolutionary subversions of empire. As such, the authority of local indigenous knowledge, as it travels throughout various contemporary circuits, is itself ironically embedded in "global" circuits. Therefore, to produce useful analytic approaches to local and transnational processes we need to aggressively pursue the role of historical formations of interconnection and fragmentation between and among transcontinental movements (Cooper 2001). By charting the ideological conditions that shape limitations of and possibilities for innovation we can understand how the imaginary is mediated by historically inscribed formations.

I have explored what relations adhere between historicity and historiography in the creation of the cultural practices that shape deterritorialized identity formation. I have explored how, when, and why various forms of meanings are introduced and how they change, and, by extension, how these changes are stabilized and incorporated into new institutional mechanisms under varying territorial, thus different political, historical, and economic conditions. I have asked how these formations, whether they are embedded in modern territorial contexts or postmodern deterritorial contexts, create meanings relevant to daily life. Ultimately, this book is engaged in anthropological explorations of knowledge production with attention to the particularities by which people use legal, religious, and historical processes of reproduction. I consider the implications of this exploration for our understanding of the concepts of culture and the geopolitics of race, ethnicity, and gender as representations of the symbolic work of how we classify difference in time and space. I am also interested in how we can better integrate anthropological method and theory developed in area studies into general theory building in the discipline. For my methodological goal has been to demarginalize "regional" knowledge developed as Americanist or Africanist in order to better comprehend how our traditionally constructed area studies fields, often substantively isolated, can be practically connected to other regions and relationally examined as a product of ongoing contact between groups of people shaped by the transnational movement of ideas, capital, resources, and human travel.

In recognizing that *anthropologies* of globalization do not necessarily entail charting interconnections everywhere, I call for more and not less innovation and teamwork in the inquiry and documentation of complex circuits and processes within and outside of the nation. My vision for the future of anthropology, therefore, involves reconfiguring nation-based area studies that have for too long overdetermined anthropological work and have shaped scholarly investments in favor of the modern nation as the basis of originary attachments. In foregrounding the need to make central alternative mappings of global connections, that is, embarking on a critical transnationalism, we need to take seriously the role that imperial designs have on the production of academic and political categories. I have argued, like others, that our dependence on nationhood as a conceptual analytic of governance and scholarly organization continues to shape postmodern geographies, but we also need to understand how people reconceptualize the relevance of the nation-state in their lives. As such, we need to understand how these designs undergird the ways that agents form or undermine national or regional coalitions—historical and religious, for example—and then we need to foreground how different moral economies are configured along historically inscribed social and regional formations.

In thinking about the future of anthropology and the increasing role that religious difference plays globally, it is my hope that anthropologists will continue to legitimate projects that are not only area-based but also mapped conceptually and that follow linkages and not just people and their governments. We need to continue to identify new ways to ensure that ethnographically localized studies are grounded in larger global linkages, and vice versa. This would require far more interrelated collaborations between cultural anthropology students and faculty than we have grown used to in the last decades of the twentieth century. Such collaborations with different theoretical and area specializations would necessarily challenge the mechanisms by which disciplines are regulated and patrolled, forcing us to think more critically about what we gain and lose in the process of studying complex multisited, transnational, and multimeasurable processes.

The issue of representation is also critical here, for often, in charting larger processes, we miss the richness of local specificities. In this study, I used narrative introductions to create a different sense of time and place and represented ritual and legal language and performance to demonstrate how mechanisms of proof were constituted as powerful tools.[1] My challenge was to capture not just the nostalgic pleasures of the lives of my informants and the power of the elite, but the feelings of discontent, of dystopia, the disagreements over and struggles for power or just to be heard and accepted. My charge was to capture the feelings of relief from the everyday laborious tasks, in the name of "tradition, halted by the beating of the town drum"—the reminder of tradition and obligation. Although moments of rupture and discontent are, in fact, irreproducible in their entirety here, the descriptions were meant to demonstrate how power is negotiated on a daily basis. In the end, Ọ̀yọ́túnjí Village networks are not simply the physical achievement of place in deterritorial contexts: Ọ̀yọ́túnjí is an ideal; it is a state of mind. We have as our task, therefore, ethnography as multisited mappings of transnational networks.

The processes of producing an Ọ̀yọ́túnjí Village, its networks, and its imaginary homeland claims are reflections of the making of daily life, our lives. The challenge today is a challenge of mapping relevant geographic scopes and understanding which institutional forces are at play. Bringing anthropological methods into the twenty-first century involves rethinking what constitutes the field, home or the *elsewhere*, and developing a conceptual framework to map the ways that people cross some boundaries within these fields, even while they reinforce others. In the case of Yoruba practices, how we study diasporic and transnational sites in which members of Yoruba religious communities are engaged in globalizing projects involves developing conceptual fields in which the area is both transregional and conceptual. The area studies model that once predetermined anthropology of the twenty-first century must be interrogated to chart sites that are at once local and historical while also conceptual and antithetical to historical hegemonies. This means we need to interrogate modern subjectivity, rethink ideologies of seeing, and chart the ways that people cross boundaries in order to theorize diasporic formations as conceptual spaces that are analytically useful for understanding claims of belonging and exclusions. It means charting contestations around boundary demarcations and mapping the ways new forms of linkages are understood both within and outside of state boundaries. This is a challenge that cannot be answered easily. The field is a complex site and areas are both transtemporal and transgeographical. Thus, whether our conclusions are produced in the spirit of mapping Yoruba communities elsewhere or configured to understand our own social worlds, it is important to recognize that the same processes inhere. If the project is an attempt to understand what is traditional or authentic, African or black, American or British, the processes of community formation are fundamentally about producing sites of difference, hierarchies of belonging, and forms of exclusions in all social worlds.

Appendix

Kingdom of Oyotunji

Alafia,

Greetings and peace. We implore all African Americans to visit Oyotunji. Oyotunji is a unique experience and historical place designated and patterned after ancient Yoruba tradition. Visit the King's Palace and our Village Museum, take a stroll down Temple Row, and be introduced to some of the ancient gods and goddesses of Southwestern Nigeria. Adupe for your interest in the Yoruba Village.

Here are the details of our Tourist Program:

Tour and Sightseeing

1. Rates per individual per tour

Adults:	$3.50
Children (6–16):	$2.50

2. Ten adults or more

Per person: $3.00

3. View of the Yoruba Temple Dancers and Drummers

with tour $75.00

4. View of African Parliament (Ogboni) in session. Must have ten or more adults and arrive by 9:00 A.M. on Mondays. Reservations are required.

5. African luncheon available upon request. Menu might include jolof rice, which is a rice cooked with fish, meat, and a variety of African spices.

6. Lecture with the King-in-State $50.00
   (45 minute lecture, 15 minute question-and-answer period)

7. Lecture with the Chiefs
    a. Male in Yoruba Society $25.00
    b. Female in Yoruba Society $25.00

8. Lodging available in Camp Compound at $3.00 per person per night. Guests must supply own bedding, lantern, and buckets (for water, etc.). Campers, tents, and small mobile homes are permitted by reservation *only*.

9. Villa Orite Guest House $10.00 per day. Has electric, linens, radio, and other comforts.

Ọyọ́túnjí Price List for Initiations and Awo òrìṣà 1991

1. Egungun Initiations $1,500.00
   (Initiations into the Egungun societies are open to all of African ancestry. Initiation into this cult will allow persons [initiated] to give ancestral pots, hold ancestral ceremonies, perform Egungun. Book list on African laws, systems, traditions, marriages, burials, customs, and religion will be given for study and tests will be administered after the three moons training period. Pots received at the time of initiation will be Getty Nimbo Ẹ́ṣu of the dead], Oya [mother of the Egúngún], and Egungun. If a person already has Oya, the price is so reduced. Also includes Ijo Egungun.)

2. Ijo Egungun or Kakiri Egungun (Parade Egungun) $800.00
   This is a ceremony performed at the demise of a family member to elevate their spirit in the spirit world.

3. Orisha Initiations $3,000.00
   Initiation into any of the Orisha priesthoods.

4. Years Ebo or Three Months Ebo $1,500.00

5. Orisha Pots with Cowries $700.00
   Includes cowries, ileki, ita.

6. Orisha Pots without Cowries $500.00
   Washed pot, ileki, no ita.

7. Eshu, Ogun, Ososi $650.00   w/Osun $700.00

8. Babaluaiye $1,500.00

9. Eshu (alone) $300.00

10. Osun (from Babalawo) $150.00

11. Ifa (Orunmila) $600.00

African Yorùbá Village Festival Calendar 1995 Kingdom of Òyótúnjí

Reading of the Year—1 January
The priests of Òyótúnjí consult the Ifá oracle to reveal the future of the United States and the world.

Olokun Festival—25–26 February
Celebration of the mysterious God of the Deep Sea and protector of the African soul.

Yorùbá New Year—20 March
Toast to the 10,037th year of the birth of Yorùbá culture.

Éṣu, Ògún, Oshosi Festival—24–26 March
Celebration of the Trickster God, War God, and Hunter God, including annual Akínkonjú Men's Rites.

Òṣun Festival—28 April–3 May
Brilliant pageants and parties for the Goddess of Love, Beauty, Riches, Spring.

Egúngún Festival—26 May–5 June
Celebration of the great ancestors; pageants featuring annual royal customs and the King's sacrifice to His ancestors.

Yemoja-Egbe Moremi Fest—24–25 June
Pageants and fertility dances for the Great Mother Goddess of the Yorùbá; celebration of Rites of Passage for Women's Society.

Ifá Festival And Yorùbá National Cultural Convention—1–4 July
Mythical festival of dances and recitations to God of Destiny; mass gathering of Yorùbás to formulate plans for continuation of Yorùbá tradition.

Ṣàngó Festival—22–23 July
Veneration of the brilliant eighth-century Alafin of ancient Òyó who became God of Thunder and Lightning.

Òbàtálá Festival—24–26 August
Stately dances and plays in celebration of the patron God of the Yorùbá Village.

King's Day—6–8 October
Grand series of elaborate processions, banquets in honor of the birthday of the King.

Oya Festival—28–29 October
Autumnal equinox venerating the fierce Royal Goddess of Death, Storm, and Niger River.

Hwedo Festival—31 October
Parade of ghosts and solemn candlelight ceremonies for the unknown dead of the African race.

Obalúaiyé Festival—21–31 December
Masquerades, archers, mischief, and dances for winter solstice and rule of Taskmaster God.

Ọ̀yọ́túnjí advertisement.

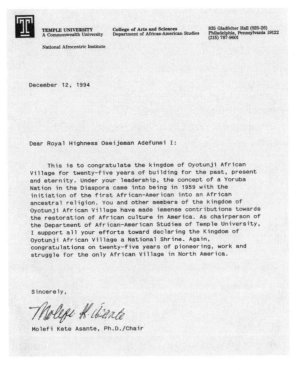

Communication from the Chair of the African Studies Department at Temple University.

AFRICAN CULTURAL RESTORATION PLAN

TAKE A STEP TOWARDS AFRICAN CULTURAL REDEMPTION

AFRICA IS THE CENTER OF THE WORLD

GOING BACK TO TRADITION IS THE FIRST STEP FORWARD

YOUR ANCESTORS ARE CALLING YOU!!!!!!!!!!

AFRICAN CIVILIZATION IS THE OLDEST CIVILIZATION

KINGDOM OF ỌYỌTUNJI

AFRICAN SOCIAL ORGANIZATION TEN STEPS TO FREEDOM

1) ANCESTOR WORSHIP
Erect an Ancestral Shrine - Light a candle for them (List all deceased members of the family). Ancestor worship is the link which keeps intact the continuity of past, present and future.

2) RACIAL IMAGE
Be a positive role model. • Take an African Name. • Wear African attire. • Make Africa the center of your world view

3) VALUES and MORAL CODES
African morals versus Foreign Morals should be studied, analyzed and explained to males, females, and children. • Rites of passage ceremonies should be constituted for each important phase of life.

4) ECONOMIC PROGRAM
Form a Business association. Begin to own businesses, become self-employed - Your children cannot inherit the job if you work for someone else!

5) EDUCATIONAL PROGRAM
Study African History. • The need for children to be educated by the community is real. We must re-educate ourselves from an African perspective.

6) LEGAL CONCEPTS
Study African social laws and customs. African culture is non-restrictive; right and wrong are relative to the situation.

7) MARITAL CODE
Study African Marriage types. There are several types in all, depending on the destinies and commitment of the people involved.

8) RECREATIONAL PROGRAM
Give your team an African name - consider uniforms in African fabric. Athletics teach confidence and discipline. Games are metaphors of life.

9) SOCIAL ORGANIZATION
Give your sorority/fraternity an African name. • Join an African Men's Society. • Join an African Women's Society. • Elders councils should be a part of all our communities.

10) ARTS PROGRAM
Have African pictures, carvings, maps, etc. in your home. • Make African arts and crafts. Artistic expressions which reflect our true selves are important statements of our development.

REMEMBER THE ANCESTORS
SUPPORT AFRICA   WEAR AFRICAN ATTIRE
SUPPORT KINGDOM OF ỌYỌTUNJI AFRICAN VILLAGE
BUY GREAT BENIN BOOKS, FILMS, TAPES
Kingdom of Ọyọtunji African Village, Hwy 17, PO Box 51, Sheldon, SC 29941

African Cultural Restoration Plan.

Notes

Preface

1   I do not use the word "ideology" to revisit Marxian debates about political-based think-
    ing, nor is it reflective of a class or a coherent system of thought. Rather, I invoke it to
    describe a sphere of logics—a domain of seeing that allows people to classify, interpret,
    and explain the world as they see it—sometimes producing contradictory results but
    shaped by particular fields of possibility through which meanings are channeled.

2   Though I do not intend my relationship to these rituals to be seen in relation to the
    supernatural efficacy of Yorùbá ritual in general, I would like to stress here that my
    experiences of various rituals during the course of my fieldwork certainly opened up a
    world of symbols and meanings that had not only socially transformative powers, but
    also psychological powers. These rituals, as Susan Harding (2000) has suggested, re-
    quire one to engage in discourses of testimonials that are substantively material. Rather
    than dismissing the contributory role of the ritual process in affecting change, or ques-
    tioning the logics of truth with which my informants understood their world, I ap-
    proached the early phase of research being conscientious of the ways agents interpreted
    and experienced meanings. I thereby recast the question not as one of the existence or
    nonexistence of the supernatural but, instead, as one of how the institutionalization of
    Yorùbá religion and ritual produces critical epistemologies for interpreting reality.

3   The very struggles of the formation of formal Christian institutions in Nigeria were
    similarly operative in the development of plantation slavery that led to the conversion
    of slaves in Cuba and that also influenced the delegitimation of non-Christian religions,
    driving various African-based cosmologies underground.

4   It marks an important historical moment in American anthropology in which many
    ethnographers believed in the sanctity of objectivity and the possibilities for under-

standing the Other through the comprehensive and systematic documentation of their history, political and kinship organization, and cultural practices.

Introduction

1 Although this is the traditional pattern, the transnational marking of òrìṣà traditions is changing what in the late twentieth century seemed to be the economic marginality of those in this category. For example, a growing number in this category, such as Dr. Wándé Abímbọ́lá and Chief Afọlábí, are transatlantic òrìṣà intellectuals able to travel between the West and Nigeria, making a living out of the teaching of Yorùbá cultural and ritual practices.

2 Just as the growth of Yorùbá transnational networks changed over time, so too have Yorùbá practices changed in the homeland; therefore, an examination of the effects of colonialism in Yorùbá traditional life shows us that the process of seeking authentic practices is futile because the very same traditional practices that are referenced by practitioners are themselves adaptations in time and space.

3 Yorùbáland is a place-name used to describe the region in West Africa where Yorùbá people predominate.

4 Circum-Atlantic is Joseph Roach's (1996) term to refer to what Robert Farris Thompson (1983) and later Paul Gilroy (1993a) have called the black Atlantic.

5 Fágbàmílà is also a prolific leader and founder of the Ifá College and the Ifá Foundation: The Home of American Ifá. Knowledge institutions, which espouse particular interpretations of òrìṣà practices, are becoming increasingly widespread.

6 As will be explored in chapter 5, Ifá divination works with sixteen *odù* (divinatory verses), which can be compared with pagan zodiac signs. It is cast with dried palm nuts that are considered holy and tied to a chain known as the *Ọ̀pẹ̀lẹ̀*. To be a diviner is to be a *babaláwo* (father of secrets), a priest of Ifá. To be a babaláwo a practitioner must be initiated and undergo many years of training in and dedication to the cult of Ifá. Similarly, other priests of òrìṣà who have not achieved the level of Ifá divination perform divination with sixteen cowry shells or other variations of four shells which they cast to derive answers to questions. However, interpretation of the òrìṣà message, though embedded in predictable odù configurations, is highly variable, for priests must use their conceptualization of the problem not only to pose questions to the oracle but also to find solutions. When cast, the Ifá divining tool is used to determine which of the sixteen basic odù will have to be interpreted.

7 The popular belief is that Ifá was the òrìṣà who was present when Olódùmarè (the chief god) was creating the world, and Ọ̀rúnmìlà, the deity of the cosmic domain, is said to cast Ifá according to the will of Olódùmarè.

8 See C. Daryll Forde (1956, 1963) in *Habitat, Economy, and Society* and his later work in southern Nigeria on the importance of secret societies and other non-kinship-based association. It was not until after the 1965 International Congress of African Historians that the African diaspora, as a subject of study, was introduced to the academy as

an intervention into the survivals discourse and as a popularized intellectual linkage between Africa and its history of African dispersal and exile.

9 For more on this, see Appadurai (1991, 1996b); Sassen (1991, 1994, 1996); Piot (1999); Holston (1999); Ong (1999); Harvey (1995, 2000, 2001); Riles (2000); Jean Comaroff and Comaroff (2001); Freeman (2000); Hutton and Giddens (2000); Hardt and Negri (2000).

1. Place, Race, and Nation

1 "Blackness" remains the sole qualification for membership into the Òyótúnjí Yorùbá secret societies.

2 The colors of the three flags are red, green, and gold; red and black; and white and black, respectively.

3 At one time many of the early residents were able to supplement their household income with government assistance payments. However, in the late 1980s, the Òyótúnjí Ògbóni council outlawed federal and South Carolina state government assistance. This new law, as well as the growing power of the Crown, made it increasingly difficult for many practitioners to make an adequate living on their religious trade alone. Unable to make ends meet, and in need of more political agency, hundreds of practitioners moved to U.S. cities, forming Yorùbá satellite communities from which to continue their religious practices.

4 Many of the practitioners lived in Òyótúnjí at one time, and others have pursued ritual initiations there over a period of time. I conducted a population tabulation of residents every three months over a one-year period and found that the population shifted from fifty-seven to forty-eight residents.

5 Note that the rural location, the signs of racial commonalities, and African practices are not in and of themselves material differences that are adequate to link life in Òyótúnjí Village to life in West Africa. Likewise, evidence of musical preference that blends West African rhythmic performers with American rap songs is not sufficient to distinguish a difference of cultural production in the United States from forms that may be simultaneously occurring in contemporary West African Yorùbá communities, even as community life, imagined as part of the Òyó Empire, is not sufficient to render these differences as signs of disjuncture with a Yorùbá tradition. Instead, signs of the inauthentic and their ability to be classified in the eyes of the beholders as legitimate are dependent on the institutional forms of remembering and forgetting that typically shape the boundaries of social distinctions. I demonstrate how ritual practices are fashioned and refined to render a useable past to those who travel to Òyótúnjí seeking assistance. The interpretative constructions of particular kinds of ancestral connections with West Africa render the meaning of the past—transatlantic slavery—central to the formation of Òyótúnjí Yorùbá traditionalism. Thus, with linkages established, the power to establish the legitimacy of an African kingdom in South Carolina lies in the personal authority generated by religious ritual conducted by the revered subject.

6 On the grounds that Africans were barbarians void of Christianity and without the mental capacity to justify their liberty.

7 In an attempt to secure rights and equal protection for all citizens of the United States, however, the Civil Rights Act of 1966 was passed by Congress many decades later. It formalized the abolition laws and also outlined the terms for guaranteeing basic rights.

8 These individual agents both influence and are influenced by the prophetic leaders. As we shall see in the last chapter, however, when they go beyond the leadership-established social norms or interventions made by Ọba practitioners, they may be repudiated or the forms of informal disapproval may be so strong that they might leave the community.

9 Santería regulations required that ritual initiations had to be presided over by babaláwo (the highest ranking priests, those of the Ifá òrìṣà). As a young priest without a congregation of qualified African-centered priests, it was difficult for the king to function in Santería religious circles with their support.

10 In the history of the demise of the Ọ̀yọ́ Empire it was a military chief excluded from the inner workings of the state, known as the *Are-Ọ́nà-Kakaǹfò*, who confronted King Aolè, rebelling against what had been identified as monarchic oppression or royal tyranny. This led to the Ọ̀yọ́ Civil War.

11 The ìká gbó district (translated as "the place of the stickers") was taken from the holy *Odù Ifa Ìká*, a divinatory verse.

12 Trinidad and Kétu Yorùbá men and women were captured by the Dahomeans, traded in Haiti and Brazil, and referred to by the Dahomean term *Nago*, from its root *Anago*, which referenced an ethnic group from the former Oahonean region of western Africa and highlighted shared traditions, customs, religions, and language.

13 It has long been documented that in the development of the modern world, trade practices have drastically affected the livelihood of communities involved in the triangular slave trade—initially those in West Africa, Europe, and the Americas. Before 1680, West African commodity exports such as palm oil, ivory, and gold were facilitated through multidirectional exchanges of short-term credit and trade. Trade transactions involved the assignment of particular types of value units and currency standards that included the cost of transportation and insurance (Eltis 1987). The initial routes for the exchange of mercantile goods led to increases in the demand for gold, ivory, and palm oil. Slave exports and imports were established in the context of the transatlantic circulation of commodities, and by the sixteenth century, the trade of slaves accounted for half of the total of goods traded with Africa (Curtin 1967).

14 In his two-volume publication, *The Modern World System*, Immanuel Wallerstein (1974, 1980) charts the geopolitical phenomenon of global trade from the sixteenth to the mid-eighteenth century. He argues that by the middle of the seventeenth century New England and Middle Atlantic merchants, as both shipbuilders and mercantile middlemen, developed a lucrative business in the triangular trading routes. In the triangle with Africa, Europe, and the Caribbean, Caribbean molasses went to the British colonies, the rum and trinkets from the northern colonies went to Africa, and African

slaves were taken to the Caribbean. Caribbean sugar and tobacco went to England, and English products went to southern Europe. Southern European wine, salt, and fruits went to England, and, again, English manufactured products such as wheat, fish, and lumber were exported to the northern colonies (1980, 237). With England and France dominating direct trade with Africa and the Caribbean islands, they developed colonies and relationships with other nations where, as direct producers and exporters, they created webs of commodity and slave exchange with other countries (241). With the rapidly growing international demand for sugar and tobacco, the plantation industry developed throughout the New World (Austen and Smith 1992, 185; Mintz 1985, 78).

15 The Dutch gained hegemonic control over mercantile trade between 1651 and 1689 and were succeeded by the English and French from 1600 to 1750. The transport of slaves to the Caribbean and South America by countries such as Spain and Portugal marked the commencement of the trade during the fifteenth and sixteenth centuries, and by the seventeenth and eighteenth centuries, the Dutch, and then the English and French, dominated trade to the New World (Curtin 1969, 15).

16 As Sidney Mintz (1985) has shown in *Sweetness and Power*, not only was sugar needed as fuel for the Industrial Revolution, but the rise of Enlightenment and industrialization increasingly required cotton for clothes that would be manufactured in Europe.

17 Though the slave trade to Cuba was officially outlawed in 1865, both slavery and the trade continued. It was only during the Ten Years' War, in 1873, that the last known slave shipment landed in Cuba. (In addition to African slaves, an estimated 150,000 to 250,000 Chinese contract laborers were taken to Cuba from 1847 to 1887, when Spain and China signed a treaty that ended the flow.) In 1880 (the year sugar production topped 700,000 tons, almost 600,000 of which was exported to the United States), the colonial authorities decreed the abolition of slavery but introduced a system akin to apprenticeship, known as *patronato*, whereby former masters would remain owners for an eight-year period. The patronato was rendered inoperative and ended earlier than originally planned, in 1886.

18 Scientific racism led to the evolutionary classification of the animal kingdom according to a Great Chain of Being. The fundamental assumption was that each racial group constituted a distinct species. Following apes, Africans were generally classified at the bottom, and other racial groupings followed in hierarchical order, from the "lower" beings to the "more evolved."

19 It is believed that the regla de ocha was encouraged to avoid slave uprisings.

20 Although there is significant agreement on the role of commodity production that propelled transatlantic slavery, there are disputes concerning the total numbers of those who were enslaved.

21 See the work of Rafael Lopez Valdes (1990). The classificatory name Lukumi (from an old Yorùbá phrase, *olùkù mi*, meaning "my friend") emerged as an early term that described the language and a common identity. This increase in exportation is according to Moreno Fraginals's (1977) data collected from Cuban plantation records during the

final period prior to the abolition of the slave trade in which large numbers of men and women from the Lukumi nation were shipped to Cuba.

22 There seemed to be religious and social similarities among the newly imported Yorùbá-speaking captives. But because of their linguistic and ethnic heterogeneity, historians of the transatlantic slave trade are in disagreement about how early Yorùbá speakers identified themselves.

23 With the birth of Enlightenment, new ideas about human value, standards of religiosity, and civil society took shape through the deployment of European civilizing missions. Different notions of black identities, as a racial typology, were produced out of Europe's encounter with Africa. This form of classification led to the institutionalization of African cultural heritage, forcing us to rethink a range of historically constituted processes. These processes emerged out of the history of racialization, political economies of slavery, and European expansionism to accumulate wealth and "discover" an unknown world. Print capital accompanied the flow of goods and materials and significantly contributed to the standardization of modern ideological conceptions of value and belonging (Anderson 1983). The goals of European Enlightenment were propelled by the early development of new global regimes of trade: books, newspapers, and magazines. However, just as access to sugar was limited, so was access to texts, and only the literate could make use of the newly developing print industry. Over time, Christian moral codes expanded and circulated in shaping the ideological standards of colonial governance within particular hierarchies of scale. Though notions of value were shaped by the relatively low prices placed on African lives, the institutional worth of African bodies as slaves was consolidated in the second half of the nineteenth century.

With the publication of Charles Darwin's (1859, 1998) *On the Origin of the Species* and the spread of scientific classifications of racial difference, racialized ranking systems permeated ideological fields of power and further perpetuated the basis for plantation slavery and consequent forms of social inequalities. These scientific justifications of racial ordering led to new discursive fields of knowledge concerned with the biological inferiority of Africans and the elevation of the meanings of whiteness. With these constructions of race as culture, a *symbolics of blood* was developed in various political, educational, and social institutions to link racial topographies of race, suggesting that particular people were predisposed to particular types of inherited behavior, to African originary descent. In such a vein, discourses that represented Africans as primitive and heathen further imposed moral injunctions that set blackness against whiteness, enforcing racial and slave-based segregation and clarifying the distinctions between citizens, colonial subjects, and slaves. These ideas, propelled by texts but inaccessible to the non-literate slave majority, combined a language of morality, family, civil society, and social progress in hierarchical distinctions of racial difference that rendered non-European knowledge production and religious practice unworthy of cultural reproduction in a "civilized" world.

24 See Matory (1994, 30) for the argument that this was done so that indirect colonial rule could be achieved more effectively.

25 On October 10, 1868, the colony embarked on a war of independence with Spain. Slave-holders such as Carlos Manuel de Céspedes freed their slaves and called for an end to Spanish rule. The struggle for Cuban nationhood was forged with Africans and former white planters alike, and in 1869 a constitution was signed and slavery was abolished. The initial declaration of the Ten Years' War, known as the Declaration of Yara, was made at a sugar mill and invoked freedom for the slaves as well as independence from Spain, reflecting the extent to which issues of abolition and independence were inter-twined. However, neither the Ten Years' War (1868–78) nor the war of 1879–80 was represented in Cuba as a reflection of mainstream popular support. Over twenty years after the abolition of slavery, the second war of independence (1895–98) became a main-stream struggle for national sovereignty from Spain. In this nation-building process blacks and whites joined forces in the military to forge an independent republic known as Cuba. Following the war for independence, Cuban national leaders focused their priorities on creating an island that was attractive to emigrants, especially from Spain. As European expansion and increasing migration from Spain shaped new terms for the entitlement to land, new forms of governance were erected through the reclassification of individuals in relation to their geographical surroundings. Notions of modernity and civilization contributed to regulating racial and ethical value with which religious norms were measured (Stepan and Gilman 1993, 181). Scientific justifications of African inferiority contributed to the racial contempt that many Europeans developed toward "darker-skinned" people. The consequent relegation of Africans to the status of an ex-ploitable labor force and the progressive development of stratified racial typologies—in which non-Aryans were identified and classified against a European cultural standard—aided the spread of European dominance. These racial institutions perpetuated norms of African inferiority through conceptual distinctions such as *modern* versus *primitive* and *civilized* versus *heathen*. Ultimately, these forms of classification led to a practice of moral regulation perpetuated through both overt and subversive forms of regulation (Saxton 1990; Dominguez 1986; Stocking 1968).

26 Unlike that of the United States during the same period, when, through the legaliza-tion of Jim Crow segregation, black people were relegated to the public and service sectors and racial segregation continued to be legal.

27 A young lawyer by the name of Fidel Castro, of Spanish (Galician) descent, disillu-sioned by the corruption of state officials under the Autentico administrations, on be-half of the Orthodox Party, led an attack on the Moncada Garrison in Santiago de Cuba in 1952. Castro was jailed but was granted amnesty and in 1955 was deported to Mexico. He led a return expedition to Cuba in 1956 to form the Rebel Army in the eastern Sierra Maestra mountains. The armed struggle had its civilian counterpart in the 26th of July Movement and, combined with the activities of other civilian groups, developed into a popular struggle for social justice that triumphed on January 1, 1959.

28 "Racial mixture" is a floating discourse that people use to highlight the ways that the newly forming Cuban state was constituted by discourses of inequality and discrimi-nation.

29 In the 1930s, some of the poor in the Cuban countryside mobilized large numbers of Afro-Cubans of the proletariat class to join in the fight for the extrication of U.S. economic interests from Cuba. Consequently, President Gerardo Machado (1925–33) was overthrown, and strong black communist leaders emerged out of a cross-racial labor movement. Government officials represented Cuba's social problems as being embedded in class disparities rather than race. Marxist socialists argued that race was lived through class relations and that addressing social economic conditions would correct racial injustices.

30 A large percentage of the new Cuban immigrants to the United States in the period leading up to the 1970s were educated and middle class and saw themselves as *mestizaje* and different from "blacks."

2. Roots Tourism and Race as Culture

1 As a committed fieldworker conducting participant observation, I quickly adjusted to Ọ̀yọ́túnjí practices, including wearing the same clothes that they wore.

2 First published in condensed form by *Reader's Digest* in 1974, and then in its entirety by Dell in January 1976, it was televised by ABC over an eight-night period in 1977.

3 By "black nationalist" and "black cultural nationalism" I mean the loosely configured conceptualization of nationalism that transcends statehood and instead converges around racial biology or symbolics of ancestry.

4 "Symbolics of blood" refers to Michel Foucault's (1978) invocation of blood as biology, thus lineage, in the *History of Sexuality*.

5 Obiagele Lake (1997), for example, suggests that "since racism continues to affect the life chances of diaspora Africans," we need to focus on racial bodies as biologically victimized objects. Indeed, racism is critical for understanding the social conditions within which agents negotiate daily life; however, there have been significant shifts in studies of race since the last decade of the twentieth century, and these days, more than ever, we need to understand the processes by which such forms are authored and legitimated. This means also examining how "victims" of racism also reproduce the same tenets of discrimination that they attempted to undermine.

6 I use the term "cultural intellectuals" similar to the ways that Antonio Gramsci (1971) used "organic intellectuals" but also incorporate traditional intellectuals in this category. For Gramsci, intellectuals are a part of everyday life, but not everyone functions as an intellectual in society. Arguing that everyone has an intellect and uses it in different ways, he demonstrated that the notion of intellectuals as a distinct social category was a myth. Thus, he identifies two types of intellectuals: traditional and organic. He commonly refers to traditional intellectuals as men of letters, the philosophers and professors. Although they like to think of themselves as independent of ruling groups, they assist with the maintenance of social order. Organic intellectuals, on the other hand, are those people who, though products of society, play a critical role in enabling the social domination of traditional intellectuals. For Gramsci, they, too, are themselves

intellectuals, and though not recognized as such, they participate in shaping cultural meanings in their world. As I demonstrate by using the term cultural intellectuals to represent both traditional and organic intellectuals, the role of producing *commonsense* explanations of the world is not just in the realm of the traditional intellectual elite, but also those nontraditional intellectuals who participate in the production of knowledge. Rather, and particularly with electronic technologies today, many types of people participate in this process, and their contributions are both part of traditionally recognized institutions of knowledge and of those forms of knowledge grounded in everyday life. Both produce cultural conceptions of the world and contribute to the shaping of local and global knowledge.

7   Their efforts ranged from educational programs and solidarity strategies to a physical return to Africa, and even though print capital was the national standard for movement building, among African American populations in the 1890s, the literacy rate among the black population was 68 percent (Bullock 1967, 172). According to government statistics, the publication and buying power of the black community even up until 1976 remained relatively low.

8   Throughout the 1950s and 1960s, in an attempt to foster diplomatic relations, the USIS sponsored a series of radio programs whose goals were to circulate anticolonial sentiments, disseminate anticommunist values, and extol the virtues of democratic freedoms. Yet even as these programs were being pursued by the United States in colonial nations, black American communist activists such as Paul Robeson, W. E. B. Du Bois, and later Angela Y. Davis critiqued what they felt were U.S. governmental contradictions surrounding the politics of racial segregation and the American rhetoric of freedom used to undermine communism. The 1960s was a period in which democratic freedom and technological advancement worked in tandem with the development of increasing linkages between newly independent African states and the U.S. federal government. By this process of spreading the virtues of democratic liberties to Third World countries, the United States shored up its economic alliances and established arrangements with various African nations, even after they had become independent, with the goal of leaving channels open for future trade and telecommunications activity. This was especially critical in the Belgian Congo, for example, which, as Penny Von Eschen (1997) pointed out in *Race against Empire*, provided two-thirds of the world's supply of raw diamonds, which were used for cutting instruments for military weapons. The United States also depended on African exports of large supplies of cobalt for building jet engines and on the African production of uranium for atomic bombs. Thus, after the independence of Indonesia and India and with the spread of communism in Asia and Cuba, African countries held increasingly strategic resources for the new technological commodities needed in the Americas. In the early 1950s, West Africa was a primary exporter of manganese, gold, tin, lead, columbite, and zinc, and East Africa was equally mineral-rich.

9   This defeat led to the abrogation of U.S. diplomatic relations with Cuba and a trade embargo against Cuba and its allies. As a result, Cuba became increasingly dependent

on its socialist allies. Once supportive of Latin American struggles, the U.S. public had to live with the heightened fear of missile attacks from a former ally about ninety miles south of Florida. In October 1962, the United States learned that the USSR had installed missiles and missile bases in Cuba. Political relations between Cuba and the United States escalated, marking the beginning of what came to be known as the Cuban Missile Crisis. President Kennedy demanded that the USSR extricate its missiles from Cuba; he then set up a naval quarantine around Cuba. Soviet Premier Khrushchev's representatives responded by indicating that if the United States would dismantle its military bases in Turkey, Russia would move the missiles from Cuba. Although the United States refused, Khrushchev agreed, a week later, to remove the missiles.

10 By 1961 more than 10,000 computers were in operation in large-scale corporate settings; ten years later, they exceeded 100,000; and by the mid-1980s, they were in many middle- and upper-middle-class American homes.

11 The New African Union Act transformed the OAU into the African Union during the transitory period 2001–2002.

12 *Brown v. Board of Education* was a landmark case of school desegregation in which the Supreme Court revisited earlier rulings of "separate but equal" doctrines established by *Plessy v. Ferguson* (163 U.S. 537) and ruled that the system of segregated public schools should be overturned in favor of racial integration.

13 The fundamental principles of becoming *black* included: (1) nurturing a positive self image, (2) reaching a state of black self-actualization, (3) seizing the power to shape black images and create new symbols of black lifestyles that would lead to the production of a new and unique form of African American culture, and (4) reclaiming black manhood and family.

14 These factors included how long slavery existed in different locations and whether and to what extent new slaves were introduced. These variables, along with many more, were introduced as a means of talking about the possibility of reinvigoration, resurgence, and independent reinvention.

15 See the U.S. Supreme Court rulings in *Plessy v. Ferguson*, *Loving v. Virgina*, and *Brown v. Board of Education* for state invocations of biology as justification for segregation.

16 Three of the most popular union workers were Jesús Menéndez, Aracelio Iglesias, and Lázaro Peña; they formed the leadership of the General Confederation of Labor. In 1938 the Communist Party was legalized and its name was soon changed to the Popular Socialist Party (PSP). Under the "united front" of World War II, when communist parties worldwide adopted a conciliatory approach to ruling bourgeois regimes, Cuba's constituent assembly, which had a number of PSP members, promulgated one of the most progressive constitutions in Latin America in 1940. From 1944 to 1952 the Auténtico (Authentic) Party was in power, led by Presidents Ramón Grau San Martín (1944–48) and Carlos Prío Socarrás (1948–52), and the intensification of the cold war set the stage for the assassinations of the foremost leaders of the General Confederation of Labor. In 1952, the next military coup by Batista's forces led to his reinstatement as president. Of the many groups opposing Batista in the 1950s, the PSP was explicitly committed

to ending racial discrimination, whereas the commitment was left implicit in the more general demands for social justice of other multiclass and multiracial movements.

17 Many black publishing houses struggled to survive in the 1970s, but because of the development of more efficient printing technologies, they tripled their output in the 1980s.

18 Compared to the 950,000 black Americans enrolled in undergraduate education in 1976, in 1980 there were 1,028,000 blacks enrolled in undergraduate study. This compares with 72,000 blacks in graduate study in 1976 and 66,000 in 1980 (U.S. Department of Education 1989; Integrated Postsecondary Education Data System 1986).

19 These included Dr. Henry Clarke, Ivan Van Sertima, and Dr. Ben-Jochannan, among hundreds of others.

20 The following is a list of African American publishing houses that spread throughout the 1970s to the present: Africa World Press and Red Sea Press, African American Images, Ananse Press, Basic Civitas Books, Beckham Publications Group, Inc., Black Classic Press, Black Words, Inc., Empak Publishing, FIRE!! Press, Fitzgerald Publishing Co. Inc., Holloway House Books, IC Publications, MG-Publishing Company, Mind Productions, Inc., Rapture Publishing, Sohaja Publishing Co., Urban Research Press, and Waverly House Publishing. Of the black-owned presses, some of their best sellers were Wade W. Nobles's (1986) *African Psychology: Toward Its Reclamation, Reascension and Revitalization*; Molefi Kete Asante's (1988) *Afrocentricity*; Maulana Karenga and Jacob Carruthers's (1986) *Kemet and the African Worldview: Research, Rescue and Restoration*; and Chancellor William's (1987) *The Destruction of Black Civilization: Great Issues of a Race from 4500 B.C. to 2000 A.D.* In the 1990s, books such as Dr. Frances Cress Welsing's (1991) *The Isis Papers: The Keys to the Colors* and Carter G. Woodson's (1933) *The Mis-Education of the Negro* dominated cultural nationalist circles.

21 Kente cloth is a Ghanian cloth that became popular in North American cities with predominantly black American populations.

22 Kwanzaa was first celebrated in 1966 in Los Angeles at the height of the Black Power movement. It was invented by Maulana Ron Karenga, a black nationalist who was interested in focusing on cultural nationalism instead of following a strictly Marxist ideological approach to black liberation.

23 The seven days of Kwanzaa are as follows: December 26, Umoja Day (unity); December 27, Kujichagulia Day (self-determination); December 28, Ujima Day (collective world and responsibility); December 29, Ujamaa Day (cooperative economics); December 30, Nia Day (purpose); December 31, Kumumba Day (creativity); January 1, Imani Day (faith). These seven days represent seven principles that were established by Karenga as the values necessary to rebuild black families and redefine the nation.

24 They began training by participating in a research study about how people's access to various technologies shapes communities' use of technology. In return for their participation, they received a donation of four computers and a $5,000 complementary grant. As a result, and by being actively engaged in Internet and Web site construction, Òyótúnjí's elementary school teachers collaborated with Web developers to design an

Ọyọ́túnjí site where their students could participate in the network of practitioners around the United States. By the end of 1996, the principal of the school used the remaining grant and community funds to buy video equipment and update the photo-copying machine.

25 Over a ten-year period (1985–95), the availability of particular rituals in Ọyọ́túnjí and the looser deterritorialized possibilities enabled willing middle-class practitioners, many of whom worked as nurses, flight attendants, hospital workers, schoolteachers, and community workers, to pursue short-term initiation.

26 By 1995, more than half of the first-generation children who lived in Ọyọ́túnjí had to find work outside the community. Five of the young men worked in construction and two of the young women left the community and enrolled in college or university. Of those who stayed or later returned, they developed their divinatory skills by going through priestly accreditation and earning their income as diviners—next to tourism, the most lucrative way to earn a living in the community.

27 The business prospectus includes the following list of average tourist spending in the state: 1975, $1.4 billion; 1985, $3.39 billion; 1986, $3.75 billion; 1987, $4.1 billion; and an estimated average of $4.5 billion in 1990 and $10 billion in 2000.

28 Unlike various African forms of governmental classifications of individual origins, which are dependent on parental origins, it is important to note here that U.S. State Department responses to multiple citizenship claims in the 1990s were not classified according to individual rights to parental origins, but on individual origins at birth or naturalization qualifications. Therefore, despite state adoptions of heritage classifica-tions as the basis for new forms of racial types and the countercitizenship claims along lines of cultural genealogies, citizenship law itself maintained a strong preoccupation with the individual and his or her rights and duties as a citizen.

3. Micropower and Ọyọ́ Hegemony

1 Members of the family disagreed with the Ọba's decision and attempted to address his appeal to literary documentation by asking the resident anthropologist to discuss with him the various ways that traditions change—even in the literature. In addressing my request, made on behalf of some of the relatives of the deceased, that the Ọba consider, for the purposes of making the rules relevant to Ọyọ́túnjí life, updating the U.S. appli-cations of Yorùbá traditions, he replied that he could not. He stated, "Our young man, brother, and friend, died a dishonorable death, and I cannot, in good faith, venerate such evil."

2 Delaney and Campbell (1969, 114–15). The authors discuss the role of Liberia and Sierra Leone in putting an end to the transatlantic slave trade.

3 Although British officials in the 1890s trained groups of Nigerians to carry out the visions of nation building within standards of civil society, an earlier class of Yorùbá-speaking people who lived in the region in the mid-1800s preceded them.

4 Ọyọ́ residents' overt religious alliances with either Christianity or Islam are often

coupled with a degree of hostility toward what they classify as "pagan traditions" conceived of as "old-time" and in mystical terms. Despite the critique of paganism, large numbers of people participate in the major festivals, regardless of their professed faith. Yorùbá òrìṣà worship and religious practices are still enmeshed in the cultural life of many traditionalists in the countryside.

5 The word *Yorùbá*, a derivative of the Hausa word *Yaraba*, referring to the people of Ọ̀yọ́, emerged outside of Nigeria. It was used in Sierra Leone by European CMS missionaries and was resignified as Yorùbá by literate Ọ̀yọ́ missionaries who claimed it as a way to describe Ọ̀yọ́ as the country of the Yorùbá.

6 This stratification of ethnicity within nationality was exacerbated during the postcolonial 1960s period of Nigerian nationalism in which ethnic, religious, and kinship subcategories were reunited with deeply penetrating forms of ethnic difference that ultimately led to fierce civil rivalries.

7 The interpretive oral descriptions of Yorùbá history, politics, and beliefs that circulated within and outside of the British colonial apparatus were diverse and shaped the narrative tropes about the Yorùbá past.

8 Their original codes of organization were either appropriated or transformed.

9 In the United States, citizenship has come to be classified according to the social contract that accompanies birth or naturalization; however, the development of notions of citizenship in Yorùbáland is deeply connected to parental patrilocal descent, in which an individual's geopolitical status at birth is secondary to his or her ancestral membership.

10 Johnson argued that missionization had advanced Yorùbá society beyond paganism and aided in its growing civility and general progress.

11 Johnson, using mythic tales and historical documentation, describes many wars and successions. His account of pre-eighteenth-century history was based on the customs and lore of the Yorùbá people. Evidence of the details of military succession in Yorùbáland before the nineteenth century is scant; however, eighteenth-century travelers wrote about the rulers of the Ọ̀yọ́ Kingdom as "a great warlike people" who from 1738 to 1747 raided Dahomey land until the Dahomey king promised to pay tribute to the Ọ̀yọ́ Empire.

Johnson also provided records about the work of Captain Clapperton, an early British explorer who recorded his observations about Yorùbá social life, and Colonel Ellis, a prolific writer whose work on Yorùbá ethnography was prominent from the end of the nineteenth into the early twentieth century.

12 Characterized here as the first significant period of war that led to the decline of the Ọ̀yọ́ Empire, the 1820 Òwu Civil War, and then the Àfọ́njá revolt against the Aláàfin at Ìlọrin (1824).

13 In the ranking system, Kakanfo is higher than Baṣọ̀run.

14 Following the death of King Aolè, Àfọ̀njá the Kakanfò and Opele the Baálè of Gbogun declared their independence and ceased exacting tribute from the local towns (Johnson 1921, 193). The downfall of the Yorùbá kingdom coincided with the beginning of tribal independence. Johnson described the post-1837 period of political struggle over Ọ̀yọ́'s

successor states. He depicts the Fulani southward invasion of Yorùbáland as symbolic of the aforementioned demise of Yorùbá dominance and of the development of the dominance of Islam in the Ọ̀yọ́ region.

15 J. D. Y. Peel (2001) describes the contest between competing centers of national power —the Yorùbá kingdoms of Benin (Bini), Dahomey (Aja), and Ọ̀yọ́—as key to understanding the rise of Yorùbá identity. The rise in Ọ̀yọ́-Yorùbá power has been described as "three brothers quarrel and their homes are invaded by strangers." The strangers signify Islamic forces that are popularly represented by Yorùbá Christians as invaders into Yorùbá territory. Fage (1970), on the other hand, emphasizes how the political system of the Ọ̀yọ́ rose to empire status in the eighteenth century, thereby enforcing particular forms of Yorùbá identity. Other scholars, such as Akínjógbìn (1967, 1972), in an attempt to demonstrate how the development of a unified conception of Yorùbá people came into being, argue that through intermarriage, common religious practices over time, and political and economic dominance the Yorùbá came to constitute a distinctive linguistic and cultural group (1972, 318–20). Regardless of the forces of power that enabled Yorùbá dominance or subordination, it is not difficult to recognize that they all share a fundamental assumption that the roots of the Yorùbá should be argued in terms of an authentic past.

16 Ilé-Ifẹ̀ is often recognized as being the originary homeland, the site of the formative development of Yorùbá cultural practices, the place where Yorùbá gods originated, and the place that the deceased are said to return to.

17 The Ifẹ̀-Modákẹ́kẹ́ crisis, one of the oldest intraethnic conflicts in Nigeria, is connected to deep-rooted conflicts over difference, land divisions, and membership: the residual collapse of the Old Ọ̀yọ́ Empire following the revolt against the Aláàfin by Àfọ̀njá, the Àrẹ-Ọ̀nà Kakanfò, the head of the Ọ̀yọ́ cavalry force; the consequent invasion of Ọ̀yọ́ by Fulani jihadists from Ìlọrin; and the subsequent wars that occurred up until 1893. Like classic contestations over homeland claims, the contemporary Ifẹ̀-Modákẹ́kẹ́ crisis is connected to the migration of Ọ̀yọ́ refugees and their resettlement at Ifẹ̀ in the 1800s. Most of the refugees headed toward Ilé-Ifẹ̀, the historic image of the city as the original home of the Yorùbá people. As the invasion of the Fulani of Ọ̀yọ́ intensified and more Ọ̀yọ́ refugees fled to Ilé-Ifẹ̀ and the surrounding communities, the mass movement of Ọ̀yọ́ refugees became more acute. The Ọ̀ọni of Ifẹ̀, once central to Yorùbá monarchies, welcomed the refugees who relocated to Ilé-Ifẹ̀. Residents of Ọ̀yọ́ who describe their history often suggest that the relationship between the Ifẹs and these Ọ̀yọ́ refugees were initially cordial. Ọ̀yọ́ people were seen as useful allies during warfare and provided military support to Ifẹ̀ residents during the Òwu War of 1825 and various invasions by Ìjẹ̀sà combatants. The Ọ̀ọni were described as having accepted more Ọ̀yọ́ refugees over time than anyone else, and those refugees contributed to the economy as workers on feudal plots who paid for their use of the land through agricultural returns. Eventually, the Ọ̀ọni created a separate settlement for those Ọ̀yọ́ refugees without a home and named the settlement Modákẹ́kẹ́, after "the cry of a nest of storks on a large tree near the site." The leader of the Ọ̀yọ́ refugees was given the title Ogunsua. The

Modákékés continued to pay royalties to the Ifę families whose land they were using, and eventually they were expected to pay for their land and claim ownership of it.

According to this narrative of movement and membership, Òyó refugees developed an identity distinct from that of the Ifę people. As described by popular accounts, over time, Ifę's political influence over Modákékę gradually diminished. They set up a separate administration and installed their Baálę as an Ọba. The Ifęs could no longer force the Òyó refugees to work on their farms, and the Modákékę saw themselves as a separate entity apart from Ilé-Ifę and therefore entitled to all the rights and privileges of a district. The popular narrative of Òyó-Modákékę aggression, therefore, often begins by explaining that Okùnadé, the Mayé, was the leader of the Yorùbá warriors who settled in Ìbàdàn in the early nineteenth century. Originally an Ifę war chief, the Mayé, seen as an autocrat by the people of Ìbàdàn and Ifę, began to claim jurisdiction over the people of Ìbàdàn. People describing the demise of his authority explain that it was challenged by Òyó citizens in Ìbàdàn and that he was expelled from the town and later murdered. The Òyó refugees then took over the political leadership of Ìbàdàn to the exclusion of their Ifę allies. The Ifę residents responded with a backlash against the Òyó refugees in Ifę. They sold some of the Òyó refugees into slavery, and, in 1839, when the Ọòni Abenila was in power, he expelled some of the refugees to regions such as Ìpetumòdù, Gbòngán, and Ìkirè in 1847.

The Ọòni who created the structure of Modákékę governance is popularly described as having been poisoned in 1849 and denied royal burial by the Ifę people. With Ifę's Ọòni dead, Ifę residents, many of whom disagreed with the consequent encroachment of Òyó people into Ifę, explained that the Ifę people attacked the Modákékés to reclaim their gains. Some of the Òyó-Modákékę people with whom I spoke, however, reported that they won the battle, and, despite this, their leaders released the Ifę prisoners caught during the battle without selling any of them into slavery. As their narrative goes, despite this "act of kindness," the Ifęs launched another attack a month after the initial defeat. The Ifęs lost again, and this time, those Ifęs who were captured by the Modákékés as prisoners of war were sold into slavery. As a result of the battles, the town was burned down and became desolate. Its principal chiefs moved to Isoya, and the Òyó-dominated people of the Ìbàdàn region seized the opportunity to extend their influence to the vacant governance of Ilé-Ifę. Historians have documented that between 1853 and 1854, Ìbàdàn tried to reconcile Modákékę and Ifę; the two parties were eventually reconciled, and Ifę became the vassal state of Ìbàdàn. The Modákékés joined the Òyó people of Ìbàdàn and again defeated the people of Ifę. The Ifę attempted to relocate the Modákékę by peace treaty; however, by 1894 this was still unsuccessful because by this time most of the Modákékę were first- and second-generation born in Ifę and had married into Ifę families.

With the development of British colonies along the Lagos coast, an established settlement took shape with a governor and district leaders. Governor William MacGregor of the Lagos colony offered to help the then Ọba, Adelekan Olubuse I of Ifę, to recover the Ifę territory taken over by Ìbàdàn and to assist in the expulsion of the Modákékés from Ifẹ. As a result of the Lagos intervention, Modákẹ́kẹ́s were made to pay taxes again to Ifẹ residents; many Modákẹ́kẹ́s objected, arguing that their ancestors worked on Ifẹ farms and paid off the price of the land over time. Nevertheless, even when these cases were brought as defenses of their land rights, many Modákẹ́kẹ́s lost.

With no legal satisfaction, another crisis unfolded in 1946 and throughout the second half of the twentieth century. In the 1990s, the conflict over the rezoning of Ifẹ local government by the Nigerian military government continued to be fueled by the contention that there was no basis to concede a separate existence to the Modákẹ́kẹ́ people as they are one of many ethnic groups in the Ilé-Ifẹ region.

18　Ọ̀banjòkó in Yorùbá means "the Ọba is in the process of sitting." It refers to the Ọba's assumption of a position of authority that requires him to leave his royal quarters and join the community.

19　Ultimately, his invocation of black American slavery served to legitimize what he posited as the long-standing connection between African Americans and Africans along the West African coast. For the Ọba, Johnson's Yorùbá also reside in the Americas. Through divinatory ritual, it is believed, African Americans have the tools to interpret the past and redeem themselves from the injustices and the betrayal of enslavement.

20　Johnson represented this as taking place through the partial eradication of non-Christian polygamy and heathenism.

21　The Ọba actually said "Baron Gaha" rather than Baṣọ́run Gáà. This "misrepresentation" is telling, if not accidental, as it might be an equation of "noble" titles.

4. Yorùbá Group Membership

1　The festival of Damballah Wedo, usually held at the end of October (the 30th or the 31st, also Halloween and otherwise known as All Fool's Day), is organized to remember the ancient ancestors of the old Dahomean and Ọ̀yọ́ Empires. Damballah Wedok, however, is also celebrated in Ọ̀yọ́túnjí during the Egúngún Festival every May.

2　Literally "all death"; the intended meaning here is "all the dead ancestors."

3　Here Nietzsche talks about the unconscious as a form of the imaginary construction of reality. He examines how the scientific paradigm is itself another form of the imaginary, and he critiques the idea of the scientific in Cartesian theory. He explores the question of fantasy and our idea of knowledge and how it is shaped by our instincts, ending with a discussion of how we can apprehend the world. He says that to live is an exercise of interpretation.

5. Yorùbá Ancestral Roots

1　A pseudonym has been used.

2　This response is often seen by Ọ̀yọ́túnjí practitioners as inappropriate and is corrected, since in the contexts of greetings, salutations, and small talk, Yorùbá is almost always used by adults.

3　My findings have confirmed that the majority of clients who participated in roots readings are told they come from noble and well-respected families of Ifá traditional worshippers. However, besides a few scattered examples of individuals (1 out of 15 roots readings), the majority of the people who are told that they emerge from royalty are those who are in the current king's family.

4　The priesthood ritual is also known in Santería circles as "making Ocha," or going under; it means that one is marrying a god.

5　For practitioner-authored books on Santería initiation, see Migene Gonzalez-Whippler (1994), *Santeria: The Religion: Faith, Rites, Magic*; Marta Moreno Vega (2000), *The Altar of My Soul: The Living Traditions of Santeria*; Lydia Cabrera (1974/1996), *Yemaya y Ochun*; Julio Garcia Cortez (Obba Bi) (2000), *The Osha: Secrets of Yoruba-Lucumi Santeria Religion in the United States and the Americas—Initiation, Rituals, Ceremonies, Orishas, Divination, Plants, Sacrifices, Cleansings, and Songs*. For Ifá initiation in Nigeria, see Wándè Abímbọ́lá (1976, 1977), and for Candomblé, see Pierre Verger (1981), *Orixas: Deuses Iorubas na Africa e no Novo Mundo*.

6　*Babaláwo* is a Yorùbá word that refers to a male high priest of Ifá. Visitors and residents in Ọ̀yọ́túnjí interested in standard initiations have to request the presence of a babaláwo.

7　Unlike the other forms of divinatory rituals, clients tend to conduct only one roots reading in a lifetime. The diviner performs this ritual to provide clients with knowledge of their paternal/maternal lineage, the specific historical explanations of their family's preslavery status, and the major calamities that led to the enslavement of their ancestors. Most important, the roots reading ritualizes the transformation of the client from an individual whose preslavery past was unknown and whose name reflected the legacy of being designated as chattel to the diviner's assignment of a new Yorùbá name to an otherwise American identity, marking the end of a sacrificial cycle.

8　There are twelve cult groups in Ọ̀yọ́túnjí, and during different times of the year each of the groups organizes a festival to venerate the òrìṣà that bears its name (e.g., the Ọ̀ṣun festival every April is organized to celebrate the òrìṣà Ọ̀ṣun). Members of each cult group conduct both a prefestival reading (to ascertain the type of offerings that should accompany the festival celebrations) and a postfestival reading (to establish whether the offerings were well received by the venerated òrìṣà). Guided by the divinatory interpretations, each group organizes one festival during a different month each year.

9　The reading of the year is a new ritual invention that is predominant throughout òrìṣà communities of the late twentieth century. For Ọ̀yọ́túnjí revivalists, the aim is to replicate the range of Southwestern Nigerian traditional divinatory ritual events performed by the king's advisors for a range of key annual cycles. The following is an example of three Readings of the Year posted on the Internet by one of the Ọ̀yọ́túnjí Affiliate communities and then two by Ọ̀yọ́túnjí Village.

　　D'afa fun Jalumi (Chicago Metro), cast by Baba S. Ifatunji, 2003. Oturupon Ose (no. 241, Ire, L'Orun T'owa, Mojale):

　　　Those who sacrifice will have sweet life. Year of blessings for Jalumi. Blessings of material wealth and social harmony. Blessings from the ancestors and egungun. Blessings from the African priesthood. Chiefs will talk. Learning will occur. Heads of arts institutions and organizations will flourish. One must be very careful how they allocate their financial holdings and earnings. If you give birth to any idea or concept, you must expect to support it financially on your own, until it is old enough or strong enough to pay its own bills. Same is true of any children you give birth to or have given birth to. Be prepared to provide for it until it can earn its own way. There will be challenges this year because there will be more ideas than resources to support them. It will be important to distinguish between party time and work time. Work is likely to come to the party. Blessings come from the heavens and through seeds that have been planted throughout the city. Be careful in parental and child relationships on all levels, especially with temple developing and forming through godchildren. If we do not do our sacrifices these temples may suffer for insufficient nourishment. Make sure that sacrifices are done on behalf of the temples. Sticking stubbornly to tradition as we find it on the road secures footing and prepares us to receive our blessings. Think carefully in order to figure your way through traps and entanglements. Stay out of ego traps. Ancestor worship will lead those who approach it fully and in African fashion to deep blessings and harmony, as well as lead them to positions of leadership or chieftaincy in the community. Think big unless your thoughts become entangled, then stop. Think big as long as you can clearly see the road and the machinery for the completion of your ideas, and be prepared to support your ideas on your own. It will be challenging year for people's egos, especially those who have not vested early in culture. The graves of our ancient ancestors will be our blessings this year, particularly those of our forefathers. Poetic battles will resolve problems. Focus on harmony rather than jealousy. Ruling òrìṣà for the city will be Oshun. Do not lie in order to assuage your ego.

Ebo [sacrifice]: Give $4.20 to a shrine of your head òrìṣà. Give a jar of honey to the ancestors.

For this year's reading for the World, the United States and African Americans as a whole click on this link: http://www.oyotunjivillage.net and connect to the Ọ̀yọ́túnjí African Village website.

Ọ̀yọ́túnjí Reading of the Year for the World, 2003:

Otura Meji speaks of a more gentle approach with the people of the world. So this year, the USA might see more solutions with a gentler approach with the nations of the world. Everybody will want to talk. The United States would benefit greatly from listening to public opinion and the leaders of other nations. Diplomats such as ambassadors will be moving around talking to people around the world, hoping to come up with solutions.

Ogunda gbe (ibi) [aka osobo—in the negative]:

Odi Fun says people of the world are angry. Odi representing various global families, ethnic groups races. Ofun says everybody is hot headed, will think their way is the correct way (too much ego). Odi Fun says people of the world will be uncompromising; no one group will want to budge from their point of view. People that believe in some kind of honest tradition that really belongs to them will be rewarded greater than those that don't. All of the important business of the world goes on in the day light hours. Sneaky and underhanded things take place at night. Ifa says terrorism is more likely to occur during the night hours. Ifa says that the only thing that can save the world is for leaders and people to become less emotional. Too many things being provoked by emotions, things not being carefully thought out, too many long-standing grudges, fixed minds on how things should go, will only nurture more emotional upheavals and spontaneous reactions. This will only impair the world's progress towards peace. If there could be less anticipation of the dreadful things happening and more anticipation of workable solutions we may get more accomplished. People of the world must seek their own cultural destinies, this will furnish them with answers. Too many different opinions are surfacing concerning world politics, without one real solution. In the direction that this mind set is taking us it will inevitably lead to war and world destruction. Ifa says, the world is headed more so on the path of war than on the path of peace. All women of the world are extremely frustrated. Older women in particular, especially those that are following their traditions will begin to speak out. They will be particularly concerned about the violation of other nations birthrights. There will be more clashes; there will be more violence. This will take place among the heads of the nations of the world. There is a need for the application of much more diplomacy, tact, this will help to sweeten things up. These people of the world must maintain their cultural ideals. This is the only chance of overcoming the osobo).

Òyótúnjí Reading for the United States, 2003. Otura Meji (Ire):

Otura Meji, the United States, with the right attitude, might be able to establish new friendships and new alliances this year. The USA should take a less arrogant attitude this year, and be kinder and sweeter to the people in the world. The USA should create a new image as a helper rather than a dictator. There is too much promoting of fear and hate. There should be more promoting of love (what ever that is). The USA must still remain open for more talking and dialog. There must be more discussion that includes other factions. This could prove to be more beneficial. This could be the year that the USA could go on record as a nation that brought peace and understanding to the world's problem. The USA must not spread untruthful propaganda this year, should not lie to the people and should not circulate half-truth rumors about the world's condition. The USA must be willing to look at the accumulated smaller problems that have brought on the bigger ones. We must face head on these un-dealt with problems of the past, even if in some cases it will mean confrontation. The USA must be willing to explore other paths, which may mean the reestablishment of certain ideals. Some of the old heads must be willing to step down. This would allow other people to come in to see what they could do.

World powers will find it difficult to oppose the USA this year, because the USA will certainly be displaying its arrogance and ego. The world has begun to look at the USA as the senior nation of the world even though it is historically untrue. The USA could be on its destiny this year, it even allows (flexing of the muscles). This can only be done with smoothness and diplomacy. The USA will have to recognize the historic GREAT SOCIETIES of the world and give them their just due. Unless there is a change in policy at home, the USA will be the instigator of most of the world's problems. The USA must take the path of peace this year. This is a bad year for the flaunting of personal egos.

10 Initiated divining priests also have relationships with priestly mentors, but because they tend to have more training than the uninitiated, they require less guidance. These diviners usually perform services for residents for bartered goods or services.

11 One could also argue that they are packaged as intellectual property and sold as history-producing commodities.

12 In 1995 all roots readings cost $100.

13 In the context of Yorùbá cultural influences as they have been shaped by African-Atlantic triangular webs in particular trade routes, the most convincing historical evidence suggests that Yorùbá (Lukumi) captives were sold not to North American, but to Caribbean and South American traders. However, Ọ̀yọ́túnjí Village revivalists' reclamation of Yorùbá ancestral membership does not constitute a miscalculation of the history of Yorùbá slave routes. Rather, the disjuncture between historical routes of trade and the symbolic roots of racial descent points out how, in the adoption of Yorùbá practices in North America, Yorùbá revivalists inscribe onto the past the complexities of the historical present.

6. Family, Status, and Legal Institutionalism

1 During the summer of 1995, there were a total of seven chiefs in the Ọ̀yọ́túnjí community. There is one ruling king, the Ọba, who refers to his governmental system as a democratic dictatorship.

2 The polygamy laws that exist in Ọ̀yọ́túnjí are deferential to state laws. The state of South Carolina does not recognize Ọ̀yọ́túnjí marriages as legitimate, as they are conducted by unauthorized individuals. In the United States every state has its own laws regarding who, what kinds of agents, will be certified to authorize marriages. In general, the institution of U.S. marriage has a history of being highly regulated. Not only was polygamy outlawed in the United States in 1879 (1878 *Reynolds v. United States*, 98 U.S. 145), but interracial marriage was banned, as was homosexual marriage. These state regulations of family norms are connected to state interests in the family as constitutive of the nation. Ọ̀yọ́túnjí regulations of family norms are motivated by similar interests.

3 This estimate of hundreds of thousands of New World Yorùbá revivalists includes those Yorùbá and Santería practitioners who identify themselves as taking part in Yorùbá religious practices.

4 The acronym HRG, meaning Her Royal Grace (the wife of the king), signifies royalty.

5 The trial ended at 2:05 in the early morning, after approximately 6.5 hours of deliberations, concluding with a 4–3 vote in favor of HRG Ìyá Sisilum's innocence. A few days after the trial, it became public knowledge that Ìyá Olayindo was strongly encouraged, even pressured by the king and other chiefs not only to file a letter of grievance against HRG Ìyá Sisilum, but to enter into a formal hearing against her.

6 If a chief makes an error in reciting his or her oath to the king, he or she is not only fined a nominal amount (as of 1995, the penalty ranged from $5 to $100) but suffers tremendous embarrassment.

Epilogue

1 Because the residents were not native Yorùbá speakers and generally used Yorùbá symbolically, Yorùbá words were constantly mispronounced, taking on the meanings intended by the speaker. The gaps in communication among residents, children, and visitors, the misreadings and misinterpretations, and the play of power to command understanding all fashioned the mystique and the quest for the past, the sometimes unattainable answers.

Glossary

a dúpẹ́. "Thank you."

Ààfin. A Yorùbá palace where the Ọba (king) resides

agbádá. A traditional Yorùbá gown worn by a man

agò, Olódùmarè, a júbà. "Peace, make way; God, we acknowledge you."

àjàká. The one that spreads like a plague

akíkanjú. A brave person

akwénùsi marriage. One of two forms of polygamous Dahomean marriage arrangements used by Ọ̀yọ́túnjí practitioners. This form of marriage is characterized by residents as "money-with-woman," where the man/husband is required to make dowry payments to the woman's father, thereby giving him control of the children born from that marriage.

àlàáfíà. Peace (borrowing from the Hausa language)

Àláàfin. The one who owns or occupies the palace. The king of Ọ̀yọ́ is the only figurehead that is called Àláàfin in Yorùbáland.

alagbàá. The head priest of the Egúngún society

alásè. Cook

alásẹ. The one that has authority

àlejò. A visitor

apènà. Official designation of the secretary of the Ògbóni secret society

àṣẹ. A supernatural force that can cause an action to occur. Power

aṣọ òkè. A traditional Yorùbá fabric woven in narrow strips mostly by men. Also called *aṣọẹ-òfì*

awo. Cult, diviner

ayaba. Wife of the king. Also known as *olorì*

Baálẹ̀. A paramount chief, second in command only to the Ọba *bàbá.* Father

babaláwo. An individual who has been initiated into the priestly cult of Ifá

babalóòṣà/babalóríṣà. A Yorùbá male priest

Baṣòrun. The official title for the Àláàfin of Ọ̀yọ́, one of the important traditional titles of Yorùbáland

bàtá drum. A two-headed drum shaped like an hourglass and used in Yorùbá ceremonies and for entertainment during festivals

bẹ́ẹ̀ ni. An affirmative response meaning "yes"

betrothal. The practice of arranged marriage through the promise of a child to a future husband

botanicas. A store that specializes in items used for spiritism and African-based religious practices such as Yorùbá or Haitian voodon worship. *Botanicas* are usually found in U.S. urban centers that have large populations of immigrants from places in the Caribbean such as Cuba, Puerto Rico, Haiti, and Trinidad.

bùbá. A loosely fitted top or long gown usually worn by women and classified as traditional wear

cabildos. Social and mutual aid organizations

Damballah Wedo. A Dahomean form of worship transported to the New World by slaves from the West African region once known as the Kingdom of Dahomey. In Ọ̀yọ́túnjí today, *damballah wedo* refers to ancestor spirits.

dànṣíkí. A casual top, usually worn by men

dìde. "Rise up."

djimbe. A cone-shaped drum with a wide head, indigenous to Senegal

Dókpwe. The Ọ̀yọ́túnjí village name of a corporate work group of men. Also known as *ọ̀wẹ̀*

dọ̀ọ̀bálẹ̀. To prostrate oneself to the ancestors and gods in the presence of an Ọba, chief, *ayaba,* priest, or an elder

Dowpe gan. Ọ̀yọ́túnjí men's work group

ẹ káàbọ́. "You are welcome."

ẹ kú iṣẹ́. "Congratulations." Greetings at work

Ẹgbá. The generic name for the Abẹ́òkúta people

ẹẹ̀rìndínlógún. A form of Yorùbá divination in which sixteen cowry shells are used

ẹgba. Whip (cut from slender plants)

ẹgbẹ́. A society or group of individuals who share a common identity or raison d'être

Ẹgbẹ́ Mọrèmi. The name of the Ọ̀yọ́túnjí village women's society

egúngún. A ghost masquerader. Ancestor worship

egúngún. Masquerade

Ẹlẹ́gbá. A deity in the Yorùbá pantheon characterized as being mischievous

ẹsẹ. The verse component of the Ifá divinatory corpus

Espiritismo. A Hispanic version of the African-based Kardecan spiritism

Èyò. A masquerade of the Lagos people

fìlà. A cap of any kind

gede nimbo. An ancestor. Also known as *òkú tọ́run*

gèlèdé. A kind of masquerade

HRG. Her Royal Grace, the title of the wife of the king

HRH. His Royal Highness, the king's title

ìbà ará tọ́run. Salute the bodies of heaven

ìbejì. Twins

ìbò. Divinatory lots based on two opposite alternatives of "yes" or "no"

Ifá. The Yorùbá god or deity of wisdom

ìgbàlè. sacred forested district

Ìgbìmọ̀ olóòṣà. Society of priests

Ìgbìmọ̀lóòṣà. Priestly Committee of Òrìṣà Worshippers

igbó odù. A grove or bush where Ifá ceremonies are conducted

igbóòṣà ~ ìká gbó. Forest of the Òrìṣà

ikín. Palm nuts used in divination

ilà. Tribal scarification used to signify ethnicity and clan

ilé. House

ilèkè. A beaded necklace worn around the neck

ire. Blessing

ìrùkèrè. A long, hand-held wand used by chiefs or Ọbas to signify their status. *Ìrùkèrè* were
made from the tail of a horse.

ìwòrì. Incantation

ìyá. Mother

ìyá ńlá. Great mother or grandmother

ìyá orîtẹ́. Mother on the throne

ìyálóde. Chief of the women

ìyálóòṣà. A Yorùbá female priest (*ìyálóríyà, ìyá olóríyà*)

ìyàwó. A bride or a wife

jinlè. Deep

kábíyèsí. A Yorùbá salutation to a king, which in Ọ̀yọ́túnjí is also the title of the king

Kakanfò. A title

kente. A form of weaving that is used to produce a particular form of traditional fabric that
has its origins in Ghana, West Africa

kúnlè. The Ọ̀yọ́túnjí practice of kneeling to priests and chiefs

lapa. A traditional form of clothing worn as a piece of fabric around the lower half of the
body and tied around the waist. The *lapa* is worn in Ọ̀yọ́túnjí by men and women;
however, it is worn predominantly by women.

Lukumi. From *olùkù mi*, "my friend." Now used to mean the Yorùbá in the diaspora

madrina. Santería word for godmother of òrìṣà

màmá. Mother

mestizaje. Racial mixture

mo yuba/júbà. "I acknowledge . . ."; "I salute you"; "I worship you" or "I pay homage to
you"

mulatez. Racial mixture; also mulatto status

Nàgó. Another name, now obsolete, for the Yorùbá

ó dàbọ̀. "Good bye"

o kú iṣẹ́. Greetings for the one working

Ọba. A king

Ọbalúayé. One of the deities, also called Ṣànpọ̀nná

obánjòkó. Literally, "the king sits and speaks"

Ọbàtálá. A Yorùbá deity celebrated in Ọ̀yọ́túnjí as its patron

obì. Four *kolanut* pieces (lobes) used for divination. In Ọ̀yọ́túnjí, Yorùbá practitioners use four pieces of the interior of a coconut.

obìnrin. Literally, woman. Also wife

odù. The information revealed when Ifá is consulted

odù ogbè ṣe mo jalè?. Did I steal, Odù Ogbè? (i.e., Ifá, was I dishonest?)

ogbará. Beads worn over the shoulder

Ògbóni. A secret society of landholding elders

Ògún. A deity in the Yorùbá pantheon popularly characterized as the god of iron

Ògúnsua. A title

ọkọ. Husband

Olódùmarè. The supreme being, or the supreme maker, also known as Ọlọ́run

Olókun. A deity in the Yorùbá pantheon popularly characterized as the god of the depths of the ocean

olorì. Wife of the king

olórìṣà. Òrìṣà worshippers

Ọlọ́run. Owner of heaven

Olúwa. The supreme god

ọmọ. Child

onílé. Owner of the house

oníṣègùn. A herbalist or medical doctor

ọọ́ni. The king of Ilé-Ifẹ̀

ọ̀pẹ̀lẹ̀. A divining chain used for Ifá divination by *babaláwo*

oríkì. A praise song often performed in a poetic matter

Òrìṣà. A Yorùbá sacred object of worship. Otherwise known as a deity believed to be ruled by the supreme being.

orò ìdílé. Traditional family worship

Òrúnmìlà. The Yorùbá supreme god

òṣẹ́ méjì. Name for a secret vote in Ifá

Osoba/osobo. Bad fortune. Otherwise referred to as "ibi." Often used in divinatory interpretations as the opposite of *ire* (good fortune)

Òṣun. A deity in the Yorùbá pantheon popularly characterized as the goddess of sexuality, beauty, and riches

otera. Break

Òwu. Some part of Ẹ̀gbáland

Ọya. Deified wife of Ṣàngó

òyìnbó. Commonly used to mean white man or foreigner

Ọ̀yọ́ Mèsì. "The Ọ̀yọ́ know the answer." Title for the council of elders in Ọ̀yọ́

Ọ̀yọ́túnjí. The Yorùbá town of "Ọ̀yọ́-awakes or revives/returns"

Padrino. A Spanish word for godfather

Pàtàkì. Story

regla dé ocha. Rules of the Santería

Ṣàngó. A deity in the Yorùbá pantheon characterized as the god of thunder

wọlé. "Come into the house"

xadudo marriage. One of two forms of polygamous Dahomean marriage arrangements used by Ọ̀yọ́túnjí practitioners. This form of marriage is characterized by residents as "friend custody," where the man/husband is not required to make dowry payments to the woman's family and therefore cannot legally claim control of the children born from the marriage according to Ọ̀yọ́túnjí Village laws.

Yemọja. Literally, "mother of the fish children"; a goddess of the river

yèyé; yeye. Mother

Yorùbá. A linguistic and ethnic identity popularly identified as having origins in the southwestern part of Nigeria

Bibliography

Abímbólá, Wande. 1976. *Ifa: An Exposition of Ifa Literary Corpus*. Ibadan: Oxford University Press.

———. 1977. *Ifa Divination Poetry*. New York: Nok Publishers.

Abrahams, Roger D. 1964. *Deep Down in the Jungle . . . : Negro Narrative Folklore from the Streets of Philadelphia*. Hatboro, Pa.: Folklore Associates.

Abu-Lughod, Lila. 1989. "Bedouins, Cassettes and Technologies of Public Culture." *Middle East Report* (July–August): 7–11, 47.

———. 1993. "Finding a Place for Islam: Egyptian Television and the National Interest." *Public Culture* 5(3): 493–513.

Agamben, Giorgio. 1998. *Homo Sacer: Sovereign Power and Bare Life*. Translated by Daniel Heller-Roazen. Stanford, Calif.: Stanford University Press.

Ajayi, Jacob Festus Ade, and M. Crowder, eds. 1972. *History of West Africa*. Vol. 1. New York: Columbia University Press.

———, eds 1973 *History of West Africa*. Vol. 2. New York: Columbia University Press.

Akínjógbìn, A. I. 1967. *Dahomey and Its Neighbours, 1708–1818*. Cambridge, England: Cambridge University Press.

———, ed. 1972. *Cradle of a Race: Ife from the Beginning to 1980*. Port Harcourt: Sunray Publications.

Akínnaso, Niyi F. 1981. "The Consequences of Literacy in Pragmatic and Theoretical Perspective." *Anthropology and Education Quarterly* 12(3): 163–201.

———. 1982. "The Literate Writes and the Nonliterate Chants: Written Language and Ritual Communication in Sociolinguistic Perspective." In *Linguistics and Literacy*, pp. 7–36. Edited by W. Frawley. New York: Plenum Press.

———. 1983a. *The Structure of Divinatory Speech: A Sociolinguistic Analysis of Yoruba Sixteen Cowry Divination*. Berkeley: University of California Press.

——. 1983b. "Yoruba Tradition, Names and the Transmission of Cultural Knowledge." *Names* 31(3): 139–58.

——. 1989. "One Nation, Four Hundred Languages: Unity and Diversity in Nigeria's Language Policy." *Language Problems and Language Planning* 13(2): 133–46.

——. 1992. "Schooling, Language, and Knowledge in Literate and Nonliterate Societies." *Comparative Studies in Society and History* 34(1): 68–109.

——. 1995. "Bourdieu and the Diviner: Knowledge and Symbolic Power in Yoruba Divination." In *The Pursuit of Certainty: Religious and Cultural Formulations*, pp. 234–58. Edited by W. James. London: Routledge.

Althusser, Louis. 1971. "Ideology and Ideological State Apparatuses (Notes towards an Investigation)." In *Lenin and Philosophy and Other Essays*, pp. 127–86. New York: Monthly Review Press.

Anderson, Benedict. 1983 (revised 1991). *Imagined Communities: Reflections on the Origin and Spread of Nationalism*. London: Verso.

Apter, Andrew. 1992. *Black Critics and Kings: The Hermeneutics of Power in Yoruba Society*. Chicago: University of Chicago Press.

Appadurai, Arjun. 1981. "The Past as a Scarce Resource." *Man* 16: 201–19.

——. 1991. "Global Ethnoscapes: Notes and Queries for a Transnational Anthropology." In *Recapturing Anthropology: Working in the Present*, pp. 191–211. Edited by R. G. Fox. Santa Fe: School of American Research Press.

——. 1995. "The Production of Locality." In *Counterworks: Managing the Diversity of Knowledge*. Edited by R. Fardon. London, Routledge.

——. 1996a. "Modern Colonies." In *Modernity at Large: Cultural Dimensions of Globalization*, pp. 1–85. Minneapolis: University of Minnesota Press.

——. 1996b. *Modernity at Large: Cultural Dimensions of Globalization*. Minneapolis: University of Minnesota Press.

——. 1998a. "Dead Certainty: Ethnic Violence in the Era of Globalization." *Public Culture* 10(2): 225–47.

——. 1998b. "Full Attachment." *Public Culture* 10(2): 443–49.

——. 2000. "Grassroots Globalization and the Research Imagination." *Public Culture* 12(1): 1–19.

Apter, Andrew H. 1992. *Black Critics and Kings: The Hermeneutics of Power in Yoruba Society*. Chicago: University of Chicago Press.

Arrighi, Giovanni. 1994. *The Long Twentieth Century: Money, Power, and the Origins of Our Times*. London: Verso.

Asad, Talal, ed. 1973. *Anthropology and the Colonial Encounter*. Atlantic Highlands, N.J.: Humanities Press.

Asante, Molefi Kete. 1988. *Afrocentricity*. Trenton, N.J.: African World Press.

Asiwaju, A. I. 1976. *Western Yorubaland under European Rule, 1889–1945: A Comparative Analysis of French and British Colonialism*. London: Longman.

Austen, Ralph, and Woodruff D. Smith. 1992. "Private Tooth Decay as Public Economic Virtue: The Slave Sugar Triangle, Consumerism, and European Industrialization." In

The Atlantic Slave Trade: Effects on Economies, Societies, and Peoples in Africa, the Americas, and Europe, pp. 183–203. Edited by Joseph E. Inkori and Stanley L. Engerman. Durham, N.C.: Duke University Press.

Axel, Brian Keith. 2001. *The Nation's Tortured Body: Violence, Representation, and the Formation of the Sikh "Diaspora."* Durham, N.C.: Duke University Press.

Ayọrinde, Christine. 2000. "Regla de Ocha-Ifd and the Construction of Cuban Identity." In *Identity in the Shadow of Slavery*, pp. 72–85. Edited by P. E. Lovejoy. London: Continuum.

Bakhtin, Mikhail M. 1981. *The Dialogic Imagination: Four Essays*. Austin: University of Texas Press.

Barber, Karin. 1991. *I Could Speak Until Tomorrow: Oriki, Women, and the Past in a Yoruba Town*. Edinburgh: University of Edinburgh Press.

Barthes, Roland. 1982. *The Empire of Signs*. New York: Hill and Wang.

Bascom, William. 1969a. *Ifa Divination: Communication between Gods and Men in West Africa*. Bloomington: Indiana University Press.

———. 1969b. *The Yoruba of Southwestern Nigeria*. New York: Holt, Rinehart, and Winston.

———. 1980. *Sixteen Cowries: Yoruba Divination from Africa to the New World*. Bloomington: Indiana University Press.

———. 1992. *African Folktales in the New World*. Bloomington: Indiana University Press.

Bastide, Roger. 1971. *African Civilizations in the New World*. London: C. Hurst.

———. 1978. *The African Religions of Brazil: Toward a Sociology of the Interpretation of Civilizations*. Baltimore: Johns Hopkins University Press.

Bay, Edna G. 1998. *Wives of the Leopard: Gender Politics and Culture in the Kingdom of Dahomey*. Charlottesville: University of Virginia Press.

Baylis, John, and Steve Smith, eds. 2001. *The Globalization of World Politics: An Introduction to International Relations*. 2nd ed. Oxford: Oxford University Press.

Bell, Catherine. 1992. *Ritual Theory, Ritual Practice*. New York: Oxford University Press.

Bhabha, Homi K. 1983. *The Politics of Theory: Difference, Discrimination and the Discourse of Colonialism*. Essex, England: Rochester University Press.

———. 1990. "The Third Space: Interview with Homi Bhabha." In *Identity: Community, Culture, Difference*, pp. 207–21. Edited by J. Rutherford. London: Lawrence and Wishart.

———. 1994. *The Location of Culture*. London: Routledge.

Boas, Franz. 1911. *The Mind of Primitive Man*. New York: Macmillan.

———. 1928. *Materials for the Study of Inheritance in Man*. New York: Columbia University Press.

———. 1932. *Anthropology and Modern Life*. New York: Norton.

———. 1940. *Race, Language, and Culture*. New York: Macmillan.

Borneman, J. 1997a. *Settling Accounts: Violence, Justice, and Accountability in Postsocialist Europe*. Princeton: Princeton University Press.

———. 1997b. "State, Territory, and National Identity Formation in the Two Berlins, 1945–95." In *Culture, Power, Place: Explorations in Critical Anthropology*, pp. 93–117. Edited by Akhil Gupta and James Ferguson. Durham, N.C.: Duke University Press.

Bourdieu, Pierre. 1990. *The Logic of Practice*. Stanford: Stanford University Press.

———. 1991. *Language and Symbolic Power*. Cambridge, Mass.: Harvard University Press.

———. 1993. *The Field of Cultural Production: Essays on Art and Literature*. Cambridge, England: Polity Press.

Brandon, George. 1993. *Santeria from Africa to the New World: The Dead Sell Memories*. Bloomington: Indiana University Press.

Brenneis, Donald L., and Ronald. K. S. MacCaulay, eds. 1996. *The Matrix of Language: Contemporary Linguistic Anthropology*. Boulder, Colo.: Westview Press.

Brown, David. 2003. *Santería Enthroned: Act, Ritual, and Innovation in an Afro-Cuban Religion*. Chicago: University of Chicago Press.

Bullock, Henry A. 1967. *A History of Negro Education in the South: From 1619 to the Present*. Cambridge, Mass.: Harvard University Press.

———. 1999. *On Racial Frontiers: The New Culture of Frederick Douglass, Ralph Ellison and Bob Marley*. Cambridge, Mass.: Harvard University Press.

Burawoy, Michael, ed. 2000. *Global Ethnography: Forces, Connections, and Imaginations in a Postmodern World*. Berkeley: University of California Press.

Butler, Judith. 1993. *Bodies That Matter: On the Discursive Limits of "Sex."* New York: Routledge.

Cabrera, Lydia. 1996. *Yemaya y Ochun*. Madrid: Son. (Orig. pub. 1974.)

Campbell, James. 1995. *Songs of Zion: The African Methodist Episcopal Church in the United States and South Africa*. Chapel Hill: University of North Carolina Press.

Campt, Tina. 2003. *Other Germans, Black Germans, and the Politics of Race, Gender, and Memory in the Third Reich*. Ann Arbor: University of Michigan Press.

Capone, Stefania. 1999a. "L'Afrique réinventée ou la construction de la tradition dans les cultes afro-brésiliens." *Archives européennes de sociologie* 40(1): 1–25.

———. 1999b. "Les dieux sur le Net: L'essor des religions d'origine africaine aux Etats-Unis." *L'Homme* 151: 47–74.

Castells, Manuel. 1989. *The Informational City: Information Technology, Economic Restructuring, and the Urban-Regional Process*. Oxford: Blackwell.

Castoriadis, Cornelius. 1987. *The Imaginary Institution of Society*. Cambridge, England: Polity Press.

Caton, Steven C. 1985. "The Poetic Construction of Self." *Anthropological Quarterly* 58(4): 141–45.

———. 1990. *"Peaks of Yemen I Summon": Poetry as Cultural Practice in a North Yemeni Tribe*. Berkeley: University of California Press.

Certeau, Michel de. 1984. *The Practice of Everyday Life*. Berkeley: University of California Press.

Chomsky, Noam. 1965. *Aspects of the Theory of Syntax*. Cambridge, Mass.: MIT Press.

Clarke, Kamari M. 1997. "Genealogies of Reclaimed Nobility: The Geotemporality of Yoruba Belonging." Ph.D. diss., University of Michigan.

———. 1999. " 'To Reclaim Yoruba Traditions Is to Reclaim the Gods of Africa': Reflections on the Uses of Ethnography and History in Yoruba Revivalism." In *Feminist Fields:*

Ethnographic Insights, pp. 229–42. Edited by Rae Anderson, Sally Cole, and Heather Howard. Peterborough, Canada: Broadview Press.

——. 2002. "Governmentality, Modernity, and the Historical Politics of Oyo-Hegemony in Yoruba Transnational Revivalism." In *Anthropologica: The Journal of the Canadian Anthropology Society* 44–42 (December): 271–93.

Clifford, James. 1997. *Routes: Travel and Translation in the Late Twentieth Century*. Cambridge, Mass.: Harvard University Press.

Colson, Elizabeth. 1949. *Life among the Cattle-Owning Plateau Tonga: The Material Culture of a Northern Rhodesia Native Tribe*. Livingston, Northern Rhodesia: Rhodes-Livingston Museum.

——. 1958. *Marriage and the Family among the Plateau Tonga of Northern Rhodesia*. Manchester, England: Manchester University Press.

——. 1960. *Social Organization of Gwenbe Tonga*. Manchester, England: Manchester University Press.

——. 1962. *The Plateau Tonga of Northern Rhodesia: Social and Religious Studies*. Manchester, England: Manchester University Press.

——. 1971. *The Social Consequences of Resettlement: The Impact of the Kariba Resettlement upon the Gwembe Tonga*. Manchester, England: Manchester University Press.

——. 1974. *Tradition and Contract: The Problem of Order*. Chicago: Aldine.

Colson, Elizabeth, and M. Gluckman, eds. 1951. *Seven Tribes of British Central Africa*. London: Oxford University Press.

Comaroff, Jean, and John. L. Comaroff, eds. 2001. *Millennial Capitalism and the Culture of Neoliberalism*. Durham, N.C.: Duke University Press.

Comaroff, John L. 1991. *Of Revelation and Revolution*. Chicago: University of Chicago Press.

Connerton, Paul. 1989. *How Societies Remember*. Cambridge, England: Cambridge University Press.

Cooper, Frederick. 2001. "What Is the Concept of Globalization Good For? An African Historian's Perspective." *African Affairs* 100: 189–213.

Croucher, Shiela L. 2004. *Globalization and Belonging: The Politics of Identity in a Changing World*. Lanham, Md.: Rowman and Littlefield.

Crowther, Samuel. 1968. *Gospel on the Banks of the Niger: Journals and Notices of the Native Missionaries Accompanying the Niger Expedition of 1857–1859*. London: Dawsons.

Curtin, Philip D., ed. 1967. *Africa Remembered: Narratives by West Africans from the Era of the Slave Trade*. Madison: University of Wisconsin Press.

——. 1969. *The Atlantic Slave Trade: A Census*. Madison: University of Wisconsin Press.

Darwin, Charles. 1859. *On the Origin of the Species by Means of Natural Selection, or The Preservation of Favored Races in the Struggle for Life*. London: John Murray.

——. 1998. *On the Origin of the Species by Means of Natural Selection, or The Preservation of Favored Races in the Struggle for Life*. New York: Classics of Medicine Library Division of Gryphon Editions.

Davis, Angela Y. 1983. *Women, Race and Class*. New York: Vintage Books.

Delaney, Martin R., and Robert Campbell. 1969. *Search for a Place: Black Separatism and Africa, 1860*. Ann Arbor: University of Michigan Press.

de Moraes Farias, P. F., and Karin Barber, eds. 1990. *Self-Assertion and Brokerage: Early Cultural Nationalism in West Africa*. Birmingham, England: Centre of West African Studies, University of Birmingham.

Deveau, Jean-Michel. 1989. *Le commerce rochelais face à la Révolution: Correspondance de Jean-Baptiste Nairac*. La Rochelle, France: Rumeur des âges.

Diamond, Stanley. 1974. *In Search of the Primitive: A Critique of Civilization*. New Brunswick, N.J.: Transaction.

Dominguez, Virginia R. 1986. *White by Definition: Social Classification in Creole Louisiana*. New Brunswick, N.J.: Rutgers University Press.

———. 1989. *People as Subject, People as Object: Selfhood and Peoplehood in Contemporary Israel*. Madison: University of Wisconsin Press.

Douglas, M. 1986. *How Institutions Think*. Syracuse, N.Y.: Syracuse University Press.

Drake, St. Clair and Horace Cayton. 1993. *Black Metropolis: Study of Negro Life in a Northern City*. Chicago: University of Chicago. (Orig. pub. 1945.)

Drake, St. Claire. 1987. *Black Folk Here and There: An Essay in History and Anthropology*. Los Angeles: University of California Press.

Drewal, Margaret T. 1994. *Yoruba Ritual: Performers, Play, Agency*. Bloomington: Indiana University Press.

———. 1997. "Dancing for Ògun in Yorubaland and in Brazil." In *Africa's Ogun: Old World and New*, pp. 199–234. 2nd ed. Edited by S. T. Barnes. Bloomington: Indiana University Press. (Orig. pub. 1989.)

Du Bois, W. E. B. 1903. *The Souls of Black Folk: Essays and Sketches*. Chicago: A. C. McClurg.

———. 1915. *The Negro*. New York: H. Holt.

———. 1947. *The World and Africa: An Inquiry into the Part Which Africa Has Played in World History*. New York: Viking.

Durkheim, Emile. 1915. *The Elementary Forms of the Religious Life*. New York: Free Press.

Ebron, Paulla A. 2002. *Performing Africa*. Princeton: Princeton University Press.

Ellis, Alfred B. 1894. *The Yoruba-Speaking Peoples of the Slave Coast of West Africa: Their Religion, Manners, Customs, Laws, Language, etc.* London: Chapmen and Hall.

Eltis, David. 1987. *Economic Growth and the Ending of the Transatlantic Slave Trade*. New York: Oxford University Press.

———. 1999. *Trans-Atlantic Slave Trade*. Cambridge, England: Cambridge University Press.

———. 2000. *The Rise of African Slavery in the Americas*. Cambridge, England: Cambridge University Press.

Equiano, Olaudah. 1793. *Interesting Narrative of the Life of Olaudah Equiano, or Gustavus Vassa, the African*. London: O. Equiano.

Evans-Pritchard, Edward E. 1937. *Witchcraft, Oracles, and Magic among the Azande*. Oxford: Clarendon Press.

———. 1940. *The Nuer: A Description of the Modes of Livelihood and Political Institutions of a Nilotic People*. New York: Oxford University Press.

———. 1951. *Kinship and Marriage among the Nuer*. Oxford: Clarendon Press.

———. 1956. *Nuer Religion*. New York: Oxford University Press.

Evans-Pritchard, Edward E., and Meyer Fortes, eds. 1940. *African Political Systems*. Oxford: International African Institute, Oxford University Press.

Fabian, Johannes. 1986. *Language and Colonial Power*. Berkeley: University of California Press.

———. 1991. *Time and the Work of Anthropology: Critical Essays, 1971–1991*. Philadelphia: Harwood Academic Publishers.

Fadipe, N. A. 1970. *The Sociology of the Yoruba*. Ibadan, Nigeria: Ibadan University Press.

Fage, J. D. 1970. *Africa Discovers Her Past*. London: Oxford University Press.

Falọla, Toyin, ed. 1993. *Pioneer, Patriot and Patriarch: Samuel Johnson and the Yoruba People*. Madison: University of Wisconsin Press.

———. 2001. *Nationalism and African Intellectuals*. Rochester, N.Y.: University of Rochester Press.

Featherstone, Mike, et al., eds. 1995. *Global Modernities*. London: Sage Publications.

Ferguson, James G. 2000. "Of Mimicry and Membership: Africans and the 'New World Society.'" *Society for Cultural Anthropology* 17(4): 551–69.

Forde, C. Daryll. 1941. *Marriage and Family among the Yako in South-eastern Nigeria*. London: London School of Economics and Political Science, P. Lund, Humphries and Co.

———. 1951. *Yoruba-Speaking Peoples of South-Western Nigeria*. London: International African Institute.

———. 1956. *Habitat, Economy, and Society: A Geographical Introduction to Ethnology*. London: Methuen.

———. 1963. *Habitat, Economy and Society: A Geographical Introduction to Society*. New York: E. P. Dutton.

Fortes, Meyer. 1949. *The Web of Kinship among the Tallensi: The Second Part of an Analysis of the Social Structure of a Trans-Volta Tribe*. London: Oxford University Press.

———. 1967. *Dynamics of Clanship among the Tallensi: Being the First Part of an Analysis of the Social Structure of a Trans-Volta Tribe*. London: Oxford University Press.

———. 1970. *Time and Social Structure and Other Essays*. London: University of London, Athlone Press.

Foucault, Michel. 1972. *The Archaeology of Knowledge*. Translated by A. M. Sheridan Smith. New York: Pantheon.

———. 1978. *The History of Sexuality*. Translated by Robert Hurley. New York: Pantheon.

———. 1988. *Technologies of the Self: A Seminar with Michel Foucault*. Edited by Luther H. Martin et al. Amherst: University of Massachusetts Press.

———. 1991. "Governmentality." In *The Foucault Effect: Studies in Governmentality*, pp. 87–104. Edited by G. Burchell, C. Gordon, and P. Miller. London: Harvester Wheatsheaf.

Fraginals, Manuel Moreno. 1977. *Africans en America Latina*. Mexico City: Siglo Veintiuno Editores.

Fraser, James George. 1922. *The Golden Bough: A Study in Magic and Religion*. New York: Macmillan.

Frazier, E. Franklin. 1963. *The Negro Church in America*. New York: Schocken Books.

Freeman, Carla. 2000. *High Tech and High Heels in the Global Economy: Women, Work, and Pink-Collar Identities in the Caribbean*. Durham, N.C.: Duke University Press.

Frobenius, Leo. 1913. *Voice of Africa: Being an Account of the Travels of the German Inner African Exploration Expedition in the Years 1910–1912*. London: Hutchinson and Co.

Garcia Cortez, Julio. (Obba Bi). 2000. *The Osha: Secrets of Yoruba-Lucumi Santeria Religion in the United States and the Americas—Initiation, Rituals, Ceremonies, Orishas, Divination, Plants, Sacrifices, Cleansings, and Songs*. Miami: Athelia Henrietta Press.

Garvey, Marcus. 1923. *The Philosophy and Opinions of Marcus Garvey*. New York: Universal Publishing House.

George, John Ọlawunmi. 1897. *Historical Notes on the Yòrúba Country and Its Tribes*. Nigeria.

Gilroy, Paul. 1993a. *The Black Atlantic: Modernity and Double Consciousness*. Cambridge, Mass.: Harvard University Press.

——. 1993b. *Small Acts: Thoughts on the Politics of Black Cultures*. London: Serpent's Tail.

——. 2000. *Against Race: Imagining Political Culture beyond the Color Line*. Cambridge, Mass.: Belknap Press of Harvard University Press.

Glick-Schiller, Nina, Linda Basch, and Cristina Blanc-Szanton, eds. 1992. *Towards a Transnational Perspective on Migration: Race, Class, Ethnicity, and Nationalism Reconsidered*. New York: New York Academy of Sciences.

Gluckman, Max. 1941. *Economy of the Central Barotse Plain*. Manchester, England: Manchester University Press.

——. 1943a. *Administrative Organization of the Barotse Native Authorities with a Plan for Reforming Them*. Livingston, Northern Rhodesia: Rhodes-Livingston Institute.

——. 1943b. *Essays on Lozi Land and Royal Property: I. Lozi Land Tenure, II. Property Rights of the Lozi King and the Royal Family*. Livingstone, Northern Rhodesia: Rhodes-Livingstone Institute.

——. 1948. *Analysis of Sociological Theories of Branislaw Malinowski*. Cape Town, South Africa: Oxford University Press.

——. 1959. *Custom and Conflict in Africa*. Glencoe, Ill.: Free Press.

Gollmer, C. A. 1877. *Historical Notices of Lagos, West Africa*. Pamphlet. Nigeria.

González-Wippler, Migene. 1992. *Powers of the Orishas: Santeria and the Worship of Saints*. New York: Original Publications.

——. 1994. *Santeria: The Religion—Faith, Rites, Magic*. St. Paul, Minn.: Llewellyn Publications.

Goody, Jack, ed. 1975. *Changing Social Structure in Ghana: Essays in the Comparative Sociology of a New State and an Old Tradition*. London: International African Institute.

——. 1977. *The Domestication of the Savage Mind*. Cambridge, England: Cambridge University Press.

Graburn, Nelson. 2002. "The Ethnographic Tourist." In *The Tourist as a Metaphor of the Social World*, pp. 19–39. Edited by Graham M. S. Dann. Luton, England: International Tourism Research Institute, University of Luton.

Gramsci, Antonio. 1971. *Selections from the Prison Notebooks*. New York: International Publishers.

Gregory, Steven. 1999. *Santería in New York City: A Study in Cultural Resistance*. New York: Garland.

Gupta, Akhil, and James Ferguson, eds. 1997a. *Anthropological Locations: Boundaries and Grounds of a Field Science*. Berkeley: University of California Press.

———. 1997b. "Culture, Power and Place: Ethnography at the End of an Era." In *Culture, Power, Place: Explorations in Critical Anthropology*, pp. 1–29. Edited by A. Gupta and J. Ferguson. Durham, N.C.: Duke University Press.

Halbwachs, Maurice. 1980. *The Collective Memory*. New York: Harper and Row.

Haley, Alex. 1976. *Roots: The Saga of an American Family*. New York: Dell.

Hall, Stuart. 1993. "Culture, Community, Nation." *Cultural Studies* 7(3): 349–63.

Hall, Stuart, and Paul du Gay, eds. 1996. *Questions of Cultural Identity*. London: Sage Publications.

Hall, Stuart, and Martin Jacques, eds. 1983. *The Politics of Thatcherism*. London: Lawrence and Wishart.

Hall, Stuart, et al., eds. 1995. *Modernity: An Introduction to Modern Societies*. Cambridge, England: Polity Press.

Hanks, William. 1990. *Referential Practice: Language and Lived Space among the Maya*. Chicago: University of Chicago Press.

Hansford, K., J. Bendor-Samuel, and R. Stanford. 1976. *An Index of Nigerian Languages*. No. 5 in the Series. Studies in Nigerian Languages. Accra North, Ghana: Summer Institute of Linguistics.

Harding, Susan Friend. 2000. *The Book of Jerry Falwell: Fundamentalist Language and Politics*. Princeton: Princeton University Press.

Hardt, Michael, and Antonio Negri. 2000. *Empire*. Cambridge, Mass.: Harvard University Press.

Harms, Robert. 2002. *The Diligent: A Voyage through the Worlds of the Slave Trade*. New York: Basic Books.

Harris, Joseph E., ed. 1982. *Global Dimensions of the African Diaspora*. Washington, D.C.: Howard University Press.

Hart, Keith. 1999. *The Memory Bank: Money in an Unequal World*. London: Profile.

Harvey, David. 1989a. *The Condition of Postmodernity: An Inquiry into the Origins of Cultural Change*. Oxford: Blackwell.

———. 1989b. "Modernity and Modernism." In *The Condition of Postmodernity: An Enquiry into the Origins of Cultural Change*, pp. 10–39. Oxford: Blackwell.

———. 1990. *The Condition of Postmodernity: An Enquiry into the Origins of Cultural Change*. Cambridge, Mass.: Blackwell.

———. 1995. "Globalization in Question." *Rethinking Marxism* 8(4): 1–18.

———. 1996. *Justice, Nature, and the Geography of Difference*. Malden, Mass.: Blackwell Publishers.

———. 2000. *Spaces of Hope*. Berkeley: University of California Press.

———. 2001. *Spaces of Capital: Towards a Critical Geography*. New York: Routledge.

Hegel, G. W. F. 1977. *Phenomenology of Spirit*. Oxford: Clarendon Press.

Hernandez-Reguant, Ariana. 1999. "Kwanzaa and the U.S. Ethnic Mosaic." In *Representations of Blackness and the Performance of Identities*, pp. 101–22. Edited by J. Muteba Rahier. Westport, Conn.: Greenwood.

———. 2002. "Radio Taino and the Globalization of the Cuban Culture Industries." Ph.D. diss., University of Chicago.

Herskovits, Melville J. 1941. *The Myth of the Negro Past*. New York: Harper and Brothers.

Herzfeld, M. 1992. *Social Production of Indifference: Exploring the Symbolic Roots of Western Bureaucracy*. New York: Berg.

Holloway, Joseph E., ed. 1990. *Africanisms in American Culture: Blacks in Diaspora*. Bloomington: Indiana University Press.

Holston, James, ed. 1999. *Cities and Citizenship*. Durham, N.C.: Duke University Press.

Hopkins, Anthony G. 1973. *An Economic History of West Africa*. New York: Columbia University Press.

Hurt, Carl M. 1979. *Oyotunji Village: The Yoruba Movement in America*. Washington, D.C.: University Press of America.

Hutton, Will, and Anthony Giddens, eds. 2000. *Global Capitalism*. New York: New Press.

Integrated Postsecondary Education Data System. 1986. *Fall Enrollment*. http://www.nces.ed.gov/ipeds/.

Irvine, Judith. 1996. "When Talk Isn't Cheap: Language and Political Economy." In *The Matrix of Language: Contemporary Linguistic Anthropology*, pp. 258–83. Edited by D. L. Brenneis and R. K. S. Macaulay. Boulder, Colo.: Westview Press.

James, Cyril Lionel Robert. 1963. *The Black Jacobins: Toussaint L'Ouverture and the San Domingo Revolution*. New York: Vintage Books. (Orig. pub. 1938.)

Jameson, Fredric, and Masao Miyoshi, eds. 1999. *The Cultures of Globalization*. Durham, N.C.: Duke University Press.

Johnson, Samuel. 1921. *The History of the Yorubas: From the Earliest Times to the Beginning of the British Protectorate*. London: Routledge and Kegan Paul.

Jusdanis, Gregory. 2001. *The Necessary Nation*. Princeton: Princeton University Press.

Kantorowicz, Ernst H. 1957. *The King's Two Bodies: A Study in Mediaeval Political Theology*. Princeton: Princeton University Press.

Karenga, Maulana, and Jacob Carruthers. 1986. *Kemet and the African Worldview: Research, Rescue and Restoration: Selected Papers of the Proceedings of the First and Second Conferences of the Asso*. Los Angeles: University of Sankore Press.

Karim, Iman B., ed. 1971. *The End of White World Supremacy: Four Speeches by Malcolm X*. New York: Seaver Books.

Keane, Web. 1994. "The Value of Words and the Meaning of Things in Eastern Indonesian Exchange." *Man*, n.s. 29(3): 605–29.

Klein, Herbert S. 1967. *Slavery in the Americas: A Comparative Study of Cuba and Virginia*. Chicago: University of Chicago Press.

Koh, Harold Hongju. 2002. "A United States Human Rights Policy for the Twenty-First Century." *St. Louis University Law Journal* 46: 293.

Kutzinski, Vera. 1993. *Sugar's Secrets: Race and Erotics of Cuban Nationalism*. Charlottesville: University of Virginia Press.

Lacan, Jacques. 1975. *De la Psychose Paranoiaque dans ses Rapports avec la Personnalite suivi de Premiers Ecrits sur la Paranoia*. Paris: Editions du Seuil.

——. 1988. *The Seminar of Jacques Lacan*. New York: Norton. (Orig. pub. 1975.)

Laitin, David D. 1986. *Hegemony and Culture: Politics and Religious Change among the Yoruba*. Chicago: University of Chicago Press.

Lake, Obiagele. 1997. "Diaspora African Repatriation: The Place of Diaspora Women in the Pan-African Nexus." In *Gendered Encounters: Challenging Cultural Boundaries and Social Hierarchies in Africa*. Edited by Maria Grosz and Ngate Omari H. Kokole. New York: Routledge.

Larkin, Brian. 1997. "Indian Films and Nigerian Lovers: Media and the Creation of Parallel Modernities." *Africa* 67(3): 406–40.

Latour, Bruno. 1993. *We Have Never Been Modern*. Cambridge, Mass.: Harvard University Press.

Law, Robin. 1991. *The Slave Coast of West Africa, 1550–1750: The Impact of the Atlantic Slave Trade on an African Society*. Oxford: Clarendon Press.

——. 1997. *The Oyo Empire, c. 1600–c. 1836: A West African Imperialism in the Era of the Atlantic Slave Trade*. Oxford: Oxford University Press.

Lefebvre, Henri. 1991. *The Critique of Everyday Life*. Translated by John Moore. London: Verso.

Lévi-Strauss, Claude. 1963. *Structural Anthropology*. New York: Basic Books.

Linton, Ralph. 1936. *The Study of Man: An Introduction*. New York: D. Appleton-Century.

Linton, Ralph, et al. 1935. "Memorandum of Acculturation." *Man* 35 (October): 145–48.

Llewellen, Ted. 2002. *The Anthropology of Globalization: Cultural Anthropology Enters the Twenty-First Century*. Westport, Conn.: Bergin and Garvey.

Lovejoy, P. E. 1983. *Transformations in Slavery: A History of Slavery in Africa*. Cambridge, England: Cambridge University Press.

Lusane, Clarence. 1997. *Race in the Global Era: African Americans at the Millennium*. Boston: South End Press.

Maddox, Gregory, ed. 1993. *African Nationalism and Revolution*. New York: Garland.

Mair, Lucy Philip. 1936. *Native Policies in Africa*. London: G. Routledge and Sons.

Malcolm X. 1965. *Malcolm X Speaks: Selected Speeches and Statements*. Edited by George Breitman. New York: Grove Press.

Malinowski, Bronislaw. 1922. "The Subject, Method and Scope of This Inquiry." In *Argonauts of the Western Pacific*, pp. 1–25. Prospect Heights, Ill.: Waveland Press.

——. 1932. *The Argonauts of the Western Pacific: An Account of Native Enterprise and Adventure in the Archipelagoes of Melanesian New Guinea*. London: G. Routledge and Sons.

——. 1935. *Coral Gardens and Their Magic. A Study of the Methods of Tilling the Soil and of Agricultural Rites in the Trobriand Islands*. London: G. Allen and Unwin.

Mankekar, Purnima. 1999. *Screening Culture, Viewing Politics: An Ethnography of Television, Womanhood, and Nation in Postcolonial India*. Durham, N.C.: Duke University Press.

Manning, P. 1990. *Slavery and African Life*. Cambridge, England: Cambridge University Press.

Marcus, George. E. 1995. "Ethnography in/of the World System: The Emergence of Multi-Sited Ethnography." *Annual Review of Anthropology* 24: 95–117.

———. 1998. *Ethnography through Thick and Thin*. Princeton: Princeton University Press.

———. 2000. *What Is at Stake in the Idea and Practice of Multi-Sited Ethnography?* New Haven, Conn.: Colloquium Series on Transnationalism, Area Studies, and Ethnographic Methods, Yale University.

Marcus, George E., and Michael M. J. Fischer. 1986. *Anthropology as Cultural Critique: An Experimental Moment in the Human Sciences*. Chicago: University of Chicago Press.

Martin Shaw, Carolyn. 1995. *Colonial Inscriptions: Race, Sex and Class in Kenya*. Minneapolis: University of Minnesota Press.

Martin Shaw, Carolyn, and Kamari Clarke. 1995. "Rethinking African American Cultural Politics." Paper presented at the American Anthropological Association, Washington, D.C., November.

Mason, John. 1985. *Four New World Yoruba Rituals*. Brooklyn, N.Y.: Yoruba Theological Archministry.

———. 1992. *Orin Orisa*. Brooklyn, N.Y.: Yoruba Theological Archministry.

Mason, John, and Gary Edwards. 1985. *Black Gods: Orisa Studies in the New World*. Brooklyn, N.Y.: Yoruba Theological Archministry.

Massey, Doreen. 1994. *Space, Place, and Gender*. Minneapolis: University of Minnesota Press.

Matory, J. Lorand. 1994. *Sex and the Empire That Is No More: Gender and the Politics of Metaphor in Oyo Yoruba Religion*. Minneapolis: University of Minnesota Press.

———. 1999. "The English Professors of Brazil: On the Diasporic Roots of the Yoruba Nation." *Comparative Studies in Society and History* 41(1): 72–103.

Mbembe, Achille J. 1992. "Provisional Notes on the Postcolony." *Africa* 62(1): 3–37.

———. 2001. *On the Postcolony*. Berkeley: University of California Press.

McCarthy Brown, K. 1991. *Mama Lola: A Vodou Priestess in Brooklyn*. Berkeley: University of California Press.

Meriwether, James Hunger. 2002. *Proudly We Can Be Africans: Black Americans and Africa*. Chapel Hill: University of North Carolina Press.

Middleton, John F. M. 1966. *The Effects of Economic Development on Traditional Political Systems in Africa South of the Sahara*. The Hague: Mouton.

———. 1998. *Lugbara Religion: Ritual and Authority among East African People*. Hamburg: LIT and James Currey.

Mintz, Sidney W. 1985. *Sweetness and Power: The Place of Sugar in Modern History*. New York: Viking Penguin.

Mintz, S. W., and R. Price. 1976. *An Anthropological Approach to the Afro-American Past: A Caribbean Perspective*. Philadelphia: Institute for the Study of Human Issues.

——. 1992. *The Birth of African American Culture: An Anthropological Perspective*. Boston: Beacon Press.

Mitchell, J. Clyde. 1956. *The Kalela Dance: Aspects of Social Relationships among Urban Africans in Northern Rhodesia*. Manchester, England: Manchester University Press.

Moore, Donald. 1998. "Subaltern Struggles and the Politics of Space: Remapping Resistance in Zimbabwe's Eastern Highlands." *Cultural Anthropology* 13: 344.

Moore, Robin Dale. 1997. *Nationalizing Blackness: Afrocubanismo and Artistic Revolution in Havana, 1920–1940*. Pittsburgh: University of Pittsburgh Press.

Moreno Vega, Marta. 2000. *The Altar of My Soul: The Living Traditions of Santeria*. Colorado Springs, Colo.: Random House.

Morley, David, and Kuan-Hsing Chen, eds. 1996. *Stuart Hall: Critical Dialogues in Cultural Studies*. London: Routledge.

Morton-Williams, Peter. 1960. "The Yoruba Ogboni Cult in Oyo." *Africa: Journal of the International African Institute* 30(4): 362–74.

——. 1967. "The Yoruba Kingdom of Oyo in the Nineteenth Century." In *West African Kingdoms in the Nineteenth Century*. Edited by D. Forde and P. M. Kaberry. London: Oxford University Press.

Mudimbe, Valentin Yves. 1988. *The Invention of Africa: Gnosis, Philosophy, and the Order of Knowledge*. Bloomington: Indiana University Press.

——. 1994. *The Idea of Africa*. Bloomington: Indiana University Press.

Nadel, Siegfried Frederick. 1942. *A Black Byzantium: The Kingdom of Nupe in Nigeria*. London: Oxford University Press.

——. 1965. *A Black Byzantium: The Kingdom of Nupe in Nigeria*. London: Oxford University Press.

Nader, Laura. 1971. "Up the Anthropologist: Perspectives Gained from Studying Up." In *Reinventing Anthropology*, pp. 284–311. Edited by D. H. Hymes. New York: Pantheon.

Naficy, Hamid. 1993. *The Making of Exile Cultures*. Minneapolis: University of Minnesota Press.

Neimark, Philip J. 1993. *Way of Orisa: Empowering Your Life through the Ancient African Religion of Ifa*. San Francisco: Harper Collins.

Nietzsche, Friedrich Wilhelm. 1967. *Le Gai Savoir: Fragments posthumes, 1881–1882*. Paris: Galliard.

Nobles, Wade W. 1986. *African Psychology: Toward Its Reclamation, Reascension and Revitalization*. Oakland, Calif.: Institute for the Advanced Study of Black Family Life and Culture.

O'Donnell, Guillermo A. 1998. *Counterpoints: Selected Essays on Authoritarianism and Democratization*. Notre Dame, Ind.: University of Notre Dame Press.

Òjó, Afolabi. 1966. Yoruba Culture, University of London Press LTD, Published with the University of Ife, Nigeria.

——. 1967. *Yoruba Culture: A Geographical Analysis*. London: University of London Press.

Olúpònà, J. K. 1991. *Kingship, Religion, and Rituals in a Nigerian Community: A Phenomenological Study of Ondo Yoruba Festivals*. Stockholm: Almquist and Wiksell.

——. 1997. "Report of the Conference 'Beyond Primitivism: Indigenous Religious Traditions and Modernity,' March 28–31, 1996, University of California, Davis." *Kroniklijke Brill* 44: 323–45.

——, ed. 2000. *African Spirituality: Forms, Meanings, and Expressions*. New York: Crossroad.

Ong, Aihwa. 1999. *Flexible Citizenship: The Cultural Logics of Transnationality*. Durham, N.C.: Duke University Press.

Ortiz, Fernando D. 1992. *Los cabildos y la fiesta afrocubanos del Dia de Reyes*. La Habana: Ciencias Sociales. (Orig. pub. 1912.)

Ortner, Sherry B. 1978. *Sherpas through their Rituals*. Cambridge, England: Cambridge University Press.

Ortner, Sherry B., and Harriet Whitehead, eds. 1981. *Sexual Meanings: The Cultural Construction of Gender and Sexuality*. Cambridge, England: Cambridge University Press.

Padmore, George. 1956. *Pan-Africanism or Communism? The Coming Struggle for Africa*. London: D. Dobson.

Park, Robert E. 1931. *The Problem of Cultural Differences*. New York: American Council, Institute of Pacific Relations.

——. 1938. *Readings in Race and Culture: The Caribbean/Seminar in Race and Culture*. Nashville, Tenn.: The Seminar.

——. 1949. *New Outline of the Principles of Sociology*. New York: Barnes and Noble.

——. 1950. *Race and Culture*. New York: Free Press.

Park, Robert E., and Herbert A. Miller. 1921. *Old World Traits Transplanted*. New York: Harper.

Patterson, Thomas. 1999. Change and Development in the Twentieth Century. Oxford, New York: Berg.

Payne, John Augustus. 1893. *Table of Principal Events in Yorùbá History*.

Peel, J. D. Y. 2001. Religious Encounter and the Making of the Yoruba. Bloomington: Indiana University Press.

Peirce, Charles Sanders. 1931. *Collected Papers*. Cambridge, Mass.: Harvard University Press.

Piot, Charles. 1999. *Remotely Global: Village Modernity in West Africa*. Chicago: University of Chicago Press.

Radcliffe-Brown, Alfred Reginald. 1922. *The Andaman Islanders: A Study in Social Anthropology (Anthony Wilkin Studentship Research, 1906)*. Cambridge, England: Cambridge University Press.

——. 1952. *Structure and Function in Primitive Society*. Glencoe, Ill.: Free Press.

Ranger, Terrence, and Eric Hobsbawm. 1992. *The Invention of Tradition*. Cambridge, England: Cambridge University Press.

Rappaport, Roy. 1990. *Ritual and Religion in the Making of Humanity*. Cambridge: Cambridge University Press.

Rappaport, Joanne. 1991. *The Politics of Memory: Native Historical Interpretations in the Colombian Andes*. Cambridge, England: Cambridge University Press.

Redfield, Robert. 1953. *The Primitive World and Its Transformations*. Ithaca, N.Y.: Cornell University Press.

Rifflet-Lemaire, Anika. 1970. *Jacques Lacan*. Brussels: C. Dessart.

Riles, Annelise. 2001. *The Network Inside Out*. Ann Arbor: University of Michigan Press.

Roach, Joseph. 1996. Cities of the Dead: Circum-Atlantic Performance. New York: Columbia University Press.

Rofel, Lisa. 1994. "Liberation, Nostalgia and a Yearning for Modernity." In *Engendering China: Women, Culture, and the State*, pp. 226–49. Edited by Christina K. Gilmartin. Cambridge, Mass.: Harvard University Press.

———. 1999. *Other Modernities: Gendered Yearnings in China after Socialism*. Berkeley: University of California Press.

———. 2001. "From Sacrifice to Desire: Globalization with Chinese Characteristics." Unpublished paper presented at Yale University Anthropology Colloquium.

Rutherford, Jonathan, ed. 1990. *Identity: Community, Culture, Difference*. London: Lawrence and Wishart.

Sassen, Saskia. 1991. *The Global City: New York, London, Tokyo*. Princeton: Princeton University Press.

———. 1994. *Cities in a World Economy*. Thousand Oaks, Calif.: Pine Forge Press.

———. 1996. *Losing Control? Sovereignty in an Age of Globalization*. New York: Columbia University Press.

———. 1999. *Guests and Aliens*. New York: New Press.

Sassen, Saskia. 2003 (forthcoming). *De-Nationalization: Territory, Authority and Rights in a Global Digital Age*. Princeton: Princeton University Press.

Saxton, Alexander. 1990. *The Rise and Fall of the White Republic: Class Politics and Mass Culture in Nineteenth Century America*. London: Verso.

Schneider, Jane. 1971. "Of Vigilance and Virgins: Honor, Shame and Access to Resources in Mediterranean Societies." *Ethnology* 10(1): 1–24.

Scott, David. 1991. "That Event, This Memory: Notes on the Anthropology of African Diasporas in the New World." *Diaspora* 1(3): 261–84.

Shapiro, Michael. 1994. "Moral Geographies and the Ethics of Post-Sovereignty." *Public Culture* 6(3): 482.

Siegal, Reva. 2002. "She the People: The Nineteenth Amendment, Sex Equality, Federalism, and the Family." *Harvard Law Review* 115: 947.

Silverstein, Michael. 1976. "Shifters, Linguistic Categories, and Cultural Description." In *Meaning in Anthropology*, pp. 11–55. Edited by K. H. Basso and H. A. Selby. Albuquerque: University of New Mexico Press.

Silverstein, Michael, and Greg Urban. 1996. *Natural Histories of Discourse*. Chicago: University of Chicago Press.

Skinner, Elliot P. 1992. *African Americans and U.S. Policy toward Africa, 1850–1924: In Defense of Black Nationality*. Washington, D.C.: Howard University Press.

Skinner, Elliot P., and Daniel Chu. 1965. *Glorious Age in Africa: The Story of Three Great Empires*. Garden City, N.Y.: Doubleday.

Skinner, Elliot P., and Pearl T. Robinson, eds. 1983. *Transformation and Resiliency in Africa: As Seen by Afro-American Scholars.* Washington, D.C.: Howard University Press.

Smith, Anthony. 1989. *The Origins of Nations: Ethnic and Racial Studies.* New York: Routledge.

Smith, Robert Sydney. 1969. *Kingdoms of the Yoruba.* 3rd ed. Madison: University of Wisconsin Press.

Stepan, Nancy Leys, and Sander L. Gilman. 1993. "Appropriating the Idioms of Science." In *"Racial" Economy of Science: Toward a Democratic Future*, pp. 170–93. Edited by Sandra Harding. Bloomington: Indiana University Press.

Stewart, Kathleen. 1996. *A Space on the Side of the Road: Cultural Poetics in an "Other" America.* Princeton: Princeton University Press.

Stocking, George W., Jr. 1968. *Race, Culture, and Evolution: Essays in the History of Anthropology.* New York: Free Press.

Sutton, Constance R. 1992. "Some Thoughts on Gendering and Internationalizing Our Thinking about Transnational Migrations." In *Towards a Transnational Perspective on Migration: Race, Class, Ethnicity, and Nationalism Reconsidered*, pp. 241–51. Edited by Nina Glick-Schiller, Linda Basch, and Cristina Blanc-Szanton. *Annals of the New York Academy of Sciences*, vol. 645. New York: New York Academy of Sciences.

Szwed, John F., ed. 1970. *Black America.* New York: Basic Books.

Szwed, John F., and Roger D. Abrahams, eds. 1975. *Discovering Afro-America.* Leiden: Brill.

Szwed, John F., and Novman E. Whitten, Jr., eds. 1970. *Afro-American Anthropology: Contemporary Perspectives.* New York: Free Press.

Thompson, Robert Farris. 1983. *Flash of the Spirit: African and Afro-American Art and Philosophy.* New York: Vintage Books.

Tonkin, Elizabeth. 1990. "West African Ethnographic Traditions." In *Localizing Strategies: Regional Traditions of Ethnographic Writing*, pp. 137–51. Edited by R. Fardon. Edinburgh: Scottish Academic Press.

———. 1992. *Narrating Our Past: The Social Construction of Oral History.* Cambridge, England: Cambridge University Press.

Tsing, Anna. 2000. "The Global Situation." *Cultural Anthropology* 15(3): 327–60.

Turner, Bryan S. 1996. *The Body and Society: Explorations in Social Theory.* London: Sage Publications.

Turner, Lorenzo D. 1942. "Some Contacts of the Brazilian Ex-Slaves with Nigeria, West Africa." *Journal of Negro History* 27: 55–67.

Turner, Victor W. 1957. *Schism and Continuity in an African Society: A Study of Ndembu Village Life.* Manchester, England: Manchester University Press.

———. 1969. *The Ritual Process: Structure and Anti-structure.* Chicago: Aldine.

Tylor, Edward. B. 1865. *Researches into the Early History of Mankind and the Development of Civilization.* London: J. Murray.

Tylor, Edward B. 1958. *Religion in Primitive Culture.* 2 vols. New York: Harper. (Orig. pub. 1871.)

U.S. Department of Education. 1989. *Digest of Educational Statistics*. National Center for Education Statistics. http://nces.ed.gov.

Vail, Leroy. 1989. *The Creation of Tribalism in South Africa*. Berkeley: University of California Press.

Valdez, Rafael Lopez. 1990. "Notas para el estudio etnohistorico de los esclavos lucumi en Cuba." In *Estudios afrocubanos*, pp. 311–47. Edited by L. Menendez. Havana: La Sociedad.

Van Deburg, William L. 1992. *New Day in Babylon: The Black Power Movement and American Culture, 1965–1975*. Chicago: University of Chicago Press.

Van Gennep, Arnold. 1960. *The Rites of Passage: A Classic Study of Cultural Celebrations*. Chicago: University of Chicago Press.

Verger, Pierre. 1981. *Orixas: Deuses Iorubas na Africa e no Novo Mundo*. Salvador, Brazil: Corrupio.

Von Eschen, Penny Marie. 1997. *Race against Empire: Black Americans and Anticolonialism, 1937–57*. Ithaca, N.Y.: Cornell University Press.

Wallerstein, Immanuel. 1974. *The Modern World System I: Capitalist Agriculture and the Origins of the European World-Economy in the Sixteenth Century*. San Diego: Academic Press.

——. 1980. *The Modern World System II: Mercantilism and the Consolidation of the European World-Economy, 1600–1750*. San Diego: Academic Press.

——. 1983. *Historical Capitalism*. London: Verso.

——. 1986. *Africa and the Modern World*. Trenton, N.J.: Africa World Press.

——. 1991. *Geopolitics and Geoculture: Essays on the Changing World-System*. Cambridge, England: Cambridge University Press.

Weber, Max. 1947. *The Theory of Social and Economic Organization*. New York: Oxford University Press.

——. 1958. *The Protestant Ethic and the Spirit of Capitalism*. New York: Charles Scribner's Sons.

——. 1963. *The Sociology of Religion*. Boston: Beacon Press.

——. 1968. *Economy and Society: An Outline of Interpretive Sociology*. New York: Bedminster Press.

Welsing, Frances Cress. 1991. *The Isis Papers: The Keys to the Colors*. Chicago: Third World Press.

White, Hayden. 1973. *Metahistory: The Historical Imagination in Nineteenth-Century Europe*. Baltimore: Johns Hopkins University Press.

Whitman, James Q. 2003. *Harsh Justice: Criminal Punishment and the Widening Divide between America and Europe*. New York: Oxford University Press.

William, Chancellor. 1987. *The Deconstruction of Black Civilization: Great Issues of a Race from 4500 B.C. to 2000 A.D.* Chicago: Third World Press.

Williams, Brackette F. 1990. "Nationalism, Traditionalism, and the Problem of Cultural Inauthenticity." In *Nationalist Ideologies and the Production of National Cultures*, pp. 112–29. Edited by R. G. Fox. Washington, D.C.: American Anthropological Association.

———. 1991. *Stains on My Name, War in My Veins: Guyana and the Politics of Cultural Struggle*. Durham, N.C.: Duke University Press.

Wipper, Audrey. 1972. "African Women, Fashion, and Scapegoating." *Canadian Journal of African Studies* 6(2): 329–49.

Wood, J. B. 1879. *Notes on the Construction of the Yoruba Language*. Exeter: James Townsend.

Woodson, Carter G. 1933. *The Mis-education of the Negro*. Washington, D.C.: Associated Publisher.

Worby, Eric 1994. "Maps, Names and Ethnic Games: The Epistemology and Iconography of Colonial Power in Northwestern Zimbabwe." *Journal of Southern African Studies* 24(3): 371–92.

———. 1995. "Not to Plough My Master's Field: Discourses of Ethnicity and the Production of Inequality in Botswana." *Journal of Social Studies* 67: 71–108.

———, ed. 2001. "A Redivided Land? New Agrarian Conflicts and Questions in Zimbabwe." *Journal of Agrarian Change* 1(4): 475–509.

Yái, Ọlábíyí Babalọlá. 2001. "Yoruba Religion and Globalization: Some Reflections." *Cuadernos Digitales* 15 (October): 1–21.

Young, Robert J. C. 1995. *Colonial Desire: Hybridity in Theory, Culture and Race*. London: Routledge.

Žižek, Slavoj. 1996. *Plague of Fantasies*. London: Verso.

———, ed. 1998. *Cogito and the Unconscious*. Durham, N.C.: Duke University Press.

Index

Forced migration. *See* Slavery
Foucault, Michel, 67, 234
Frobenius, Leo, 167

Garvey, Marcus, 122
Gates, Henry Louis, Jr., 115, 133, 140
Gèlèdé, 192
Gender, xvi, 258–61, 265; limits on
    women's power, 18; regulation of sexes,
    xix–xx, 44; segregated sex organiza-
    tion, 44
Genealogies, 118
Geographical scales of globalization, 16–18
Geotemporality, definition of, 160
Gilroy, Paul, 47, 161, 184
Globalization, 16–18, 32–36
God, 4, 20. *See also* Olódùmarè
Gupta, Akil, and James Ferguson, 11, 24,
    29, 33

Harvey, David, xxvi, 117, 126
Hegemony, 18, 62, 67, 159
Heritage tourism, 37, 143, 149
Hernandez- Reguant, Ariana, 67, 199
Herskovits, Melville J. (*The Myth of the
    Negro Past*), 132, 134
Heterosexuality, xix, xx, 44, 262
Hierarchies of prestige, xvi, 55, 70–71, 87,
    129; Ọba prestige, 272; Social order-
    ing, 95
Historiography, xxv, 16, 179
History, xxiii, 64–65, 87–89, 175, 178–83;
    manipulation of historical knowledge,
    115
Homosexuality, xix, xx, 262
HRG Ìyá Sisilum, 267–68, 270, 273–75
Hunt, Carl, 5
Hybridity, 16, 62

Ìbà ará t'ọ̀run, 218
Identity politics, xvi, xxvi, 46

Ifá, 60, 77, 233; divination system, 20–21,
    43; reading, 20–21, 43; reading of the
    year, 60
Ìgbàlè, 82
Ìgbìmọ̀lóṣà, 192
Igbó odù, 240–41
Ilà, 108
Ilé, 97
Ilé Ifẹ̀, xxiv, 7, 55, 91, 181, 183
Ilèkẹ̀, 51
Imagined communities, 35, 37, 68
Improvisation, 188–90
Incantation, 202–6, 233
Indexicality, 54, 65
Individuals, as social actors, xxii, 33
Initiation ceremony, xxii, 78
Ire, 233
Islam, 130, 179
Ìyánífá Olúfadékẹ́, 18
Ìyá Olayindo, 274–75
Ìyá Sisilum, 267–68, 270, 273–75

Johnson, Samuel, 158, 172–73, 178–79, 181,
    186, 257

Kábíyèsí, 78, 192
Kakanfò Ọ̀yabi, 180
King, Serge (HRH Ọba Ofuntola
    Oseigeman Adelabu Adéfúmni I), 72
Kinship relations, 28
Knowledge, 8, 170–74; changes in mean-
    ing, 141; knowledge production, 36;
    transmission of, 36, 279; transmission of
    divinatory, xvii, 190, 198, 236
Kwanzaa, 145

Lagos, Nigeria, 107
Language practices: in Nigeria, 168–69; in
    Ọ̀yọ́túnjí, 43, 53, 79, 190, 213–15
Law, in Ọ̀yọ́túnjí, 78, 79

Kamari Maxine Clarke is an Associate Professor of Anthropology
at Yale University and a Research Associate at the Yale
Law School.

Library of Congress Cataloging-in-Publication Data
Clarke, Kamari Maxine.
Mapping Yorùbá networks : power and agency in the making of
transnational communities / Kamari Maxine Clarke.
Includes bibliographical references and index.
ISBN 0-8223-3330-9 (cloth : alk. paper)
ISBN 0-8223-3342-2 (pbk. : alk. paper)
1. Yorùbá (African people)—South Carolina—Ọ̀yọ́túnjí
African Village—Migrations. 2. Yorùbá (African people)—
South Carolina—African Village—Ethnic identity.
3. Yorùbá (African people)—South Carolina—Ọ̀yọ́túnjí
African Village—Rites and ceremonies. 4. African Americans—
South Carolina—Ọ̀yọ́túnjí African Village—Ethnic identity.
5. African Americans—South Carolina—Ọ̀yọ́túnjí African Village—
Rites and ceremonies. 6. Culture and tourism—South Carolina—
Ọ̀yọ́túnjí African Village. 7. Ọ̀yọ́túnjí African Village (S.C.)—
History. 8. Ọ̀yọ́túnjí African Village (S.C.)—Social life and
customs. I. Title.
E194.Y66C53 2004   305.896'333—dc22   2004001301